MPLS and VPN Architectures

Jim Guichard, CCIE #2069

Ivan Pepelnjak, CCIE #1354

CISCO SYSTEMS

CISCO PRESS®

Cisco Press
201 West 103rd Street
Indianapolis, IN 46290 USA

MPLS and VPN Architectures

Jim Guichard, CCIE #2069

Ivan Pepelnjak, CCIE #1354

Copyright© 2001 Cisco Press

Cisco Press logo is a trademark of Cisco Systems, Inc.

Published by:
Cisco Press
201 West 103rd Street
Indianapolis, IN 46290 USA

Printed in the United States of America 1 2 3 4 5 6 7 8 9 0   03 02 01

1st Printing October 2000

Library of Congress Cataloging-in-Publication Number: 00-105168

ISBN: 1-58705-002-1

Warning and Disclaimer

This book is designed to provide information about Multiprotocol Label Switching (MPLS) and Virtual Private Networks (VPN). Every effort has been made to make this book as complete and as accurate as possible, but no warranty or fitness is implied.

The information is provided on an "as is" basis. The author, Cisco Press, and Cisco Systems, Inc., shall have neither liability nor responsibility to any person or entity with respect to any loss or damages arising from the information contained in this book or from the use of the discs or programs that may accompany it.

The opinions expressed in this book belong to the authors and are not necessarily those of Cisco Systems, Inc.

Feedback Information

At Cisco Press, our goal is to create in-depth technical books of the highest quality and value. Each book is crafted with care and precision, undergoing rigorous development that involves the unique expertise of members from the professional technical community.

Readers' feedback is a natural continuation of this process. If you have any comments regarding how we could improve the quality of this book, or otherwise alter it to better suit your needs, you can contact us through email at ciscopress@mcp.com. Please make sure to include the book title and ISBN in your message.

We greatly appreciate your assistance.

Trademark Acknowledgments

All terms mentioned in this book that are known to be trademarks or service marks have been appropriately capitalized. Cisco Press or Cisco Systems, Inc., cannot attest to the accuracy of this information. Use of a term in this book should not be regarded as affecting the validity of any trademark or service mark.

Publisher	John Wait
Executive Editor	John Kane
Cisco Systems Program Manager	Bob Antsey
Managing Editor	Patrick Kanouse
Acquisitions Editor	Kathy Trace
Development Editor	Allison Beaumont Johnson
Copy Editors	Krista Hansing
	Theresa Wehrle
Technical Editors	Stefano Previdi
	Dan Tappan
	Emannuel Guillain
Team Coordinator	Amy Lewis
Book Designer	Gina Rexrode
Cover Designer	Louisa Klucznik
Compositor	Steve Gifford
Indexer	Tim Wright

CISCO SYSTEMS

CISCO PRESS

Corporate Headquarters
Cisco Systems, Inc.
170 West Tasman Drive
San Jose, CA 95134-1706
USA
http://www.cisco.com
Tel: 408 526-4000
    800 553-NETS (6387)
Fax: 408 526-4100

European Headquarters
Cisco Systems Europe s.a.r.l.
Parc Evolic, Batiment L1/L2
16 Avenue du Quebec
Villebon, BP 706
91961 Courtaboeuf Cedex
France
http://www-europe.cisco.com
Tel: 33 1 69 18 61 00
Fax: 33 1 69 28 83 26

**Americas
Headquarters**
Cisco Systems, Inc.
170 West Tasman Drive
San Jose, CA 95134-1706
USA
http://www.cisco.com
Tel: 408 526-7660
Fax: 408 527-0883

Asia Headquarters
Nihon Cisco Systems K.K.
Fuji Building, 9th Floor
3-2-3 Marunouchi
Chiyoda-ku, Tokyo 100
Japan
http://www.cisco.com
Tel: 81 3 5219 6250
Fax: 81 3 5219 6001

Cisco Systems has more than 200 offices in the following countries. Addresses, phone numbers, and fax numbers are listed on the Cisco Connection Online Web site at http://www.cisco.com/offices.

Argentina • Australia • Austria • Belgium • Brazil • Canada • Chile • China • Colombia • Costa Rica • Croatia • Czech Republic • Denmark • Dubai, UAE Finland • France • Germany • Greece • Hong Kong • Hungary • India • Indonesia • Ireland • Israel • Italy • Japan • Korea • Luxembourg • Malaysia Mexico • The Netherlands • New Zealand • Norway • Peru • Philippines • Poland • Portugal • Puerto Rico • Romania • Russia • Saudi Arabia • Singapore Slovakia • Slovenia • South Africa • Spain • Sweden • Switzerland • Taiwan • Thailand • Turkey • Ukraine • United Kingdom • United States • Venezuela

About the Authors

Jim Guichard is a senior network design consultant within Global Solutions Engineering at Cisco Systems. During the last four years at Cisco, Jim has been involved in the design, implementation, and planning of many large-scale WAN and LAN networks. His breadth of industry knowledge, hands-on experience, and understanding of complex internetworking architectures have enabled him to provide a detailed insight into the new world of MPLS and its deployment. If you would like to contact Jim, he can be reached at jguichar@cisco.com.

Ivan Pepelnjak, CCIE, is the executive director of the Technical Division with NIL Data Communications (www.NIL.si), a high-tech data communications company focusing on providing high-value services in new-world Service Provider technologies.

Ivan has more than 10 years of experience in designing, installing, troubleshooting, and operating large corporate and service provider WAN and LAN networks, several of them already deploying MPLS-based Virtual Private Networks. He is the author or lead developer of a number of highly successful advanced IP courses covering MPLS/VPN, BGP, OSPF, and IP QoS. His previous publications include *EIGRP Network Design Solutions*, by Cisco Press.

About the Technical Reviewers

Stefano Previdi joined Cisco in 1996 after 10 years spent in network operations. He started in the Technical Assistance Center as a routing protocols specialist and then moved to consulting engineering to focus on IP backbone technologies such as routing protocols and MPLS. In 2000, he moved to the IOS engineering group as a developer for the IS-IS routing protocol.

Dan Tappan is a distinguished engineer at Cisco Systems. He has 20 years of experience with internetworking, starting with working on the ARPANET transition from NCP to TCP at Bolt, Beranek and Newman. For the past several years, Dan has been the technical lead for Cisco's implementation of MPLS (tag switching) and MPLS/VPNs.

Emmanuel Gillain has been with Cisco Systems since 1997. He got his CCIE certification in 1998 and currently is a systems engineer in EMEA on the Global Telco Team. His responsibilities include presales and technical account management for major global service providers. He helps in identifying business opportunities from a technical standpoint and provides presales and technical support. He earned a five-year degree in electrical engineering in 1995 and worked for two years at France Telecom/Global One.

Dedications

This book is dedicated to our families for their continuous support during the time when we were writing this book.

Acknowledgments

Our special thanks go to Stefano Previdi, from the Cisco Service Provider technical consulting team. One of the MPLS pioneers, he introduced us both to the intricacies of MPLS architecture and its implementation in IOS. He was also kind enough to act as one of the reviewers, making sure that this book thoroughly and correctly covers all relevant MPLS aspects.

Every major project is a result of teamwork, and this book is no exception. We'd like to thank everyone who helped us in the long writing process—our development editor, Allison Johnson, who helped us with the intricacies of writing a book; the rest of the editorial team from Cisco Press; and especially our technical reviewers, Stefano Previdi, Dan Tappan, and Emannuel Guillan. They not only corrected our errors and omissions, but they also included several useful suggestions based on their experience with MPLS design and implementation.

Finally, this book would never have been written without the continuous support and patience of our families, especially our wives, Sadie and Karmen.

Contents at a Glance

Contents

MPLS Technology and Configuration

CHAPTER 1

Multiprotocol Label Switching (MPLS) Architecture Overview

Traditional IP packet forwarding analyzes the destination IP address contained in the network layer header of each packet as the packet travels from its source to its final destination. A router analyzes the destination IP address independently at each hop in the network. Dynamic routing protocols or static configuration builds the database needed to analyze the destination IP address (the routing table). The process of implementing traditional IP routing also is called *hop-by-hop destination-based unicast routing*.

Although successful, and obviously widely deployed, certain restrictions, which have been realized for some time, exist for this method of packet forwarding that diminish its flexibility. New techniques are therefore required to address and expand the functionality of an IP-based network infrastructure.

This first chapter concentrates on identifying these restrictions and presents a new architecture, known as *Multiprotocol Label Switching (MPLS)*, that provides solutions to some of these restrictions. The following chapters focus first on the details of the MPLS architecture in a pure router environment, and then in a mixed router/ATM switch environment.

Scalability and Flexibility of IP-based Forwarding

To understand all the issues that affect the scalability and the flexibility of traditional IP packet forwarding networks, you must start with a review of some of the basic IP forwarding mechanisms and their interaction with the underlying infrastructure (local- or wide-area networks). With this information, you can identify any drawbacks to the existing approach and perhaps provide alternative ideas on how this could be improved.

Network Layer Routing Paradigm

Traditional network layer packet forwarding (for example, forwarding of IP packets across the Internet) relies on the information provided by network layer routing protocols (for example, Open Shortest Path First [OSPF] or Border Gateway Protocol [BGP]), or static routing, to make an independent forwarding decision at each hop (router) within the network. The forwarding decision is based solely on the destination unicast IP address. All packets for the same destination follow the same path across the network if no other equal-cost paths exist. Whenever a router has two equal-cost paths toward a destination, the packets toward the destination might take one or both of them, resulting in some degree of load sharing.

NOTE   Enhanced Interior Gateway Routing Protocol (EIGRP) also supports non–equal-cost load sharing although the default behavior of this protocol is equal-cost. You must configure EIGRP *variance* for non–equal-cost load balancing. Please see *EIGRP Network Design Solutions* (ISBN 1-57870-165-1), from Cisco Press for more details on EIGRP.

Load sharing in Cisco IOS can be performed on a packet-by-packet or source-destination-pair basis (with Cisco Express Forwarding [CEF] switching) or on a destination basis (most of the other switching methods).

Routers perform the decision process that selects what path a packet takes. These network layer devices participate in the collection and distribution of network-layer information, and perform Layer 3 switching based on the contents of the network layer header of each packet. You can connect the routers directly by point-to-point links or local-area networks (for example, shared hub or MAU), or you can connect them by LAN or WAN switches (for example, Frame Relay or ATM switches). These Layer 2 (LAN or WAN) switches unfortunately do not have the capability to hold Layer 3 routing information or to select the path taken by a packet through analysis of its Layer 3 destination address. Thus, Layer 2 (LAN or WAN) switches cannot be involved in the Layer 3 packet forwarding decision process. In the case of the WAN environment, the network designer has to establish Layer 2 paths manually across the WAN network. These paths then forward Layer 3 packets between the routers that are connected physically to the Layer 2 network.

LAN Layer 2 paths are simple to establish—all LAN switches are transparent to the devices connected to them. The WAN Layer 2 path establishment is more complex. WAN Layer 2 paths usually are based on a point-to-point paradigm (for example, virtual circuits in most WAN networks) and are established only on request through manual configuration. Any routing device (ingress router) at the edge of the Layer 2 network that wants to forward Layer 3 packets to any other routing device (egress router) therefore needs to either establish a direct connection across the network to the egress device or send its data to a different device for transmission to the final destination.

Consider, for example, the network shown in Figure 1-1.

Figure 1-1   *Sample IP Network Based on ATM Core*

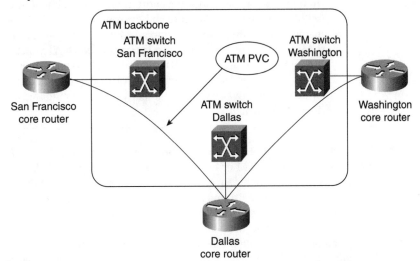

The network illustrated in Figure 1-1 is based on an ATM core surrounded by routers that perform network layer forwarding. Assuming that the only connections between the routers are the ones shown in Figure 1-1, all the packets sent from San Francisco to or via Washington must be sent to the Dallas router, where they are analyzed and sent back over the same ATM connection in Dallas to the Washington router. This extra step introduces delay in the network and unnecessarily loads the CPU of the Dallas router as well as the ATM link between the Dallas router and the adjacent ATM switch in Dallas.

To ensure optimal packet forwarding in the network, an ATM virtual circuit must exist between any two routers connected to the ATM core. Although this might be easy to achieve in small networks, such as the one in Figure 1-1, you run into serious scalability problems in large networks where several tens or even hundreds of routers connect to the same WAN core.

The following facts illustrate the scalability problems you might encounter:

- Every time a new router is connected to the WAN core of the network, a virtual circuit must be established between this router and any other router, if optimal routing is required.

Note   In Frame Relay networks, the entire configuration could be done within the Layer 2 WAN core and the routers would find new neighbors and their Layer 3 protocol addresses through the use of LMI and Inverse ARP. This also is possible on an ATM network through the use óf Inverse ARP, which is enabled by default when a new PVC is added to the configuration of the router, and ILMI, which can discover PVCs dynamically that are configured on the local ATM switch.

- With certain routing protocol configurations, every router attached to the Layer 2 WAN core (built with ATM or Frame Relay switches) needs a dedicated virtual circuit to every other router attached to the same core. To achieve the desired core redundancy, every router also must establish a routing protocol adjacency with every other router attached to the same core. The resulting full-mesh of router adjacencies results in every router having a large number of routing protocol neighbors, resulting in large amounts of routing traffic. For example, if the network runs OSPF or IS-IS as its routing protocol, every router propagates every change in the network topology to every other router connected to the same WAN backbone, resulting in routing traffic proportional to the *square* of the number of routers.

Note   Configuration tools exist in recent Cisco IOS implementations of IS-IS and OSPF routing protocols that allow you to reduce the routing protocol traffic in the network. Discussing the design and the configuration of these tools is beyond the scope of this book (any interested reader should refer to the relevant Cisco IOS configuration guides).

- Provisioning of the virtual circuits between the routers is complex, because it's very hard to predict the exact amount of traffic between any two routers in the network. To simplify the provisioning, some service providers just opt for lack of service guarantee in the network—zero Committed Information Rate (CIR) in a Frame Relay network or Unspecified Bit Rate (UBR) connections in an ATM network.

The lack of information exchange between the routers and the WAN switches was not an issue for traditional Internet service providers that used router-only backbones or for traditional service providers that provided just the WAN services (ATM or Frame Relay virtual circuits). There are, however, several drivers that push both groups toward mixed backbone designs:

- Traditional service providers are asked to offer IP services. They want to leverage their investments and base these new services on their existing WAN infrastructure.

- Internet service providers are asked to provide tighter quality of service (QoS) guarantees that are easier to meet with ATM switches than with traditional routers.

- The rapid increase in bandwidth requirements prior to the introduction of optical router interfaces forced some large service providers to start relying on ATM technology because the router interfaces at that time did not provide the speeds offered by the ATM switches.

It is clear, therefore, that a different mechanism must be used to enable the exchange of network layer information between the routers and the WAN switches and to allow the switches to participate in the decision process of forwarding packets so that direct connections between edge routers are no longer required.

Differentiated Packet Servicing

Conventional IP packet forwarding uses only the IP destination address contained within the Layer 3 header within a packet to make a forwarding decision. The hop-by-hop destination-only paradigm used today prevents a number of innovative approaches to network design and traffic-flow optimization. In Figure 1-2, for example, the direct link between the San Francisco core router and the Washington core router forwards the traffic entering the network in any of the Bay Area Points-of-Presence (POPs), although that link might be congested and the links from San Francisco to Dallas and from Dallas to Washington might be only lightly loaded.

Figure 1-2   *Sample Network that Would Benefit from Traffic Engineering*

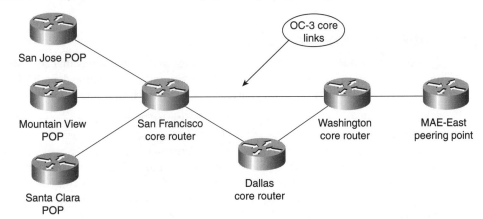

Although certain techniques exist to affect the decision process, such as Policy Based Routing (PBR), no single scalable technique exists to decide on the full path a packet takes across the network to its final destination. In the network shown in Figure 1-2, the policy-based routing must be deployed on the San Francisco core router to divert some of the Bay Area to Washington traffic toward Dallas. Deploying such features as PBR on core routers could severely reduce the performance of a core router and result in a rather unscalable network design. Ideally, the edge routers (for example, the Santa Clara POP in Figure 1-2) can specify over which core links the packets should flow.

NOTE   Several additional issues are associated with policy-based routing. PBR can lead easily to forwarding loops as a router configured with PBR deviates from the forwarding path learned from the routing protocols. PBR also is hard to deploy in large networks; if you configure PBR at the edge, you must be sure that *all* routers in the forwarding path can make the *same* route selection.

Because most major service providers deploy networks with redundant paths, a requirement clearly exists to allow the ingress routing device to be capable of deciding on packet forwarding, which affects the path a packet takes across the network, and of applying a *label* to that packet that indicates to other devices which path the packet should take.

This requirement also should allow packets that are destined for the same IP network to take separate paths instead of the path determined by the Layer 3 routing protocol. This decision also should be based on factors other than the destination IP address of the packet, such as from which port the packet was learned, what quality of service level the packet requires, and so on.

Independent Forwarding and Control

With conventional IP packet forwarding, any change in the information that controls the forwarding of packets is communicated to all devices within the routing domain. This change always involves a period of convergence within the forwarding algorithm.

A mechanism that can change how a packet is forwarded, without affecting other devices within the network, certainly is desirable. To implement such a mechanism, forwarding devices (routers) should not rely on IP header information to forward the packet; thus, an additional label must be attached to a forwarded packet to indicate its desired forwarding behavior. With the packet forwarding being performed based on labels attached to the original IP packets, any change within the decision process can be communicated to other devices through the distribution of new labels. Because these devices merely forward traffic based on the attached label, a change should be able to occur without any impact at all on any devices that perform packet forwarding.

External Routing Information Propagation

Conventional packet forwarding within the core of an IP network requires that external routing information be advertised to all transit routing devices. This is necessary so that packets can be routed based on the destination address that is contained within the network layer header of the packet. To continue the example from previous sections, the core routers in Figure 1-2 would have to store all Internet routes so that they could propagate packets between Bay Area customers and a peering point in MAE-East.

NOTE   You might argue that each major service provider also must have a peering point somewhere on the West coast. That fact, although true, is not relevant to this discussion because you can always find a scenario where a core router with no customers or peering partners connected to it needs complete routing information to be able to forward IP packets correctly.

This method has scalability implications in terms of route propagation, memory usage, and CPU utilization on the core routers, and is not really a required function if all you want to do is pass a packet from one edge of the network to another.

A mechanism that allows internal routing devices to *switch* the packets across the network from an ingress router toward an egress router without analyzing network layer destination addresses is an obvious requirement.

Multiprotocol Label Switching (MPLS) Introduction

Multiprotocol Label Switching (MPLS) is an emerging technology that aims to address many of the existing issues associated with packet forwarding in today's Internetworking environment. Members of the IETF community worked extensively to bring a set of standards to market and to evolve the ideas of several vendors and individuals in the area of *label switching*. The IETF document *draft-ietf-mpls-framework* contains the framework of this initiative and describes the primary goal as follows:

The primary goal of the MPLS working group is to standardize a base technology that integrates the label swapping forwarding paradigm with network layer routing. This base technology (label swapping) is expected to improve the price/performance of network layer routing, improve the scalability of the network layer, and provide greater flexibility in the delivery of (new) routing services (by allowing new routing services to be added without a change to the forwarding paradigm).

NOTE   You can download IETF working documents from the IETF home page (www.ietf.org). For MPLS working documents, start at the MPLS home page (www.ietf.org/html.charters/mpls-charter.html).

The MPLS architecture describes the mechanisms to perform label switching, which combines the benefits of packet forwarding based on Layer 2 switching with the benefits of Layer 3 routing. Similar to Layer 2 networks (for example, Frame Relay or ATM), MPLS assigns *labels* to packets for transport across packet- or cell-based networks. The forwarding mechanism throughout the network is *label swapping*, in which units of data (for example, a packet or a cell) carry a short, fixed-length label that tells switching nodes along the packets path how to process and forward the data.

The significant difference between MPLS and traditional WAN technologies is the way labels are assigned and the capability to carry a stack of labels attached to a packet. The concept of a label stack enables new applications, such as Traffic Engineering, Virtual Private Networks, fast rerouting around link and node failures, and so on.

Packet forwarding in MPLS is in stark contrast to today's connectionless network environment, where each packet is analyzed on a hop-by-hop basis, its layer 3 header is checked, and an independent forwarding decision is made based on the information extracted from a network layer routing algorithm.

The architecture is split into two separate components: the *forwarding* component (also called the *data plane*) and the control component (also called the *control plane*). The forwarding component uses a label-forwarding database maintained by a label switch to perform the forwarding of data packets based on labels carried by packets. The control component is responsible for creating and maintaining label-forwarding information (referred to as *bindings*) among a group of interconnected label switches. Figure 1-3 shows the basic architecture of an MPLS node performing IP routing.

Figure 1-3   *Basic Architecture of an MPLS Node Performing IP Routing*

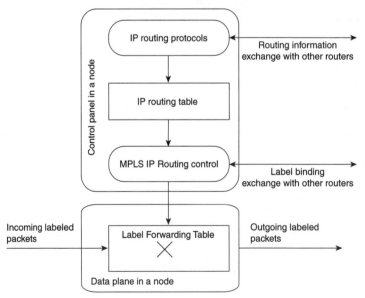

Every MPLS node must run one or more IP routing protocols (or rely on static routing) to exchange IP routing information with other MPLS nodes in the network. In this sense, every MPLS node (including ATM switches) is an IP router on the control plane.

Similar to traditional routers, the IP routing protocols populate the IP routing table. In traditional IP routers, the IP routing table is used to build the IP forwarding cache (fast switching cache in Cisco IOS) or the IP forwarding table (Forwarding Information Base [FIB] in Cisco IOS) used by Cisco Express Forwarding (CEF).

In an MPLS node, the IP routing table is used to determine the label binding exchange, where adjacent MPLS nodes exchange labels for individual subnets that are contained within the IP routing table. The label binding exchange for unicast destination-based IP routing is performed using the Cisco proprietary Tag Distribution Protocol (TDP) or the IETF-specified Label Distribution Protocol (LDP).

The MPLS IP Routing Control process uses labels exchanged with adjacent MPLS nodes to build the Label Forwarding Table, which is the forwarding plane database that is used to forward labeled packets through the MPLS network.

MPLS Architecture—The Building Blocks

As with any new technology, several new terms are introduced to describe the devices that make up the architecture. These new terms describe the functionality of each device and their roles within the MPLS domain structure.

The first device to be introduced is the *Label Switch Router (LSR)*. Any router or switch that implements label distribution procedures and can forward packets based on labels falls under this category. The basic function of label distribution procedures is to allow an LSR to distribute its label bindings to other LSRs within the MPLS network. (Chapter 2, "Frame-mode MPLS Operation," discusses label distribution procedures in detail.)

Several different types of LSR exist that are differentiated by what functionality they provide within the network infrastructure. These different types of LSR are described within the architecture as *Edge-LSR*, *ATM-LSR*, and *ATM edge-LSR*. The distinction between various LSR types is purely architectural—a single box can serve several of the roles.

An Edge-LSR is a router that performs either label imposition (sometimes also referred to as *push* action) or label disposition (also called *pop* action) at the edge of the MPLS network. Label imposition is the act of prepending a label, or a stack of labels, to a packet in the ingress point (in respect of the traffic flow from source to destination) of the MPLS domain. Label disposition is the reverse of this and is the act of removing the last label from a packet at the egress point before it is forwarded to a neighbor that is outside the MPLS domain.

Any LSR that has any non-MPLS neighbors is considered an Edge-LSR. However, if that LSR has any interfaces that connect through MPLS to an ATM-LSR, then it also is considered to be an ATM edge-LSR. Edge-LSRs use a traditional IP forwarding table, augmented with labeling information, to label IP packets or to remove labels from labeled packets before sending them to non-MPLS nodes. Figure 1-4 shows the architecture of an Edge-LSR.

Figure 1-4  *Architecture of an Edge-LSR*

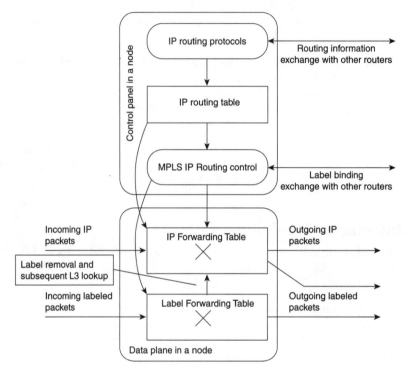

An Edge-LSR extends the MPLS node architecture from Figure 1-3 with additional components in the data plane. The standard IP forwarding table is built from the IP routing table and is extended with labeling information. Incoming IP packets can be forwarded as pure IP packets to non-MPLS nodes or can be labeled and sent out as labeled packets to other MPLS nodes. The incoming labeled packets can be forwarded as labeled packets to other MPLS nodes. For labeled packets destined for non-MPLS nodes, the label is removed and a Layer 3 lookup (IP forwarding) is performed to find the non-MPLS destination.

An ATM-LSR is an ATM switch that can act as an LSR. The Cisco Systems, Inc. LS1010 and BPX family of switches are examples of this type of LSR. As you see in the following chapters, the ATM-LSR performs IP routing and label assignment in the control plane and forwards the data packets using traditional ATM cell switching mechanisms on the data plane. In other words, the ATM switching matrix of an ATM switch is used as a Label Forwarding Table of an MPLS node. Traditional ATM switches, therefore, can be redeployed as ATM-LSRs through a software upgrade of their control component.

Table 1-1 summarizes the functions performed by different LSR types. Please note that any individual device in the network can perform more than one function (for example, it can be Edge-LSR and ATM edge-LSR at the same time).

Table 1-1   *Actions Performed by Various LSR Types*

LSR Type	Actions Performed by This LSR Type
LSR	Forwards labeled packets.
Edge-LSR	Can receive an IP packet, perform Layer 3 lookups, and impose a label stack before forwarding the packet into the LSR domain.
	Can receive a labeled packet, remove labels, perform Layer 3 lookups, and forward the IP packet toward its next-hop.
ATM-LSR	Runs MPLS protocols in the control plane to set up ATM virtual circuits. Forwards labeled packets as ATM cells.
ATM edge-LSR	Can receive a labeled or unlabeled packet, segment it into ATM cells, and forward the cells toward the next-hop ATM-LSR.
	Can receive ATM cells from an adjacent ATM-LSR, reassemble these cells into the original packet, and then forward the packet as a labeled or unlabeled packet.

Label Imposition at the Network Edge

Label imposition has been described already as the act of prepending a label to a packet as it enters the MPLS domain. This is an edge function, which means that packets are labeled before they are forwarded to the MPLS domain.

To perform this function, an Edge-LSR needs to understand where the packet is headed and which label, or stack of labels, it should assign to the packet. In conventional layer 3 IP forwarding, each hop in the network performs a lookup in the IP forwarding table for the IP destination address contained in the layer 3 header of the packet. It selects a next hop IP address for the packet at each iteration of the lookup and eventually sends the packet out of an interface toward its final destination.

NOTE   Some forwarding mechanisms, such as CEF, allow the router to associate each destination prefix known in the routing table to the adjacent next-hop of the destination prefix, thus solving the recursive lookup problem. The whole recursion is resolved while the router populates the cache or the forwarding table and not when it has to forward packets.

Choosing the next hop for the IP packet is a combination of two functions. The first function partitions the entire set of possible packets into a set of IP destination prefixes. The second function maps each IP destination prefix to an IP next hop address. This means that each destination in the network is reachable by one path in respect to traffic flow from one ingress device to the destination egress device (multiple paths might be available if load balancing is performed using equal-cost paths or unequal-cost paths as with some IGP protocols, such as Enhanced IGRP).

Within the MPLS architecture, the results of the first function are known as *Forwarding Equivalence Classes (FECs)*. These can be visualized as describing a group of IP packets that are forwarded in the same manner, over the same path, with the same forwarding treatment.

NOTE   A Forwarding Equivalence Class might correspond to a destination IP subnet, but also might correspond to any traffic class that the Edge-LSR considers significant. For example, all interactive traffic toward a certain destination or all traffic with a certain value of IP precedence might constitute an FEC. As another example, an FEC can be a subset of the BGP table, including all destination prefixes reachable through the same exit point (egress BGP router).

With conventional IP forwarding, the previously described packet processing is performed at each hop in the network. However, when MPLS is introduced, a particular packet is assigned to a particular FEC just once, and this is at the edge device as the packet enters the network. The FEC to which the packet is assigned is then encoded as a short fixed-length identifier, known as a label.

When a packet is forwarded to its next hop, the label is prepended already to the IP packet so that the next device in the path of the packet can forward it based on the encoded label rather than through the analysis of the Layer 3 header information. Figure 1-5 illustrates the whole process of label imposition and forwarding.

NOTE   The actual packet forwarding between the Washington and MAE-East routers might be slightly different from the one shown in Figure 1-5 due to a mechanism called *penultimate hop popping (PHP)*. Penultimate hop popping arguably might improve the switching performance, but does not impact the logic of label switching. Chapter 2 covers this mechanism and its implications.

Figure 1-5   *MPLS Label Imposition and Forwarding*

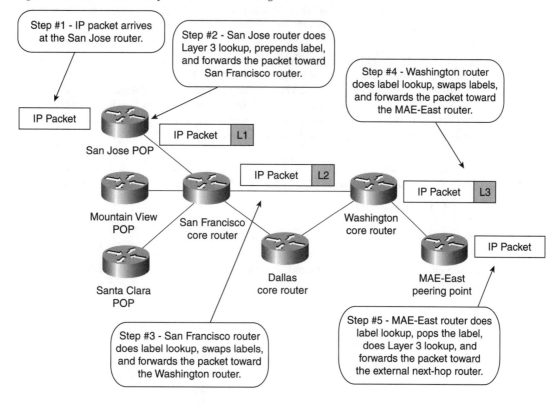

MPLS Packet Forwarding and Label Switched Paths

Each packet enters an MPLS network at an ingress LSR and exits the MPLS network at an egress LSR. This mechanism creates what is known as an *Label Switched Path (LSP)*, which essentially describes the set of LSRs through which a labeled packet must traverse to reach the egress LSR for a particular FEC. This LSP is unidirectional, which means that a different LSP is used for return traffic from a particular FEC.

The creation of the LSP is a connection-oriented scheme because the path is set up prior to any traffic flow. However, this connection setup is based on topology information rather than a requirement for traffic flow. This means that the path is created regardless of whether any traffic actually is required to flow along the path to a particular set of FECs.

As the packet traverses the MPLS network, each LSR swaps the incoming label with an outgoing label, much like the mechanism used today within ATM where the VPI/VCI is swapped to a different VPI/VCI pair when exiting the ATM switch. This continues until the last LSR, known as the egress LSR, is reached.

Each LSR keeps two tables, which hold information that is relevant to the MPLS forwarding component. The first, known in Cisco IOS as the *Tag Information Base (TIB)* or *Label Information Base (LIB)* in standard MPLS terms, holds all labels assigned by this LSR and the mappings of these labels to labels received from any neighbors. These label mappings are distributed through the use of label-distribution protocols, which Chapter 2 discusses in more detail.

Just as multiple neighbors can send labels for the same IP prefix but might not be the actual IP next hop currently in use in the routing table for the destination, not all the labels within the TIB/LIB need to be used for packet forwarding. The second table, known in Cisco IOS as the *Tag Forwarding Information Base (TFIB)* or *Label Forwarding Information Base (LFIB)* in MPLS terms, is used during the actual forwarding of packets and holds only labels that are in use currently by the forwarding component of MPLS.

NOTE   Label Forwarding Information Base is the MPLS equivalent of the switching matrix of an ATM switch.

Using Cisco IOS terms and Cisco Express Forwarding (CEF) terminology, the Edge-LSR architecture in Figure 1-4 can be redrawn as shown in Figure 1-6 (Edge-LSR was chosen because its function is a superset of non–Edge-LSR).

Figure 1-6   *Edge-LSR Architecture Using Cisco IOS Terms*

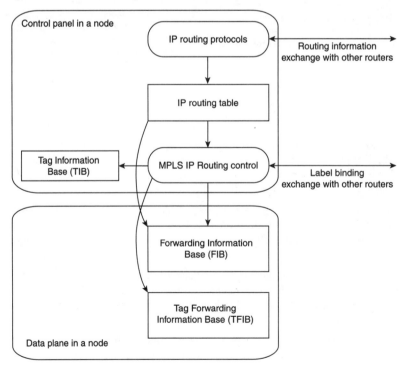

Other MPLS Applications

The MPLS architecture, as discussed so far, enables the smooth integration of traditional routers and ATM switches in a unified IP backbone (IP+ATM architecture). The real power of MPLS, however, lies in other applications that were made possible, ranging from traffic engineering to peer-to-peer Virtual Private Networks. All MPLS applications use control-plane functionality similar to the IP routing control plane shown in Figure 1-6 to set up the label switching database. Figure 1-7 outlines the interaction between these applications and the label-switching matrix.

Figure 1-7   *Various MPLS Applications and Their Interactions*

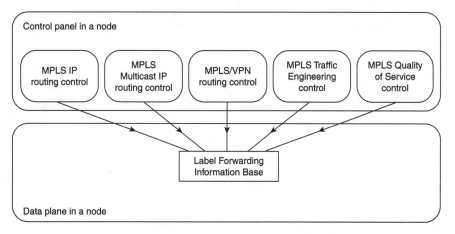

Every MPLS application has the same set of components as the IP routing application:

- A database defining the Forward Equivalence Classes (FECs) table for the application (the IP routing table in an IP routing application)

- Control protocols that exchange the contents of the FEC table between the LSRs (IP routing protocols or static routing in an IP routing application)

- Control process that performs label binding to FECs and a protocol to exchange label bindings between LSRs (TDP or LDP in an IP routing application)

- Optionally, an internal database of FEC-to-label mapping (Label Information Base in an IP routing application)

Each application uses its own set of protocols to exchange FEC table or FEC-to-label mapping between nodes. Table 1-2 summarizes the protocols and the data structures.

The next few chapters cover the use of MPLS in IP routing; Part II, "MPLS-based Virtual Private Networks," covers the Virtual Private Networking application.

Table 1-2   *Control Protocols Used in Various MPLS Applications*

Application	FEC Table	Control Protocol Used to Build FEC Table	Control Protocol Used to Exchange FEC-to-Label Mapping
IP routing	IP routing table	Any IP routing protocol	Tag Distribution Protocol (TDP) or Label Distribution Protocol (LDP)
Multicast IP routing	Multicast routing table	PIM	PIM version 2 extensions
Application	FEC Table	Control Protocol Used to Build FEC Table	Control Protocol Used to Exchange FEC-to-Label Mapping
VPN routing	Per-VPN routing table	Most IP routing protocols between service provider and customer, Multiprotocol BGP inside the service provider network	Multiprotocol BGP
Traffic engineering	MPLS tunnels definition	Manual interface definitions, extensions to IS-IS or OSPF	RSVP or CR-LDP
MPLS Quality of Service	IP routing table	IP routing protocols	Extensions to TDP LDP

Summary

Traditional IP routing has several well-known limitations, ranging from scalability issues to poor support of traffic engineering and poor integration with Layer 2 backbones already existing in large service provider networks. With the rapid growth of the Internet and the establishment of IP as the Layer 3 protocol of choice in most environments, the drawbacks of traditional IP routing became more and more obvious.

MPLS was created to combine the benefits of connectionless Layer 3 routing and forwarding with connection-oriented Layer 2 forwarding. MPLS clearly separates the control plane, where Layer 3 routing protocols establish the paths used for packet forwarding, and the data plane, where Layer 2 label switched paths forward data packets across the MPLS infrastructure. MPLS also simplifies per-hop data forwarding, where it replaces the Layer 3 lookup function performed in traditional routers with simpler label swapping. The simplicity of data plane packet forwarding and its similarity to existing Layer 2 technologies enable traditional WAN equipment (ATM or Frame Relay switches) to be redeployed as MPLS nodes (supporting IP routing in the control plane) just with software upgrades to their control plane.

The control component in the MPLS node uses its internal data structure to identify potential traffic classes (also called Forward Equivalence Classes). A protocol is used between control components in MPLS nodes to exchange the contents of the FEC database and the FEC-to-label mapping. The FEC table and FEC-to-label mapping is used in Edge-LSRs to label ingress packets and send them into the MPLS network. The Label Forwarding Information Base (LFIB) is built within each MPLS node based on the contents of the FEC tables and the FEC-to-label mapping exchanged between the nodes. The LFIB then is used to propagate labeled packets across the MPLS network, similar to the function performed by an ATM switching matrix in the ATM switches.

The MPLS architecture is generic enough to support other applications besides IP routing. The simplest additions to the architecture are the IP multicast routing and quality of service extensions. The MPLS connection-oriented forwarding mechanism together with Layer 2 label-based look ups in the network core also has enabled a range of novel applications, from Traffic Engineering to real peer-to-peer Virtual Private Networks.

CHAPTER 2

Frame-mode MPLS Operation

In Chapter 1, "Multiprotocol Label Switching (MPLS) Architecture Overview," you saw the overall MPLS architecture as well as the underlying concepts. This chapter focuses on one particular application: unicast destination-based IP routing in a pure router environment (also called Frame-mode MPLS because the labeled packets are exchanged as frames on Layer 2). Chapter 3, "Cell-mode MPLS Operation," focuses on the unicast destination-based IP routing in the ATM environment (also called Cell-mode MPLS because the labeled packets are transported as ATM cells).

This chapter first focuses on the MPLS data plane, assuming that the labels were somehow agreed upon between the routers. The next section explains the exact mechanisms used to distribute the labels between the routers, and the last section covers the interaction between label distribution protocols, the Interior Gateway Protocol (IGP), and the Border Gateway Protocol (BGP) in a service provider network.

Throughout the chapter, we refer to the generic architecture of an MPLS Label Switch router (LSR), as shown in Figure 2-1, and use the sample service provider network (called SuperNet) shown in Figure 2-2 for any configuration or debugging printouts.

The SuperNet network uses unnumbered serial links based on loopback interfaces that have IP addresses from Table 2-1.

Table 2-1   *Loopback Addresses in the SuperNet Network*

Router	Loopback Interface
San Jose	172.16.1.1/32
Mountain View	172.16.1.2/32
Santa Clara	172.16.1.3/32
San Francisco	172.16.1.4/32
Dallas	172.16.2.1/32
Washington	172.16.3.1/32
New York	172.16.3.2/32
MAE-East	172.16.4.1/32

Figure 2-1 *Edge-LSR Architecture*

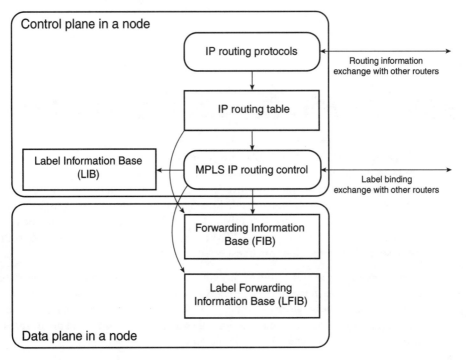

Figure 2-2 *SuperNet Service Provider Network*

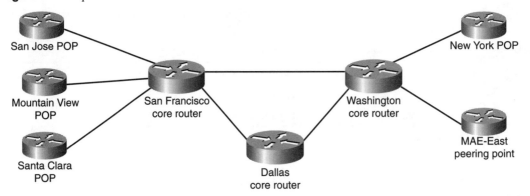

Frame-mode MPLS Data Plane Operation

Chapter 1 briefly described the propagation of an IP packet across an MPLS backbone. There are three major steps in this process:

- The Ingress Edge-LSR receives an IP packet, classifies the packet into a forward equivalence class (FEC), and labels the packet with the outgoing label stack corresponding to the FEC. For unicast destination-based IP routing, the FEC corresponds to a destination subnet and the packet classification is a traditional Layer 3 lookup in the forwarding table.

- Core LSRs receive this labeled packet and use label forwarding tables to exchange the inbound label in the incoming packet with the outbound label corresponding to the same FEC (IP subnet, in this case).

- When the Egress Edge-LSR for this particular FEC receives the labeled packet, it removes the label and performs a traditional Layer 3 lookup on the resulting IP packet.

Figure 2-3 shows these steps being performed in the SuperNet network for a packet traversing the network from the San Jose POP toward a customer attached to the New York POP.

Figure 2-3 *Packet Forwarding Between San Jose POP and New York Customer*

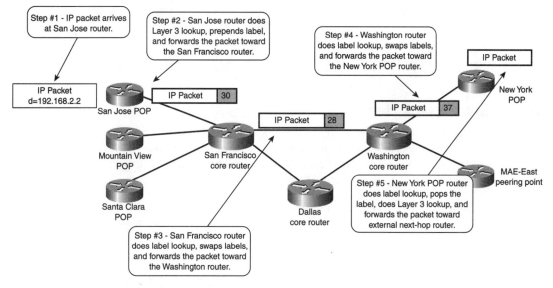

The San Jose POP router receives an IP packet with the destination address of 192.168.2.2 and performs a traditional Layer 3 lookup through the IP forwarding table (also called Forwarding Information Base [FIB]).

NOTE   Because Cisco Express Forwarding (CEF) is the only Layer 3 switching mechanism that
uses the FIB table, CEF must be enabled in all the routers running MPLS *and* all the ingress
interfaces receiving unlabeled IP packets that are propagated as labeled packets across an
MPLS backbone must support CEF switching.

The core routers do not perform CEF switching—they just switch labeled packets—but
they still must have CEF enabled globally for label allocation purposes.

The entry in the FIB (shown in Example 2-1) indicates that the San Jose POP router should
forward the IP packet it just received as a labeled packet. Thus, the San Jose router imposes
the label "30" into the packet before it's forwarded to the San Francisco router, which
brings up the first question: Where is the label imposed and how does the San Francisco
router know that the packet it received is a labeled packet and not a pure IP packet?

Example 2-1   *CEF Entry in the San Jose POP Router*

```
SanJose#show ip cef 192.168.2.0
192.168.2.0/24, version 11, cached adjacency to Serial1/0/1
0 packets, 0 bytes
  tag information set
    local tag: 29
    fast tag rewrite with Se1/0/1, point2point, tags imposed: {30}
  via 172.16.1.4, Serial1/0/1, 0 dependencies
    next hop 172.16.1.4, Serial1/0/1
    valid cached adjacency
    tag rewrite with Se1/0/1, point2point, tags imposed: {30}
```

MPLS Label Stack Header

For various reasons, switching performance being one, the MPLS label must be inserted in
front of the labeled data in a frame-mode implementation of the MPLS architecture. The
MPLS label thus is inserted between the Layer 2 header and the Layer 3 contents of the
Layer 2 frame, as displayed in Figure 2-4.

Figure 2-4   *Position of the MPLS Label in a Layer 2 Frame*

Unlabeled IP packet in
Layer 2 frame

Layer 2 frame	
Layer 3 data (IP packet)	Layer 2 header

Labeled IP packet in
Layer 2 frame

Layer 2 frame		
Layer 3 data (IP packet)	MPLS label (shim header)	Layer 2 header

Due to the way an MPLS label is inserted between the Layer-3 packet and the Layer-2 header, the MPLS label header also is called the *shim header*. The MPLS label header (detailed in Figure 2-5) contains the MPLS label (20 bits), the class-of-service information (three bits, also called *experimental bits*, in the IETF MPLS documentation), and the eight-bit Time-to-Live (TTL) field (which has the identical functions in loop detection as the IP TTL field) and one bit called the *Bottom-of-Stack* bit.

NOTE   Please see Chapter 5, "Advanced MPLS Topics," for a detailed discussion on loop detection and prevention in an MPLS (both frame-mode and cell-mode) environment.

Figure 2-5   *MPLS Label Stack Header*

The Bottom of Stack bit implements an MPLS label stack, which Chapter 1 defined as a combination of two or more label headers attached to a single packet. Simple unicast IP routing does not use the label stack, but other MPLS applications, including MPLS-based Virtual Private Networks or MPLS Traffic Engineering, rely heavily on it.

With the MPLS label stack header being inserted between the Layer 2 header and the Layer 3 payload, the sending router must have some means to indicate to the receiving router that the packet being transmitted is not a pure IP datagram but a labeled packet (an MPLS datagram). To facilitate this, new protocol types were defined above Layer 2 as follows:

- In LAN environments, labeled packets carrying unicast and multicast Layer 3 packets use ethertype values 8847 hex and 8848 hex. These ethertype values can be used directly on Ethernet media (including Fast Ethernet and Gigabit Ethernet) as well as part of the SNAP header on other LAN media (including Token Ring and FDDI).

- On point-to-point links using PPP encapsulation, a new Network Control Protocol (NCP) called MPLS Control Protocol (MPLSCP) was introduced. MPLS packets are marked with PPP Protocol field value 8281 hex.

- MPLS packets transmitted across a Frame Relay DLCI between a pair of routers are marked with Frame Relay SNAP Network Layer Protocol ID (NLPID), followed by a SNAP header with type ethertype value 8847 hex.

- MPLS packets transmitted between a pair of routers over an ATM Forum virtual circuit are encapsulated with a SNAP header that uses ethertype values equal to those used in the LAN environment.

NOTE   For more details on MPLS transport across non-MPLS WAN media, see Chapter 4, "Running Frame-mode MPLS Across Switched WAN Media."

Figure 2-6 shows the summary of all the MPLS encapsulation techniques.

Figure 2-6   *Summary of MPLS Encapsulation Techniques*

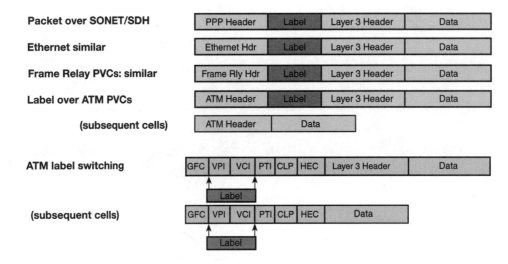

The San Jose router in the example shown in Figure 2-3 inserts the MPLS label in front of the IP packet just received, encapsulates the labeled packet in a PPP frame with a PPP Protocol field value of 8281 hex, and forwards the Layer 2 frame toward the San Francisco router.

Label Switching in Frame-mode MPLS

After receiving the Layer 2 PPP frame from the San Jose router, the San Francisco router immediately identifies the received packet as a labeled packet based on its PPP Protocol field value and performs a label lookup in its Label Forwarding Information Base (LFIB).

NOTE   LFIB also is called Tag Forwarding Information Base (TFIB) in older Cisco documentation.

The LFIB entry corresponding to inbound label 30 (and displayed in Example 2-2) directs the San Francisco router to replace the label 30 with an outbound label 28 and to propagate the packet toward the Washington router.

Example 2-2   *LFIB Entry for Label 30 in the San Francisco Router*

```
SanFrancisco#show tag forwarding-table tags 30 detail
Local  Outgoing     Prefix              Bytes tag  Outgoing    Next Hop
tag    tag or VC    or Tunnel Id        switched   interface
30     28           192.168.2.0/24      0          Se0/0/1     172.16.3.1
          MAC/Encaps=14/18, MTU=1504, Tag Stack{28}
          00107BB59E2000107BEC6B008847 0001C000
       Per-packet load-sharing
```

The labeled packet is propagated in a similar fashion across the SuperNet backbone until it reaches the New York POP, where the LFIB entry tells the New York router to pop the label and forward the unlabeled packet (see Example 2-3).

Example 2-3   *LFIB Entry in the New York Router*

```
NewYork#show tag forwarding-table tags 37 detail
Local  Outgoing     Prefix              Bytes tag  Outgoing    Next Hop
tag    tag or VC    or Tunnel Id        switched   interface
37     untagged         192.168.2.0/24 0           Se2/1/3     192.168.2.1
          MAC/Encaps=0/0, MTU=1504, Tag Stack{}
       Per-packet load-sharing
```

A Cisco router running Cisco IOS software and operating as an MPLS LSR in Frame-mode MPLS can perform a number of actions on a labeled packet:

- **Pop tag**—Removes the top label in the MPLS label stack and propagates the remaining payload as either a labeled packet (if the bottom-of-stack bit is zero) or as an unlabeled IP packet (the Tag Stack field in the LFIB is empty).

- **Swap tag**—Replaces the top label in the MPLS label stack with another value (the Tag Stack field in the LFIB is one label long)

- **Push tag**—Replaces the top label in the MPLS label stack with a set of labels (the Tag Stack field in the LFIB contains several labels).

- **Aggregate**—Removes the top label in the MPLS label stack and does a Layer 3 lookup on the underlying IP packet. The removed label is the bottom label in the MPLS label stack; otherwise, the datagram is discarded.

- **Untag**—Removes the top label in the MPLS label stack and forwards the underlying IP packet to the specified IP next-hop. The removed label is the bottom label in the MPLS label stack; otherwise, the datagram is discarded.

MPLS Label Switching with Label Stack

The label switching operation is performed in the same way regardless of whether the labeled packet contains only one label or a label stack several labels deep. In both cases, the LSR switching the packet acts only on the top label in the stack, ignoring the other labels. This function enables a variety of MPLS applications where the edge routers can agree on packet classification rules and associated labels without knowledge of the core routers.

For example, assume that the San Jose router and the New York router in the SuperNet network support MPLS-based Virtual Private Networks and that they have agreed that network 10.1.0.0/16, which is reachable through the New York router, is assigned a label value of 73. The core routers in the SuperNet network (San Francisco and Washington) are not aware of this.

To send a packet to a destination host in network 10.1.0.0/16, the San Jose router builds a label stack. The bottom label in the stack is the label agreed upon with the New York router, and the top label in the stack is the label assigned to the IP address of the New York router by the San Francisco router. When the network propagates the packet (as displayed in Figure 2-7), the top label is switched exactly like in the example where a pure IP packet was propagated across the backbone and the second label in the stack reaches the New York router intact.

Figure 2-7 *Label Switching with the MPLS Label Stack*

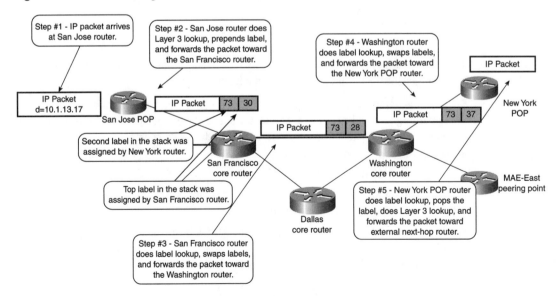

Label Bindings and Propagation in Frame-mode MPLS

The previous section identifies the mechanisms necessary to forward labeled packets between the LSRs using framed interfaces (LAN, point-to-point links, or WAN virtual circuits). This section focuses on FEC-to-label bindings and their propagation between LSRs over framed interfaces.

Cisco IOS software implements two label binding protocols that can be used to associate IP subnets with MPLS labels for the purpose of unicast destination-based routing:

- **Tag Distribution Protocol (TDP)**—Cisco's proprietary protocol available in IOS software release 11.1CT, as well as 12.0 and all subsequent IOS releases

- **Label Distribution Protocol (LDP)**—IETF standard label binding protocol available in 12.2T release

TDP and LDP functionally are equivalent and can be used concurrently within the network, even on different interfaces of the same LSR. Due to their functional equivalence, this section shows only TDP debugging and monitoring commands.

To start MPLS packet labeling for unicast IP packets and associated protocols on an interface, use the commands in Table 2-2.

Table 2-2   *IOS Configuration Commands Used to Start MPLS on an Interface*

Task	IOS Command
Start MPLS packet labeling and run TDP on the specified interface.	**tag-switching ip**
Start MPLS packet labeling on the specified interface. TDP is used as the default label distribution protocol. Note: This command is equivalent to the tag-switching ip command:	**mpls ip**
Select the label distribution protocol on the specified interface.	**mpls label-distribution [ldp | tdp | both]**

LDP/TDP Session Establishment

When you start MPLS on the first interface in a router, the TDP/LDP process is started and the Label Information Base (LIB) structure is created. The router also tries to discover other LSRs on the interfaces running MPLS through TDP hello packets. The TDP hello packets are sent as broadcast or multicast UDP packets, making LSR neighbor discovery automatic. The **debug tag tdp transport** command can monitor the TDP hellos. Example 2-4 shows the TDP process startup and Example 2-5 illustrates the successful establishment of a TDP adjacency.

NOTE	The **debug mpls** commands replace the **debug tag** commands in IOS images with LDP support.

Example 2-4 *TDP Startup After the First Interface Is Configured for MPLS*

```
SanFrancisco#debug tag tdp transport
TDP transport events debugging is on
SanFrancisco#conf t
Enter configuration commands, one per line.  End with CNTL/Z.
SanFrancisco(config)#interface serial 1/0/1
SanFrancisco(config-subif)#tag-switching ip                         .

1d20h: enabling tdp on Serial1/0/1
1d20h: tdp: 1<tdp_start: tdp_process_ptr = 0x80B7826C
1d20h: tdp: tdp_set_intf_id: intf 0x80E49B74, Serial1/0/1, not tc-atm, intf_id 0
1d20h: enabling tdp on Serial1/0/1
1d20h: tdp: Got TDP Id
1d20h: tdp: Got TDP TCP Listen socket
1d20h: tdp: tdp_hello_process tdp inited
1d20h: tdp: tdp_hello_process start hello for Serial1/0/1
1d20h: tdp: Got TDP UDP socket
```

Example 2-5 *TDP Neighbor Discovery*

```
1d20h: tdp: Send hello; Serial1/0/1, src/dst 172.16.1.4/255.255.255.255, inst_id 0
1d20h: tdp: Rcvd hello; Serial1/0/1, from 172.16.1.1 (172.16.1.1:0), intf_id 0, opt
0x4
1d20h: tdp: Hello from 172.16.1.1 (172.16.1.1:0) to 255.255.255.255, opt 0x4
```

There also might be cases where an adjacent LSR wants to establish an LDP or TDP session with the LSR under consideration, but the interface connecting the two is not configured for MPLS due to security or other administrative reasons. In such a case, the debugging printout similar to the printout shown in Example 2-6 indicates ignored hello packets being received through interfaces on which MPLS is not configured.

Example 2-6 *Ignored TDP Hello*

```
1d20h: tdp: Ignore Hello from 172.16.3.1, Serial0/0/1; no intf
```

After the TDP hello process discovers a TDP neighbor, a TDP session is established with the neighbor. TDP sessions are run on the well-known TCP port 711; LDP uses TCP port 646. TCP is used as the transport protocol (similar to BGP) to ensure reliable information delivery. Using TCP as the underlying transport protocol also results in excellent flow control properties and good adjustments to interface congestion conditions. Example 2-7 shows the TDP session establishment.

Example 2-7   *TDP Session Establishment*

```
1d20h: tdp: New adj 0x80EA92D4 from 172.16.1.1 (172.16.1.1:0), Serial1/0/1
1d20h: tdp: Opening conn; adj 0x80EA92D4, 172.16.1.4 <-> 172.16.1.1
1d20h: tdp: Conn is up; adj 0x80EA92D4, 172.16.1.4:11000 <-> 172.16.1.1:711
1d20h: tdp: Sent open PIE to 172.16.1.1 (pp 0x0)
1d20h: tdp: Rcvd open PIE from 172.16.1.1 (pp 0x0)
```

After a TDP session is established, it's monitored constantly with TDP keepalive packets to ensure that it's still operational. Example 2-8 shows the TDP keepalive packets.

Example 2-8   *TDP Keepalives*

```
1d20h: tdp: Sent keep_alive PIE to 172.16.1.1:0 (pp 0x0)
1d20h: tdp: Rcvd keep_alive PIE from 172.16.1.1:0 (pp 0x0)
```

The TDP neighbors and the status of individual TDP sessions also can be monitored with **show tag tdp neighbor** command, as shown in Example 2-9. This printout was taken at the moment when the San Jose router was the only TDP neighbor of the San Francisco router.

Example 2-9   *Show Tag TDP Neighbor Printout*

```
SanFrancisco#show tag-switching tdp neighbor
  Peer TDP Ident: 172.16.1.1:0; Local TDP Ident 172.16.1.4:0
  TCP connection: 172.16.1.1.711 - 172.16.1.4.11000
                  State: Oper; PIEs sent/rcvd: 4/4; ; Downstream
                  Up time: 00:01:05
                  TDP discovery sources:
                    Serial1/0.1
    Addresses bound to peer TDP Ident:
    172.16.1.1
```

The command displays the TDP identifiers of the local and remote routers, the IP addresses and the TCP port numbers between which the TDP connection is established, the connection uptime and the interfaces through which the TDP neighbor was discovered, as well as all the interface IP addresses used by the TDP neighbor.

NOTE   The TDP identifier is determined in the same way as the OSPF or BGP identifier (unless controlled by the **tag tdp router-id** command)—the highest IP address of all loopback interfaces is used. If no loopback interfaces are configured on the router, the TDP identifier becomes the highest IP address of any interface that was operational at the TDP process startup time.

| NOTE | The IP address used as the TDP identifier *must be reachable* by adjacent LSRs; otherwise, the TDP/LDP session cannot be established. |

Label Binding and Distribution

As soon as the Label Information Base (LIB) is created in a router, a label is assigned to every Forward Equivalence Class known to the router. For unicast destination-based routing, the FEC is equivalent to an IGP prefix in the IP routing table. Thus, a label is assigned to every prefix in the IP routing table and the mapping between the two is stored in the LIB.

| NOTE | Labels are not assigned to BGP routes in the IP routing table. The BGP routes use the same label as the interior route toward the BGP next hop. For more information on MPLS/BGP integration, see the section, "MPLS Interaction with the Border Gateway Protocol," later in this chapter. |

The Label Information Base is always kept synchronized to the IP routing table—as soon as a new non-BGP route appears in the IP routing table, a new label is allocated and bound to the new route. The **debug tag tdp bindings** printouts show the subnet-to-label binding. Example 2-10 shows a sample printout.

Example 2-10   *Sample Label-to-prefix Bindings*

```
SanFrancisco#debug tag-switching tdp bindings
TDP Tag Information Base (TIB) changes debugging is on
1d20h: tagcon: tibent(172.16.1.4/32): created; find route tags request
1d20h: tagcon: tibent(172.16.1.4/32): lcl tag 1 (#2) assigned
1d20h: tagcon: tibent(172.16.1.1/32): created; find route tags request
1d20h: tagcon: tibent(172.16.1.1/32): lcl tag 26 (#4) assigned
1d20h: tagcon: tibent(172.16.1.3/32): created; find route tags request
1d20h: tagcon: tibent(172.16.1.3/32): lcl tag 27 (#6) assigned
1d20h: tagcon: tibent(172.16.1.2/32): created; find route tags request
1d20h: tagcon: tibent(172.16.1.2/32): lcl tag 28 (#8) assigned
1d20h: tagcon: tibent(192.168.1.0/24): created; find route tags request
1d20h: tagcon: tibent(192.168.1.0/24): lcl tag 1 (#10) assigned
1d20h: tagcon: tibent(192.168.2.0/24): created; find route tags request
1d20h: tagcon: tibent(192.168.2.0/24): lcl tag 29 (#12) assigned
```

Because the LSR assigns a label to each IP prefix in its routing table as soon as the prefix appears in the routing table, and the label is meant to be used by other LSRs to send the labeled packets toward the assigning LSR, this method of label allocation and label distribution is called *independent control* label assignment, with *unsolicited downstream* label distribution:

- The label allocation in routers is done regardless of whether the router has received a label for the same prefix already from its next-hop router or not. Thus, label allocation in routers is called *independent control*.

- The distribution method is unsolicited because the LSR assigns the label and advertises the mapping to upstream neighbors regardless of whether other LSRs need the label. The on-demand distribution method is the other possibility. An LSR assigns only a label to an IP prefix and distributes it to upstream neighbors when asked to do so. Chapter 3 discusses this method in more detail.

- The distribution method is downstream when the LSR assigns a label that other LSRs (upstream LSRs) can use to forward labeled packets and advertises these label mappings to its neighbors. Initial tag switching architecture also contains provisions for upstream label distribution, but neither the current tag switching implementation nor the MPLS architecture needs this type of distribution method.

All label bindings are advertised immediately to all other routers through the TDP sessions. The advertisements also can be examined by means of debugging commands, as shown in Example 2-11. The printout was taken on the San Francisco router after the route toward 192.168.2.0/24 was propagated from New York to San Francisco via the IGP and entered into the San Francisco LSR's routing table.

Example 2-11 *IP Prefix-to-label Binding Propagation Through TDP*

```
1d20h: tagcon: adj 172.16.1.1:0 (pp 0x80EA98E4): advertise 192.168.2.0/24, tag 29
(#12)
1d20h: tagcon: adj 172.16.3.1:0 (pp 0x80EA98E4): advertise 192.168.2.0/24, tag 29
(#12)
1d20h: tagcon: adj 172.16.2.1:0 (pp 0x80EA98E4): advertise 192.168.2.0/24, tag 29
(#12)
1d20h: tagcon: adj 172.16.1.2:0 (pp 0x80EA98E4): advertise 192.168.2.0/24, tag 29
(#12)
1d20h: tagcon: adj 172.16.1.3:0 (pp 0x80EA98E4): advertise 192.168.2.0/24, tag 29
(#12)
1d20h: tdp: Sent bind PIE to 172.16.1.1:0 (pp 0x80EA98E4)

... rest deleted ...
```

As you can see from the printout, the San Francisco router announces its IP prefix-to-label binding to all TDP neighbors, regardless of whether they are upstream or downstream. Even more, the binding also is sent to the next-hop router, so there is no split-horizon processing in TDP or LDP.

The adjacent LSRs receive prefix-to-label mappings, store them in their LIB, and use them in their FIB or LFIB if the mapping has been received from their downstream neighbor, which is the next-hop for the particular FEC in question. This storage method is called *liberal retention mode* as opposed to *conservative retention mode*, where an LSR retains only the labels assigned to a prefix by its current downstream routers.

NOTE   There are a number of possible combinations between the three label allocation parameters (unsolicited versus on-demand distribution, independent versus ordered control, and liberal versus conservative retention), but the routers running Cisco IOS software always use unsolicited distribution, independent control, and liberal retention over Frame-mode MPLS interfaces. The fixed set of parameters should not prevent the router from interoperating through LDP with other devices that use a different default. For more details on which combinations work and which ones don't, please refer to the IETF LDP documentation.

The **show tag-switching tdp bindings** command can display all the label mappings generated by a router or received from its TDP neighbors. Example 2-12 displays the result of that command for IP prefix 192.168.2.0/24 on the San Francisco router.

Example 2-12   *Label Information Base Entry on San Francisco Router*

```
SanFrancisco#show tag-switching tdp bindings 192.168.2.0
  tib entry: 192.168.2.0/24, rev 7
                    local binding:  tag: 30
                    remote binding: tsr: 172.16.1.1:0, tag: 33
                    remote binding: tsr: 172.16.1.2:0, tag: 35
                    remote binding: tsr: 172.16.1.3:0, tag: 23
                    remote binding: tsr: 172.16.2.1:0, tag: 59
                    remote binding: tsr: 172.16.3.1:0, tag: 28
SanFrancisco#
```

A router might receive TDP bindings from a number of neighbors, but uses only a few of them in the forwarding tables as follows:

- The label binding from the next-hop router is entered in the corresponding FIB entry. If the router doesn't receive the label binding from the next-hop router, the FIB entry specifies that the packets for that destination should be sent unlabeled.

- If the router receives a label binding from the next-hop router, the local label and the next-hop label are entered in the LFIB. If the next-hop router didn't assign a label to the corresponding prefix, the outgoing action in LFIB is unlabeled. Example 2-13 shows both cases.

NOTE   A router that has no label for a specific IP prefix from the next-hop router marks the prefix as unlabeled if it is not a directly connected interface or is not a summary route. If the route is connected directly or is a summary route, an additional Layer 3 lookup is needed and a router assigns a null label to that prefix due to a mechanism called *Penultimate Hop Popping*, which is covered in the next section.

Example 2-13   *Label Forwarding Information Base on San Francisco Router*

```
SanFrancisco#show tag forwarding-table tags 30-31
Local   Outgoing     Prefix           Bytes tag  Outgoing    Next Hop
tag     tag or VC    or Tunnel Id     switched   interface
30      28           192.168.2.0/32   0          Se0/0/1     172.16.3.1
31      untagged     192.168.100.4/32 0          Se1/0/3     172.16.1.3
```

Convergence in a Frame-mode MPLS Network

An important aspect in MPLS network design is the convergence time of the network. Some MPLS applications (for example, an MPLS/VPN or BGP design based on MPLS) do not work correctly unless a labeled packet can be sent all the way through from the ingress Edge-LSR to the egress Edge-LSR. In these applications, the convergence time needed by an Interior Gateway Protocol (IGP) to converge around a failure in the core network could be increased by the label propagation delay.

In a Frame-mode MPLS network, using liberal retention mode in combination with independent label control and unsolicited downstream label distribution minimizes the TDP/LDP convergence delay. Every router using liberal retention mode usually has label assignments for a given prefix from all its TDP/LDP neighbors, so it can always find a proper outgoing label following the routing table convergence without asking its new next-hop router for the label assignment.

NOTE   Unfortunately the immediate TDP/LDP convergence happens only when a link fails. When a link is reestablished, the IGP adjacency and convergence usually happens before the TDP adjacency is set up and the labels are exchanged, resulting in the temporary incapability to forward labeled packets until the labels are exchanged.

The next set of examples, based on a failure scenario (the link between Washington and San Francisco fails) in the SuperNet network, illustrate the immediate convergence. The examples observe only the route toward network 192.168.100.2/32, which is attached to the New York router.

The **show** command printouts (see Example 2-14) in the initial state indicate that the target route is reachable through interface Serial0/0/1 through next-hop 172.16.3.1.

Example 2-14   *TDP, LFIB, and FIB Entries Prior to Link failure*

```
SanFrancisco#show tag-switching tdp binding 192.168.100.2 32
    tib entry: 192.168.100.2/32, rev 10
          local binding:  tag: 28
          remote binding: tsr: 172.16.2.1:0, tag: 28
          remote binding: tsr: 172.16.3.1:0, tag: 32

SanFrancisco#show tag-switching forwarding 192.168.100.2
Local  Outgoing    Prefix           Bytes tag  Outgoing   Next Hop
tag    tag or VC   or Tunnel Id     switched   interface
28     32          192.168.100.2/32 0          Se0/0/1    point2point
SanFrancisco#show ip cef 192.168.100.2
192.168.100.2/32, version 76, attached
0 packets, 0 bytes
  tag information set, shared, unshareable
    local tag: 28
  via Serial0/0/1, 9 dependencies
    valid adjacency
    tag rewrite with Se0/0/1, point2point, tags imposed: {32}
```

Immediately following the link failure, the LFIB is scanned to clean up any entries that used the failed interface as the outgoing interface (see Example 2-15)

Example 2-15   *LFIB Scan Following a Link Failure*

```
SanFrancisco#sh debug
IP routing:
  IP routing debugging is on
Tag Switching:
  TDP Tag Information Base (TIB) changes debugging is on
  TDP tag and address advertisements debugging is on
  Cisco Express Forwarding related TFIB services debugging is on

SanFrancisco#
3d03h: %LINK-5-CHANGED: Interface Serial0/0/1, changed state to down
3d03h: %LINEPROTO-5-UPDOWN: Line protocol on Interface Serial0/0/1, changed state
to down
3d03h: TFIB: fib scan start:needed:1,unres:0,mac:0,mtu:0,loadinfo:0,scans aborted 0
3d03h: TFIB: fib check cleanup for 192.168.100.2/32,index=0,return_value=0
3d03h: TFIB: fib_scanner_walk,reslve path 0 of 192.168.100.2/32
3d03h: TFIB: resolve tag rew,prefix=192.168.100.2/32,has tag_info,no parent
3d03h: TFIB: finish fib res 192.168.100.2/32:index 0,parent outg tag no parent
3d03h: TFIB: set fib rew: pfx 192.168.100.2/32,index=0,add=1,tag_rew->adj=Serial 0/
0/1
3d03h: TFIB: Update TFIB for 192.168.100.2/32, fib no loadinfo, tfib no loadinfo,
per_pkt,resolved=1
3d03h: TFIB: fib_scanner_end
```

The failed interface then is removed from the routing table and the associated routes are removed from the IP routing table. Because no alternative equal-cost route toward 192.168.100.2/32 currently exists, the route is removed completely from the routing table and the associated entry is deleted from the LFIB (see Example 2-16).

Example 2-16 *Routing Table and LFIB Cleanup*

```
3d03h: RT: interface Serial0/0/1 removed from routing table
3d03h: RT: delete route to 192.168.100.2 via 0.0.0.0, Serial0/0/1
3d03h: RT: no routes to 192.168.100.2, flushing
3d03h: TFIB: tfib_fib_delete,192.168.100.2/32,fib->count=1
3d03h: TFIB: fib complete delete: prefix=192.168.100.2/32,inc tag=28,del info=1
3d03h: TFIB: deactivate tag rew for 192.168.100.2/32,index=0
3d03h: TFIB: Update TFIB for 192.168.100.2/32, fib no loadinfo, tfib no loadinfo
, per_pkt,resolved=0
3d03h: TFIB: set fib rew: pfx 192.168.100.2/32,index=0,add=0,tag_rew->adj=Serial 0/
0/1
```

An alternate route to 192.168.100.2 goes through the Denver router. The OSPF process immediately installs the alternate route in the routing table. Corresponding CEF and LFIB entries are created and the LFIB entry gets the label assigned by 172.16.2.1 (the Denver router) as its outgoing label. The new LFIB entry is installed without any TDP/LDP interaction with any TDP/LDP neighbors (see Example 2-17).

Example 2-17 *Alternate Route Is Installed in the Routing Table*

```
3d03h: RT: add 192.168.100.2/32 via 172.16.2.1, ospf metric [110/21]
3d03h: TFIB: post table chg,ROUTE_UP 192.168.100.2/32,loadinfo ct=1
3d03h: TFIB: find_rt_tgs,192.168.100.2/32,meth 1,res_next_hop=172.16.2.1, Se0/0/2
,next_hop 172.16.2.1
3d03h: TFIB: route tag chg 192.168.100.2/32,idx=0,inc=28,outg=28,enabled=0x1
3d03h: TFIB: create tag info 192.168.100.2/32,inc tag=28,has no info
3d03h: TFIB: resolve tag rew,prefix=192.168.100.2/32,has tag_info,no parent
3d03h: TFIB: finish fib res 192.168.100.2/32:index 0,parent outg tag no parent
3d03h: TFIB: set fib rew: pfx 192.168.100.2/32,index=0,add=1,tag_rew->adj=FastEt
hernet0/0
3d03h: TFIB: Update TFIB for 192.168.100.2/32, fib no loadinfo, tfib no loadinfo
, per_pkt,resolved=1
```

As the last step, all entries from the TDP neighbor 172.16.3.1 (the Washington router), which is no longer reachable, are removed from the Label Information Base (see Example 2-18)

Example 2-18 *LIB Entries Received from Washington Router Are Removed*

```
3d03h: tagcon: tibent(192.168.100.2/32): rem tag 1 from 172.16.3.1:0 removed
3d03h: tagcon: no route_tag_change for: 192.168.100.2/32
       for tsr 172.16.3.1:0: tsr is not next hop
3d03h: TFIB: resolve recursive: share rewrite of parent 192.168.100.2/32
```

Penultimate Hop Popping

An egress Edge-LSR in an MPLS network might have to perform two lookups on a packet received from an MPLS neighbor and destined for a subnet outside the MPLS domain. It must inspect the label in the label stack header, and it must perform the label lookup just to realize that the label has to be popped and the underlying IP packet inspected. An additional Layer 3 lookup must be performed on the IP packet before it can be forwarded to its final destination. Figure 2-8 shows the corresponding process in the SuperNet network.

Figure 2-8 *Double Lookup in New York POP Router*

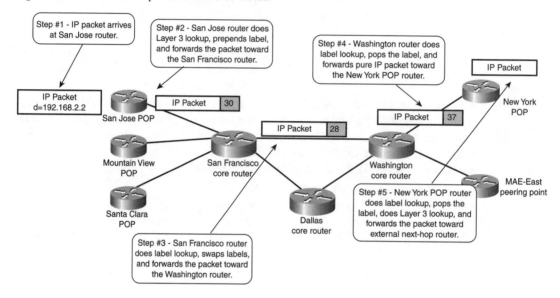

The double lookup in the New York POP router might reduce the performance of that node. Furthermore, in environments where MPLS and IP switching is realized in hardware, the fact that a double lookup might need to be performed can increase the complexity of the hardware implementation significantly. To address both issues, *Penultimate Hop Popping (PHP)* was introduced into the MPLS architecture.

NOTE	Penultimate Hop Popping is used only for directly connected subnets or aggregate routes. In the case of a directly connected interface, Layer 3 lookup is necessary to obtain the correct next-hop information for a packet that is sent toward a directly connected destination. If the prefix is an aggregate, a Layer 3 lookup also is necessary to find a more specific route that then is used to route the packet toward its correct destination. In all other cases, the Layer 2 outbound packet information is available within the LFIB and, therefore, a Layer 3 lookup is not necessary and the packet can be label switched.

With penultimate hop popping, the Edge-LSR can request a label pop operation from its upstream neighbors. In the SuperNet network, the Washington router pops the label from the packet (Step 4 in Figure 2-9) and sends a pure IP packet to the New York router. Then the New York router does a simple Layer 3 lookup and forwards the packet to its final destination (Step 5 in Figure 2-9).

Figure 2-9 *Penultimate Hop Popping in the SuperNet Network*

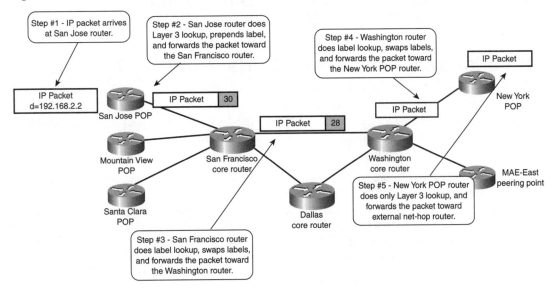

Penultimate hop popping is requested through TDP or LDP by using a special label value (1 for TDP, 3 for LDP) that also is called the *implicit-null* value.

When the egress LSR requests penultimate hop popping for an IP prefix, the local LIB entry in the egress LSR and the remote LIB entry in the upstream LSRs indicate the **imp-null** value (see Example 2-19) and the LFIB entry in the penultimate LSR indicates a tag pop operation (see Example 2-20).

Example 2-19 *LIB Entries in Edge LSR and Penultimate LSR*

```
NewYork#show tag tdp binding 192.168.2.0 24
  tib entry: 192.168.2.0/24, rev 10
      local binding:  tag: imp-null(1)
      remote binding: tsr: 172.16.3.1:0, tag: 28

Washington#show tag tdp binding 192.168.2.0 24
  tib entry: 192.168.2.0/24, rev 10
      local binding:  tag: 28
      remote binding: tsr: 172.16.3.2:0, tag: imp-null(1)
      remote binding: tsr: 172.16.1.4:0, tag: 30
      remote binding: tsr: 172.16.2.1:0, tag: 37
```

Example 2-20 *LFIB Entry in Washington Router*

```
Washington#show tag forwarding tags 28
Local  Outgoing    Prefix        Bytes tag  Outgoing   Next Hop
tag    tag or VC   or Tunnel Id  switched   interface
26     Pop tag     192.168.2.0/24  0                   Se0/0/2    point2point
```

MPLS Interaction with the Border Gateway Protocol

In the section "Label Binding and Distribution," earlier in this chapter, you saw that a label is assigned to every IP prefix in the IP routing table of a router acting as LSR, the only exception being routes learned through the Border Gateway Protocol (BGP). No labels are assigned to these routes and the ingress Edge-LSR uses the label assigned to the BGP next hop to label the packets forwarded toward BGP destinations.

To illustrate this phenomenon, assume that the MAE-East router in the SuperNet network receives a route for network 192.168.3.0 from a router in Autonomous System 4635. The route is propagated throughout the SuperNet network with the MAE-East router from AS4635 being the BGP next-hop. When looking in the BGP table on the San Jose router and in the corresponding FIB table entries, you can see that the same label (28) is used to label the packets for the BGP destination and for the BGP next-hop (see Example 2-21).

Example 2-21 *BGP and FIB Entries on the San Jose Router*

```
SanJose#show ip bgp 192.168.3.0
BGP routing table entry for 192.168.3.0/24, version 2
Paths: (1 available, best #1, table Default-IP-Routing-Table)
  4635
    192.168.100.2 (metric 21) from 172.16.4.1 (172.16.4.1)
      Origin IGP, metric 0, localpref 100, valid, internal, best
SanJose#show ip cef 192.168.3.0
192.168.3.0/24, version 52, cached adjacency 172.16.1.4
0 packets, 0 bytes
```

Example 2-21   *BGP and FIB Entries on the San Jose Router (Continued)*

```
  tag information from 172.16.1.4/32, shared
    local tag: 39
    fast tag rewrite with Se1/0/1, 172.16.1.4, tags imposed: {28}
  via 192.168.100.2, 0 dependencies, recursive
    next hop 172.16.1.4, Serial1/0/1 via 172.16.1.4/32
    valid cached adjacency
    tag rewrite with Se1/0/1, 172.16.1.4, tags imposed: {28}
SanJose#show ip cef 192.168.100.2
192.168.100.2/32, version 26, cached adjacency 172.16.1.4
0 packets, 0 bytes
  tag information set, shared
    local tag: 39
    fast tag rewrite with Se1/0/1, 172.16.1.4, tags imposed: {28}
  via 192.168.100.2, 0 dependencies, recursive
    next hop 172.16.1.4, Serial1/0/1 via 172.16.1.4/32
    valid cached adjacency
    tag rewrite with Se1/0/1, 172.16.1.4, tags imposed: {28}
```

The interaction between MPLS, IGP, and BGP gives a network designer a completely new approach to network design. Traditionally, BGP had to be run on every router in the core of a service provider network to enable proper packet forwarding. For example, BGP information from MAE-East had to be propagated to every core router in the SuperNet network (Washington, Denver, and San Francisco). If that were not the case, the core routers could not route the packets toward the BGP destination, as illustrated in Figure 2-10.

Figure 2-10   *Connectivity Loss in Network with No BGP on Core Routers*

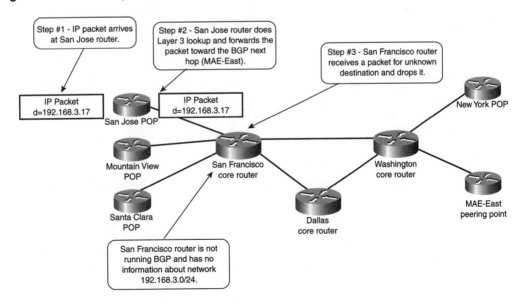

If, however, the SuperNet network runs MPLS, the San Jose router propagates the packet toward a BGP destination as a labeled packet with the label associated with the BGP next hop. Because the BGP next-hop should always be announced in the IGP the network is running, all intermediate routers must have an incoming-to-outgoing label mapping for that destination in their LFIB already and must propagate the labeled packet toward the egress LSR (MAE-East) but need not run BGP. Figure 2-11 displays the whole process.

Figure 2-11 *Packet Propagation Toward BGP Destination in MPLS-enabled Network*

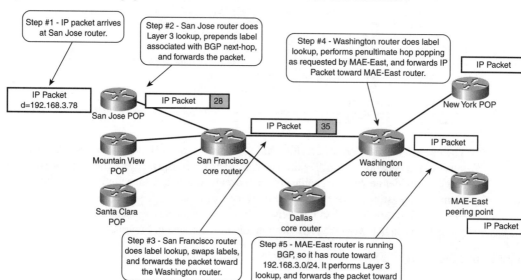

The removal of the BGP process from the core routers in a service provider network has a number of benefits:

* The routing tables in the core routers become much more stable because the core routers do not process route flaps in the Internet.

* Memory requirements for the core routers are reduced because they do not have to store the Internet routes (around 70,000 to 80,000 routes, consuming between 20 to 40 MB of memory in the router).

* The route processor CPU utilization on the core routers is reduced greatly because they do not have to process BGP updates.

MPLS deployment, even in a pure router-based service provider IP backbone, is therefore highly recommended. Chapter 13, "Guidelines for the Deployment of MPLS/VPN," looks further at the removal of BGP within the core of a service provider network and the advantages this brings, especially in a VPN environment.

Summary

This chapter discusses MPLS operation over interfaces where labeled packets are sent encapsulated in Layer 2 frames (Frame-mode MPLS operation).

Label Switch Routers (LSRs) use Label Distribution Protocol (LDP, an IETF standard) or Tag Distribution Protocol (TDP, a Cisco pre-standard) to exchange IP prefix-to-label bindings. A Label Information Base (LIB, also called a Tag Information Base [TIB]) stores these bindings, which are used to build the Forwarding Information Base (FIB) entries in ingress Edge-LSRs as well as Label Forwarding Information Base (LFIB, also called Tag Forwarding Information Base [TFIB]) in all MPLS nodes. Cisco IOS supports both label distribution protocols, and you can use both in the same network, even on separate interfaces of the same LSR.

The **tag-switching ip** or **mpls ip** interface configuration command enables MPLS on a Frame-mode interface. In IOS releases supporting LDP, the desired label distribution protocol must be selected using the **mpls label-distribution** command. These commands start TDP or LDP on the specified interface. TDP/LDP finds other LSRs attached to the same subnet through TDP/LDP hello packets sent as UDP packets to broadcast or multicast IP addresses. When the neighboring LSRs are discovered, a TDP/LDP session is established using TCP as the transport protocol to ensure the reliable delivery of label mappings.

The IOS implementation of LSR on Frame-mode interfaces assigns labels to IP prefixes as soon as they appear in the routing table, even though the LSR hasn't received a corresponding label from its downstream neighbor, because it can always perform a Layer 3 lookup if needed. The router is thus working in independent control allocation mode, as opposed to ordered control allocation, where a device assigns only labels to those prefixes where a downstream label already exists in the LIB.

When running MPLS over Frame-mode interfaces, a Cisco router immediately propagates allocated labels to its TDP/LDP neighbors. This distribution method is called unsolicited downstream distribution, as opposed to downstream on demand distribution, where the upstream routers explicitly ask the downstream routers for specific labels.

A Cisco router acting as an LSR stores all label mappings received from its TDP/LDP neighbors. This storage method is called liberal retention mode as opposed to conservative retention mode where the LSR stores only labels received from its next hop downstream routers. The liberal retention mode uses more memory but enables instantaneous TDP/LDP convergence following the routing protocol convergence after a failure in the network.

After the LSRs in an MPLS network have exchanged label mappings, the ingress LSR can label the incoming data packets. The ingress LSR inserts a label stack header between the Layer 2 header and the IP header. For unicast destination-only IP routing, the label stack header usually contains only one label, but the MPLS architecture also supports stacked labels used by other MPLS applications, such as traffic engineering or Virtual Private Networks. The labeled packets are distinguished from the unlabeled IP packets by using different ethertype codes on LAN media and a different PPP Protocol field value.

Network designers usually consider MPLS only as a technology that allows seamless integration of IP routers and ATM switches or enables additional applications, such as MPLS Traffic Engineering or MPLS/VPN. They usually don't realize they can gain significant simplifications by deploying MPLS in any network that runs BGP as its exterior routing protocol. Deploying MPLS in a network running BGP allows you to remove BGP routing from core routers (non–Edge-LSRs), resulting in a network design that is more stable, requires less memory on the core routers, and prevents high CPU utilization due to BGP update processing on the core routers.

CHAPTER 3

Cell-mode MPLS Operation

In Chapter 2, "Frame-mode MPLS Operation," you saw how MPLS is run between Layer 3 switching devices (routers) across Frame-mode interfaces. The routers running MPLS exchange pure IP packets (for control protocols) as well as labeled IP packets (forwarded or non-adjacent locally sourced traffic) over the same link. They also perform label switching by examining the label header in front of the IP packet.

When trying to fit the MPLS architecture into the limitations of ATM technology, a number of obstacles must be overcome:

- There is no mechanism for direct exchange of IP packets between two adjacent MPLS nodes over an ATM interface. All data exchange over an ATM interface must take place over an ATM virtual circuit (VC).

- ATM switches cannot perform MPLS label lookup or Layer 3 lookup. The only capability of an ATM switch is to map the incoming VC in a cell to an outgoing VC and an outgoing interface.

NOTE   In the ATM world, a pair of values—the virtual path identifier (VPI) and the virtual circuit identifier (VCI)—identify the VC. These values are local to an incoming or outgoing interface; the same VPI/VCI value denotes a different VC when used on a different interface.

The VC lookup operation in an ATM switch is exceedingly simple: The incoming interface and the VPI/VCI value in the incoming cell are used to look up the outgoing interface and the outgoing VPI/VCI value.

The ATM technology design and architecture present a number of challenges to an ATM implementation of MPLS technology, all of which will be discussed in this chapter:

- Control-plane IP packets cannot be exchanged directly over an ATM interface. A control VC must be established between adjacent MPLS nodes to exchange control-plane packets.

- ATM switches cannot perform label lookup. The top label in the label stack must be translated into the VPI/VCI value.

- ATM switches cannot perform Layer 3 lookup. The label allocation and distribution procedures must be modified to make sure that an ATM switch will never have to perform Layer 3 lookup.

Additional limitations of ATM technology become apparent in the area of loop detection and prevention techniques. These limitations and corresponding solutions will be discussed in Chapter 5, "Advanced MPLS Topics."

The ATM implementation of MPLS technology uses several terms that are specific to the ATM world and that will be used throughout this chapter:

- **Label Switching Controlled ATM interface** (LC-ATM interface) is an interface on a router or an ATM switch in which the VPI/VCI value is assigned through MPLS control protocols (TDP or LDP).

- **ATM-LSR** is an ATM switch that runs MPLS protocols on the control plane and performs MPLS forwarding between LC-ATM interfaces on the data plane by means of traditional ATM cell switching.

- **Frame-based LSR** is an LSR that forwards complete frames between its interfaces. A typical example of a frame-based LSR is a traditional router. A frame-based LSR can also have a number of LC-ATM interfaces, but it performs only frame-based label switching based on label stack, not cell switching like an ATM-LSR.

- **ATM-LSR domain** is a set of ATM-LSRs interconnected by LC-ATM interfaces.

- **ATM edge-LSR** is a frame-based LSR with at least one LC-ATM interface.

Throughout the chapter, a sample network (shown in Figure 3-1) will be used for configuration or debugging printouts. The network in this figure is identical to the network in Chapter 2, with the core routers being replaced by ATM switches. The IP addressing in this network is the same as the IP addressing in the SuperNet network of Chapter 2; refer to Chapter 2 for IP address assignment in the SuperCell network.

Figure 3-1 *SuperCell Network—ATM Implementation*

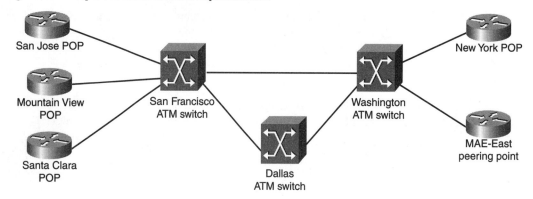

Control-plane Connectivity Across an LC-ATM Interface

MPLS architecture requires that the control planes of adjacent LSRs have pure IP connectivity to exchange label binding as well as other control packets (for example, routing protocol hello packets and routing updates), as shown in Figure 3-2.

Figure 3-2   *Information Exchange Between Adjacent LSRs*

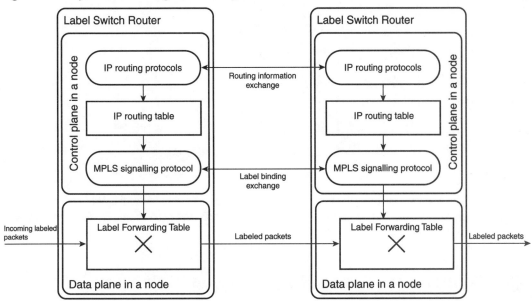

In Frame-mode MPLS, this requirement is easily met because the routers can send and receive IP packets as well as labeled packets over any Frame-mode interface, whether LAN or WAN. The ATM switches, however, do not have this capability.

There are two ways of guaranteeing pure IP connectivity between the ATM-LSRs:

- Through an out-of-band connection, such as an Ethernet connection between the switches.

- Through an in-band management VC, similar to the way that ATM Forum protocols (User-Network Interface [UNI] or Integrated Local Management Interface [ILMI]) are implemented. The detailed architecture of this solution is shown in Figure 3-3.

NOTE   The current LC-ATM IETF specification specifies only the in-band management VC, and the IOS implementation of MPLS on the ATM platforms implements only this method. The in-band management VC is also used for other control purposes, such as for IP routing protocol traffic.

Figure 3-3   *MPLS Control Virtual Circuit Architecture*

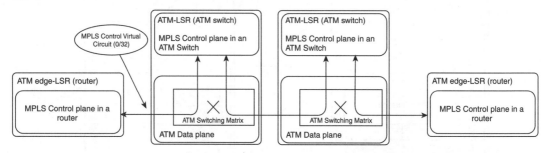

The MPLS control VC is by default configured on VC 0/32 and must use LLC/SNAP encapsulation of IP packets as defined in RFC 1483 (the corresponding IOS keyword is **aal5snap**).

MPLS Control-plane Connectivity in Cisco IOS Software

The control-plane connectivity in Cisco IOS software is established as soon as MPLS is configured on an ATM interface of a router or an ATM switch. The configuration mechanisms are slightly different, though:

- On a router, you create an LC-ATM interface by configuring a separate ATM subinterface with the interface type **tag-switching**, as displayed in Example 3-1, and by configuring MPLS on that subinterface.

- On a switch, you simply configure MPLS on an ATM interface, similar to the way that MPLS is configured on Frame-mode router interfaces, as displayed in Example 3-2.

NOTE   Configuration commands in Example 3-2 are valid only for IOS-based switches, including LightStream 1010, Catalyst 8510, and Catalyst 8540, but not the BPX series of switches.

Example 3-1   *Configuring LC-ATM Interface in a Router*

```
SanJose#configure terminal
SanJose(config)#interface atm 2/0/0.1 tag-switching
SanJose(config-if)#ip unnumbered loopback 0
SanJose(config-if)#tag-switching ip
```

Example 3-2   *Configuring LC-ATM Interface in an IOS-based ATM Switch*

```
SanFrancisco#configure terminal
SanFrancisco(config)#interface atm 2/1/3
SanFrancisco(config-if)#ip unnumbered loopback 0
SanFrancisco(config-if)#tag-switching ip
```

NOTE   It is highly recommended that you configure a loopback interface on every LSR to have a stable TDP/LDP LSR ID. The subnet mask of the loopback interface should be set to 255.255.255.255 to reduce the address space usage and to prevent undesired side effects when using OSPF as your routing protocol. The LC-ATM interfaces should be unnumbered and based on loopback interfaces. If multiple loopback interfaces will be used on the LSR, the TDP/LDP LSR ID should be explicitly configured using the **tag-switching tdp router-id** or **mpls ldp router-id** commands.

The status of an LC-ATM interface can be easily verified by using the **show tag-switching interface detail** command, similar to Example 3-3. The printout displays whether MPLS is enabled on an interface (IP tagging enabled) and whether the TDP/LDP session with a neighbor is already established (tagging operational). The printout also gives you the maximum MTU, the VPI/VCI value of the control VC, and the VPI range for label allocation.

Example 3-3   *show tag-switching interface detail Command*

```
SanFrancisco#show tag-switching interface detail
Interface ATM0/0/3:
        IP tagging enabled
        TSP Tunnel tagging not enabled
        Tagging operational
        MTU = 4470
        ATM tagging: Tag VPI = 1, Control VC = 0/32
```

NOTE	The VC used to exchange routing updates and TDP/LDP messages can also be displayed with the **show atm vc** command. Using this command to verify that the VC with the VPI/ VCI value 0/32 is established is a good initial step in ATM MPLS troubleshooting. If this VC is not active, the interface is not working in LC-ATM mode.

Control-plane Implementation in an ATM Switch

With the deployment of MPLS in the ATM-LSRs, the central processor of an ATM switch must support MPLS signaling and VC setup protocols in addition to the traditional ATM Forum signaling protocols such as UNI and PNNI. The two sets of protocols run transparently side by side, as shown in Figure 3-4. (This mode of operation is sometimes also called the *ships-in-the-night* approach.)

Figure 3-4   *Signaling Protocols Running in an ATM Switch*

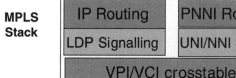

In some ATM switches, the additional functionality required by the MPLS protocol stack can be implemented in the existing control processor of the switch. These ATM switches include LightStream 1010, Catalyst 8510, and Catalyst 8540 from Cisco Systems.

Other ATM switches cannot be directly upgraded with new firmware that would support MPLS. In these cases, an external MPLS controller can be added to the switch to support the additional functionality. The communication between the switch and the external controller supports only simple operations such as setting up a VC, and all the internode MPLS signaling is processed by the external controller.

Cisco Systems' implementation of an external controller is the Label Switch Controller (LSC) for the BPX family of ATM switches. The LSC attaches to the BPX through a standard ATM interface. The Virtual Switch Interface (VSI) protocol running between the LSC and the ATM switch supports the VC additions and deletions. All the higher-layer MPLS operations (exchanging routing updates, building routing tables, exchanging labels through TDP or LDP) are performed by the external controller that utilizes the control VC 0/32.

Labeled Packet Forwarding Across an ATM-LSR Domain

The forwarding of a labeled packet across an ATM-LSR domain is straightforward and is performed in three distinct steps:

1 The ingress ATM edge-LSR receives a labeled or unlabeled packet, performs a Forwarding Information Base (FIB) or Label Forwarding Information Base (LFIB) lookup, and finds the outgoing VPI/VCI value, which it uses as the outgoing label. The labeled packet is segmented into ATM cells and is sent toward the next ATM-LSR. The VPI/VCI value found during the label lookup phase is put into the ATM cell header of each cell.

Note	From this moment until the labeled packet exits the ATM-LSR domain, the label lookup is performed purely based on VPI/VCI values, not on the MPLS label header. The MPLS label header is still present in the labeled packet, however, because it is needed to retain additional header fields, such as bottom-of-stack, Time-to-Live (TTL), and experimental bits.

2 ATM-LSRs switch cells based on the VPI/VCI value in the ATM cell header. The switching mechanism is the same as traditional ATM cell switching, and the MPLS label allocation and distribution mechanisms are responsible for establishing proper inbound/outbound VPI/VCI mappings.

3 The egress ATM edge-LSR reassembles the cells into a labeled packet, performs the label lookup, and forwards the packet toward its next-hop LSR. The label lookup is based on the VPI/VCI values of the incoming cells, not on the top-of-stack label in the MPLS label header. This is because the ATM-LSRs between the edges of the ATM-LSR domain have changed only the VPI/VCI values, not the labels inside the ATM cells.

NOTE	Because the top-of-stack label is not used by the egress edge ATM-LSR, it is set to 0 by the ingress ATM edge-LSR before the labeled packet is segmented in ATM cells.

The major differences between frame-based label switching and cell-based label switching are listed here:

- Label lookup in frame-based label forwarding is performed based on the top-of-stack label in the MPLS label header. In cell-based forwarding, the lookup is performed on the VPI/VCI values in the ATM cell headers.

- The switching mechanism in cell-based label switching is traditional ATM cell switching based on VPI/VCI values in the cell headers. MPLS label stack is completely ignored by ATM-LSRs.

- The top-of-stack label in the MPLS label header is set to 0 by the ingress ATM edge-LSR.

Label Allocation and Distribution Across an ATM-LSR Domain

Label allocation and distribution across an ATM-LSR domain could use the same procedure as the frame-based MPLS world. However, such an implementation would quickly face severe scalability limitations because each label allocated across an LC-ATM interface corresponds to an ATM VC. (Each label has unique VPI/VCI value, and each VPI/VCI value identifies a distinct ATM VC.)

The number of ATM VCs supported across an ATM interface varies between platforms but is rarely higher than approximately 4000 VCs on edge devices (routers), with some hardware platforms supporting only approximately 1000 VCs (for example, PA-A1 port adapter for 7000-series routers). The very small number of VCs supported over an ATM interface makes these circuits a scarce resource that must be tightly controlled. Therefore, the label allocation and distribution over ATM interfaces must be highly conservative.

To ensure that the number of VCs allocated over LC-ATM interfaces stays minimal, upstream LSRs trigger label allocation and distribution over LC-ATM interfaces. An upstream LSR that needs a label to forward labeled packets toward its next hop would explicitly request a label from its downstream LSR.

NOTE   In most MPLS implementations (including Cisco IOS) of LC-ATM, the labels are requested based on the routing table contents, not on actual data flow, which is the standard MPLS behavior: MPLS is control-driven, not data-driven. These implementations request a label for every destination where the next hop is reachable across the LC-ATM interface.

The downstream LSR could simply allocate a label and respond to the request from the upstream LSR with a corresponding reply message. Under some circumstances, this action would require the downstream LSR to have Layer 3 lookup capability (such as if the downstream LSR would have no further downstream label for the requested destination), which is not the case with ATM switches. Therefore, the ATM switches never respond to a label allocation request unless they already have a corresponding downstream label allocated. If the ATM-LSR has no downstream label that would correspond to the request received from the upstream LSR, it would recursively request a label from its downstream neighbor and reply to the upstream LSR only after receiving a label from the downstream LSR.

The label allocation and distribution process across the ATM-LSR domain has the following characteristics:

- Label allocation in devices with Layer 3 lookup capabilities (routers) is done regardless of whether the router has already received a label for the same prefix from its next-hop router. Label allocation in routers is thus called *independent control*.

- Label allocation in devices with no Layer 3 lookup capabilities (ATM switches) is performed only if a corresponding downstream label has already been allocated. Label allocation in ATM switches is thus called *ordered control*.

- The distribution method over LC-ATM interfaces is *downstream on demand* because an LSR assigns a label across the LC-ATM interface only when that label is specifically requested by an upstream LSR.

To illustrate label allocation and distribution procedures across the ATM-LSR domain, an example from the SuperCell network will be used. The label allocation process for destination X, which is reachable through the New York POP in the SuperCell network, is illustrated in Figure 3-5.

Figure 3-5   *Label Allocation in an ATM-LSR Domain*

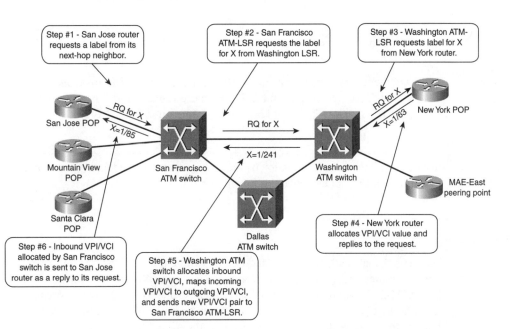

The label allocation and distribution in the SuperCell network is performed in a series of steps:

1 The San Jose router needs a label for destination X. Its routing table indicates that destination X is reachable through an LC-ATM interface, so it requests a label for this destination from its downstream ATM-LSR.

2 The San Francisco ATM-LSR is a classical ATM switch operating in ordered control mode, so it requests a label from the Washington ATM switch.

3 Similarly, the Washington ATM switch requests a label from the New York router.

4 The New York router operates in independent control mode and can immediately allocate a label (free VC on its LC-ATM interface) for the requested destination. If the New York router already has a downstream label for destination X, it enters the mapping between the allocated VPI/VCI pair and downstream label in its Label Forwarding Information Base (LFIB). Otherwise, it associates a **pop** operation with the allocated VPI/VCI pair. The VPI/VCI pair allocated to destination X is sent back to the Washington ATM switch in a TDP/LDP reply packet.

5 After receiving the downstream label allocation, the Washington ATM switch allocates a label for its upstream LSR (yet again, a free VC on the ATM interface leading toward the San Francisco ATM switch) and enters the mapping between the newly allocated VPI/VCI pair and the VPI/VCI pair that it has received from the New York router in its ATM switching matrix. The newly allocated VPI/VCI pair (1/241) is sent to the San Francisco ATM switch in a TDP/LDP reply packet.

6 The San Francisco ATM switch performs a similar operation, allocates another VPI/VCI pair (1/85), and sends that pair as the label for destination X to the San Jose router.

7 After receiving a reply to its label allocation request, the San Jose router can enter the VPI/VCI pair received from the San Francisco switch in its Forwarding Information Base (FIB) and in its Label Forwarding Information Base (LFIB).

NOTE   See Chapter 2 for more information on the processing performed on a router after receiving a label mapping from its downstream neighbor.

VC Merge

Based on the label allocation and distribution rules outlined in the previous section, you might consider a label optimization technique across an ATM-LSR domain. For example, if an ATM-LSR has already received a label for a destination from its downstream neighbor, it might reuse the same downstream label when another upstream LSR asks for the label binding for the same destination. For example, the ATM-LSR in Figure 3-6 might reuse the label already allocated by the router at the right for destination 171.68.0.0/16 when the bottom-left router asks for a label toward that destination.

Figure 3-6   *Potential Optimization of ATM Label Allocation*

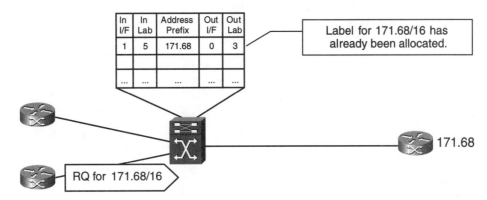

However, if the ATM-LSR tried such an optimization technique, the downstream router would be faced with a tough problem as soon as the ATM cells started arriving simultaneously from both routers at the left, as illustrated in Figure 3-7.

Figure 3-7   *Cell Interleaving Problem in an ATM-LSR Domain*

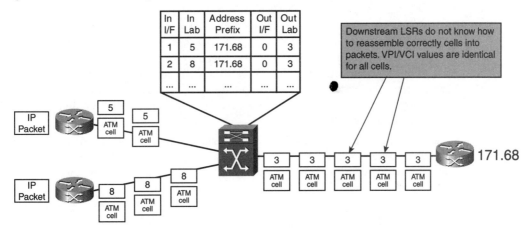

The ATM switch has no means of ensuring that the cells arriving simultaneously from many sources will not be interleaved if they are mapped to the same VC toward the destination. The egress edge LSR obviously cannot resolve the cell interleave because the AAL5 encapsulation used by MPLS contains no additional header fields that would be of any help.

AAL5 encapsulation assumes that the cells from different frames will not be interleaved over a VC.

To prevent the cell interleave problem, the ATM-LSR must ask its downstream neighbor for a new label every time an upstream neighbor asks for a label toward any destination, even though it already has some labels allocated for that same destination. This process and the corresponding cell flow are illustrated in Figure 3-8.

Figure 3-8 *Cell Flow with Multiple Labels Assigned for the Same Destination*

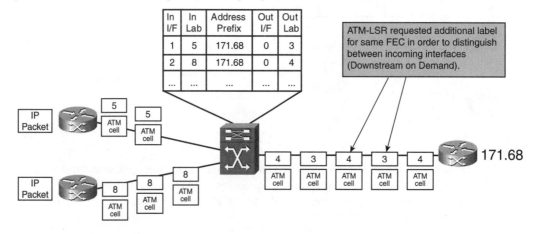

With small hardware modifications, some ATM switches can ensure that two cell flows converging on the same outgoing VC will never get interleaved. These switches buffer incoming ATM cells until they receive a cell with the end-of-frame bit set in the ATM cell header. Then they transmit all the buffered cells on the outgoing VC. This operation effectively turns an ATM switch almost into a frame-based forwarding device, as the additional buffering increases the latency across the switch as well as the buffering requirements of the switch.

The serialization of incoming cell flows onto a single outgoing VC is called *virtual circuit merge* (VC merge) and allows the ATM-LSRs that support this function to share the same outbound label for a destination among many inbound labels allocated for multiple upstream LSRs, as illustrated in Figure 3-9.

The ATM VC merge function drastically reduces the number of labels allocated across an ATM-LSR domain. For example, consider an IP backbone network in which 100 edge routers are interconnected across an ATM network. Further assume that each edge router announces only 10 subnets into the ATM network (in other words, the router is the egress edge LSR for only 10 destinations). In a traditional ATM MPLS implementation, such a router would have to allocate 10 labels for each ingress router, resulting in 1000 VCs just to support labeled packet forwarding from its upstream neighbors. However, if the ATM network supports VC merge functionality, the egress edge router must allocate only 10 labels because the ATM switches can reuse these labels for all upstream routers.

Figure 3-9   *ATM VC Merge*

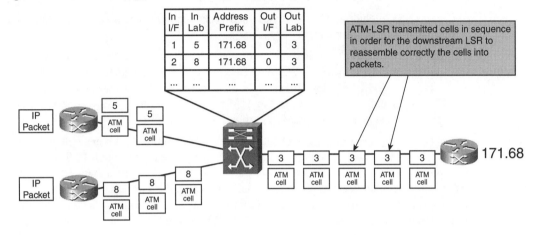

Convergence Across an ATM-LSR Domain

In Chapter 2, you saw that an MPLS deployment in a router-only network does not increase the overall convergence time of the network after a network failure (the convergence time does increase following recovery of a link—see Chapter 2 for more details). On the other hand, the convergence in ATM networks can change considerably when deploying MPLS. In a traditional ATM network, the convergence time consisted of the following components:

- An edge router had to detect an adjacent router failure through ATM signaling, ATM operation-and-maintenance (OAM) cells, or routing protocol timeouts (dead timer or hold timer).

- The edge router detecting the adjacent router failure immediately propagated the change in network topology to all other routers.

- In link-state protocols, all the routers had to recompute a new network topology, usually after a slight delay.

When the ATM network is migrated toward MPLS, the convergence time of the network consists of the following components:

- An LSR must detect an adjacent LSR failure. This process is usually very quick because the adjacent LSRs linked with point-to-point links and the physical layer indicates line failure very quickly.

- The LSR must propagate change in network topology to other LSRs. This process takes longer in MPLS networks because the number of routing devices between the edges of the ATM network has increased. All ATM switches that were transparent to IP routing in traditional ATM networks now act as IP routers.

- All LSRs, including ATM switches, must recalculate the new network topology and change their routing tables.

- If the next-hop for a destination has changed, an ATM edge-LSR must request new labels for these destinations. Other ATM-LSRs must propagate these label requests across the ATM-LSR domain, more so if VC merge is not used and each request must be propagated all the way across the ATM network to the egress ATM edge-LSR. This is an extra step that is not needed in traditional ATM networks.

When comparing the convergence of a traditional ATM-based IP backbone with the MPLS-based IP+ATM backbone, you can see that the convergence time in the MPLS-based backbone usually increases because the extra steps were not performed in the traditional IP backbone. The other benefits of MPLS usually outweigh this concern, but the increased convergence time is still a parameter that you must take into account when planning the migration of your ATM backbone toward an MPLS-enabled IP+ATM backbone.

Summary

In this chapter, we've discussed the specifics of running MPLS across ATM networks. The MPLS architecture allows MPLS to be deployed in ATM networks with no hardware upgrades to the ATM switches.

NOTE   A hardware upgrade is usually needed to support VC merge functionality in the ATM switches because the traditional ATM switches have no equivalent function.

ATM switches do need new control software in the control processors that support MPLS signaling. Some switches cannot support the increased demands, resulting in the need for an external controller (Label Switch Controller) that provides MPLS support for such a switch.

The MPLS forwarding and label allocation procedures were slightly modified to support the ATM environment:

- Cell-based label switching is performed purely based on VPI/VCI values in ATM cell headers to support the existing ATM infrastructure. The top-of-stack MPLS label is thus encoded in the ATM cell header.

- Even though the top-of-stack label is moved into the ATM cell header, the MPLS stack in the labeled packet is still intact because it is needed to support additional MPLS functionality such as MPLS experimental bits or the TTL field. The label in the top entry of the MPLS label header is set to 0 because it is not used across an ATM network.

- Label distribution in an ATM network is based on downstream-on-demand procedures to minimize VC usage across LC-ATM interfaces.

- Traditional ATM switches must request a label from the downstream LSR before they can allocate a label to an upstream LSR and establish inbound-to-outbound VPI/VCI mapping in the ATM switching matrix. A new label must be requested from the downstream LSR for each upstream request to prevent cell interleave problems.

- Advanced ATM switches support VC merge, additional cell buffering that prevents cell interleave problems. These switches can use the same downstream label for all upstream neighbors, resulting in significant savings of VCs used across LC-ATM interfaces.

The downstream-on-demand label distribution in ATM networks also affects the convergence time of ATM-based MPLS networks. The overall convergence time usually increases because new labels must be requested and allocated following the convergence of an IP routing protocol.

CHAPTER 4.

Running Frame-mode MPLS Across Switched WAN Media

The previous two chapters showed that you can deploy MPLS using different modes of operation. Chapter 2, "Frame-mode MPLS Operation," details how MPLS operates across framed interfaces, and Chapter 3, "Cell-mode MPLS Operation," shows how MPLS operates natively across ATM media.

The Layer 2 infrastructure, which provides the media over which Frame-mode MPLS can operate, often can be supplied through the use of switched WAN technology, such as Frame Relay or ATM. You can run MPLS in Cell-mode across ATM but not when using Frame Relay or when the ATM structure is built using traditional ATM Forum PVCs. This means that it must be possible to run Frame-mode MPLS across these types of interfaces so you can deploy MPLS end-to-end across the network.

This chapter considers the deployment of MPLS across Frame Relay interfaces and ATM PVCs. It also considers the use of Frame-mode and Cell-mode MPLS across the same physical interface; this functionality can be useful during a migration to the MPLS architecture, as you'll learn in Chapter 6, "MPLS Migration and Configuration Example."

Frame-mode MPLS Operation Across Frame Relay

Frame Relay is a widely deployed switched WAN technology that provides, in its basic form, a connection-oriented protocol between a service provider switch port and a customer premises equipment (CPE) device. This means basically that a session, or virtual circuit (VC), must be established before any data flow can commence across the Frame Relay network. The VC acts as a point-to-point link for purposes of data forwarding between connected CPE devices.

Using these VCs, you can establish MPLS forwarding and label distribution between two endpoint devices in exactly the same way as over any other type of interface that operates in Frame-mode. This means that the label distribution across the interface is unsolicited downstream with independent label control. Figure 4-1 provides an example of this type of connectivity.

Figure 4-1   *MPLS Connectivity Across Frame Relay PVCs*

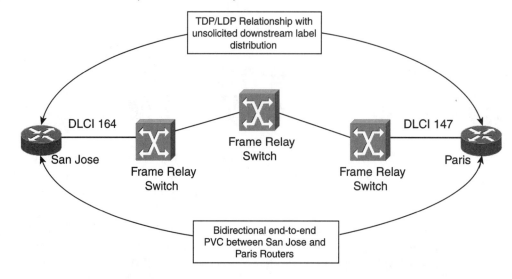

Figure 4-1 illustrates two routers connected across a Frame Relay network. If you concentrate on the San Jose router, you can see that it addresses the VC using a Data Link Connection Identifier (DLCI) of 164 and uses this VC to exchange routing protocol information and to learn and distribute MPLS label forwarding information. From this router's perspective, any routes learned from its routing protocol neighbor across this VC (Paris in this case) have a next-hop forwarding address pointing to the Paris router.

When the San Jose router builds its LFIB, it uses the labels that it received across its TDP/LDP session with the Paris router to forward traffic to any FECs that it determines are reachable via the Paris router. You can see the relevant configuration of the San Jose router in Example 4-1.

Example 4-1   *MPLS Across Frame Relay Router Configuration*

```
hostname San Jose
!
interface serial 1/0
 description ** interface to Paris
 no ip address
 encapsulation frame-relay
!
interface Serial0/1.1 point-to-point
 ip address 146.4.1.18 255.255.255.252
 tag-switching ip
 frame-relay interface-dlci 164
```

To confirm the TDP relationship between the two routers, use the **show tag-switching tdp neighbor** command, as shown in Example 4-2. This command confirms that your TDP session is established across the Frame Relay interface and that unsolicited downstream label distribution is in effect.

Example 4-2 *Confirmation of TDP Relationship Between Two LSRs Across Frame Relay*

```
San Jose# show tag-switching tdp neighbor
Peer TDP Ident: 194.22.15.1:0; Local TDP Ident 194.22.15.2:0
        TCP connection: 194.22.15.1.711 - 194.22.15.2.11363
        State: Oper; PIEs sent/rcvd: 124/123; ; Downstream
        Up time: 01:43:37
        TDP discovery sources:
          Serial0/1.1
        Addresses bound to peer TDP Ident:
          146.4.1.17    196.7.25.1      194.22.15.1    10.2.1.13
```

There are two ways to encapsulate IP packets across a Cisco Systems, Inc., implementation of Frame Relay. The first is to use Cisco encapsulation (the default) and the second is to use RFC 1490 (IETF) encapsulation. MPLS forwarding and control functions across either encapsulation. Figure 4-2 shows the two encapsulation methods and how the MPLS information is added to the frame.

Figure 4-2   *MPLS Encapsulation Across Frame Relay*

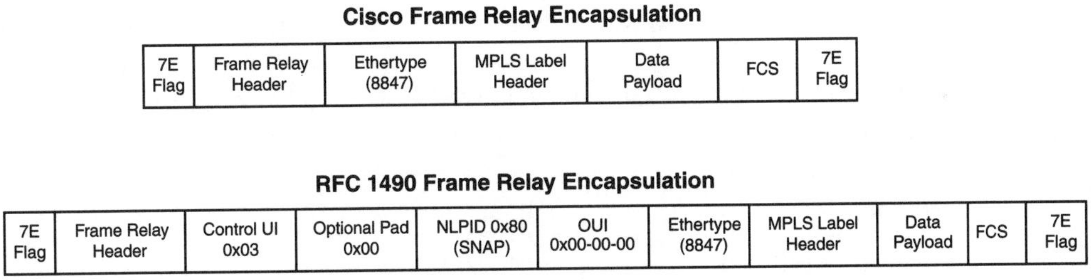

Cisco Frame Relay Encapsulation

7E Flag	Frame Relay Header	Ethertype (8847)	MPLS Label Header	Data Payload	FCS	7E Flag

RFC 1490 Frame Relay Encapsulation

7E Flag	Frame Relay Header	Control UI 0x03	Optional Pad 0x00	NLPID 0x80 (SNAP)	OUI 0x00-00-00	Ethertype (8847)	MPLS Label Header	Data Payload	FCS	7E Flag

Frame-mode MPLS Operation Across ATM PVCs

In certain circumstances, such as during a transition to a full IP+ATM MPLS environment, or if transit ATM switches do not support MPLS, it might be desirable to run MPLS in Frame-mode across ATM PVCs. This is a perfectly valid configuration although it suffers from the same scaling issues (due to the high number of VCs) as running IP over ATM in an overlay mode.

This type of connectivity, from an MPLS perspective, is essentially the same as described within the previous Frame Relay section. The label allocation scheme uses independent mode, and the distribution of labels uses unsolicited downstream. Figure 4-3 shows an example of this type of connectivity.

Figure 4-3 *MPLS Connectivity Across ATM PVCs*

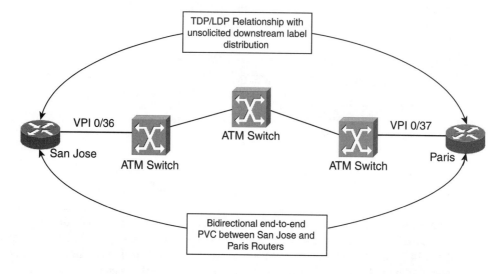

You can see from Figure 4-3 that the San Jose and Paris routers are connected across a point-to-point ATM PVC. Again, using the **show tag-switching tdp neighbor** command confirms that unsolicited downstream label distribution is in effect across the interface and, therefore, MPLS is operating in Frame-mode. You can see this output in Example 4-3 and you can see the relevant configuration of the San Jose router in Example 4-4.

Example 4-3 *Confirmation of TDP Relationship Between Two LSRs Across an ATM PVC*

```
San Jose# show tag-switching tdp neighbor
Peer TDP Ident: 194.22.15.1:0; Local TDP Ident 194.22.15.2:0
      TCP connection: 194.22.15.1.711 - 194.22.15.2.11064
      State: Oper; PIEs sent/rcvd: 6557/6559; ; Downstream
      Up time: 3d23h
      TDP discovery sources:
       ATM0/0/0.1
      Addresses bound to peer TDP Ident:
        146.4.1.17     196.7.25.1       194.22.15.1     10.2.1.13
```

Example 4-4 *MPLS Across ATM PVC Router Configuration*

```
interface ATM0/0/0
 no ip address
 !
interface ATM0/0/0.1 point-to-point
 description ** interface to Paris
 ip address 146.4.1.18 255.255.255.252
 pvc 0/36
```

Example 4-4 *MPLS Across ATM PVC Router Configuration (Continued)*

```
  encapsulation aal5snap
  !
  tag-switching ip
```

NOTE   Running MPLS across an ATM Forum PVC requires AAL5SNAP encapsulation on that PVC. AAL5MUX encapsulation does not work because packets of two different protocols (pure IP control packets and labeled data packets) are exchanged over the same VC. Chapter 2 details the specific encapsulation across ATM.

Frame-mode and Cell-mode MPLS Across the Same ATM Interface

It might be desirable in some deployments of the MPLS architecture to run both Frame-mode and Cell-mode MPLS across the same physical ATM interface, for example when linking two private MPLS-enabled ATM networks across a public ATM network that offers only ATM Forum PVC services. You can see how this feature can be used in the migration of an ATM network toward MPLS in the migration example in Chapter 6.

This type of connectivity is possible through the use of sub-interfaces with different sub-interface types on the router's ATM interface configuration. These sub-interfaces can be configured to run Cell-mode MPLS (sub-interface type *tag-switching*), or they can be configured to run Frame-mode (sub-interface type **point-to-point**). Figure 4-4 illustrates this technique.

The example topology in Figure 4-4 shows that the San Jose and Paris routers have a point-to-point PVC connection between them but they also run Cell-mode MPLS directly with the MPLS ATM switch. This is achieved through the use of two separate ATM sub-interfaces. Example 4-5 shows the configuration of the San Jose router in this environment.

Example 4-5 *Configuration of Frame-mode and Cell-mode MPLS on the Same ATM Interface*

```
interface ATM0/0/0
 no ip address
 !
interface ATM0/0/0.1 point-to-point
 description ** ATM PVC interface to Paris
 ip address 146.4.1.18 255.255.255.252
 pvc 0/36
  encapsulation aal5snap
  !
 tag-switching ip
 !
interface ATM0/0/0.2 tag-switching
 description ** cell-mode interface to adjacent ATM-LSR
 ip unnumbered Loopback0
 tag-switching ip
```

Figure 4-4 *Frame-mode and Cell-mode MPLS Across the Same ATM Interface*

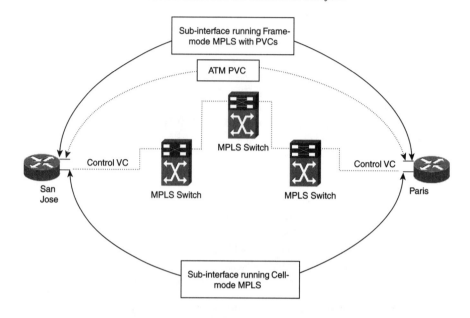

Summary

In this chapter, you see how you can run MPLS across traditional WAN media, be it a Frame Relay network or an ATM network supporting only ATM Forum permanent VCs. In both cases, MPLS runs directly between routers connected to the WAN network and the WAN switches are not aware of MPLS being transported across the WAN network.

MPLS over a Frame Relay network or an ATM Forum PVC is configured as Frame-mode MPLS and the LDP/TDP session is established directly between routers connected to the WAN network. The routers use standard Frame-mode label allocation and distribution procedures and forward labeled packets as frames with the standard label header (like any other datagrams, these frames obviously are transported as cells across the ATM network).

There are several benefits gained by running MPLS in Frame-mode across a WAN network:

- You can use the existing WAN infrastructure for transporting labeled packets.

- You can run MPLS across ATM networks that are not yet MPLS-enabled or across public ATM networks that do not support MPLS services.

- The migration of ATM networks toward MPLS becomes simple as the Frame-mode MPLS between routers offers a very convenient first transitional step.

The drawback of running MPLS across a WAN network in Frame-mode is also obvious—you're again faced with the scalability issues of the large WAN networks discussed in Chapter 1, "Multiprotocol Label Switching (MPLS) Architecture Overview."

CHAPTER 5

Advanced MPLS Topics

Up until this point, this book has concentrated on explaining the concepts and mechanisms that make up the Multiprotocol Label Switching (MPLS) architecture. This chapter aims to provide further information on some more advanced topics that you face when deploying this architecture.

The guidelines presented in this chapter are specific to the MPLS architecture and are relevant to any deployment, regardless of whether advanced features, such as VPN, are used within the infrastructure. You can find further guidelines that are important for the successful deployment of the MPLS/VPN architecture in Chapter 13, "Guidelines for the Deployment of MPLS/VPN."

You have seen already how MPLS labels are distributed between adjacent TDP/LDP neighbors. However, it might be necessary to restrict the distribution of this information to certain neighbors, or even to block the advertisement of the information altogether. This chapter looks at this facility and analyzes why this feature can be useful when deploying MPLS. This chapter also looks at how the Cisco Systems, Inc., implementation of the MPLS architecture can deal with large packets across certain types of media that have a maximum transmission unit (MTU) that does not allow the addition of MPLS labels, by default, to packets that are larger than 1500 bytes.

Last, this chapter analyzes how MPLS can detect and prevent forwarding loops, and determines how aggregation of IP routing information can affect the functionality of the network.

Controlling the Distribution of Label Mappings

In Chapter 2, "Frame-mode MPLS Operation," you saw that an Interior Gateway Protocol (IGP) is used within an MPLS network to discover IP prefix information, which is associated with a particular forwarding equivalent class (FEC). After the LSR discovers this information, a label might be assigned to the FEC and advertised to all upstream LDP/TDP neighbors, depending on whether downstream or downstream-on-demand label distribution mode is in operation.

The decision of whether to assign a label to an FEC is based on which control mode is in operation. There are two such modes: *ordered* and *independent*. Chapter 2 shows that when you deploy ordered LSP control, which is the default mode for an ATM-LSR, an LSR binds only a label to a particular FEC if it is the egress LSR for that FEC, or if it has received a label binding already from the next-hop LSR for that FEC. When you use independent mode, which is the default when using Frame-mode MPLS, an LSR binds a label to an FEC independently of the label it has to receive from the next-hop LSR. This is similar to link-state IP routing, where each router builds its routing table independently.

Because of the way labels bind to FECs, it is not possible within the MPLS architecture to restrict which FECs have labels associated to them and which do not. Therefore, if label switching to a particular FEC is not desirable (which may be the case during a migration to the MPLS architecture), you need a mechanism that can filter the advertisement of label mappings so that an upstream LSR neighbor does not receive label mapping for a particular FEC. Without this label mapping information, the upstream LSR cannot label switch to the destination FEC and, therefore, must route packets based on the IP routing table information. Figure 5-1 illustrates this technique.

Figure 5-1   *Control of Label Distribution Between Adjacent LSRs*

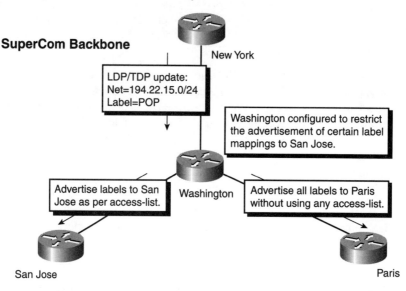

You can see from Figure 5-1 that the Washington LSR is configured to restrict the advertisement of label mappings to the San Jose LSR but not the Paris LSR. This configuration is achieved through the use of the **tag-switching advertise-tags** global command. Table 5-1 shows the syntax of this command.

Table 5-1   *tag-switching advertise-tags Command Syntax*

Command	Purpose
tag-switching advertise-tag [**for** *access-list-for-definition-prefixes*] [**to** *access-list-for-TDP/LDP-peers*]	Filter label mappings to TDP/LDP peers based on destination prefixes specified in a standard access-list

Table 5-1 shows that two arguments exist for the **tag-switching advertise-tags** command. The **for** argument uses an access-list that specifies the destination IP prefixes that either must be permitted or denied. The **to** argument uses an access-list to specify to which TDP/LDP neighbors the previous **for** argument should be applied. The access list specified in the **to** argument should match the TDP/LDP identifier of the neighbor. This identifier can be displayed with the **show tag-switching tdp neighbor** command, as shown in Example 5-1, where the neighbor TDP identifier is highlighted in the printout.

NOTE   It is important to ensure that stable addresses are used for the TDP/LDP identifier. Therefore, make sure a loopback address is available for use as the identifier. If multiple loopbacks are used, use the **tag-switching tdp router-id** command to specify which loopback address to use as the TDP/LDP identifier.

You can see the necessary configuration for the Washington LSR in Example 5-2.

Example 5-1   *tag-switching tdp neighbor Command*

```
washington# show tag-switching tdp neighbor

Peer TDP Ident: 194.22.15.2:0; Local TDP Ident 194.22.15.3:0
        TCP connection: 194.22.15.2.12226 - 194.22.15.3.711
        State: Oper; PIEs sent/rcvd: 122/117; ; Downstream
        Up time: 01:37:24
        TDP discovery sources:
          ATM0/0/0.1
        Addresses bound to peer TDP Ident:
          10.1.1.13       194.22.15.2
```

Example 5-2   *tag-switching advertise-tags Configuration Example*

```
hostname Washington
!
tag-switching advertise-tags for 1 to 2
tag-switching tdp router-id Loopback0
!
interface Loopback0
 ip address 194.22.15.3 255.255.255.255
!
interface ATM0/0/0
 no ip address
 no atm ilmi-keepalive
!
interface ATM0/0/0.1 point-to-point
 description ** interface to San Jose **
 ip address 10.1.1.14 255.255.255.252
 atm pvc 1 20 20 aal5snap
 tag-switching ip
!
interface Ethernet0/1/0
 description ** interface to Paris **
 ip address 10.2.1.22 255.255.255.252
 tag-switching ip
!
interface POS2/0/0
 description ** interface to New York **
 ip address 10.1.1.21 255.255.255.252
 tag-switching ip
!
access-list 1 permit 194.22.15.0 0.0.0.255
access-list 1 deny    any
access-list 2 deny 195.22.15.1
```

The **tag-switching advertise-tags** command can be used only when running Frame-mode MPLS. This means that if the link between two LSRs is via an LC-ATM interface, then the filtering of label mappings is not possible.

NOTE   It is worth noting that you can use an ATM interface within the configuration of the Washington router and to connect to the San Jose router. However, this interface is not an LC-ATM interface; therefore, a traditional ATM Forum PVC is configured across the interface between the two routers. In this case, the router uses Frame-mode for that particular interface, although it is an ATM interface, and therefore the **tag-switching advertise-tags** command works.

The reason for this restriction is that when running across an LC-ATM interface, the router uses ordered LSP control mode and downstream-on-demand label distribution. When using this mode of operation, interface resources are used as labels. In the case of ATM, these are VPI/VCI pairs and are known as label virtual circuits (LVCs). Chapter 3, "Cell-mode MPLS Operation," discusses LVCs. The consequence of this is that if the advertisement of label mappings were filtered, then all traffic across the link would be sent across the control virtual circuit (VPI 0 VCI 32). This is because the destination prefix would be shown as *untagged* within the LFIB and any traffic toward that prefix would be routed. Because the next-hop for the destination prefix of the packet would point toward the downstream neighbor that is reachable via the control virtual circuit, all traffic would follow this path. This is not a desirable function because this virtual circuit is used for control messaging and routing protocol traffic and is not intended to carry IP traffic.

MPLS Encapsulation Across Ethernet Links

One of the issues surrounding the use of MPLS encapsulation is the deployment of Ethernet links (Ethernet, Fast Ethernet, or Gigabit Ethernet) within the topology using any supported Ethernet encapsulation: Ethernet II, 802.3 (with or without an 802.2 header), or SNAP. Each media type has a maximum frame size of 1518 octets (not including preamble or Start Frame Delimiter [SFD]) with a payload size ranging from 46 octets to 1500 octets (1492 in the case of SNAP encapsulation).

Previous chapters illustrate that the use of MPLS within the network causes a packet to grow in size, which is due to the addition of labels onto the label stack. Each label header entry is 4 octets in length. This means that if a packet of 1500 octets payload is received, and a label header is pushed onto the stack, then the frame needs to be forwarded with a 1504-octet payload. Because of the restriction to the maximum frame size across the various Ethernet media types, this could cause a problem because the MTU on these links is smaller than the presented packet size.

NOTE	The Gigabit Ethernet standard currently limits the frame size to 1518 octets although some vendors now support jumbo frames, where the data field can extend to 4470 or 9000 octets. Extending the length of the Ethernet frame data field results in not being able to uniquely determine whether a particular sized packet is an 802.3 or Ethernet Type II encapsulated packet. This is because the type/length field is interpreted as *length* if it is less than 1535 octets (therefore, it is an 802.3, 802.3 plus 802.2, or SNAP frame) and as *type* if it is greater than 1535 octets (therefore, the encapsulation is Ethernet II). The consequence of this is that large frames across Ethernet-type media with Ethernet II encapsulation work well but not across any other encapsulation. Further studies are ongoing to determine how to handle encapsulations other than Ethernet II across Gigabit Ethernet although no firm conclusions are available at the time of writing this book.

IP MTU Path Discovery

Most IP hosts today support the use of the Path MTU discovery mechanism, as documented in RFC 1191, "Path MTU Discovery." The mechanism described in the RFC allows an IP host to discover dynamically the maximum allowable MTU size along the path from source to destination.

The basic idea behind Path MTU Discovery is that a source host initially assumes that the Path MTU of a particular connection is the MTU of its first hop, and sends all datagrams on that path with the DF (do not fragment) bit set. No datagram is sent that is bigger than the MTU of the first hop. Hosts that do not use these procedures should not send datagrams larger than 576 octets.

NOTE   In the case of Transmission Control Protocol (TCP), when a session is established with a remote device, the Maximum Segment Size option is negotiated. The two devices involved in the session establishment exchange their TCP Maximum Segment Size (MSS) values, which normally are determined as the local MTU value minus 40 octets (IP header and TCP header). The smaller of the two MSS values is used for the Path MTU during the discovery process.

When a router receives a packet that is larger than the MTU of the outgoing interface toward the destination contained in the incoming packet, and the DF bit is set on the packet, it sends an ICMP destination unreachable message with a code of 4 (fragmentation needed and DF set) back to the source of the packet. The Path MTU discovery process relies on the receipt of these messages to determine the maximum packet size that can be sent across the path to a particular destination. Figure 5-2 illustrates this process.

Figure 5-2   *Path MTU Discovery Mechanism*

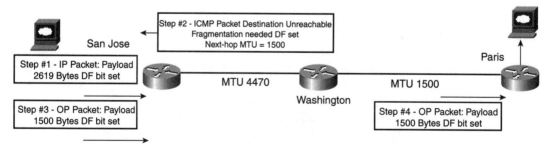

When you deploy these procedures, packets can be sent successfully across an MPLS backbone without fragmentation. However, each LSR can fragment labeled or non-labeled packets if they are larger than the outgoing MTU, as long as the DF bit is not set. If the DF bit is set, the LSR conforms to the Path MTU discovery mechanism by sending an ICMP destination unreachable message with the "fragmentation needed and DF set" code.

All this would be fine if everyone conformed to the previously described mechanisms. However, the reality is that some hosts do not use Path MTU discovery and send datagrams that are larger than 576 Octets. Furthermore, some firewalls drop ICMP unreachable messages, which effectively breaks the MTU discovery mechanism. Because of these issues, a further mechanism that allows frames with a payload greater than 1500 octets is needed within an MPLS environment to ensure that packets can be sent successfully across the network.

NOTE   Some of the issues with MTU discovery are discussed in further detail in *draft-ietf-tcpimpl-pmtud*. You can find this draft at the IETF web site at www.ietf.org/ids.by.wg/tcpimpl.html.

Cisco Systems introduced a workaround for these issues that allows an Ethernet port on a router to support MPLS packets that have a payload larger than 1500 octets. This is achieved by increasing the MTU of the Ethernet port to 1526 octets, which constitutes the standard maximum Ethernet frame size of 1518 octets plus 8 octets for two levels of MPLS labels. This amount of labels is adequate at this time, and supports the introduction of MPLS and MPLS-enabled VPNs, but does not support an arbitrary label stack depth. Further study is ongoing and the label stack depth may be increased in the future to allow the introduction of services that require a label stack depth greater than two. This workaround is relevant to packets that are received with their DF (Do not fragment) bit set. In *draft-ietf-mpls-label-encaps,* this increase in payload size is known as the "True Maximum Frame Payload Size."

For packets that do *not* have their DF bit set, the previously mentioned draft specifies that every LSR should support a configuration parameter known as the "Maximum Initially Labeled IP Datagram Size." (See section 3.2 of *draft-ietf-mpls-label-encaps*.) This parameter is used on the ingress to the MPLS domain so that the packet can be fragmented at the edge of the network if it is larger than the configured maximum labeled MTU size. This means that the MTU size needs to be established for all backbone links so that this value can be decided. The advantage of this is that the packet is fragmented prior to entry into the MPLS domain and does not require further fragmentation within the MPLS backbone.

In the Cisco MPLS implementation, this parameter is configured using the **tag-switching mtu** command on the output interface. This command defaults to the interface MTU size. If packets arrive that are too big, as specified by the **tag-switching mtu** command, to be sent without fragmentation somewhere within the MPLS network, and they do *not* have the DF bit set, then they are fragmented prior to transmission out of the outbound interface. The advantage of this is that fragmentation need not occur within the MPLS domain and is restricted to the edge of the network.

NOTE   The **tag-switching mtu** command also is required in conjunction with the increase of the maximum Ethernet MTU size ("True Maximum Frame Payload Size"). If you do not set this command, any arriving packets that have a payload size larger than the default maximum frame size for the outgoing interface (in the case of Ethernet II, for example, this size is 1500 octets when MPLS labels are pushed onto the stack) are dropped and an ICMP message is sent back to the source. This occurs even though the interface can support this larger frame size. For this reason, set this command on all Ethernet interfaces that will be configured to carry MPLS-encapsulated packets.

NOTE   Ethernet interfaces are not the only interfaces where the MTU is smaller than the resultant frame size after MPLS labels have been added. This means that the **tag-switching mtu** command is not restricted to Ethernet interfaces only and should be configured for any interface where the maximum MTU configured for the interface is likely to be exceeded.

Ethernet Switches and MPLS MTU

As discussed in the previous section, the MTU of IP packets increases by 4 octets for each MPLS label appended to the packet. Whichever MPLS facility is used (base MPLS, VPN, or Traffic Engineering), an MPLS packet can exceed the maximum Ethernet frame size of 1518 octets. The previous section showed that this problem has been somewhat resolved by changes to the LSR to make it capable of transmitting a frame that is larger than 1518 octets.

This workaround is fine if the LSRs are connected through back-to-back Ethernet cabling. However, if you use a Layer 2 switch to provide the Ethernet segment, then this device also must be capable of forwarding frames that are greater than 1518 octets. In most—but not all—cases, this is not actually the reality and the switch drops the frame and reports a GIANT.

NOTE   Some Cisco Layer 2 switches support giant frames by default and some do not. If they do not, several workarounds exist to enable switches to pass the frames. You can obtain these workarounds from the Cisco Systems Inc., TAC (Technical Assistance Center) on request.

MPLS Loop Detection and Prevention

An important issue to consider when deploying the MPLS architecture is its capability to detect and prevent forwarding loops within the topology. A forwarding loop in an IP network is the process by which a router forwards a packet down the incorrect path (as far as its neighbor is concerned) to a particular destination based on the information contained in its routing table. This can happen during a convergence transition when dynamic routing protocols are used, or through the misconfiguration of the routers so that one router points to another router that is not actually the correct next-hop for a particular destination.

In terms of the MPLS architecture, you must consider both the control plane and the data plane, and how loop prevention is deployed in both a Frame-mode and Cell-mode backbone. You also must understand how each can detect, and deal with, forwarding loops.

Loop Detection and Prevention in Frame-mode MPLS

As shown in Chapter 2, labels are assigned to particular FECs using independent control mode when running MPLS across a Frame-mode implementation. When you use this mode, labels are assigned to FECs based on whether the FEC exists within the routing table of the LSR. Using these label assignments, you can establish Label Switched Paths (LSPs) across the MPLS network. Building on this knowledge, you can understand how each LSR can detect, and prevent, forwarding loops.

Frame-mode: Data Plane Loop Detection

In a standard IP-routed network, forwarding loops can be detected by examining the TTL field of an incoming IP packet. Using this field, each router in the packet's path decrements its value by 1; if the field reaches 0, the packet is dropped and the forwarding loop is broken. Figure 5-3 illustrates this mechanism.

Figure 5-3   *Loop Detection Using TTL in an IP Network*

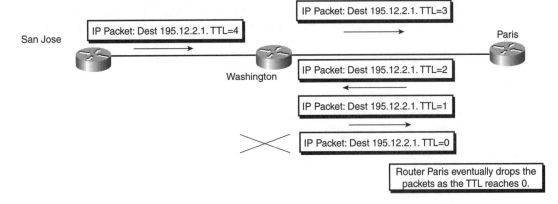

As Figure 5-3 shows, a loop has been formed between the Washington and Paris routers. Because each router decrements the TTL field by 1, the loop eventually is discovered and the looping packet is dropped (by the Paris router in the example). This same mechanism is used within the data plane of a Frame-mode implementation of MPLS. Each LSR along a particular LSP decrements the TTL field of the MPLS header whenever it forwards an incoming MPLS frame, and drops any packets that reach a 0 TTL.

NOTE   This also is true of an ATM interface that is *not* running MPLS directly with any ATM switches. This is because a PVC across this interface is treated as one hop, although it might traverse a series of ATM switches.

Frame-mode: Control Plane Loop Prevention

The detection of forwarding loops is obviously a very necessary function. However, it also is necessary that the LSR be capable of preventing these forwarding loops before they occur. This prevention activity must be achieved within the control plane because this is where Label Switched Paths (LSPs) are created.

In a standard IP-routed network, the prevention of forwarding loops is the job of the interior routing protocol. Because each LSR in a Frame-mode implementation of MPLS uses these same routing protocols to populate its routing table, the information that is used to form the LSPs within the network is the same as with a standard IP-routed network. For this reason, a Frame-mode implementation of MPLS relies on the routing protocols to make sure the information contained in the routing table of the LSR is loop-free, in exactly the same way as a standard IP-routed network.

Loop Detection and Prevention in Cell-mode MPLS

When you deploy MPLS across ATM switches and routers that run LC-ATM interfaces, the mechanisms used for loop detection and prevention in a Frame-mode deployment are not adequate for this type of environment. This is because there is no concept of TTL within an ATM cell header and a different method achieves the allocation and distribution of labels. Therefore, new mechanisms specific to the ATM environment are necessary so that MPLS can be deployed successfully across this type of network.

To see how the detection and prevention of loops is deployed within an ATM environment, consider both the MPLS control plane and the MPLS data plane to see how they differ from the Frame-mode implementation.

Cell-mode: Control Plane Loop Detection/Prevention

As discussed in Chapter 2, "Frame-mode MPLS Operation," when MPLS is deployed across LC-ATM interfaces and ATM switches, the control plane uses downstream-on-demand label distribution procedures with ordered label allocation by default. This means that the allocation and distribution of labels occurs based on request rather than on the presence of a particular FEC in the routing table of the ATM-LSR. You also saw that you can use independent label allocation on ATM-LSRs, which means that an ATM-LSR can allocate a label for each FEC independently of whether it already received a label mapping from a downstream ATM-LSR neighbor. In either case, a label request message is sent on demand to the downstream neighbor for a particular FEC to ask for a label mapping for that FEC. A significant difference exists between the two methods: When you use independent control mode, the ATM-LSR returns a label mapping immediately to the source of the label request message, whereas when you use ordered control mode, the ATM-LSR waits for a label mapping from its downstream neighbor before allocating and sending its own label mapping to the source of the label request message.

The consequence of both of these methods is that although the ATM-LSR still relies on the interior routing protocol to populate its routing table, it also must rely on the successful completion of signaling mechanisms to be able to create a Label Switched Path (LSP) to a particular FEC. To understand why this could be an issue, and why the control plane of MPLS running in Cell-mode has been enhanced, review how to achieve label distribution and allocation (using ordered control for simplicity), through the example shown in Figure 5-4.

Figure 5-4   *Downstream-on-demand and Ordered Control Mode*

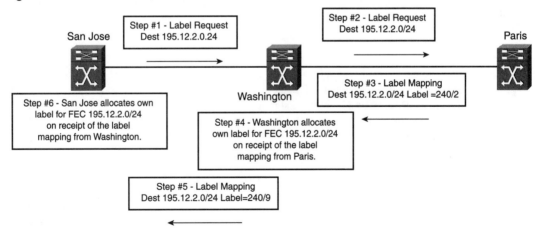

As you can see in Figure 5-4, when the San Jose ATM edge-LSR wants to set up an LSP to FEC 195.12.2.0/24, it checks its local routing table to find the next-hop for the FEC. After it determines this next-hop (by examining the LDP/TDP neighborship information), it can find which LDP/TDP neighbor has this next-hop as one of its directly connected interfaces. The San Jose ATM edge-LSR then sends a label request message to its next-hop downstream neighbor, the Washington ATM-LSR in the example. This label request message travels across the MPLS network, hop by hop, and eventually reaches the egress ATM-LSR for FEC 195.12.2.0/24, which is the Paris ATM-LSR in the example.

The Paris ATM-LSR sends a label mapping message upstream in response to the label request message, which cascades back down the LSP until reaching the ingress ATM-LSR. When this process is complete, the LSP is ready to pass traffic. This method works fine except that it is possible for either the label request or the label mapping messages to be forwarded continually between ATM-LSRs due to incorrect routing information. This is the same situation as in the previous TTL example, and it constitutes a forwarding loop of the control information. This certainly is undesirable, so extra mechanisms are necessary within the control plane to prevent this from happening.

NOTE   The possibility of a control information forwarding loop is apparent only when you deploy non–merge-capable ATM-LSRs. This is because an ATM-LSR becomes a merging ATM-LSR when it must merge at least two LSPs to the same FEC and it is configured to support VC merge. Therefore, when the first label request is received for a particular FEC, only one of the preceding conditions is met and non-merging ATM-LSR procedures are used. If both conditions are met, no further label request message is sent, regardless of whether a label mapping is received for the initial label request.

This mechanism is provided through the use of a hop-count TLV, which contains a count of the number of ATM-LSRs that the label request or label mapping message traversed. When an ATM-LSR receives a label request message, if it is not the egress ATM-LSR for the FEC contained within the message or does not have a label for the FEC, it initiates its own label request message and sends it to the next-hop ATM-LSR. This next-hop ATM-LSR again is determined by the analysis of the routing table.

NOTE   The current Cisco TDP implementation uses a hop-count object as part of the TDP label request and label mapping messages. This mechanism is the same as the LDP hop-count TLV that is specified in section 2.8, "Loop Detection" of *draft-ieft-mpls-ldp*, which is supported by the Cisco implementation of LDP.

If the original label request message contained a hop-count object/TLV, the ATM-LSR also includes one in its own label request message but increments the hop-count by 1. This is the inverse of the TTL operation, where the TTL is decreased by one although the same concept of a maximum number of hops is used. When an ATM-LSR receives a label-mapping message, if that message contains a hop-count object/TLV, this object/TLV hop-count is also incremented by 1 when the local label mapping is sent upstream.

When an ATM-LSR detects that the hop-count has reached a configured maximum value (254 in the Cisco implementation), it considers that the message has traversed a loop. It then sends a "Loop Detected Notification" message back to the source of the label request, or label mapping, message. Using this mechanism, a forwarding loop can be detected and subsequently prevented. Figure 5-5 illustrates this process.

Figure 5-5   *Hop-count Object/TLV Processing*

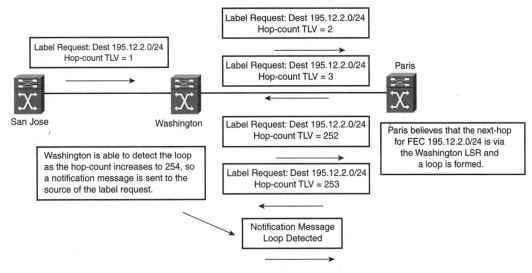

One problem with the hop-count method of loop detection is that potentially the time to discover the loop might be large based on the principle that the hop-count might need to increase to 254 before the loop is detected.

NOTE   The default hop-count within the Cisco implementation is 254 hops. You can change this, however, using the **tag-switching atm maxhops** command. Using this command, you can reduce the maximum number of hops, thus reducing the amount of time that potentially might be needed to detect a loop in the control information.

For this reason, *draft-ietf-mpls-ldp* provides a path vector mechanism through the use of the path-vector TLV, which can detect a loop based on the path that the message traversed. This is similar in concept to the way that BGP-4 detects loops within an AS_PATH, but in the case of MPLS, the LSR identifier is used. Using this mechanism, each ATM-LSR appends its LSR identifier to the path-vector list whenever it propagates a message that contains the path-vector TLV. If a message is received that contains the ATM-LSR's own LSR identifier within the path-vector list, the loop is detected and a "Loop Detected Notification" is sent back to the source of the message. Figure 5-6 shows this process.

Figure 5-6   *Path-Vector TLV Loop Prevention Mechanism*

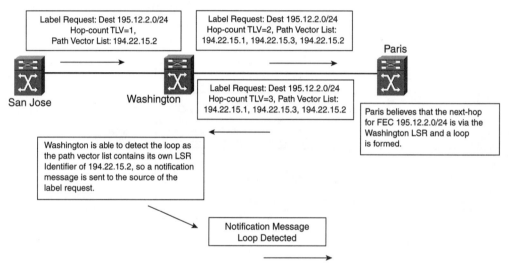

As Figure 5-6 shows, the LSR identifier of each ATM-LSR is added to the label request message as it proceeds through the network. Due to incorrect routing information, the Washington ATM-LSR believes that the next-hop for FEC 195.12.2.0/24 is via the Paris ATM-LSR, but the Paris ATM-LSR believes the next-hop for FEC 195.12.2.0/24 is via the Washington ATM-LSR. This constitutes a loop. The Washington ATM-LSR can detect this loop because it sees its own LSR identifier in the label request message.

Cell-mode––Data Plane Loop Detection

You learned already that an ATM cell header does not have any concept of TTL. This means that the mechanisms already described for the detection of forwarding loops in a Frame-mode MPLS implementation cannot be used when running in Cell-mode. In the previous section, however, you saw that forwarding loops within the control plane can be prevented through the use of a hop-count object/TLV in the label request/mapping messages exchanged between ATM-LSRs. The consequence of this is that each ATM-LSR has the information necessary to determine the number of hops necessary to reach the ATM egress point of an LSP, and this information can be used within the data plane of the Cell-mode MPLS deployment. Figure 5-7 shows the propagation of hop-count information between ATM-LSRs.

Figure 5-7 *Hop-count Propagation Between ATM-LSRs*

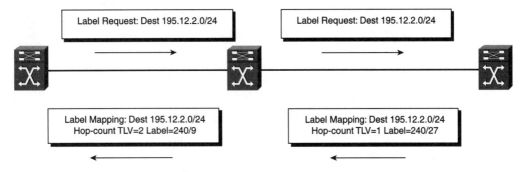

The example shown in Figure 5-7 shows that the San Jose ATM edge-LSR can determine that to reach the egress point of the LSP for FEC 195.12.2.0/24, a packet must traverse 2 hops. Armed with this information, the San Jose ATM edge-LSR can process the TTL field of an incoming IP packet prior to the segmentation of the packet into ATM cells. Figure 5-8 shows this process.

Figure 5-8 *IP Packet TTL Processing Prior to SAR Process*

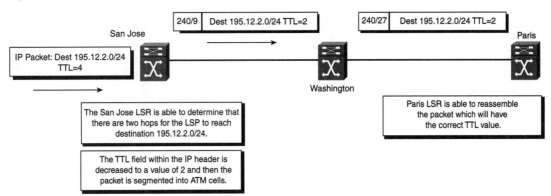

Figure 5-8 shows that when an IP packet destined for a host on network 195.12.2.0/24 arrives at the San Jose ATM edge-LSR, the IP TTL is decreased by the number of hops necessary to reach the end point of the LSP during the segmentation of the packet into cells. When the Paris ATM-LSR reassembles the original IP packet, the TTL field contained in the IP header contains the correct TTL value that reflects the number of hops the packet traversed.

The problem with this approach, however, is that anomalies are produced when using traceroute across the ATM portion of the network. Reducing the MPLS/IP TTL by 1 is sufficient to prevent forwarding loops. In the Cisco implementation of the MPLS architecture, the ATM edge-LSR decreases the TTL by 1—regardless of the number of hops—prior to the segmentation of the frame into cells. By using this method, you can rely on TTL for regions of the network that are frame-forwarded, including the edge of the ATM cloud, and you can assume that control procedures (as discussed in the previous section) prevent loops within the ATM portion of the network.

Traceroute Across an MPLS-enabled Network

The traceroute facility is a useful troubleshooting tool that allows you to trace the path a packet takes from an IP source to an IP destination. This tool is used extensively in the IP community and, therefore, its importance warrants discussion in this book.

Although the MPLS architecture does not change the inherent behavior of the traceroute facility, it does handle the forwarding of traceroute packets slightly differently to a normal IP network. In a normal IP environment, the Cisco implementation of traceroute works as illustrated in Figure 5-9.

Figure 5-9   *Operation of Traceroute Across an IP Network*

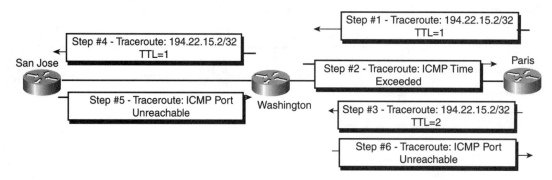

As Figure 5-9 shows, the operation of traceroute across an IP network can be summarized as follows. These steps constitute the use of traceroute both within an IP network and within an MPLS-enabled network:

Step 1   The source of the traceroute sends an IP packet to a particular destination with a Time-to-Live (TTL) of 1 and a destination UDP port of 33434 (Step 1).

Step 2   The first router in the path of the packet sends an Internet Control Message Protocol (ICMP) "Time Exceeded" message back to the source of the packet. This is because the TTL of the IP packet reaches zero after the router decrements it by 1 (Step 2).

Step 3   The source sends a second packet, this time with a TTL of 2. The first hop router routes this packet. When it reaches the second router in the path, an ICMP "Time Exceeded" message is sent again (Step 3 and Step 4).

Step 4   This process continues (with the source incrementing the TTL by 1 on each iteration), until it reaches the final destination of the packet, or a maximum number of hops is reached (the default value is 30 hops). The final destination router (or host) sends an ICMP "Port Unreachable" message back to the source. Using the ICMP response messages, the source can tell whether the response is from a transit router or from the final destination of the packet (Step 5 and Step 6).

This process certainly is adequate in a normal IP backbone where all transit routers carry external routes. However, as discussed in Chapter 2, it is desirable in an MPLS network to not carry external routing information and just to label switch traffic to the BGP next-hop of these external destinations. This presents a couple of problems with the use of traceroute:

- Traceroute relies on the fact that the source address of the traceroute packet is reachable by any router that needs to respond to the packet with an ICMP message.

- TTL propagation must be possible across the network for traceroute to function.

NOTE   This issue is discussed fully in *draft-ietf-mpls-label-encaps*, section 2.3.2, "Tunneling Private Addresses Through a Public Backbone."

Because the source address might not be reachable (for example, when running VPN or when the core of the network does not carry BGP routes) in an MPLS environment, you can re-use the label stack from the original packet to label switch the ICMP message back to the source. This means that the packet can be sent to the original destination, which then can forward the packet back across the MPLS network to the original source of the packet. In the example shown in Figure 5-9, this behavior causes the Washington router to forward the ICMP "Time Exceeded" message (Step 2 in Figure 5-9) to the San Jose router, which then forwards the packet back to the Washington router with a label stack to reach the Paris router. Figure 5-10 shows this process.

Figure 5-10 *Traceroute in an MPLS Environment*

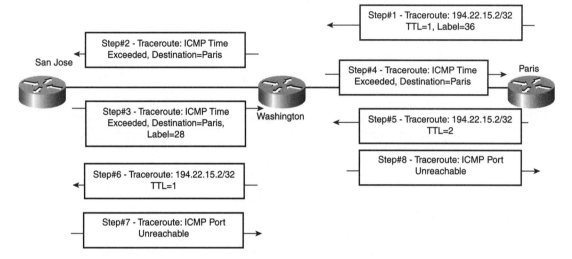

Figure 5-10 shows that although the TTL of the incoming packet (Step 1) reaches zero, the Washington router can direct the ICMP "Time Exceeded" message back to the Paris router by using the original label stack of the packet. Example 5-3 provides some debug output to show this process in action. The addresses shown are 10.2.1.21 (the address of the Paris router interface connecting it to Washington), 10.1.1.13 (the address of the San Jose router interface connecting it to Washington), and 194.22.15.2 (the loopback interface address on the San Jose router).

Example 5-3 *Traceroute Across an MPLS Network*

```
Paris# debug ip icmp
Paris# traceroute 194.22.15.2

Type escape sequence to abort.
Tracing the route to 194.22.15.2

  1 10.2.1.22 4 msec 0 msec 0 msec
  2 10.1.1.13 4 msec *  0 msec

ICMP: dst (10.2.1.21) port unreachable rcv from 10.1.1.13
ICMP: dst (10.2.1.21) port unreachable rcv from 10.1.1.13

Washington# debug ip icmp
Washington# debug tag packet

TAG: Et0/1/0: recvd: CoS=0, TTL=1, Tag(s)=36
TAG: AT0/0/0.1: xmit: (no tag)

ICMP: time exceeded (time to live) sent to 10.2.1.21 (dest was 194.22.15.2)
```

Example 5-3   *Traceroute Across an MPLS Network (Continued)*

```
TAG: Et0/1/0: recvd: CoS=0, TTL=1, Tag(s)=36
TAG: AT0/0/0.1: xmit: (no tag)

ICMP: time exceeded (time to live) sent to 10.2.1.21 (dest was 194.22.15.2)

TAG: Et0/1/0: recvd: CoS=0, TTL=1, Tag(s)=36
TAG: AT0/0/0.1: xmit: (no tag)

ICMP: time exceeded (time to live) sent to 10.2.1.21 (dest was 194.22.15.2)

TAG: Et0/1/0: recvd: CoS=0, TTL=2, Tag(s)=36
TAG: AT0/0/0.1: xmit: (no tag)

TAG: Et0/1/0: recvd: CoS=0, TTL=2, Tag(s)=36
TAG: AT0/0/0.1: xmit: (no tag)

TAG: Et0/1/0: recvd: CoS=0, TTL=2, Tag(s)=36
TAG: AT0/0/0.1: xmit: (no tag)

San Jose# debug ip icmp

ICMP: dst (194.22.15.2) port unreachable sent to 10.2.1.21
ICMP: dst (194.22.15.2) port unreachable sent to 10.2.1.21
```

NOTE   *draft-ietf-mpls-icmp* describes an extension to the traceroute facility to include MPLS label information. This is a useful extension and provides information not only on the path a packet takes, but also on the MPLS labels used throughout that path.

Although the previous description provides all the necessary functionality for traceroute to work in a Frame-mode MPLS environment, you also need to consider the effects of traceroute across an MPLS network that is constructed with ATM-LSRs in the topology.

Chapter 1, "Multiprotocol Label Switching (MPLS) Architecture Overview," defines an ATM-LSR as an LSR with a number of LC-ATM interfaces that forward cells between these interfaces using labels carried in the VPI/VCI field. The consequence of this is that TTL is not available in the header of an ATM cell and, therefore, cannot be manipulated at each hop in the network. For this reason, when ATM-LSRs are within the path, the ATM portion of the network is treated as one IP hop.

NOTE	*draft-ietf-mpls-atm* discusses the manipulation of the TTL in an ATM environment in section 10, "TTL Manipulation."

NOTE	You can disable the TTL in a Frame-mode network using the [**no**] **tag-switching ip propagate-ttl** command. Chapter 13 discusses this command in detail.
	When this command is disabled, the IP TTL field is not copied into the MPLS TTL field during label imposition—a value of 255 is copied instead. This action effectively disables traceroute across the MPLS network and the output of the **traceroute** command shows only non-MPLS hops (hops where the packet is IP-forwarded) within the output.

NOTE	Because each ICMP "Time Exceeded" message is propagated using the original label stack of the packet, the delay output shown in the traceroute is no longer meaningful because it does not reflect an accurate delay encountered by packets traversing the backbone.

Route Summarization Within an MPLS-enabled Network

In any IP-based deployment, whether using standard IP routing protocols or running IP across an MPLS network, route summarization is an important part of the network structure. Route summarization provides the mechanism necessary to reduce the size of the Layer 3 routing table by *bundling* a number of prefixes into a less specific summary route, which helps reduce the amount of memory required by devices in the network but also helps reduce the overhead when computing paths through the network topology.

In an MPLS deployment, this summarization can help reduce the number of labels because only one label is necessary for the summary route. You can see an example of this summarization, and relevant label distribution, in Figure 5-11.

You can see in Figure 5-11 that the Washington LSR receives two /24 prefixes, 174.24. 9.0/24 and 174.24.10.0/24, from the Paris LSR via its internal routing protocol. The Washington LSR is configured to send a summary route, 174.24.0/16, which covers both of the more specific routes that it learned from the Paris LSR.

Figure 5-11 *Route Summarization in an MPLS Network*

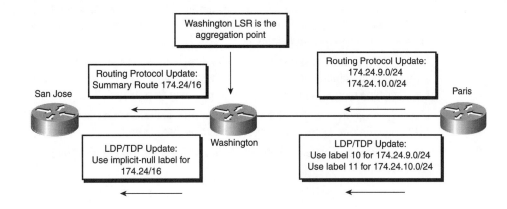

Using this configuration, the Washington LSR becomes the aggregation point for LSPs that use the summary route. This means that each LSP that uses the summary route needs to terminate on the Washington LSR. The result is that the Washington LSR needs to examine the second-level label of each packet and, depending on what it finds, depends on the action that is taken. If a label exists, the LSR switches the packet based on this label. If a label does not exist, the LSR needs to examine the Layer 3 header information so it can reclassify the packet.

Because of the necessity to reclassify packets at the aggregation point, it is imperative that the device that provides the aggregation not be an ATM switch. This is because an ATM switch has no hardware to process Layer 3 information with which to reclassify any packets and just uses the incoming VPI/VCI as reference to determine the outgoing port, and the outgoing VPI/VCI that should be used for the incoming cell.

NOTE   Summarization also has major implications when used in an MPLS/VPN environment. Chapter 13 discusses this in more detail.

Summary

This chapter discussed advanced MPLS topics that are not necessarily needed to successfully deploy an MPLS backbone, but could become very useful during advanced network design or troubleshooting.

You can control several advanced mechanisms in Cisco IOS:

- Controlled label distribution, where you can fine-tune which packets are label-switched and which packets are IP-routed by controlling which labels an LSR announces to its upstream neighbors

- MPLS MTU on a LAN segment in combination with increased physical MTU on the same segment, which allows maximum-sized IP packets to be propagated across Ethernet-type media as giant frames without being fragmented

- IP TTL propagation, with which you can control whether an end-host connected to an MPLS network can perform a traceroute across that network

- **atm maxhops** parameter, which allows you to fine-tune loop prevention in ATM environments

CHAPTER 6

MPLS Migration and Configuration Case Study

The previous chapters discussed the theory and configuration of the MPLS architecture within a Frame-mode and Cell-mode implementation. Now that this theory is clear, we should consider a case study that provides a migration example for both a router and an ATM-based backbone so that we can put the theory into practice.

Although this chapter provides a suggested basic migration path, this does not mean that other approaches cannot be taken or that all relevant topics are covered. For instance, we will not consider network management or accounting because both of these areas are too broad for meaningful discussion within this chapter. However, you should be aware that each of these topics should be fully investigated before migration. We will look at network management in some detail in chapters that follow and explore some suggested techniques to assist in successful deployment within an MPLS environment, especially in the case where advanced services such as virtual private networks are used. In the case of IP accounting, you should be aware that tools such as NetFlow work purely on IP packets, not MPLS packets. This means that care must be taken to enable these tools on interfaces that will receive IP packets so that accounting of customer traffic is successful.

Migration of the Backbone to a Frame-mode MPLS Solution

We will consider within this chapter a theoretical service provider backbone network—let's call it TransitNet—that currently provides Internet transit to several large customers. This Internet access is obtained through two separate external BGP peering points to upstream service providers. For the first part of the case study, we will consider a backbone made up purely of routers, without any ATM switch involvement. This router-based topology can be seen in Figure 6-1.

Although Figure 6-1 does not show all the physical network structure (this is not necessary within the scope of this discussion), it does provide an illustration of the BGP structure of the TransitNet backbone network.

Figure 6-1   *TransitNet Backbone Network Topology*

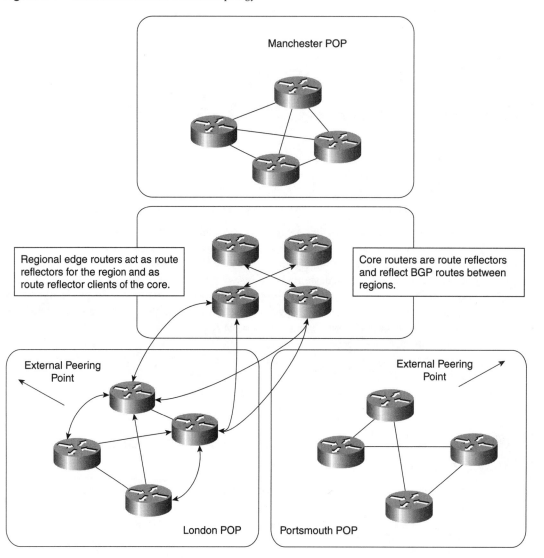

Each regional POP within the backbone has a requirement to carry BGP information that has been learned from the two external peering points located in the London and Portsmouth POPs. Furthermore, all TransitNet customer routes are carried within BGP, so there is also a requirement to run BGP in each POP so that customer routes can be propagated across the backbone network and be advertised to external BGP peers.

All external and customer routing information must be advertised throughout the topology so that all transit routers are capable of successfully routing traffic. Because of this requirement, a complex BGP structure that includes route reflection both within the POPs and also within the core of the network is necessary. Figure 6-1 shows each of the necessary iBGP sessions for one of the TransitNet POPs and highlights the complex hierarchical route reflection topology. This topology includes reflection within the POP from access-layer routers to the distribution-layer routers. Each distribution-layer router is a route reflector for clients within the POP (access-layer router) and is itself a client of the core route reflectors. Each core route reflector is fully meshed with every other core route reflector, and its role is to reflect routes from one POP to all other core routers and POPs.

NOTE	We will discuss route reflection and BGP design considerations further in Chapter 12, "Advanced MPLS/VPN Topics." If you need in-depth details of the Border Gateway Protocol, its functional elements such as route reflectors, or usage guidelines for BGP deployment on the Internet, turn to *Internet Routing Architectures*, Second Edition, by Bassam Halabi (Cisco Press).

The TransitNet service provider has decided to migrate its backbone toward an MPLS-based infrastructure because it does not want to carry external BGP information within the core of its network. The service provider also wants to remove the complexity of the routing protocol structure, which requires multiple BGP peering sessions and the deployment of multiple BGP route reflectors. In addition, the service provider wants to provide more advanced services, such as virtual private networks, to its customers at a later date, as well as the capability to distribute this traffic across its backbone using traffic engineering.

We have already seen that one of the consequences of a migration to the MPLS architecture is the capability to remove the requirement to carry BGP information within the core of the network. This was fully discussed in Chapter 2, "Frame-mode MPLS Operation." This is not always an obvious reason to migrate to an MPLS topology, but it certainly has major advantages and fits in very well with the objectives of the TransitNet service provider.

Pre-migration Infrastructure Checks

Before any migration to an MPLS solution can occur, whether across a pure router network or a network that consists of ATM switches, certain pre-migration steps must be completed.

As we have already discussed in the previous section, one of the advantages of running MPLS within the core of a service provider network is the capability to remove BGP information from transit routers. This means that all customer routes must be carried within BGP, which is good design practice for several reasons:

- BGP is the only protocol that can scale to a large number of routes; this is one of the design goals of the protocol.

- As external routing is carried within BGP, the internal routing structure of the network is protected from outside influence such as route flapping.

- Quality of service policy can be distributed using BGP (such as QoS policy propagation for BGP [QPPB]) so that differentiated service can be provided to individual customers using the BGP community attribute.

- The injection of a large number of routes into the IGP reduces the performance of the protocol and leads to stability and scalability issues.

NOTE   The migration of customer routes into BGP is covered in more detail in Chapter 13, "Guidelines for the Deployment of MPLS/VPN."

The configuration of the internal BGP sessions should include the use of the **next-hop-self** command (in conjunction with **update-source loopback xx**) within the BGP configuration so that the BGP next hop of the customer routes is one of the loopback interface addresses of the advertising edge router. This is necessary so that customer interface addresses do not have to be redistributed in the IGP of the service provider. This also provides a more stable environment for the BGP sessions between edge routers.

Cisco Express Forwarding (CEF) Requirements

After all external routes are carried within BGP, the next premigration step is to enable Cisco Express Forwarding (CEF) on all routers within the network. CEF is a fundamental requirement of the Cisco implementation of the MPLS architecture and must be enabled globally on all routers.

It is not necessary to enable CEF on all interfaces within the backbone—only on those that will perform label imposition, such as inbound interfaces on edge LSRs. However, if there is no particular reason to disable CEF on an interface, then we recommend that it be enabled across the network on all interfaces. To enable CEF globally, use the command **ip cef** or **ip cef distributed** (if distributed CEF on the 75xx series is required). To disable CEF on an interface basis, use the **no ip route-cache cef** or **no ip route-cache distributed** commands.

NOTE   If distributed CEF is disabled on an interface, then CEF switching of packets will still occur, although this will occur on the 75xx RSP rather than the interface. If CEF switching must be disabled for the 75xx interface completely, then the command **no ip route-cache cef** is also required.

Addressing the Internal BGP Structure

Because certain routers within the TransitNet network will no longer be required to hold BGP routes after the migration to MPLS, it is necessary to build the relevant infrastructure to support the new BGP design. This new structure can be seen in Figure 6-2.

Figure 6-2   *TransitNet MPLS BGP Peering Structure*

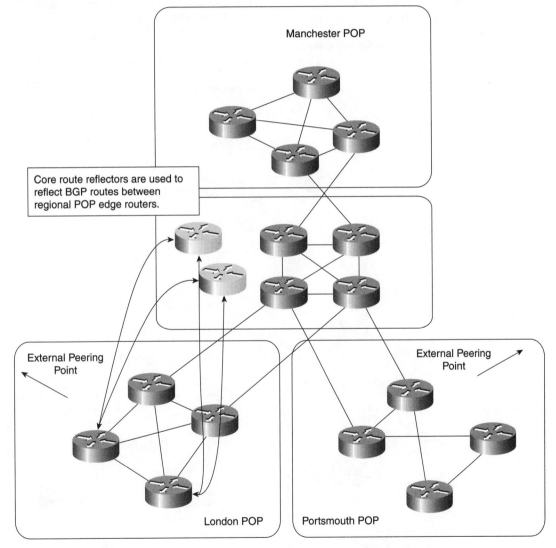

Figure 6-2 shows the desired topology, where BGP is enabled only on edge routers. These routers run iBGP sessions with core route reflectors so that all external routes can be distributed successfully between edge routers. All transit routers are now BGP-free and purely label switch packets across the backbone.

To be able to achieve this topology, and to provide a smooth migration to the MPLS solution, it is necessary as a migration step to run multiple BGP sessions from the edge routers. This can be seen in Figure 6-3, which shows the necessary old and new iBGP sessions for both of the edge routers within the London POP.

Figure 6-3   *TransitNet iBGP Session Requirements*

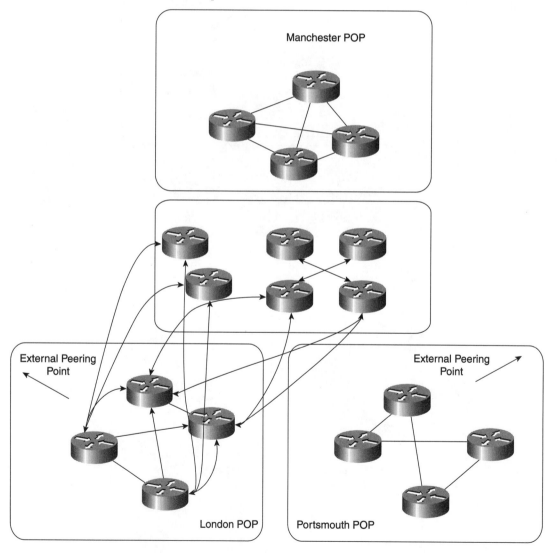

This type of migration approach has some implications—most notably, the increase in the memory requirements of BGP routers because they will need to house multiple BGP sessions and learn several copies of the same routes. However, if a smooth transition is required and memory is not an issue for a short-term migration phase, then this type of migration approach provides a seamless transition from one BGP topology to another.

NOTE   Our sample topology uses separate route reflectors for the migration. This is not strictly necessary because the existing route reflectors could be used as long as separate addresses are used for the iBGP sessions. (It is not possible to have multiple iBGP sessions between the same set of addresses.)

The addition of further BGP peering sessions on the edge routers does not present a problem for the BGP protocol. This is because the attributes of the routes are exactly the same; the only difference is that they have been reflected to the edge router from a different route reflector. This means that when the backbone routers are capable of label switching packets, the current BGP sessions can be removed without the danger of losing traffic.

Migration of Internal Links to MPLS

The next step in the migration process is to enable MPLS. The size of the MPLS deployment can range from just one link to the whole of the network, and from a limited subset of prefixes to all internal prefixes in the network.

Whichever deployment choice is taken (all the pre-migration steps will have been completed at this time), the **tag-switching ip** command (or the **mpls ip** command, if the Cisco Systems, Inc., LDP implementation is used) is the only one necessary on an interface basis to allow MPLS to function between the adjacent LSRs (unless these links are Ethernet links—see the accompanying note). As we have seen in previous chapters, using this command allows the LSR to build a TDP/LDP relationship with any adjacent LSRs and to distribute label bindings across the resultant TCP sessions.

NOTE   If MPLS is to be deployed across Ethernet links, the additional command **tag-switching mtu** is necessary within the interface configuration. For further information on the use of this command, refer to Chapter 5, "Advanced MPLS Topics."

WARNING   Caution must be taken if a partial migration to an MPLS-based solution approach is used and external routing information is carried within BGP. In this environment, it is absolutely essential to make sure that any routers within the backbone that do *not* run MPLS (or that do run MPLS, but with a restricted distribution of labels) have the necessary routing information to be capable of forwarding packets that arrive without labels.

In our sample topology, the service provider has adopted a two-stage migration plan for the TransitNet backbone. The first stage is the migration of the network core to an MPLS solution; the second stage is the migration of each POP. Both of these migration steps can be seen in Figure 6-4. Obviously many combinations exist for a successful migration, but because there are no special requirements within the TransitNet backbone to restrict which prefixes are used for label switching, the chosen migration steps are appropriate to achieve a quick and successful transition.

NOTE   If it is necessary to restrict which prefixes will be used for label switching, you should refer to the section "Controlling the Distribution of Label Mappings," in Chapter 5.

The first-stage migration includes the enabling of MPLS on all backbone links, which include all core routers and the links from each POP border router into the core. The consequence of this is that each of the POP border routers must still hold BGP routes although the core routers do not need BGP routing information anymore because they will label switch all traffic.

Figure 6-4 shows all the necessary BGP sessions for the London POP. Each of the core routers is used to reflect routes between POP sites, so the BGP peering structure is essentially the same, even though the core routers do not actually need the BGP information for successful connectivity between POPs.

NOTE   An alternative approach to the method shown in Figure 6-4 is to remove BGP from the core completely and define a scheme in which one level of route reflection is used for all edge devices. This reduces the complexity of the BGP design because hierarchical route reflection is no longer a requirement. This also helps to improve BGP convergence time because a BGP route is required to traverse fewer hops. This type of scheme is adequate for many designs, although the scheme shown in Figure 6-4 will be necessary in larger topologies, where the number of BGP speakers and session requirements is high, to allow the BGP topology to scale.

Figure 6-4   *TransitNet Migration Strategy*

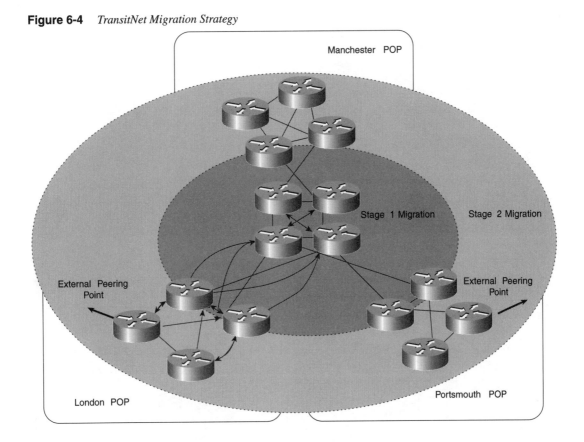

The second-stage migration involves enabling MPLS within each POP in the network. This could be achieved within a select number of POPs, or within every POP. When this migration stage is complete, all traffic entering a POP will be label-switched across the TransitNet backbone to the egress edge router that originated the route within BGP.

Removal of Unnecessary BGP Peering Sessions

When all of the links within the TransitNet backbone have been enabled for MPLS, the last step of the migration is to remove any unnecessary BGP sessions. With the introduction of new route reflectors to propagate routes between POPs, the core routers are no longer needed to perform the route reflection task. They also do not need to carry BGP routes because they will label-switch all traffic that is directed toward external destinations. This is also true of the border routers within each POP.

Figure 6-5 shows the necessary BGP sessions, with all unnecessary sessions removed.

Figure 6-5 *Final TransitNet BGP Peering Structure*

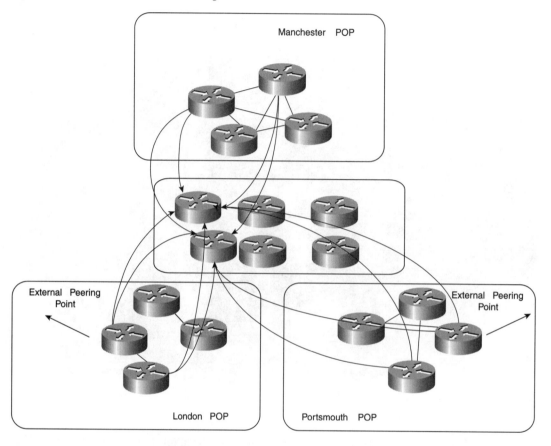

Migration of an ATM-based Backbone to Frame-mode MPLS

Our previous migration example assumed that the backbone of the service provider network is made up purely of routers, interconnected through point-to-point or shared media links. This is certainly the easiest topology to migrate to an MPLS solution, but what if the backbone is made up of routers, interconnected across ATM switches via PVCs? This is certainly not an uncommon type of topology, so we should consider how this type of topology could be migrated to MPLS.

Figure 6-6 provides an example of this type of connectivity and shows that the TransitNet backbone is connected through a full mesh of ATM PVCs in the core of the network.

Figure 6-6   *TransitNet Backbone Topology Using ATM Switches*

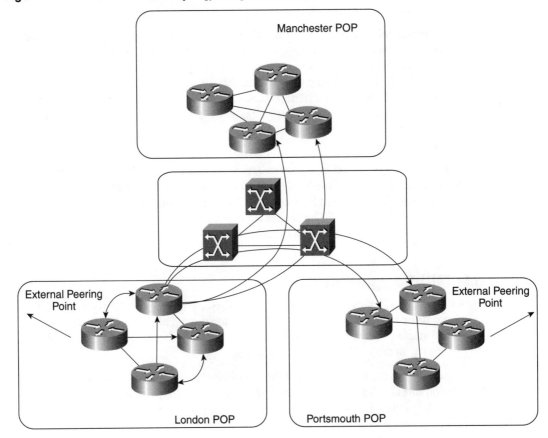

This figure shows only the relevant PVCs for one of the London POP border routers, but if optimal, any-to-any connectivity is a requirement, then all other border routers within the core of the network will require a PVC with all other border routers.

The TransitNet service provider has essentially two choices with this type of connectivity. First, it could opt to migrate the ATM switches to MPLS and run IP+ATM within the backbone, creating a point-to-point type topology in which each of the border routers requires only a single connection (or multiple connections, for redundancy) into the ATM network, rather than multiple virtual circuits to other border routers. Second, the service provider could choose to deploy MPLS across the existing infrastructure and run either PVCs or permanent virtual path connections (PVPs) between ATM edge LSRs. Neither of these methods (PVCs and PVPs) are good long-term solutions, however, because they suffer from the scaling issues that we have already described, despite the use of VP tunnels that allows the ATM edge LSR to use different VCs for different FECs, rather than sending all traffic across the same PVC.

As an interim migration step, the TransitNet service provider has chosen to deploy the second option and to run MPLS across its existing PVCs. This is exactly the same type of connectivity that we examined in Chapter 4, "Running Frame-mode MPLS Across Switched WAN Media." Using this method, the service provide can enable MPLS across the whole backbone and pass IP traffic across the ATM PVCs using Frame-mode MPLS. This is no different than our previous example of the migration of a router-only backbone, and it provides a simple first-stage migration of the existing backbone to an MPLS-based solution.

As a second-stage migration, the service provider either can migrate the existing ATM infrastructure to a frame-based-only topology by simply bypassing the ATM switches and adding further frame-based LSRs, connected with point-to-point links such as POSIP, or it can migrate the existing ATM switches to provide support for MPLS and integrate the IP and ATM networks into one IP+ATM solution.

Cell-mode MPLS Migration

A migration to Cell-mode MPLS from a PVC-based topology is more involved than the migration of a router-only frame-based MPLS topology. This type of migration requires several stages to allow the existing infrastructure to be switched over to the new MPLS topology with minimal disruption to IP traffic.

In the previous section, we saw that the TransitNet backbone was converted to an MPLS solution across ATM PVCs as a temporary measure. This type of solution involves all the scaling issues that we have already discussed, so a migration to a full Cell-mode implementation is desirable.

As part of the migration, all existing ATM PVCs must be maintained so that minimal disruption to traffic is achieved. In the case of the TransitNet backbone, in which the ATM topology is provided through use of Cisco BPX switches, this can be achieved by partitioning the ATM link from the ATM edge LSR to the BPX ATM-LSR so that both MPLS- and standards-based ATM PVCs can coexist across the same physical media. Figure 6-7 shows this topology.

Figure 6-7   *Coexistence of MPLS and ATM PVCs*

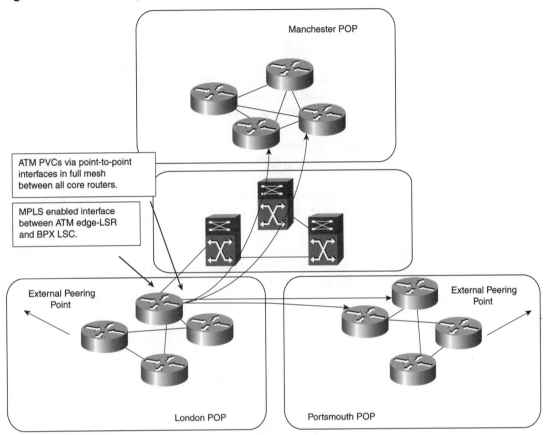

As Figure 6-7 shows, each BPX (or LS1010) switch can be converted to an MPLS-aware switch while maintaining the existing PVC-based topology. Using this method of migration, the following steps can be used to provide a staged transfer of traffic onto the new MPLS solution:

- Enable the ATM switch for participation in the MPLS topology. This will include all necessary software upgrades, configuration of the switches (including the partitioning of the switch trunks), and the addition and configuration of a Label Switch Controller (LSC) in the case of BPX implementations.

- When the ATM switch is ready for participation in the MPLS topology, each interface that will carry both MPLS and ATM PVC traffic must be configured. On the BPX, this includes the partitioning of the physical interface to carry MPLS traffic in one partition and AuroRoute traffic in the other partition. On the LS1010, this includes the configuration of the PVCs (which will already exist) and the enabling of MPLS on the physical interface.

- The next step is the configuration of the ATM edge LSR. Because it is necessary to continue to use the existing PVCs during the migration, a further subinterface must be configured that will be used to carry MPLS traffic. The IGP cost of this interface must be higher than the interface that will carry the PVC traffic so that the PVC-based interface is always preferred over the MPLS interface. Multiple hops will exist across the MPLS path, so the cost of the MPLS interface should, in most cases, be greater by default, and no further configuration will be necessary.

- When everything is configured and MPLS functionality is tested across the ATM network, the last stage of the migration is to increase the IGP cost of the PVC interface so that the MPLS-enabled interface is preferred. This will cause labels to be requested from the downstream ATM-LSR, and label switching of traffic will be achieved.

NOTE   For a discussion and configuration examples of running both MPLS and PVCs across the same ATM interface, refer to Chapter 4.

Summary

In this chapter, you've seen several potential migration strategies from classical IP backbones toward MPLS-enabled backbones. These strategies should serve only as a starting point for your own migration strategy, of course, because every network has its own specific requirements. Regardless of which strategy is adopted, a number of common steps must be followed in every network migration toward an MPLS-enabled backbone.

Start with these preparatory steps:

Step 1   Determine the required software and firmware versions for all network devices in your network, based on their hardware configuration.

Step 2   Determine memory requirements and any other potential upgrade requirements for all network devices in your network.

Step 3   Determine the impact that MPLS might have on your network management system, specifically in areas of accounting and billing. You might use NetFlow or IP accounting on the core routers, which will cease to function as soon as these routers start forwarding labeled packets.

Step 4   Test the target software version on your typical hardware platforms in a controlled lab environment to ensure that the software will be stable in your target network.

Step 5   Based on the upgrade requirements, you might decide to perform partial or full migration. (This decision is even more important if you have ATM switches in your network.)

Migrate your router-based network to MPLS by following these steps:

Step 1   Upgrade your network devices to the target software version. Verify that your network is stable.

Step 2   If you're running BGP in your network and you plan to remove BGP from your core routers after the migration to an MPLS infrastructure, design your new BGP structure and implement it in parallel with your old structure.

Step 3   Migrate the router part of your network. For networks using an ATM core infrastructure, retain the traditional ATM PVC setup and run MPLS over the ATM Forum PVCs as an interim step.

Step 4   Verify that your network is stable and performs label switching as planned. Verify that the core routers forward only labeled packets.

Step 5   Remove BGP from the core routers if needed. Verify that the network still performs as planned.

The following additional steps must be performed if you're migrating ATM switches toward MPLS as well:

Step 1   Migrate the ATM part of your network by upgrading ATM switches and establishing a parallel Cell-mode MPLS infrastructure. Verify that the Cell-mode MPLS infrastructure performs as expected.

Step 2   Using IGP cost, move your traffic from ATM Forum PVCs toward a Cell-mode MPLS infrastructure. Verify that the Cell-mode MPLS works as planned.

Step 3   Remove ATM Forum PVCs from your ATM network.

MPLS-based Virtual Private Networks

CHAPTER 7

Virtual Private Network (VPN) Implementation Options

A Virtual Private Network (VPN) is defined loosely as a network in which customer connectivity amongst multiple sites is deployed on a shared infrastructure with the same access or security policies as a private network. With the recent advent of marketing activities surrounding the term VPNs, from new technologies supporting VPNs to a flurry of VPN-enabled products and services, you might think that the VPN concept is a major technology throughput. However, as is often the case, VPN is a concept that is more than 10-years old and is well known in the service provider market space.

The new technologies and products merely enable more reliable, scalable, and more cost-effective implementation of the same product. With the cost reduction and enhanced scalability associated with new VPN technologies, it's not surprising that VPN services are among the major drivers for Multiprotocol Label Switching (MPLS) deployment in service provider and enterprise networks.

Before discussing a technology (VPN services based on MPLS) designed to solve a problem (cost-effective VPN implementation), it's always advantageous to focus on the problem first, which is what we do in this chapter.

This chapter gives you an overview of VPN services, common VPN terminology, and detailed classification of various VPN usages and topologies that are encountered most often. This chapter also provides an overview of technologies that were used traditionally to implement Virtual Private Networks either on individual service provider backbones or over the public Internet.

Virtual Private Network Evolution

Initial computer networks were implemented with two major technologies: *leased lines* for permanent connectivity and *dial-up lines* for occasional connectivity requirements. Figure 7-1 shows a typical network from those days.

Figure 7-1 *Typical Computer Network from 15 Years Ago*

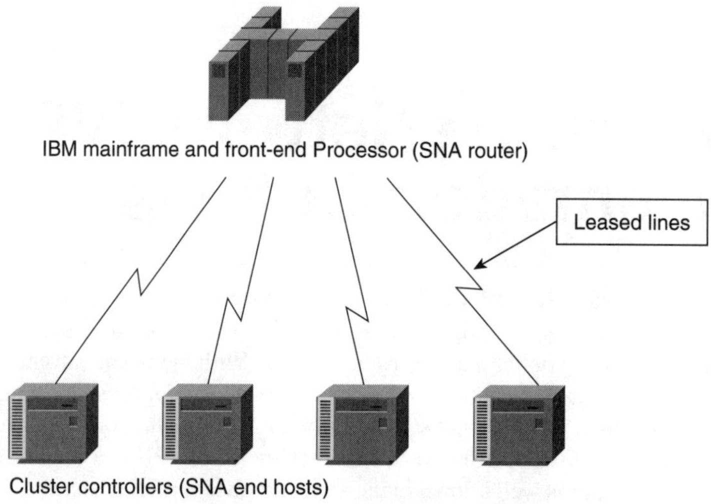

IBM mainframe and front-end Processor (SNA router)

Leased lines

Cluster controllers (SNA end hosts)

The initial computer network implementation provided the customers with good security (capturing data off leased lines requires dedicated equipment and physical access to the wires), but did not provide cost-effective implementation due to two reasons:

- The typical traffic profile between any two sites in a network varies based on the time of day, the day of the month, and even the season (for example, traffic at retail stores increases around Christmas season).

- The end-users always request fast responses, resulting in a high bandwidth requirement between sites, but the dedicated bandwidth available on the leased lines is used only part of the time (when the users are active).

These two reasons prompted the data communication industry and service providers to develop and implement a number of statistical multiplexing schemas that provided the customers with a service that was almost an equivalent to leased lines. This service was cheaper, however, due to the statistical benefits the service provider could achieve from a large customer base. The first *virtual* private networks were based on such technologies as X.25 and Frame Relay, and, later, SMDS and ATM. Figure 7-2 shows a typical VPN built with these technologies (for example, Frame Relay).

As you can see in Figure 7-2, the overall VPN solution has a number of components:

- The service provider is the organization that owns the infrastructure (the equipment and the transmission media) that provides emulated leased lines to its customers. The service provider in this scenario offers a customer a *Virtual Private Network Service*.

Figure 7-2   *Typical Frame Relay Network*

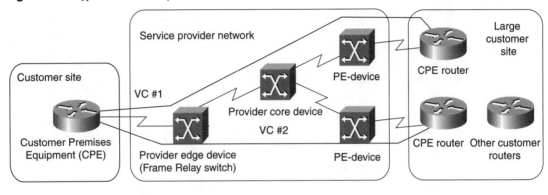

- The customer connects to the service provider network through a *Customer Premises Equipment (CPE)* device. The CPE is usually a Packet Assembly and Disassembly (PAD) device that provides plain terminal connectivity, a bridge, or a router. The CPE device is also sometimes called a *Customer Edge (CE)* device.

- The CPE device is connected through transmission media (usually a leased line, but could also be a dial-up connection) to the service provider equipment, which could be an X.25, Frame Relay, or ATM switch, or even an IP router. The edge service provider device is sometimes called the *Provider Edge (PE)* device.

- The service provider usually has additional equipment in the core of the service provider network (also called the *P-network*). These devices are called *P-devices* (for example, P-switches or P-routers).

- A contiguous part of the customer network is called a *site*. A site can connect to the P-network through one or several transmission lines, using one or several CPE and PE devices, based on the redundancy requirements.

- The emulated leased line provided to the customer by the service provider in the overlay VPN model (see the section, "Overlay and Peer-to-peer VPN Model," later in this chapter for more details) frequently is called a *Virtual Circuit (VC)*. The VC can be either constantly available (*Permanent Virtual Circuit [PVC]*) or established on demand (*Switched Virtual Circuit [SVC]*). Some technologies used special terms for VCs, for example Data Link Connection Identifier (DLCI) in Frame Relay.

- The service provider can charge either a flat rate for the VPN service, which normally depends on the bandwidth available to the customer, or a usage-based rate, which can depend on the volume of data exchanged or the duration of data exchange.

Modern Virtual Private Networks

With the introduction of new technologies in the service provider networks and new customer requirements, the VPN concept became more and more complex. Vendors introduced different and often conflicting terms, which further increased the complexity. The modern VPN services thus can span a variety of technologies and topologies. The only way to cope with this diversity is to introduce VPN classification, which you can do using four criteria:

- The business problem a VPN is trying to solve. The major classes of business problems are intracompany communication (lately, also called *intranet*), inter-company communication (also called *extranet*), and access for mobile users (also called *Virtual Private Dialup Network*).

- The OSI layer at which the service provider exchanges the topology information with the customer. Major categories here are the *overlay model*, where the service provider provides the customer with only a set of point-to-point (or multipoint) links between the customer sites, and the *peer model*, where the service provider and the customer exchange Layer 3 routing information.

- The Layer 2 or Layer 3 technology used to implement the VPN service within the service provider network, which can be X.25, Frame Relay, SMDS, ATM, or IP.

- The topology of the network, which can range from simple hub-and-spoke topology to fully meshed networks and multilevel hierarchical topologies in larger networks.

Business Problem-based VPN Classification

The three business problems a typical organization is trying to solve with a Virtual Private Network are:

- Intra-organizational communication (intranet).

- Communication with other organizations (extranet).

- Access of mobile users, home workers, remote office, and so on, through inexpensive dial-up media (Virtual Private Dial-up Network)

The three types of VPN solutions usually span most of the topologies and technologies offered by VPN service providers, but differ greatly in the level of security required in their implementation.

Intra-organizational communications usually are not protected well by the end hosts or the firewalls. The VPN service used to implement intra-organizational communication therefore must offer high levels of isolation and security. Intra-organizational communications also require guaranteed quality of service for mission-critical processes.

These are the two major reasons why we don't see many organizations using Internet, which cannot offer end-to-end quality of service, isolation, or security, as the infrastructure for their intra-organizational communications. Intranet VPNs were thus usually implemented with traditional technologies like X.25, Frame Relay, or ATM.

Inter-organizational communications frequently take place between central sites of the organizations—usually using dedicated security devices, such as firewalls or encryption gear similar to the setup demonstrated in Figure 7-3. These communications also might have less stringent quality of service requirements. This set of requirements makes the Internet more and more suitable for inter-organizational communications; therefore, it's no surprise that more and more business-to-business traffic takes place over the Internet.

Figure 7-3 *Typical Extranet Setup*

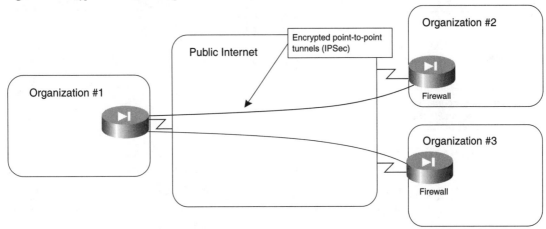

Remote user access into a corporate network, typically from changing or unknown locations, is always riddled with security issues, which have to be resolved on an end-to-end basis using such technologies as encryption or one-time passwords. Thus, the security requirements for VPDN services were never as high as the requirements for Intranet communications. It's no surprise that most of the VPDN services today are implemented on top of Internet Protocol (IP), either over the Internet or using the private backbone of a service provider, as illustrated in Figure 7-4. The protocols used to implement VPDN service over IP include Layer 2 Forwarding (L2F) or Layer 2 Transport Protocol (L2TP).

Figure 7-4   *Service Provider Offering Separate VPDN Backbone*

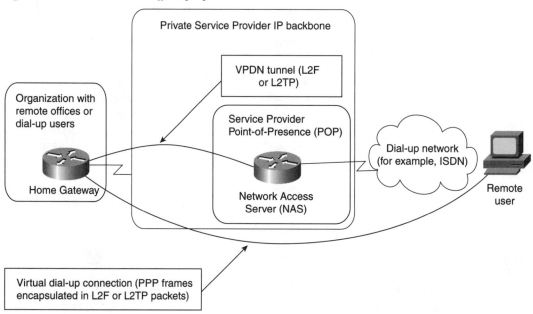

The VPDN technology uses a number of special terms that are unique to the VPDN world:

- **Network Access Server (NAS)**—The Remote Access Server (RAS) managed by the service provider that accepts the customer call, performs the initial authentication, and forwards the call (via L2F or L2TP) to the customer's gateway.

- **Home Gateway**—A customer-managed router that accepts the call forwarded by the NAS, performs additional authentication and authorization, and terminates the PPP session from the dial-up user. The PPP session parameters (including network addresses, such as an IP address) are negotiated between the dial-up user and the home gateway; NAS only forwards frames of Point-to-Point Protocol (PPP) between the two.

NOTE   The details of VPDN, L2F, and L2TP are beyond the scope of this book. Please refer to *RFC 2341 Cisco Layer Two Forwarding (Protocol) "L2F"* and *RFC 2661 Layer Two Tunneling Protocol "L2TP"* for additional information on these topics.

Overlay and Peer-to-peer VPN Model

Two VPN implementation models have gained widespread use:

- The overlay model, where the service provider provides emulated leased lines to the customer.

- The peer-to-peer model, where the service provider and the customer exchange Layer 3 routing information and the provider relays the data between the customer sites on the optimum path between the sites and without the customer's involvement.

NOTE	One might argue that the case where the customer and the provider use the same Layer 2 technology (for example, Frame Relay or ATM switches) also constitutes a peer-to-peer model, but because we focus on Layer 3 VPN services here, we will not consider this scenario. Similarly, a humorous person might call a leased line service a Layer 1 peer-to-peer model.

Overlay VPN Model

The overlay VPN model is the easiest to understand because it provides very clear separation between the customer's and the service provider's responsibilities:

- The service provider provides the customer with a set of emulated leased lines. These leased lines are called VCs, which can be either constantly available (PVCs) or established on demand (SVCs). Figure 7-5 shows the topology of a sample overlay VPN and the VCs used in it.

Figure 7-5   *Sample Overlay VPN Network*

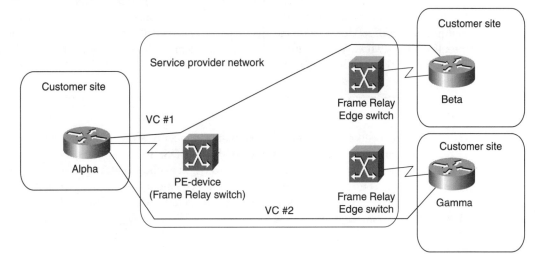

- The customer establishes router-to-router communication between the Customer Premises Equipment (CPE) devices over the VCs provisioned by the service provider. The routing protocol data is always exchanged between the customer devices, and the service provider has no knowledge of the internal structure of the customer network. Figure 7-6 shows the routing topology of the VPN network in Figure 7-5.

Figure 7-6   *Routing in Sample Overlay VPN Network*

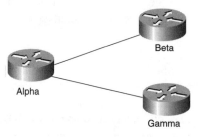

The QoS guarantees in the overlay VPN model usually are expressed in terms of bandwidth guaranteed on a certain VC (Committed Information Rate or CIR) and maximum bandwidth available on a certain VC (Peak Information Rate or PIR). The committed bandwidth guarantee usually is provided through the statistical nature of the Layer 2 service but depends on the overbooking strategy of the service provider. This means that the committed rate is not actually guaranteed although the provider can provision a Minimum Information Rate (MIR) that effectively is nailed up across the Layer 2 infrastructure.

NOTE   The committed bandwidth guarantee is also only a guarantee of the bandwidth between two points in the customer network. Without a full traffic matrix for all traffic classes, it's hard for the customer to engineer guarantees in most overlay networks. It's also hard to provide multiple classes of service because the service provider cannot differentiate the traffic in the middle of the network. Working around this by creating multiple connections (for example, Frame Relay PVCs) between the customer sites only increases the overall cost of the network.

Overlay VPN networks can be implemented with a number of switched WAN Layer 2 technologies, including X.25, Frame Relay, ATM, or SMDS. In the last years, overlay VPN networks also have been implemented with IP-over-IP tunneling, both in private IP backbones and over the public Internet. The two most commonly used IP-over-IP tunneling methods are Generic Route Encapsulation (GRE) tunneling and IP Security (IPSec) encryption.

NOTE	This book does not discuss the various Layer 2 and Layer 3 overlay VPN technologies in detail because they are covered well in other Cisco Press publications and are beyond the scope of this book. For more information on Layer 2 WAN technologies, please refer to *Internetworking Technologies Handbook*, Second Edition, from Cisco Press (ISBN 1-57870-102-3). For a description of IP-over-IP tunneling and IPSec encryption, please see *RFC 1702 – Generic Routing Encapsulation over IPv4 networks*, *RFC 2401 – Security Architecture for the Internet Protocol*, and *Enhanced IP Services for Cisco Networks* from Cisco Press (ISBN 1-57870-106-6).

Although it's relatively easy to understand and implement, the overlay VPN model nevertheless has a number of drawbacks:

- It's well suited to non-redundant configurations with a few central sites and many remote sites, but becomes exceedingly hard to manage in a more meshed configuration (see also the section, "Typical VPN Network Topologies," later in this chapter for more details).

- Proper provisioning of the VC capacities requires detailed knowledge of site-to-site traffic profiles, which are usually not readily available.

Last but not least, the overlay VPN model, when implemented with Layer 2 technologies, introduces another unnecessary layer of complexity into the New World Service Provider networks that are mostly IP-based, thus increasing the acquisition and operational costs of such a network.

Peer-to-peer VPN Model

The peer-to-peer VPN model was introduced a few years ago to alleviate the drawbacks of the overlay VPN model. In the peer-to-peer model, the Provider Edge (PE) device is a router (PE-router) that directly exchanges routing information with the CPE router. Figure 7-7 shows a sample peer-to-peer VPN, which is equivalent to the VPN in Figure 7-5.

NOTE	The *Managed Network* service offered by many service providers, where the service provider also manages the CPE devices, is not relevant to this discussion because it's only a repackaging of another service. The Managed Network provider concurrently assumes the role of the VPN service provider (providing the VPN infrastructure) and part of the VPN customer role (managing the CPE device).

Figure 7-7 *Sample Peer-to-peer VPN*

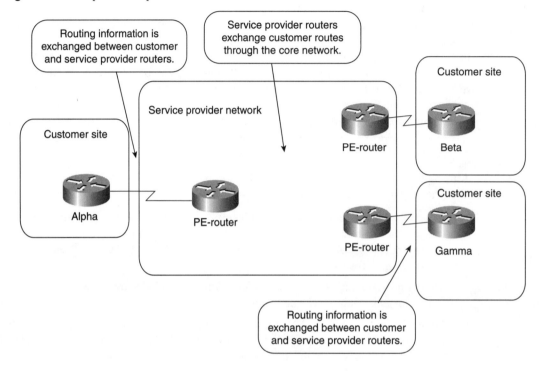

NOTE   Please note that this section describes the non-MPLS approach to peer-to-peer VPN as currently deployed by several large service providers and the complexities associated with it. The MPLS-based peer-to-peer VPN approach is described in the next chapter.

The peer-to-peer model provides a number of advantages over the traditional overlay model:

- Routing (from the customer's perspective) becomes exceedingly simple, as the customer router exchanges routing information with only one (or a few) PE-router, whereas in the overlay VPN network, the number of neighbor routers can grow to a large number.

- Routing between the customer sites is always optimal, as the provider routers know the customer's network topology and can thus establish optimum inter-site routing.

- Bandwidth provisioning is simpler because the customer has to specify only the inbound and outbound bandwidths for each site (Committed Access Rate [CAR] and Committed Delivery Rate [CDR]) and not the exact site-to-site traffic profile.

- The addition of a new site is simpler because the service provider provisions only an additional site and changes the configuration on the attached PE-router. Under the overlay VPN model, the service provider must provision a whole set of VCs leading from that site to other sites of the customer VPN.

Prior to an MPLS-based VPN implementation, two implementation options existed for the peer-to-peer VPN model:

- The shared-router approach, where several VPN customers share the same PE-router.

- The dedicated-router approach, where each VPN customer has dedicated PE-routers.

Shared-router Approach to Peer-to-peer VPN Model

In the shared-router approach, several customers can be connected to the same PE-router. Access lists have to be configured on every PE-CE interface on the PE-router to ensure isolation between VPN customers, to prevent a VPN customer from breaking into another VPN network, or to prevent a VPN customer from performing a denial-of-service attack on another VPN customer. Figure 7-8 illustrates a sample shared-router configuration.

Figure 7-8   *Peer-to-peer VPN Model: Shared Router Configuration*

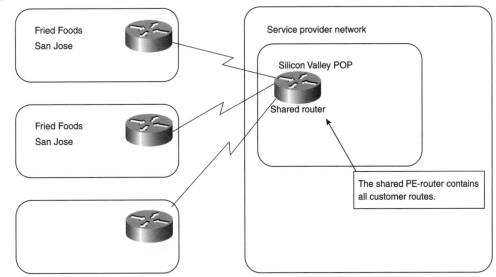

Fried Foods
San Jose

Service provider network

Silicon Valley POP

Shared router

Fried Foods
San Jose

The shared PE-router contains all customer routes.

Let's assume that the customers shown in Figure 7-8 use the address space and routing protocols from Table 7-1.

Table 7-1 *Peer-to-peer Shared-router Example—Address Space*

Customer Name	Address Space	Routing Protocol
FriedFoods (Customer #75)	155.13.0.0/16	RIP
GeneralMining (Customer #98)	195.166.16.0/20	OSPF (area 3)

To ensure the isolation between the customers, the configuration from Example 7-1 would have to be entered in the POP-router in Figure 7-8.

Example 7-1 *POP-router Configuration*

```
interface serial 0/0/1
 description FriedFoods - San Jose Site
 ip address 153.13.254.1 255.255.255.252
! The IP address on WAN link is an address from Customer's address space
 ip access-group FriedFoods in
 ip access-group FriedFoods out
!
interface serial 0/0/2
 description FriedFoods - Santa Clara Site
 ip address 153.13.254.5 255.255.255.252
 ip access-group FriedFoods in
 ip access-group FriedFoods out
!
interface serial 0/1/3
 description GeneralMining - Mountain View Site
 ip address 195.166.31.17 255.255.255.252
 ip access-group GeneralMining in
 ip access-group GeneralMining out
!
router rip
 network 153.13.0.0
!
router ospf 1
 network 195.166.31.17 0.0.0.0 area 3
!
ip access-list FriedFoods
   permit ip 155.13.0.0 255.255.0.0 153.13.0.0 255.255.0.0
!
ip access-list GeneralMining
   permit ip 195.166.16.0 255.255.240.0 195.166.16.0 255.255.240.0
```

Dedicated-router Approach to Peer-to-peer Model

In the dedicated-router approach to the peer-to-peer model, every VPN customer has their own dedicated PE routers (as detailed in Figure 7-9) and, thus, has access only to the routes contained within the routing table of that PE router.

Figure 7-9   *Peer-to-peer VPN Model: Dedicated Router Configuration*

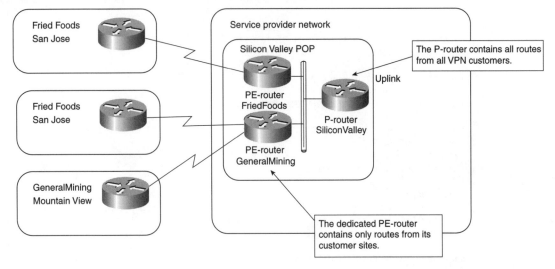

The dedicated-router model uses routing protocols to create per-VPN routing tables on PE routers. The routing tables on PE-routers contain only the routes advertised by the VPN customer connected to them, resulting in almost perfect isolation between the VPN customers (assuming that the IP source routing is disabled). The routing in the dedicated-router model can be implemented as follows:

- Any routing protocol is run between the PE-router and the CE-router.

- BGP is run between the PE-router and the P-router.

- The PE-router redistributes routes received from the CE-router into BGP, marked with the customer ID (BGP community), and propagates the routes to the P-routers. P-routers thus contain all the routes from all VPN customers.

- P-routers propagate only routes with the proper BGP community to the PE-routers. The PE-routers thus receive only the routes that originated from the CE-routers in their VPN.

Relevant parts of PE-router and P-router configuration for the Service Provider Point-of-Presence (POP) shown in Figure 7-9 (assuming the address space and the routing protocols from Table 7-1) can be found in Example 7-2 and Example 7-3.

Example 7-2   *PE-router Configuration*

```
hostname PE-router-FriedFoods
!
interface serial 0/0/1
 description FriedFoods – San Jose Site
 ip address 153.13.254.1 255.255.255.252
```

continues

Example 7-2 *PE-router Configuration (Continued)*

```
!
interface serial 0/0/2
 description FriedFoods - Santa Clara Site
 ip address 153.13.254.5 255.255.255.252
!
interface FastEthernet 2/0/0
 description Intra-POP LAN
 ip address 10.13.1.2 255.255.255.0
!
router rip
 network 153.13.254.1
 version 2
 redistribute bgp 111 subnets
!
router bgp 111
 no auto-summary
 redistribute rip route-map ToBGP-FriedFoods
 neighbor 10.13.1.1 remote-as 111
!
route-map ToBGP-FriedFoods permit 10
 set community 111:75
```

Example 7-3 *P-router Configuration*

```
hostname P-Router-Silicon-Valley-POP
!
interface FastEthernet 0/1/0
 description Intra-POP LAN
 ip address 10.13.1.1 255.255.255.0
!
router bgp 111
 neighbor 10.13.1.2 remote-as 111
 neighbor 10.13.1.2 route-reflector-client
 neighbor 10.13.1.2 route-map VPN-FriedFoods out
!
route-map VPN-FriedFoods permit 10
 match community-list 75
!
ip community-list 75 permit 111:75
```

Comparison of Peer-to-peer Models

As you easily can deduce from Example 7-1, the shared-router peer-to-peer model is very hard to maintain because it requires the deployment of potentially long and complex access lists on almost every router interface. The dedicated-router approach, although simpler to configure and maintain, becomes very expensive for the service provider when it tries to serve a large number of customers with geographically dispersed sites.

Both peer-to-peer models also share several common drawbacks that prevent their widespread usage:

- All the customers share the same IP address space, preventing the customers from deploying private IP addresses according to RFC 1918. The customers must use either public IP addresses or private IP addresses allocated to them by the service provider.

- The customers cannot insert the default route into their VPN. This limitation prevents certain routing optimizations and prevents the customers from getting Internet access from another service provider.

In addition to these two drawbacks, the shared-router model suffers from additional complexity when several customers use the routing protocols (RIP, RIPv2, BGP, and IS-IS) where multiple instances are not supported in Cisco IOS.

Typical VPN Network Topologies

The VPN topology required by an organization should be dictated by the business problems the organization is trying to solve. However, several well-known topologies appear so often that they deserve to be discussed here. As you can see, the same topologies solve a variety of different business issues in different vertical markets or industries.

The VPN topologies discussed here can be split into three major categories:

- Topologies influenced by the overlay VPN model, which include hub-and-spoke topology, partial or full-mesh topology, and hybrid topology.

- Extranet topologies, which include any-to-any Extranet and Central Services Extranet.

- Special-purpose topologies, such as VPDN backbone and Managed Network topology.

Hub-and-spoke Topology

The most commonly encountered topology is a hub-and-spoke topology, where a number of remote offices (spokes) are connected to a central site (hub), similar to the setup in Figure 7-10. The remote offices usually can exchange data (there are no explicit security restrictions on inter-office traffic), but the amount of data exchanged between them is negligible. The hub-and-spoke topology is used typically in organizations with strict hierarchical structures, for example, banks, governments, retail stores, international organizations with small in-country offices, and so on.

NOTE	When deploying VPNs based on Layer 2 technologies, such as Frame Relay or ATM, the hub-and-spoke VPN topology is more common than you might expect. This is based purely on business needs due to higher costs or increased routing complexity associated with other topologies that use these types of technologies. In other words, there are many examples where the customer could benefit from a different topology but has nonetheless chosen the hub-and-spoke topology for cost or complexity reasons.

With increased redundancy requirements, the simple hub-and-spoke topology from Figure 7-10 often is enhanced with an additional router at the central site (shown in Figure 7-11) or with a backup central site, which is then linked with the primary central site through a higher-speed connection (shown in Figure 7-12).

Figure 7-10 *Hub-and-spoke Topology*

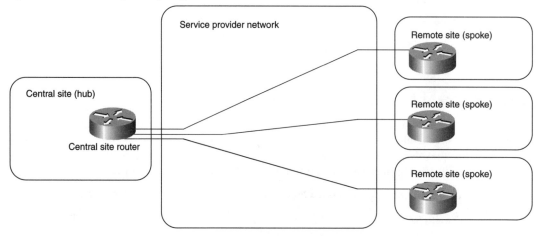

Figure 7-11 *Hub-and-spoke Topology with Two Central Routers*

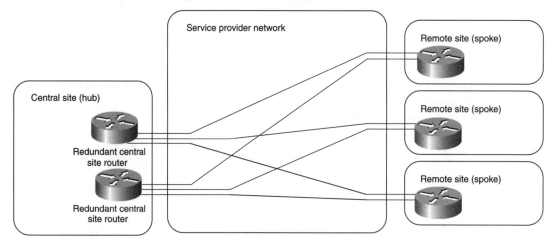

Implementing redundant hub-and-spoke topology with an overlay VC–based VPN model always poses a number of challenges. Each hub site requires a VC to at least two central routers. These VCs could be provisioned in primary-backup configuration or in load-sharing configuration with a number of drawbacks of one or the other solution:

- In primary-backup configuration, the backup VC is unused while the primary VC is active, resulting in unnecessary expenses incurred by the customer.

- In load-sharing configuration, the spoke site encounters reduced throughput if one of the VCs (or one of the central routers) fails. The load-sharing configuration is also not appropriate for the topologies with a backup central site similar to the one in Figure 7-12.

Figure 7-12 *Hub-and-spoke Topology with Two Central Sites*

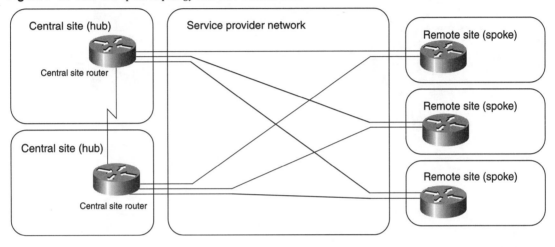

The higher-quality service providers try to meet the redundancy requirements of their customers with an enhanced service offering called *shadow PVC*. With a shadow PVC, the customer gets two virtual circuits for the price of one on the condition that they can use only one VC for data traffic at a time (a small amount of traffic is allowed on the second PVC to enable routing protocol exchanges over the second PVC).

Redundancy requirements can further complicate hub-and-spoke topology with the introduction of dial-backup features. The dial backup solution implemented within the service provider network (for example, an ISDN connection backing up a Frame-Relay leased line, as shown in Figure 7-13) is transparent to the customer, but it does not offer true end-to-end redundancy because it cannot detect all potential failures (for example, CPE or routing protocol failures). The true end-to-end redundancy in an overlay VPN model can be achieved only by CPE devices establishing a dial-up connection outside the VPN space.

Usually, simple hub-and-spoke topology transforms into multilevel topology as the network grows. The multilevel topology can be a recursive hub-and-spoke topology, similar to the one shown in Figure 7-14, or a hybrid topology, which is discussed later in this section. The network restructuring can be triggered by scalability restrictions of IP routing protocols or by application-level scalability issues (for example, the introduction of a three-tier client-server approach).

Figure 7-13 *Dial Backup Solution Within Service Provider Network*

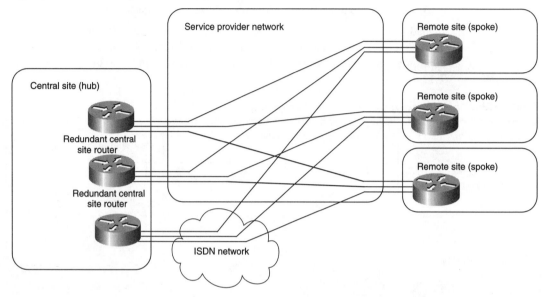

Figure 7-14 *Multilevel Hub-and-spoke Topology*

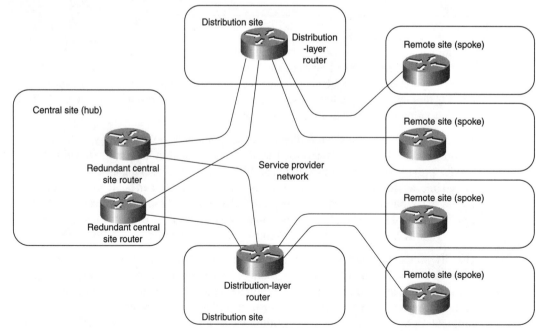

The hub-and-spoke topology implemented with an overlay VPN model is well suited to environments where the remote offices mostly exchange data with the central sites and not with each other, as the data exchanged between the remote offices always gets transported via the central site. If the amount of data exchanged between the remote offices represents a significant proportion of the overall network traffic, partial-mesh or full-mesh topology might be more appropriate.

Partial- or Full-mesh Topology

Not all customers can implement their networks with the hub-and-spoke topology discussed in the previous section for a variety of reasons, for example:

- The organization might be less hierarchical in structure, requiring data exchange between various points in the organization.

- The applications used in the organization need peer-to-peer communication (for example, messaging or collaboration systems).

- For some multinational corporations, the cost of hub-and-spoke topology might be excessive due to the high cost of international links.

In these cases, the overlay VPN model best suited to the organization's needs would be a partial-mesh model, where the sites in the VPN are connected by VCs dictated by traffic requirements (which eventually are dictated by business needs). If not all sites have direct connectivity to all other sites (like the example in Figure 7-15), the topology is called a *partial mesh*; if every site has a direct connection to every other site, the topology is called a *full mesh*.

NOTE   Not many full-mesh networks are implemented due to the very high cost of this approach and the complexity introduced by the high number of VCs. With this type of topology, the number of VCs = $[(n-1) \times n) \div 2]$ where n is equal to the number of attached devices.

Most of the customers have to settle for a partial mesh topology, which usually is affected by compromises and external parameters, such as link availability and the cost of VCs.

Figure 7-15 *Partial-mesh Example*

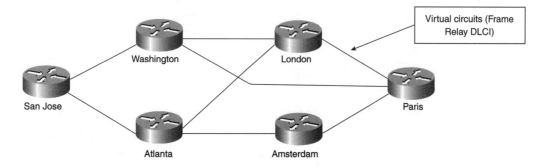

Provisioning a full-mesh topology is pretty simple—you just need a traffic matrix indicating the bandwidth required between a pair of sites in the VPN and you can start ordering the VCs from the service provider. Provisioning a partial mesh, on the other hand, can be a real challenge, as you have to do the following:

1 Figure out the traffic matrix.

2 Propose a partial-mesh topology based on a traffic matrix (for example, install a VC only between sites with high traffic requirements) and redundancy requirements.

3 Determine exactly over which VCs the traffic between any two sites will flow. This step also might involve routing protocol tuning to make sure the traffic flows over the proper VCs.

4 Size the VCs according to the traffic matrix and the traffic aggregation achieved over the VCs.

NOTE   The routing protocol issues in larger (usually multinational) partial meshes can grow to the proportion where it's extremely hard to predict the traffic flows without using such advanced simulation tools as Netsys. It is not unheard of to see customers who are forced to migrate to Border Gateway Protocol (BGP) just to handle the traffic engineering problems in their partial-mesh topologies.

Hybrid Topology

Large VPN networks built with an overlay VPN model tend to combine hub-and-spoke topology with the partial-mesh topology. For example, a large multinational organization might have access networks in each country implemented with a hub-and-spoke topology, whereas the international core network would be implemented with a partial-mesh topology. Figure 7-16 shows an example of such an organization.

Figure 7-16 *Hybrid Topology Example*

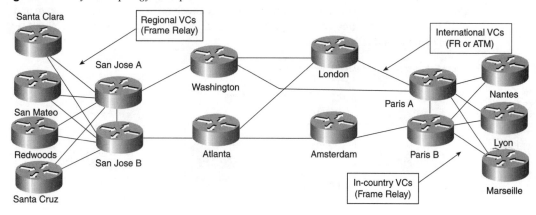

The best approach to the hybrid topology design is to follow the modular network design approach:

- Split the overall network into core, distribution, and access networks.

- Design the core and access parts of the network individually (for example, dual hub-and-spoke with dial backup in the access network, partial mesh in the core network).

- Connect the core and access networks through the distribution layer in a way that isolates them as much as possible. For example, a local loop failure in a remote office somewhere should not be propagated into the core network. Likewise, the remote office routers should not see a failure of one of the international links.

Simple Extranet Topology

The Intranet topologies discussed so far are concerned mostly with the physical and logical topology of the VPN network, as dictated by the VC technology by which the overlay VPN model is implemented. In the extranet topologies, we focus more on the security requirements of the VPN network, which then can be implemented with a number of different topologies, either with the overlay or peer-to-peer VPN model.

The traditional extranet topology would be an extranet allowing a number of companies to perform any-to-any data exchange. The examples could include communities of interest (for example, airline companies, airplane manufacturers, and so on) or supply chain (for example, car manufacturer and all its suppliers).

The data in such an extranet can be exchanged between any numbers of sites—the extranet itself imposes no restriction on the data exchange. Usually, each site is responsible for its own security, traffic filtering, and firewalling. The only reason to use an extranet instead of the public Internet is quality of service guarantees and sensitivity of the data exchanged over such a VPN network, which still is more resilient to data capture attacks than the generic Internet.

If the Extranet is implemented by a peer-to-peer VPN model (like the example Extranet in Figure 7-17), each organization specifies only how much traffic it's going to receive and send from each of its sites; thus, the provisioning on the customer and service provider side is very simple and effective.

Figure 7-17 *Sample Extranet Implemented with Peer-to-peer VPN Model*

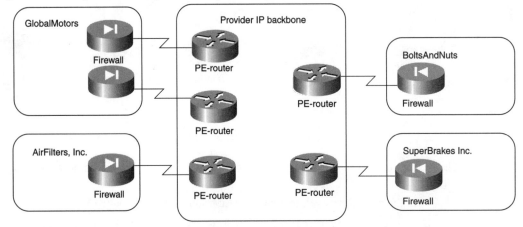

In the overlay VPN model, however, the traffic between sites is exchanged over point-to-point VCs, similar to the example in Figure 7-18.

Figure 7-18 *Sample Extranet Implemented with Overlay VPN Model*

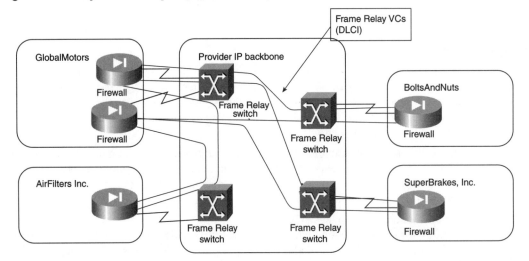

In the extranet topology similar to that in Figure 7-18, each participating organization usually pays for the VCs it uses. Obviously, only the most necessary VCs are installed to minimize the cost. Furthermore, participants in such a VPN would try to prevent transit traffic between other participants from flowing over VCs for which they pay, usually resulting in partial connectivity between the sites in the extranet and sometimes even resulting in interesting routing problems. The peer-to-peer VPN model is therefore the preferred way of implementing an any-to-any extranet.

Central-services Extranet

Extranets linking organizations that belong to the same community of interest are often pretty open, allowing any-to-any connectivity between the organizations. Dedicated-purpose extranets (for example, a supply chain management network linking a large organization with all its suppliers) tend to be more centralized and allow communication only between the organization sponsoring the extranet and all other participants, resembling the example shown in Figure 7-19.

Other examples of such an extranet include stock exchange networks, where every broker can communicate with the stock exchange, but not with other brokers or financial networks built in some countries between the central bank and the commercial banks. Although the purposes of such extranets can vary widely, they all share a common concept: a number of different users receive access to a *central service* (application, server, site, network, and so on).

Figure 7-19 *Supply Chain Management Extranet*

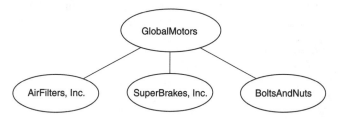

The security in the central services extranet typically is provided by the central organization sponsoring the extranet. Other participants with mission-critical internal networks (for example, stock brokers or commercial banks) also might want to implement their own security measures (for example, a firewall between their internal network and the extranet).

Similar to any other VPN network, the central services extranet can be implemented with either peer-to-peer or overlay VPN model. In this case, however, the peer-to-peer model has definitive disadvantages, because the service provider must take great care that the participants of the extranet cannot reach each other.

The implementation of the central services extranet by an overlay VPN model, on the contrary, is extremely straightforward:

- VCs between all the participants and the central site are provisioned. The size of each VC corresponds to the traffic requirements between the participant and the central site.

- The central site announces subnets available only at the central site to the other participants.

- The central site filters traffic received by other participants to make sure a routing problem or purposeful theft-of-service attack does not influence the stability of the VPN.

Following these three steps, the VPN network from Figure 7-19 is transformed into a VC topology in Figure 7-18.

NOTE   Under the any-to-any extranet model, the network in Figure 7-18 would have a limited number of VCs (resulting in a redundant hub-and-spoke topology) due to cost constraints. Under the central services extranet model, the same VPN would have the same number of VCs due to security restrictions. This example thus represents an interesting case where a number of different requirements can dictate the same VC topology.

A slightly more complex central services extranet topology might contain a number of servers, dispersed across several sites, and a number of client sites accessing those servers, similar to the setup in Figure 7-20. Typical examples that would require this topology are Voice over IP networks, where a number of users access common gateways in different cities (or countries) but are not allowed to see each other.

Figure 7-20 *Central Services Extranet with a Large Number of Server Sites*

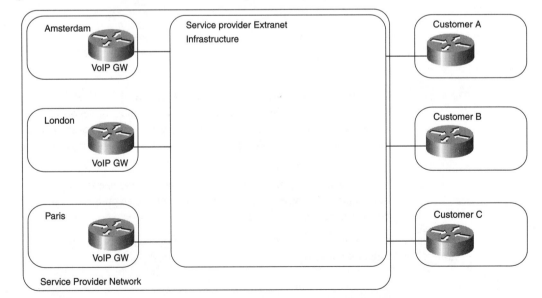

Such an extranet also can be implemented with either the peer-to-peer VPN model or the overlay VPN model. The number of VCs required in the overlay VPN model (a separate VC is required from each client site to each server site) and the corresponding provisioning complexity usually prevents the deployment of an overlay VPN model in these scenarios. A more manageable setup would use either a peer-to-peer model or a combination of both models, as illustrated in Figure 7-21.

Figure 7-21 *Combination of Peer-to-peer VPN with Overlay VPN*

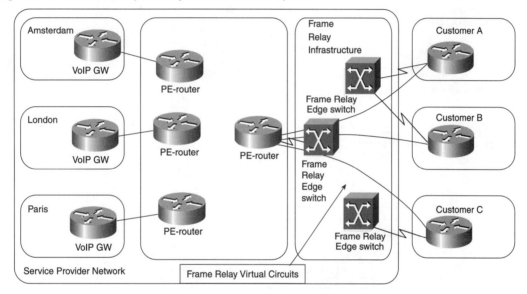

Logically, the network in Figure 7-21 uses a peer-to-peer VPN model, with distribution routers acting as PE routers of the peer-to-peer model. The actual physical topology differs from the logical view: The distribution routers are linked with the customer sites (CE routers) through the overlay VPN model (for example, Frame Relay network).

VPDN Topology

The Virtual Private Dial-up Network (VPDN) service (also described in the section, "Business Problem-based VPN Classification," earlier in this chapter) usually is implemented by tunneling PPP frames exchanged between the dial-up user and his home gateway in IP packets exchanged between the network access server, as shown in Figure 7-22.

The dial-up user and the home gateway establish IP (or IPX, Appletalk, and so on) connectivity over the tunneled PPP link and exchange data packets over it. Figure 7-23 details the protocol stack used between various parts of the VPDN solution.

Figure 7-22 *End-to-end Connectivity in a VPDN Solution*

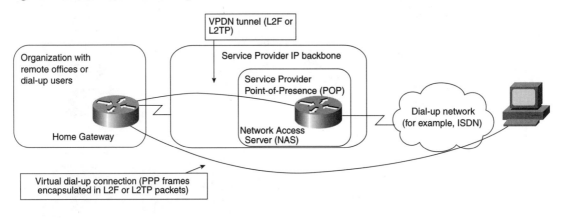

Figure 7-23 *Protocol Stack in a VPDN Solution*

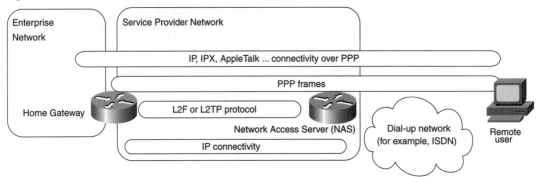

Every VPDN solution requires an underlying IP infrastructure to exchange tunneled PPP frames between the NAS and the home gateway. In the simplest possible scenario, the public Internet can be used as the necessary infrastructure. When the security requirements are stricter, a virtual private network could be built to exchange the encapsulated PPP frames. The resulting structure is thought to be complex by some network designers, because they try to understand the whole picture in all details at once. As always, the complexity can be reduced greatly through proper decoupling:

- The NAS and the home gateway use whatever IP infrastructure is available to exchange the VPDN data, which can be thought of as an application sitting on the top of the IP stack. Consequently, the internal structure of the underlying IP network does not affect the exchange of the application data, and the contents of the application data (IP packets in PPP frames encapsulated in a VPDN envelope) does not interact with the routers providing the IP service.

- The underlying IP network is effectively a central services extranet with many server sites (Network Access Servers) and a home gateway acting as client sites. This infrastructure can be implemented in any number of ways, from pure overlay VPN model to pure peer-to-peer model.

Managed Network VPN Topology

The last VPN topology discussed in this chapter is the topology used by service providers to manage the customer-premises routers in a managed network service (see also the comments on the managed network service in the section, "Peer-to-peer VPN Model," earlier in this chapter). In a typical setup, shown in Figure 7-24, the service provider provisions a number of routers at customer sites, connecting them through VCs implemented with Frame Relay or ATM and builds a separate hub-and-spoke topology connecting every customer router with the Network Management Center (NMC).

Figure 7-24 *Typical Managed Network Topology*

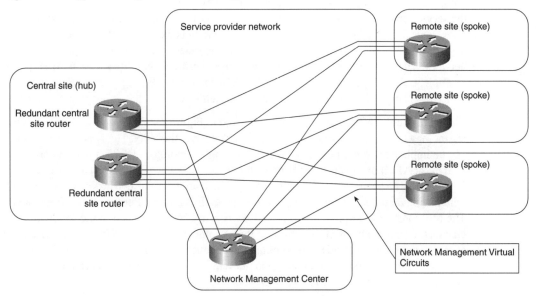

The VPN topology used in the customer part of the network can be any topology supported with the underlying VPN model, ranging from hub-and-spoke to full-mesh topology. The topology used in the CPE management part of the network effectively would be a central services extranet topology with the customer routers acting as clients and the Network Management Center being the central site of the management extranet.

As already explained in the "Central-services Extranet" section earlier in this chapter, such a topology is easiest to implement with a hub-and-spoke topology of the overlay VPN model, which also explains why most Managed Network service providers use the setup in Figure 7-24.

NOTE   The Managed Network topology can also be implemented with various peer-to-peer VPN technologies, although it's not as simple as with the overlay VPN model. Chapter 11, "Advanced MPLS/VPN Topologies," describes an example of a managed network implemented with MPLS/VPN technology.

Summary

VPNs can be classified in a variety of ways. The broadest technological classification is based on the way the routing information is exchanged in the VPN. In the peer-to-peer VPN model, the customer routing information is exchanged between the customer routers and the service provider routers. In the overlay VPN model, the service provider provides only VCs (logical leased lines) and the routing information is exchanged directly between the edge customer routers. The two models can be combined in a large service provider network: The peer-to-peer VPN model might use overlay VPN in its access parts (for example, connecting customers to the provider edge routers through Frame Relay) or its core (for example, linking provider routers through ATM).

The more detailed VPN classification (displayed in Figure 7-25) focuses on the underlying technology that is used to transport Layer 3 packets over the VPN. The overlay VPN model can be implemented with Layer 2 WAN switching technologies (X.25, Frame Relay, SMDS, or ATM) or Layer 3 tunneling technologies (IP-over-IP, IPSec). The peer-to-peer VPN model can be implemented traditionally with complex routing tricks or IP access lists, both having a number of shortcomings outlined in the section, "Peer-to-peer VPN Model." The Multiprotocol Label Switching (MPLS)–based VPNs, described in the following chapters, overcome most of the shortcomings of other peer-to-peer VPN technologies, allowing the service providers to combine the benefits of the peer-to-peer model (simpler routing, simpler implementation of customer requirements) with the security and the isolation inherent in the overlay VPN model.

Figure 7-25 *VPN Classification Based on Underlying Technology*

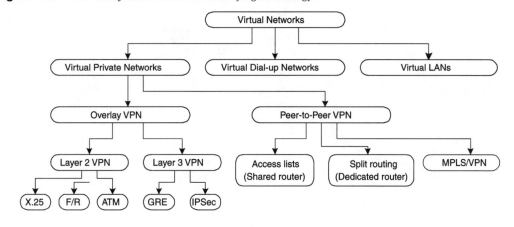

CHAPTER 8

MPLS/VPN Architecture Overview

In the previous chapter, you learned about virtual private network (VPN) evolution; two major VPN models, overlay VPN and peer-to-peer VPN; and the major technologies used to implement both VPN models.

The overlay VPN model, most commonly used in a service provider network, dictates that the design and provisioning of virtual circuits across the backbone must be complete prior to any traffic flow. In the case of an IP network, this means that even though the underlying technology is connectionless, it requires a connection-oriented approach to provision the service.

From a service provider's point of view, the scaling issues of an overlay VPN model are felt most when having to manage and provision a large number of circuits/tunnels between customer devices. From a customer's point of view, the Interior Gateway Protocol design is typically extremely complex and also difficult to manage.

On the other hand, the peer-to-peer VPN model suffers from lack of isolation between the customers and the need for coordinated IP address space between them.

With the introduction of Multiprotocol Label Switching (MPLS), which combines the benefits of Layer 2 switching with Layer 3 routing and switching, it became possible to construct a technology that combines the benefits of an overlay VPN (such as security and isolation among customers) with the benefits of simplified routing that a peer-to-peer VPN implementation brings. The new technology, called MPLS/VPN, results in simpler customer routing and somewhat simpler service provider provisioning, and makes possible a number of topologies that are hard to implement in either the overlay or peer-to-peer VPN models. MPLS also adds the benefits of a connection-oriented approach to the IP routing paradigm, through the establishment of label-switched paths, which are created based on topology information rather than traffic flow.

| NOTE | This introduction might lead you to believe that any overlay VPN implementation can be replaced with an MPLS/VPN implementation. Unfortunately, that is not true. MPLS/VPN currently supports only IP as the Layer 3 protocol. Other protocols, such as IPX and AppleTalk, still must be tunneled across an IP backbone. |

The MPLS/VPN architecture provides the capability to commission an IP network infrastructure that delivers *private* network services over a *public* infrastructure. This is the same type of service that has already been described in the previous chapter. However, the mechanisms used to provision the service are different. The MPLS/VPN technology is quite complex in itself and will be covered in a series of chapters. In this chapter, you'll see the basic MPLS/VPN concepts without going into too many details that would clutter the overall picture. In the next chapter, the detailed operation of MPLS/VPN is explained, along with the relevant configuration information to be able to provision a simple Intranet topology based on the MPLS/VPN architecture.

Case Study: Virtual Private Networks in SuperCom Service Provider Network

As with all complex topics, the MPLS/VPN concepts are best explained through use of a case study. Imagine a service provider (let's call it SuperCom) that is offering VPN services based on MPLS/VPN technologies. The service provider has two points of presence (POP), a U.S. POP in the San Jose area and a French POP in the Paris area. The POPs are linked through a core router located in Washington, D.C.

The service provider has two customers: FastFood, with headquarters in San Jose and branch offices in Santa Clara and Lyon; and EuroBank, with headquarters in Paris and branch offices in Chartres and San Francisco. The FastFood company has a number of other branch offices (for example, in Santa Cruz and Monterey) that are linked directly with the FastFood central site. The whole network is shown in Figure 8-1.

According to the terminology introduced in Chapter 7, "Virtual Private Network (VPN) Implementation Options," the routers in Figure 8-1 have the following roles:

- San Jose and Paris routers link the SuperCom network with its customers; they are thus provider edge (PE) routers.

- The Washington router does not have any customer connection; therefore, it's a provider (P) router.

- Customer routers connected to the SuperCom network—FastFood routers in San Jose, Santa Clara, and Lyon, as well as EuroBank routers in San Francisco, Paris, and Chartres—are customer edge (CE) routers.

- The FastFood routers in Santa Cruz and Monterey have no connection to the SuperCom network; they are customer (C) routers. All the networks connected directly to the FastFood San Jose site (Santa Cruz and Monterey networks) form a customer network (C-network) and represent a single site to the SuperCom network. The service provider does not care (and does not need to know) about the internal structure of that site.

Figure 8-1   *SuperCom Network and Its Customers*

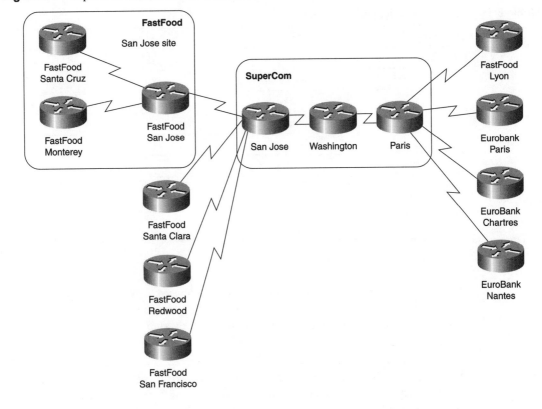

Let's assume that both companies, FastFood and EuroBank, follow the same addressing convention—the central sites use public IP addresses, whereas all the remote sites use private IP address space (network 10.0.0.0).

NOTE   The addressing scheme used by these corporations is seen more often in real customer networks, more so in cases in which the customer didn't acquire a significant portion of public IP address space several years ago.

The IP addresses used by these two companies are summarized in Table 8-1.

Table 8-1   *Address Space of FastFood and EuroBank*

Company	Site	Subnet
FastFood	San Jose	195.12.2.0/24
	Santa Clara	10.1.1.0/24
	Redwood	10.1.2.0/24
	Santa Cruz	10.1.3.0/24
	Monterey	10.1.4.0/24
	Lyon	10.2.1.0/24
EuroBank	Paris	196.7.25.0/24
	Chartres	10.2.1.0/24
	Nantes	10.2.2.0/24
	San Francisco	10.1.1.0/24

The SuperCom service provider would like to offer IP-based VPN service based on the peer-to-peer model (not a number of IP-over-IP tunnels), but it cannot do so easily because the address space of sites connected to the same router overlap.

NOTE   The service provider would encounter a similar (but not so obvious) problem if the address space overlap occurred between customers connected to different POPs. The traditional peer-to-peer model requires strict uniqueness of IP address space.

SuperCom can traditionally solve the overlapping addresses issue in three ways:

- It can persuade the customers to renumber their networks. Most customers would not be willing to do that and would rather find another service provider.

- It can implement the VPN service with IP-over-IP tunnels, where the customer IP addresses are hidden from the service provider routers.

- It can implement a complex network address translation (NAT) scheme that would translate customer addresses into a different (but unique) set of addresses at the provider edge router and then translate those addresses back to the customer addresses before the packet would be sent from the egress PE-router to the CE router. Although such a solution is technically feasible, the administrative overhead is prohibitively large.

VPN Routing and Forwarding Tables

The overlapping addresses, usually resulting from usage of private IP addresses in customer networks, are one of the major obstacles to successful deployment of peer-to-peer VPN implementations. The MPLS/VPN technology provides an elegant solution to the dilemma: Each VPN has its own routing and forwarding table in the router, so any customer or site that belongs to that VPN is provided access only to the set of routes contained within that table. Any PE-router in an MPLS/VPN network thus contains a number of per-VPN routing tables and a global routing table that is used to reach other routers in the provider network, as well as external globally reachable destinations (for example, the rest of the Internet). Effectively, a number of virtual routers are created in a single physical router, as displayed in Figure 8-2 for the case of San Jose router of SuperCom network.

NOTE   The relationship between virtual private networks and VPN routing and forwarding tables as explained in the previous paragraph is a slight simplification of the actual relationship between these two concepts. Nevertheless, it is true in cases where each site (or customer) belongs only to one VPN. The additional complexity introduced by overlapping VPNs or sites belonging to more than one VPN is explained in the section "Overlapping Virtual Private Networks," later in this chapter.

The concept of virtual routers allows the customers to use either global or private IP address space in each VPN. Each customer site belongs to a particular VPN, so the only requirement is that the address space be unique within that VPN. Uniqueness of addresses is not required among VPNs except where two VPNs that share the same private address space want to communicate.

More structures are associated with each virtual router than just the virtual IP routing table:

- A forwarding table that is derived from the routing table and is based on CEF technology.
- A set of interfaces that use the derived forwarding table.
- Rules that control the import and export of routes from and into the VPN routing table. These rules were introduced to support overlapping VPNs and are explained later in this chapter.
- A set of routing protocols/peers, which inject information into the VPN routing table. This includes static routing.
- Router variables associated with the routing protocol that is used to populate the VPN routing table.

Figure 8-2 *Virtual Routers Created in a PE-router*

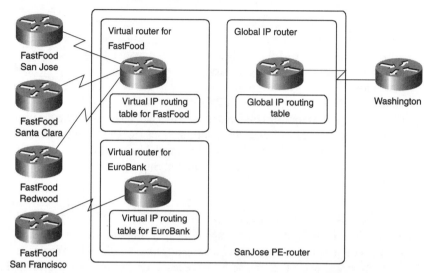

The usage of these structures is explained in the rest of this chapter, and the detailed operation of each of them is explained in the next chapters.

The combination of the VPN IP routing table and associated VPN IP forwarding table is called VPN routing and forwarding instance (VRF).

NOTE	You might think that there is no difference between an IP routing table and an IP forwarding table—and usually that's true. In an MPLS environment, the only minor difference between them is the fact that the IP forwarding table also contains MPLS encapsulation information.
	A major difference between the two tables arises in cases where an IP route refers to a next hop that is not directly connected. In that case, the routing table will contain the next-hop information, but not the outgoing interface or the IP address of the downstream router. The forwarding table will contain all the information needed to forward the packet toward the destination. For example, with the configuration in Example 8-1, the routing table lists the next hop for network 10.0.0.0/8 as 1.0.0.1 (as shown in Example 8-2), while the forwarding table contains the real next hop (the IP address of the downstream router), as shown in Example 8-3.

Example 8-1 *Sample Configuration with Recursive IP Routing*

```
ip route 10.0.0.0 255.0.0.0 1.0.0.1
ip route 1.0.0.1 255.255.255.255 2.0.0.2
!
interface serial 0
ip address 2.0.0.1 255.0.0.0
```

Example 8-2 *IP Routing Table for the Recursive IP Routing Example*

```
mpls router# show ip route
...
       1.0.0.0/32 is subnetted, 1 subnets
S        1.0.0.1 [1/0] via 2.0.0.2
C      2.0.0.0/8 is directly connected, Serial0
S      10.0.0.0/8 [1/0] via 1.0.0.1
...
```

Example 8-3 *CEF Forwarding Table Entry for Recursive IP Routing Example*

```
mpls router# show ip cef 10.0.0.0

10.0.0.0/8, version 87
0 packets, 0 bytes
  via 1.0.0.1, 0 dependencies, recursive
    next hop 2.0.0.2, Serial0 via 1.0.0.1/32
```

In the SuperCom case, the San Jose router contains three IP routing and forwarding tables—one table per customer and a global table used to forward non-VPN IP packets and to route VPN packets between PE-routers.

Overlapping Virtual Private Networks

The SuperCom example might lead you to believe that a VPN is associated with a single VRF in a PE-router. Although that would be true in the case where the VPN customer needs no connectivity with other VPN customers, the situation might become more complex and require more than one VRF per VPN customer.

Imagine that SuperCom wants to extend its service offering with a Voice over IP (VoIP) service with gateways to the public voice network located in San Jose and Paris, as shown in Figure 8-3. The VoIP gateways were placed in a separate VPN to enhance the security of the newly created service. The IP addresses of these gateways are shown in Table 8-2.

Table 8-2 *IP Addresses of VoIP Gateways in SuperCom Network*

VoIP Gateway Location	VoIP Gateway IP Address
San Jose	212.15.23.12
Paris	212.15.27.35

Figure 8-3 *VoIP Gateways in SuperCom Network*

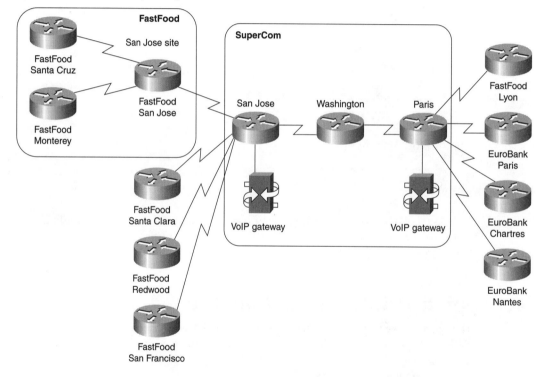

Both EuroBank and FastFood decided to use the service, but only from their central sites—the branch offices have no need for international voice connectivity. This requirement leads to an interesting problem: The central sites of both organizations need to be in two VPNs: the corporate VPN to reach their remote sites and the VoIP VPN to reach the VoIP gateways. The connectivity requirements are illustrated in Figure 8-4.

Figure 8-4   *VPN Connectivity Requirements in SuperCom Network*

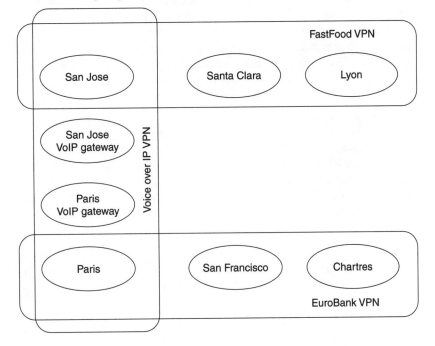

NOTE   The connectivity requirements in Figure 8-4 are a simplification of the requirements that you would encounter in a real service provider network. Most often, for security reasons, the customers using a common service (for example, VoIP gateways) will not see each other, but only the gateways or servers providing the service that they are using.

To support connectivity requirements similar to those in Figure 8-4, the MPLS/VPN architecture supports the concept of *sites*, where a VPN is made up of one or multiple sites. A VPN is essentially a collection of sites sharing common routing information, which means that a site may belong to more than one VPN if it holds routes from separate VPNs. This provides the capability to build intranets and extranets, as well as any other topology described in Chapter 7. A VPN in the MPLS/VPN architecture can therefore be pictured as a community of interest or a closed user group, which is dictated by the routing visibility that the site will have.

The VRF concept introduced in the previous section must be modified to support the concept of sites that can reside in more than one VPN. For example, the central site of

FastFood and EuroBank cannot use the same VRF as all other FastFood or EuroBank sites connected to the same PE-router. The central site of EuroBank, for example, needs to access the VoIP gateways, so the routes toward these gateways must be in the VRF for that site, whereas the same routes will not be in the Chartres' site VRF. Therefore, the MPLS/VPN architecture unbundles the concept of VRF from the concept of VPN. The VRF is simply a collection of routes that should be available to a particular site (or set of sites) connected to a PE-router. These routes can belong to more than one VPN.

NOTE   You might be inclined at this moment to jump from a one-VPN-one-VRF model to the other extreme: one-site-one-VRF model. Although that model is theoretically correct and supports any VPN topology, it leads to more complex configurations of the PE-routers that are harder to maintain and that also use more memory. Therefore, it is recommended to keep the number of VRFs to a minimum (for example, one VRF for the customer's central site and another VRF for all remote offices connected to the same PE-router).

The relationship between the VPNs, sites, and VRFs can be summarized in the following rule, which should be used as the basis for any VRF definition in an MPLS/VPN network.

NOTE   All sites that share the same routing information (usually this means that they belong to the same set of VPNs), that are allowed to communicate directly with each other, and that are connected to the same PE-router can be placed in a common VRF.

Using this rule, the minimum set of VRFs in the SuperCom network is the one outlined in Table 8-3.

Table 8-3   *VRFs in the PE-routers in the SuperCom Network*

PE-router	VRF	Sites in the VRF	VRF Belongs to VPNs
San Jose	FastFood_Central	FastFood SanJose site	FastFood, VoIP
	FastFood	FastFood Santa Clara site FastFood Redwood site	FastFood
	EuroBank	EuroBank San Francisco site	EuroBank
	VoIP	San Jose VoIP gateway	VoIP
Paris	FastFood	FastFood Lyon site	FastFood
	EuroBank_Central	EuroBank Paris site	EuroBank, VoIP

Table 8-3 *VRFs in the PE-routers in the SuperCom Network (Continued)*

PE-router	VRF	Sites in the VRF	VRF Belongs to VPNs
	EuroBank	EuroBank Chartres site	EuroBank
		EuroBank Nantes site	
	VoIP	Paris VoIP gateway	VoIP

Route Targets

A careful reader might start asking an interesting question: If there is no one-to-one mapping between VPN and VRF, how does the router know which routes need to be inserted into which VRF? This dilemma is solved by the introduction of another concept in the MPLS/VPN architecture: the *route target*. Every VPN route is tagged with one or more route targets when it is exported from a VRF (to be offered to other VRFs). You can also associate a set of route targets with a VRF, and all routes tagged with at least one of those route targets will be inserted into the VRF.

NOTE The *route target* is the closest approximation to a *VPN identifier* in the MPLS/VPN architecture. In most VPN topologies, you can equate them, but in other topologies (usually a central services topology), a single VPN might need more than one route target for successful implementation.

NOTE The route target is a 64-bit quantity, the format of which is explained in the next chapter. For simplicity reasons, we will use names for route targets in this chapter.

The SuperCom network contains three VPNs and thus requires three route targets. The association between route targets and VRFs in the SuperCom network is outlined in Table 8-4.

Table 8-4 *Correspondence Between VRFs and Route Targets in SuperCom Network*

PE-router	VRF	Sites in the VRF	Route Target Attached to Exported Routes	Import Route Targets
San Jose	FastFood_ Central	FastFood SanJose site	FastFood, VoIP	FastFood, VoIP

continues

Table 8-4   *Correspondence Between VRFs and Route Targets in SuperCom Network (Continued)*

PE-router	VRF	Sites in the VRF	Route Target Attached to Exported Routes	Import Route Targets
	FastFood	FastFood Santa Clara site	FastFood	FastFood
		FastFood Redwood site		
	EuroBank	EuroBank San Francisco site	EuroBank	EuroBank
	VoIP	San Jose VoIP gateway	VoIP	VoIP
Paris	FastFood	FastFood Lyon site	FastFood	FastFood
	EuroBank_ Central	EuroBank Paris site	EuroBank, VoIP	EuroBank, VoIP
	EuroBank	EuroBank Chartres site	EuroBank	EuroBank
		EuroBank Nantes site		
	VoIP	Paris VoIP gateway	VoIP	VoIP

NOTE   Based on Table 8-4, you might assume that the route targets attached to routes exported from a VRF always match the set of import route targets of a VRF. Although that's certainly true in simpler VPN topologies, there are widespread VPN topologies (for example, central services VPN) in which this assumption is not true.

Propagation of VPN Routing Information in the Provider Network

The previous sections have explained MPLS/VPN architecture from a single PE-router standpoint. Two issues have yet to be addressed:

- How will the PE-routers exchange information about VPN customers and VPN routes between themselves?

- How will the PE-routers forward packets originated in customer VPNs?

This section addresses inter-PE routing; the next section briefly describes the forwarding mechanism.

Two fundamentally different ways exist for approaching the VPN route exchange between PE-routers:

- The PE-routers could run a different routing algorithm for each VPN. For example, a copy of OSPF or EIGRP could be run for each VPN. This solution would face serious scalability problems in service provider networks with a large number of VPNs. It would also face interesting design challenges when asked to provide support for overlapping VPNs.

- The PE-routers run a single routing protocol to exchange all VPN routes. To support overlapping address spaces of VPN customers, the IP addresses used by the VPN customers must be augmented with additional information to make them unique.

NOTE   To illustrate the scalability issues that might arise from deploying one routing algorithm per VPN, consider the case where the SuperCom network would have to support more than 100 VPN customers connected to the San Jose and Paris routers with OSPF as the routing protocol. The PE-routers in the SuperCom network would run more than 100 independent copies of OSPF routing process (if that were technically possible), with each copy sending hello packets and periodic refreshments over the network. Because you cannot run more than one copy of OSPF over the same link, you would have to configure per-VPN subinterfaces (for example, using Frame Relay encapsulation) on the link between San Jose (or Paris) and Washington, resulting in an extremely complex network similar to the one shown in Figure 8-5. You would also have to run 100 different SPF algorithms and maintain 100 separate topology databases in the service provider routers.

The second approach was chosen as the building block of MPLS/VPN technology. IP subnets advertised by the CE-routers to the PE-routers are augmented with a 64-bit prefix called a *route distinguisher* to make them unique. The resulting 96-bit addresses are then exchanged between the PE-routers using a special address family of Multiprotocol BGP (hereby referred to as MP-BGP). There were several reasons for choosing BGP as the routing protocol used to transport VPN routes:

- The number of VPN routes in a network can become very large. BGP is the only routing protocol that can support a very large number of routes.

- BGP, EIGRP, and IS-IS are the only routing protocols that are multiprotocol by design (all of them can carry routing information for a number of different address families). IS-IS and EIGRP, however, do not scale to the same number of routes as BGP. BGP is also designed to exchange information between routers that are not directly connected. This BGP feature supports keeping VPN routing information out of the provider core routers (P-routers).

• GP can carry any information attached to a route as an optional BGP attribute. What's more, you can define additional attributes that will be transparently forwarded by any BGP router that does not understand them. This property of BGP makes propagation of route targets between PE-routers extremely simple.

Figure 8-5   *SuperCom Network with One IGP per VPN*

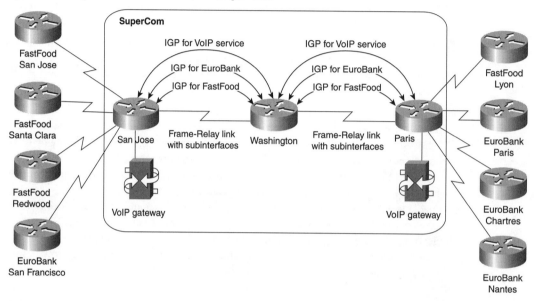

Multiprotocol BGP in the SuperCom Network

To illustrate the interaction of per-VPN routing protocols with the MP-BGP used in the service provider network core, consider the case of the FastFood customer in the SuperCom network. Let's assume that the San Jose site is using OSPF to interact with the SuperCom backbone, the Lyon and Santa Clara sites are using RIP, and the Redwood site is using no routing protocol—there is a static route configured on the San Jose PE-router and the default route configured on the Redwood router. The routing protocols used in FastFood VPN are shown in Figure 8-6.

NOTE   The Washington router (the P-router in the SuperCom network) is not involved in the MP-BGP. As you'll see in the next section, the forwarding model used in MPLS/VPN does not require the P-routers to make any routing decisions based on VPN addresses; they just forward packets based on the label value attached to the packet. The P-routers, therefore, do not need to carry the VPN routes, resulting in even better scalability.

Figure 8-6   *Routing Protocols Used in FastFood VPN*

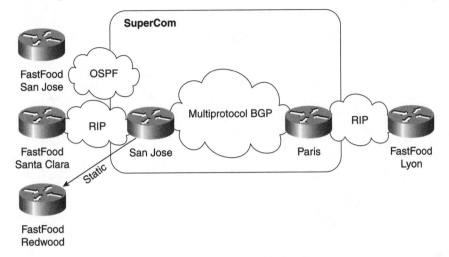

The San Jose PE-router collects routing information from the San Jose site using a per-VPN OSPF process. Similarly, the information from the Santa Clara site is collected using a per-VPN RIP process. This process is marked as Step 1 in Figure 8-7.

NOTE	The routing protocol used within a VPN network must be limited to the VPN in question. If the same routing protocol would be used in different VPNs, the possibility of using overlapping IP addresses between VPNs would be lost, and there would be potential route leakage between VPNs.

To support overlapping VPNs, the routing protocol must be limited to a single VPN routing and forwarding (VRF) table. Each PE-router must be configured so that any routing information learnt from an interface can be associated with a particular VRF. This is done through the standard routing protocol process and is known as the *routing context*. A separate routing context is used per VRF.

Some routing protocols (for example, RIP) support several instances (or routing contexts) of the same protocol, with each instance running in a different VRF. Other protocols (for example, OSPF) require a separate copy of the routing protocol process for each VRF.

The information gathered by various routing protocols in the San Jose PE-router, as well as the static routes configured on the San Jose router, is redistributed into MP-BGP. VPN addresses are augmented with the route distinguishers at the moment of redistribution. The route export route target specified in the originating VRF is also attached to the route. The resulting 96-bit routing information is propagated by MP-BGP to the Paris router (Step 2 in Figure 8-7).

Figure 8-7 *Routing Protocol Operation in SuperCom Network*

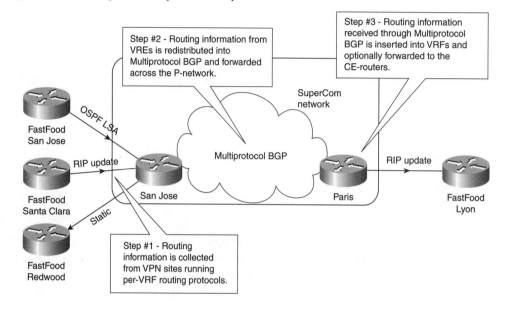

The Paris router, after receiving MP-BGP routes, inserts the received routes into various VRF tables based on the route target attribute attached to each individual route. The route distinguisher is dropped from the 96-bit route when the route is inserted into the VRF, resulting yet again in a traditional IP route. Finally, the routing information received through BGP is redistributed into the RIP process and is passed on to the Lyon site through RIP updates (Step 3 in Figure 8-7).

WARNING	Similar to the redistribution of VRF routes into MP-BGP, the redistribution of routes received over the service provider backbone back into the per-VRF routing process is not automatic, unless this process is BGP; it must be manually configured if the redistribution is required by the routing design.
	Contrary to the traditional BGP operation in which the internal BGP routes are not allowed to be redistributed into other routing protocols, this restriction is lifted in the MPLS/VPN environment. The VPN routes received by a PE-router through an internal MP-BGP session from another PE-router can be redistributed into other routing protocols.

VPN Packet Forwarding

In the previous section, you saw that the IP addresses used within a VPN must be prepended with a 64-bit prefix called a route distinguisher (RD) to make them unique.

Similarly, when the VPN-originated IP packets are forwarded across the service provider backbone (the P-network), they must be augmented to make them uniquely recognizable. Yet again, several technology options are possible:

- The IP packet is rewritten to include 96-bit addresses in the packet header. This operation would be slow and complex.

- The IP packet is tunneled across the network in VPN-over-IP tunnels. This choice would make MPLS/VPN as complex as traditional IP-over-IP VPN solutions using the overlay VPN model.

With the introduction of MPLS, a third technology option was made possible: Each VPN packet is labeled by the ingress PE-router with a label uniquely identifying the egress PE-router, and is sent across the network. All the routers in the network subsequently switch labels without having to look into the packet itself. The preparatory steps for this process are illustrated in Figure 8-8.

Each PE-router needs a unique identifier (a host route—usually the loopback IP address is used), which is then propagated throughout the P-network using the usual IGP (Step 1). This IP address is also used as the BGP next-hop attribute of all VPN routes announced by the PE-router. A label is assigned in each P-router for that host route and is propagated to each of its neighbors (Step 2). Finally, all other PE-routers receive a label associated with the egress PE-router through an MPLS label distribution process (Step 3). After the label for the egress PE-router is received by the ingress PE-router, the VPN packet exchange can start.

Figure 8-8 *VPN Packet Forwarding—Preparatory Steps*

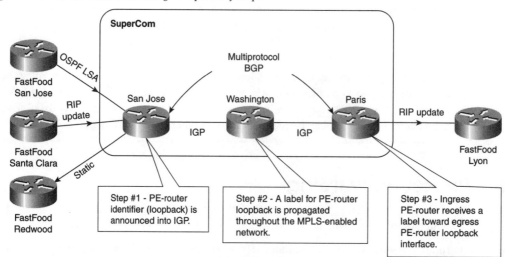

However, when the egress PE-router receives the VPN packet, it has no information to tell it which VPN the packet is destined for. To make the communication between VPN sites unique, a second set of labels is introduced, as illustrated in Figure 8-9.

Each PE-router allocates a unique label for each route in each VPN routing and forwarding (VRF) instance (Step 1). These labels are propagated together with the corresponding routes through MP-BGP to all other PE-routers (Step 2). The PE-routers receiving the MP-BGP update and installing the received routes in their VRF tables (see Figure 8-7 for additional details) also install the label assigned by the egress router in their VRF tables. The MPLS/VPN network is now ready to forward VPN packets.

When a VPN packet is received by the ingress PE-router, the corresponding VRF is examined, and the label associated with the destination address by the egress PE-router is fetched. Another label, pointing toward the egress PE-router, is obtained from the global forwarding table. Both labels are combined into an MPLS label stack, are attached in front of the VPN packet, and are sent toward the egress PE-router.

All the P-routers in the network switch the VPN packet based only on the top label in the stack, which points toward the egress PE-router. Because of the normal MPLS forwarding rules, the P-routers never look beyond the first label and are thus completely unaware of the second label or the VPN packet carried across the network.

Figure 8-9 *VPN Label Allocation*

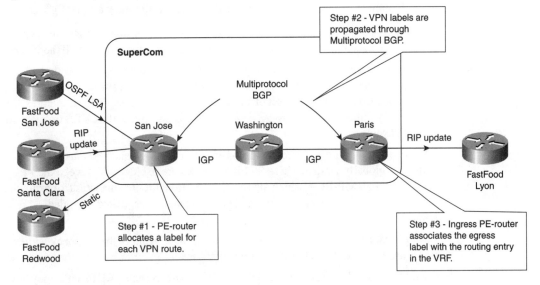

The egress PE-router receives the labeled packet, drops the first label, and performs a lookup on the second label, which uniquely identifies the target VRF and sometimes even the outgoing interface on the PE-router. A lookup is performed in the target VRF (if needed), and the packet is sent toward the proper CE-router.

NOTE The egress PE-router assigns labels to VPN routes in such a way that the need for additional Layer 3 lookup in the target VRF is minimized. The additional Layer 3 lookup is needed only for summary VPN routes advertised between the PE-routers.

The router just before the egress PE-router might also remove the first label in the label stack through a mechanism called *penultimate hop popping*. Refer to Chapter 2, "Frame-mode MPLS Operation," for a detailed description of this mechanism.

In the best case (no summary VPN routes and network topology that supports penultimate hop popping), the egress PE-router would perform only a single label lookup, resulting in maximum forwarding performance.

Summary

Virtual Private Networks (VPN) based on Multiprotocol Label Switching (MPLS) combine the benefits of the overlay VPN model, such as isolation and security, with the benefits of the peer-to-peer VPN model, such as simplified routing, easier provisioning, and better scalability. A number of mechanisms are needed to successfully meet all these goals:

- Each VPN needs a separate VPN routing and forwarding instance (VRF) in each PE-router to guarantee isolation and enable usage of uncoordinated private IP addresses.

- To support overlapping VPN topologies, the VRFs can be more granular than the VPNs and can participate in more than one VPN at a time. An attribute called a route target is needed to identify the set of VPNs in which a particular VRF participates. For maximum flexibility, a set of route targets can be associated with a VRF or attached to a VPN route.

- VPN IP addresses are prepended with 64-bit route distinguishers to make VPN addresses globally unique. These 96-bit addresses are exchanged between the PE-routers through MP-BGP, which also carries additional route attributes (for example, the route target) by means of optional BGP route attributes, called extended communities.

- Each PE-router needs a unique router ID (host route—usually the loopback address) that is used to allocate a label and enable VPN packet forwarding across the backbone.

- Each PE-router allocates a unique label to each route in each VRF (even if they have the same next hop) and propagates these labels together with 96-bit VPN addresses through MP-BGP.

- Ingress PE-routers use a two-level MPLS label stack to label the VPN packets with a VPN label assigned by the egress PE-router and an IGP label identifying the PE-router assigned through the regular MPLS label distribution mechanisms. The label stack is prepended to the VPN packet, and the resulting MPLS packet is forwarded across the P-network.

CHAPTER 9

MPLS/VPN Architecture Operation

In the previous chapter, we introduced the key mechanisms and features that make up the MPLS/VPN architecture. You learned that the VPN service is established through the use of Virtual Routing and Forwarding Instances (VRFs) into which specific VPN customer routing information is placed through import mechanisms that utilize the Route Target BGP extended community. This VPN routing information is identified uniquely through the use of a Route Distinguisher and is distributed among service provider edge routers, known as Provider Edge (PE) routers, through the use of Multiprotocol BGP extensions.

Now that you clearly understand the basic concepts of the MPLS/VPN architecture, you can understand how to implement this architecture in terms of design and through the configuration of the service provider backbone infrastructure. You also can learn further details on the mechanisms required to achieve this, so that you can fully understand the architecture and how it is implemented. This chapter concentrates on these goals and provides a more detailed description of these mechanisms, some of which you already saw presented in their basic format in Chapter 8, "MPLS/VPN Architecture Overview."

This chapter also introduces the basic configuration steps that are necessary in all deployments of the architecture. To assist in the explanation of these configuration steps, we use a case study to show a basic Intranet topology. This case study highlights the basic VPN service, with no advanced feature deployment. For simplicity and ease of understanding, Chapter 10, "Provider Edge (PE) to Customer Edge (CE) Connectivity Options," covers more advanced configuration steps and VPN customer-to-service provider connectivity options (that are used in some deployments of the MPLS/VPN architecture).

Two requirements exist for a PE-router in respect to the advertisement of routes:

* Advertise routes to attached CE-devices
* Advertise routes that have been learned from these CE-devices across the MPLS/VPN backbone

This chapter covers only the second requirement of how the routes are propagated between PE-routers across the MPLS/VPN backbone. Chapter 10 covers the first requirement.

Case Study: Basic MPLS/VPN Intranet Service

One of the simplest VPN topologies you can provision using the MPLS/VPN architecture
is an Intranet between multiple sites that belong to the same organization. This topology is
the basic VPN network structure that provides any-to-any connectivity between sites using
the enhanced peer-to-peer model discussed in Chapter 7, "Virtual Private Network (VPN)
Implementation Options." Using the same mechanisms you use to build the Intranet
topology, you can add more advanced services and connectivity requirements.

Figure 9-1 shows an example of this type of topology, which is used as a case study
throughout this chapter.

Figure 9-1   *Basic MPLS/VPN Intranet Topology Structure*

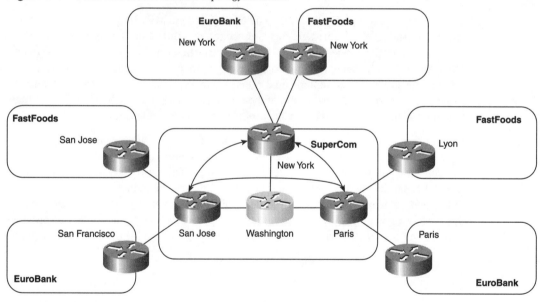

In Figure 9-1, you can see that the SuperCom MPLS/VPN backbone has two VPN
customers: EuroBank and FastFoods. The EuroBank organization has sites in San
Francisco, New York, and Paris. The FastFoods organization has sites in San Jose, New
York, and Lyon. Both customer sites have the any-to-any, non-redundant, Intranet VPN
service from the SuperCom MPLS/VPN backbone, with only one CE-to-PE connection.

The SuperCom service provider learns routes from both VPN customers through a combination of RIP Version 2 and static routing. The EuroBank San Francisco site and the FastFoods San Jose site both use RIP Version 2 to communicate with the MPLS/VPN backbone, whereas the FastFoods Lyon/New York and EuroBank Paris/New York sites use static routing.

Table 9-1 shows the relevant address space for both VPN customers, and the loopback addresses used by the SuperCom backbone for BGP sessions.

Table 9-1   *Address Space for VPN Customers and Service Provider Loopbacks*

Company	Site	Subnet
FastFoods	San Jose	195.12.2.0/24
	New York	10.2.2.0/24
	Lyon	10.2.1.0/24
EuroBank	San Francisco	10.2.1.0/24
	New York	10.1.2.0/24
	Paris	196.7.25.0/24
SuperCom	Paris (Loopback 0)	194.22.15.1/32
	San Jose (Loopback 0)	194.22.15.2/32
	New York (Loopback 0)	194.22.15.3/32

To provision this VPN service across the MPLS/VPN backbone, follow these steps:

1 Define and configure the VRFs.

2 Define and configure the route distinguishers.

3 Define and configure the import and export policies.

4 Configure the PE-to-CE links.

5 Associate the CE-interfaces to the previously defined VRFs.

6 Configure the Multiprotocol BGP.

Throughout the rest of this chapter, you examine in more detail each of these mechanisms and you can follow the configuration of the SuperCom San Jose PE-router (refer to Figure 9-1) to learn how to provision the basic MPLS/VPN architecture.

Configuration of VRFs

The first step in provisioning a VPN service based on the MPLS architecture is to define and configure the Virtual Routing and Forwarding Instances (VRFs). Chapter 8 explains VRFs in detail.

In the case study, this means you configure a VRF for the EuroBank and FastFoods VPN customers. You attach each PE-router in the MPLS/VPN backbone to a site that wants to receive routes from a specific VPN, so the PE-router must have the relevant VRF configuration for that VPN. Because the SuperCom San Jose, New York, and Paris PE-routers all attach to EuroBank and FastFoods sites, the VRF configuration for these specific VPN customers must exist on all the PE-routers.

You can achieve this configuration by using the **ip vrf** *vrf-name* command. Example 9-1 shows the configuration for the FastFoods VRF on the SuperCom San Jose PE-router.

Example 9-1   *Configuration of the VRF*

```
San Jose(config)# ip vrf FastFoods
San Jose(config-vrf)#
```

NOTE   The name of the VRF used in the **ip vrf** *vrf-name* command is case sensitive.

The command shown in Example 9-1 creates the relevant VRFs and unique CEF forwarding and routing tables. However, the VRFs are not fully provisioned yet and do not contain any routes. You must configure the VRFs further to provide routes for the tables and to create associated MPLS labels.

When you enter the **ip vrf** *vrf-name* command, the router moves into the **vrf configuration** sub-mode. Now you can configure the variables associated with this VRF, such as the route distinguisher and the import and export policies.

Example 9-2 shows the initial configuration, including the creation of all relevant VRFs for the SuperCom San Jose PE-router.

Example 9-2   *Initial VRF Configuration for the SuperCom San Jose PE-router*

```
hostname San Jose
!
ip vrf EuroBank
!
ip vrf FastFoods
```

Route Distinguishers and VPN-IPv4 Address Prefixes

The previous chapter identifies the requirements for advertising customer VPN routes across the MPLS/VPN backbone between PE-routers, and for importing these routes into VPN-specific routing tables (referred to as VRFs). Chapter 8 also identified that the Border Gateway Protocol (BGP) is the protocol of choice to achieve this aim due to its capability of handling a large number of routes and its flexibility to carry optional parameters (known as *attributes*) without extensively changing the protocol. These factors make the protocol very adaptable and well-suited for use with the MPLS/VPN architecture.

BGP, in its standard format, can handle only IPv4 routes. In the MPLS/VPN architecture, because each VPN must be capable of using (although it is not necessary) the same IP prefixes as other VPNs (as long as they do not communicate), it is necessary to prepend a route distinguisher to the IPv4 address. This requires extensions to the BGP protocol so that VPN information can remain unique within the MPLS/VPN backbone and so that BGP speakers can identify routing updates that do not carry standard IPv4 prefix information. Multiprotocol (MP-BGP) and VPN-IPv4 routing information provide these extensions.

NOTE   Although you can use MP-BGP with internal and external peers, the rest of this chapter refers to this protocol as *MP-iBGP* because sessions between PE-routers exist via interior BGP (iBGP) within the same MPLS/VPN domain.

Although MP-iBGP provides the capability of identifying and propagating non-IPv4 routing information, you first need to investigate how VPN routes are represented and how you can make each route unique among multiple sets of VPN customers. This is necessary so the BGP decision process on PE-routers can keep different VPN information separate; only comparable routes are subjected to the same route selection process. A route distinguisher and a VPN-IPv4 address (refer to Chapter 8), provide this functionality.

You have seen already that one of the requirements of the MPLS/VPN architecture is that all customer routes be unique within the backbone but not restrict the use of private IP addresses. These routes need to be unique so that MP-iBGP can treat the same prefix from two separate VPNs as non-comparable routes.

MP-iBGP (as with standard BGP-4) selects one single path among all possible paths describing a route to a given destination (network and mask). Therefore, MP-iBGP on its own cannot work correctly if customers use the same address space (which happens in the case of private address usage).

Figure 9-2 shows the problem faced when the SuperCom New York PE-router receives two identical IPv4 updates. In this case, the PE-router chooses the best route between the two routes received based on the standard BGP decision process. This means that a mechanism is needed so that MP-iBGP does not consider identical (thus comparable) routes as belonging to different VPNs, even if these routes carry the same IPv4 Network Layer Reachability Information (NLRI).

Figure 9-2 *PE-router Comparison of BGP routes*

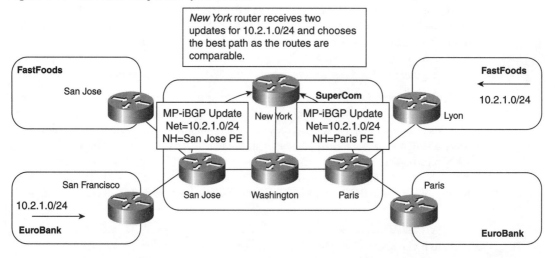

This mechanism consists of prepending a sequence of 64 bits in front of the IPv4 address that is contained in the MP-iBGP update. This sequence of bits is called a *route distinguisher* and it is different for each VPN (or for a subset of sites within a VPN) so that the addresses contained within all VPNs are unique within the MPLS/VPN backbone. BGP considers an IPv4 address as non-comparable with another IPv4 address that has the same network and mask if the route distinguishers are different.

As discussed in Chapter 8, a VPN-IPv4 (or VPNv4 address) is the combination of the IPv4 address and the route distinguisher. Combining the route distinguisher and the IPv4 address makes the IPv4 route globally unique across the MPLS/VPN network. Figure 9-3 illustrates how the PE-router now can distinguish between the same two IPv4 routes and can treat them as separate entities belonging to separate VPNs.

Figure 9-3 shows that when the New York PE-router receives an update about 10.2.1.0/24 from the San Jose and Paris PE-routers, these updates are now non-comparable because a route distinguisher was prepended to the prefix. The update received from the San Jose PE-router is for prefix **100:26:10.2.1.0/24** and the update received from the Paris PE-router is for prefix **100:27:10.2.1.0/24**. Example 9-3 shows the representation of these routes on the New York router.

Figure 9-3   *PE-router Comparison of VPN-IPv4 Routes*

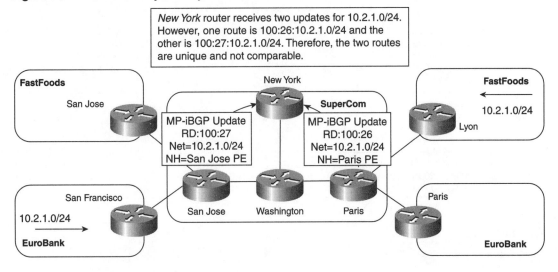

> *New York* router receives two updates for 10.2.1.0/24. However, one route is 100:26:10.2.1.0/24 and the other is 100:27:10.2.1.0/24. Therefore, the two routes are unique and not comparable.

Example 9-3   *PE-router Comparison of VPN-IPv4 Routes*

```
New York# show ip bgp vpnv4 vrf EuroBank 10.2.1.0
BGP routing table entry for 100:27:10.2.1.0/24, version 9
Paths: (1 available, best #1, table EuroBank)
  Advertised to non peer-group peers:
  194.22.15.1
  2
    194.22.15.2 from 194.22.15.2(194.22.15.2)
      Origin IGP, metric 0, localpref 100, valid, external, best
      Extended Community: RT:100:27

New York# show ip bgp vpnv4 vrf FastFoods 10.2.1.0
BGP routing table entry for 100:26:10.2.1.0/24, version 7
Paths: (1 available, best #1, table FastFoods)
  Advertised to non peer-group peers:
  194.22.15.2
  2
    194.22.15.1 from 194.22.15.1 (194.22.15.1)
      Origin IGP, metric 0, localpref 100, valid, external, best
      Extended Community: RT:100:26
```

Although the route distinguisher mechanism provides you with a solution that allows VPN customers to use the same private addressing scheme, it does not solve the problem of multiple customers within the same VPN using the same addressing scheme within their sites. To understand why, consider what happens by looking at the example in Figure 9-4.

Figure 9-4 *Same Private Address Usage Within a VPN*

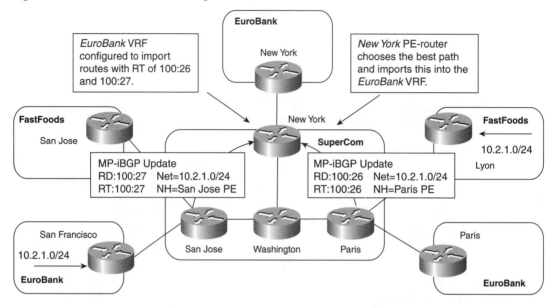

Figure 9-4 shows that the New York PE-router receives an MP-iBGP update for subnet 10.2.1.0/24 from two separate VPNs, in this case, the EuroBank and FastFoods VPNs. The EuroBank VPN is configured to import any routes that contain the route targets of 100:26 or 100:27. This means that it imports any routes from members of the EuroBank or FastFoods VPNs as they export their routes using these route targets.

The New York PE-router compares the two routes to determine which one to import into the EuroBank VRF; depending on which one is chosen, connectivity to the other VPN site is lost. For example, if the New York PE-router determines that the MP-iBGP update for 10.2.1.0/24 received from the Paris PE-router is the best path, then connectivity from the EuroBank New York site to destinations within subnet 10.2.1.0/24 in the EuroBank San Francisco site are lost. For this reason, the design of the MPLS/VPN architecture was restricted to limit the use of overlapping address ranges to VPNs that do not communicate with each other across the MPLS backbone if they share the same set of addresses within their sites.

NOTE The incapability to have overlapping address ranges is not a restriction of the MPLS/VPN architecture. This problem occurs in a standard IP routing scenario if the same set of routes is used at different VPN sites. If full connectivity between VPNs is required, the address ranges should be unique, or Network Address Translation (NAT) could be deployed.

Configuration of the Route Distinguisher

Each VRF within the PE-router configuration needs to have an associated route distinguisher, which might or might not be related to a particular site or VPN membership of that site. In the most common case, where a site belongs only to one intranet VPN, it is technically possible, and recommended, to use a unique route distinguisher for the VPN. However, if this site at some point in the future will become a member of an extranet VPN, do not take this approach because it might incur configuration issues when trying to provision the extranet VPN.

For example, suppose a different route distinguisher is used for each VPN. If a particular site wants to be a member of multiple VPNs, it is not possible to identify which route distinguisher to use for the site because it belongs to more than one VPN.

Therefore, for network topologies other than the simple intranet model, use the same route distinguisher per VRF, rather than per VPN, to avoid this type of conflicting configuration and to reduce the memory requirements of the PE-router. In the case of an extranet VPN, this means the VRF that makes up the VPN uses the same route distinguisher regardless of the particular VPN site to which the VRF belongs.

When you deploy certain topologies, you might need to extend the same route distinguisher per-VRF model to a scheme that uses a unique route distinguisher on each VRF within the VPN. One such topology is the hub-and-spoke, or common services topology, which is described in detail in Chapter 11, "Advanced MPLS/VPN Topologies." This type of topology sometimes requires that each spoke (or a user of the common service) use a different route distinguisher depending on whether the topology is distributed or local to the hub PE-router.

You must establish the assignment of a particular value to the route distinguisher for each VRF on the PE-router. The structure of this value can be either ASN:nn or IP-address:nn. We recommend the use of ASN:nn with an Autonomous System Number (ASN) that is assigned by the Internet Assigned Numbers Authority (IANA) so that it is unique between service providers. Use the IP-address:nn format only when the MPLS/VPN network uses a private AS number but the VPN-IPv4 addresses are propagated beyond the private AS (for example, when exchanging VPN routes between different service providers).

Because the customers who use the routes contained within the VRF also can attach to other MPLS/VPN service providers, it is important to use the ASN of the service provider as the first two bytes of the route distinguisher format to avoid using the same VPN-IPv4 addresses in separate MPLS/VPN domains.

NOTE   Even when you use the ASN:nn format for the route distinguisher, it is important to note that the route distinguisher does not have any semantics and is interpreted only by BGP as a sequence of bits (part of the whole VPN-IPv4 address).

The service provider assigns the value of the second portion of the route distinguisher. As recommended earlier, this value normally should be unique per VRF, although in some cases, such as the simple intranet example in this chapter, it can be unique per-VPN customer. Separate route distinguishers are not necessary for this type of topology, because no potential routing issues (caused by the bad assignment of route distinguishers) must be overcome. Therefore, in the case study example, you can allocate a route distinguisher based on which VPN customer connects via the interface. This means that the value of the route distinguisher is the same for each VRF that belongs to (or, more accurately, contains routes for) a particular intranet VPN. Table 9-2 lists the assigned values for each SuperCom VPN customer.

Table 9-2   *SuperCom Route Distinguisher Definitions*

VPN Customer	Service Provider ASN	Unique Value	Route Distinguisher
FastFoods	100	26	100:26
EuroBank	100	27	100:27

You can configure the route distinguisher for the VRF within the **vrf configuration** sub-mode using the command **rd** *ASN:nn|IP-address:nn* as shown in Example 9-4. This example also shows that a unique routing table for this VRF is created.

Example 9-4   *Route Distinguisher Configuration Example*

```
San Jose(config)#ip vrf FastFoods
San Jose(config-vrf)#rd 100:26
San Jose(config-vrf)#^Z

San Jose# show ip route vrf FastFoods
Codes: C - connected, S - static, I - IGRP, R - RIP, M - mobile, B - BGP
       D - EIGRP, EX - EIGRP external, O - OSPF, IA - OSPF inter area
       N1 - OSPF NSSA external type 1, N2 - OSPF NSSA external type 2
       E1 - OSPF external type 1, E2 - OSPF external type 2, E - EGP
       i - IS-IS, L1 - IS-IS level-1, L2 - IS-IS level-2, ia - IS-IS
       inter area
       * - candidate default, U - per-user static route, o - ODR
       P - periodic downloaded static route

Gateway of last resort is not set
```

The same configuration is necessary for the SuperCom New York and Paris PE-routers. Example 9-5 shows the expanded configuration of the SuperCom San Jose PE-router.

Example 9-5   *SuperCom San Jose PE-router Configuration—Addition of RD*

```
hostname San Jose
!
ip vrf EuroBank
 rd 100:27
```

Example 9-5   *SuperCom San Jose PE-router Configuration—Addition of RD (Continued)*

```
!
ip vrf FastFoods
 rd 100:26
```

BGP Extended Community Attribute

You have seen already that each PE-router learns routes from across the MPLS/VPN backbone and from attached customer sites. These routes are populated into VPN-specific routing tables. Any routes learned from customers are advertised across the MPLS/VPN backbone through the use of MP-iBGP, and any routes learned via MP-iBGP are placed into the VRFs of interested parties. To achieve this, each PE-router needs information that tells it how to process any routes it receives. This information not only tells the PE-router into which VRF the routes should be imported but also what information it should append to the route when advertising to other PE-routers.

Chapter 8 introduced the concept of a route target and briefly explained how this entity determines which VRF, and thus which VPN sites, should receive the route. Although the route target provides the mechanisms to identify which VRFs should receive the routes, it does not provide a facility that can prevent routing loops. These loops could occur if routes learned from a site are advertised back to that site. To prevent this, the *Site of Origin (SOO)*, another concept in the MPLS/VPN architecture identifies which site originated the route and, therefore, should not receive the route from any PE-routers.

NOTE   The SOO is not necessary if the MPLS/VPN backbone is repairing a partitioned site. In this case, routes learned from one portion of the site should be advertised to another portion of the site at a different PE location.

The BGP Extended Community attribute applies both of these concepts to the MPLS/VPN architecture. This attribute is described in *draft-ramachandra-bgp-ext-communities*, which you can find on the IETF Web site at www.ietf.org.

This draft defines a new transitive optional BGP attribute, which contains a set of *Extended Communities* that define the site from where the VPN-IPv4 address was learned (the *route origin*) and the set of routers to which the route should be exported (the *route target*). The extended community attribute enables the closed user group functionality and is set by the PE-routers, via configuration, to define the import and export policies on a per site/VRF basis. Before you consider the specific details of this attribute, we should briefly review how it is used within the MPLS/VPN architecture.

Route Target BGP Extended Community

As mentioned, the BGP extended communities draft specifies two new communities defined as the route target and the route origin. The Cisco implementation of the draft uses both of these communities. The route origin, referred to as the SOO by the Cisco implementation, prevents routing loops between sites, and the route target extended community defines the import and export policies that a particular VRF uses.

The extended community is attached to a BGP route the same way standard BGP communities or any other BGP attributes are. The MP-iBGP update propagates the extended community along with other BGP attributes between PE-routers, and its value determines to which VRF or set of VRFs to import the route. Careful definition of the route target extended community values provides the flexibility to provision many different VPN topologies. One such topology, which uses the MPLS/VPN backbone from the case study, helps to show the basic operation of the route target (see Figure 9-5).

Figure 9-5   *Route Target BGP Extended Community Usage*

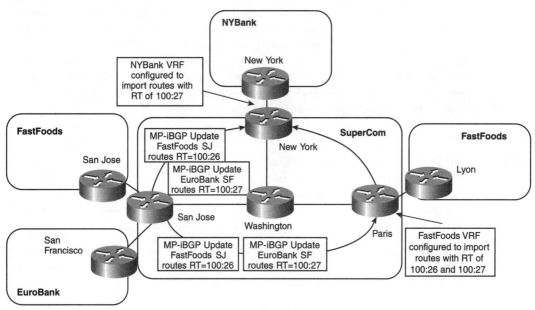

Figure 9-5 shows that the SuperCom San Jose PE-router exports routes for the FastFoods VPN with a route target of 100:26 and for the EuroBank VPN with a route target of 100:27. The NYBank VRF on the SuperCom New York router imports routes with a route target of 100:27. This means that it contains only routes for the EuroBank San Francisco site. The FastFoods VRF on the SuperCom Paris router imports routes with a route target of 100:26

and 100:27. This means that it contains routes for the FastFoods San Jose site and for the EuroBank San Francisco site.

NOTE

Figure 9-5 also shows an interesting example of how one site within a VPN can hold routes that are not contained in another site of the same VPN. The Paris PE-router imports routes with a route target of 100:26 and 100:27. This means that the FastFoods Lyon site has routes that belong to the EuroBank San Francisco site and the FastFoods San Jose site. However, neither the EuroBank or FastFoods VRFs on the San Jose PE-router are configured to import both route target values. They contain only routes that belong to their particular VPN because the Paris PE-router does not re-advertise routes from within its VRF that it learned via iBGP (standard iBGP rules).

Configuration of Import and Export Policies

The last step in the configuration of each VRF is the addition of import and export policies for the VRF to use. These policies are used to populate routes into the VRF and to advertise routes out of the VRF.

The route target BGP Extended Community dictates the policies used by the VRF. The route target must be configured to specify the routes, which contain this specific route target value, that are imported into the VRF, and the route target that is added to the routes that are exported from the VRF. The **route-target** command, the syntax of which is shown in Example 9-6, controls this within the VRF configuration.

Example 9-6   *Route Target VRF Configuration Command*

```
San Jose(config-vrf)#route-target ?
  ASN:nn or IP-address:nn  Target VPN Extended Community
  both                     Both import and export Target-VPN community
  export                   Export Target-VPN community
  import                   Import Target-VPN community
```

Use the **export** and **import** keywords with the **route-target** command to specify separately the export and import policies for each VRF. Usually, the default export and import policies are the same so you can specify both using one command, either **route-target ASN:nn** or **route-target both ASN:nn** (both commands achieve the same results). This is the case in the sample topology, where both the EuroBank and FastFoods VRFs need to export their routes with a route target that is imported by other members of their organization's VPN.

Example 9-7 shows the relevant configuration of the SuperCom San Jose PE-router, for the EuroBank and FastFoods VPN customer VRFs.

Example 9-7   *SuperCom San Jose PE-router Configuration—Import/Export*

```
hostname San Jose
!
ip vrf EuroBank
 rd 1:27
 route-target export 100:27
 route-target import 100:27
!
ip vrf FastFoods
 rd 1:26
 route-target export 100:26
 route-target import 100:26
```

If you need to add more than one route target to any routes that are exported from the VRF, use the **route-target export** command multiple times within the VRF configuration. This command defines the set of VPN route target extended communities that can attach to any routes exported from the VRF into VPN-IPv4 NLRIs in MP-BGP updates. Likewise, you can use the **route-target import** command to specify which routes to import into the VRF. If a received route contains any of the route target values listed in the import list, then that route is eligible for import into the VRF.

Site of Origin BGP Extended Community

The route origin extended community is referred to as the *SOO* in the Cisco implementation of the MPLS/VPN architecture; therefore, we use this description throughout this book.

The SOO prevents routing loops when a site is multihomed to the MPLS/VPN backbone, and, in addition, that site uses the AS-override feature. This is achieved by identifying the site from where the route was learned, based on its SOO, so that it is not re-advertised back to that site from a PE-router somewhere else in the MPLS/VPN backbone.

NOTE   Chapter 10 discusses the AS-override feature in more detail.

NOTE   The SOO is not necessary if the MPLS/VPN backbone is used to repair a partitioned site that is multihomed and uses the AS-override feature. SOO also is used only if BGP is used to achieve the PE to CE connectivity.

Figure 9-6 illustrates this concept, and shows a site connected to two separate PE-routers and the behavior of the PE-router when a route is received that contains a SOO extended community that matches the one configured for the VRF.

Figure 9-6   *SOO BGP Extended Community*

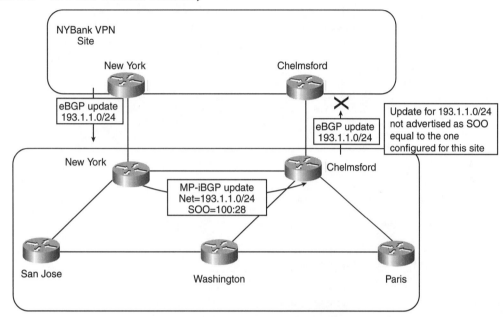

Figure 9-6 shows that the SuperCom Chelmsford PE-router receives an MP-iBGP update for 193.1.1.0/24 from the New York PE-router. This update contains a SOO of 100:28, which is the one configured for the NYBank VRF on the Chelmsford PE-router. Because of this, the route is not advertised to the NYBank Chelmsford CE-router.

Configuration of the SOO

The SOO extended community is configured using a route-map on each PE-router. Because it is required only in a multihomed environment, you do not need for this chapter's simple intranet case study example or if you run a PE to CE protocol other than BGP.

Example 9-8 shows a configuration for the New York PE-router shown in Figure 9-6. The route-map can be applied to routes learned through a particular VRF, regardless of whether these routes were learned via BGP (they could be learned through redistribution from another protocol into BGP).

Example 9-8   *Configuration of the SOO Extended Community*

```
router bgp 1
 no synchronization
 no bgp default ipv4-unicast
 neighbor 194.22.15.4 remote-as 1
 neighbor 194.22.15.4 update-source loopback0
 !
 address-family ipv4 vrf NYBank
 neighbor 192.168.65.5 remote-as 250
 neighbor 192.168.65.5 activate
 neighbor 192.168.65.5 route-map setsoo in
 no auto-summary
 no synchronization
 exit-address-family
 !
 address-family vpnv4
 neighbor 194.22.15.4 activate
 neighbor 194.22.15.4 send-community extended
 no auto-summary
 exit-address-family
 !
 route-map setsoo permit 10
 set extcommunity soo 100:28
```

Example 9-9 shows that the subnet 193.1.1.0/24, learned from the NYBank New York CE-router by the SuperCom New York PE-router, contains the SOO 100:28.

Example 9-9   *SOO Extended Community Example*

```
New York# show ip bgp vpnv4 vrf NYBank 193.1.1.0
BGP routing table entry for 1:27:193.1.1.0/24, version 14
Paths: (1 available, best #1, table NYBank)
  Advertised to non peer-group peers:
  194.22.15.4
  2
    192.168.65.5 from 192.168.65.5 (195.12.2.1)
      Origin IGP, metric 0, localpref 100, valid, external, best
      Extended Community: SoO:100:28 RT:100:27
```

BGP Extended Community Attribute Format

Now that you know how the BGP extended community attribute is used in the MPLS/VPN architecture, you can learn how this attribute is structured.

Each of the extended community attributes has a defined community type code of 16 and is encoded as an 8-octet value. The first two octets define the attribute type, and the next six octets hold the value of the attribute. Types 0 through 0x7FFF inclusive are assignable by the Internet Assigned Numbers Authority (IANA), and types 0x8000 through 0xFFFF inclusive are vendor-specific.

The route target extended community has a type code of 0x0002 or 0x0102, and the SOO extended community has a type code of 0x0003 or 0x0103. The structure of the value field (and the way the value field is displayed) depends on the high order byte of the type field. See Figure 9-7.

Figure 9-7   *BGP Extended Community Attribute Format*

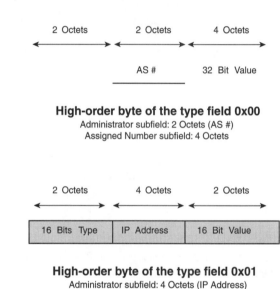

A route can carry both the standard BGP Communities attribute as defined in RFC1997 and the extended BGP Communities attribute as defined in *draft-ramachandra-bgp-ext-communities.* It also can carry multiple community attributes through the use of the **additive** keyword in the case of standard communities and through the use of route-maps when exporting the VRF routes in the case of extended communities. Cisco IOS 12.1 allows the **additive** keyword to be used with extended communities.

Basic PE to CE Link Configuration

To provide a VPN service, the PE-router needs to be configured so that any routing information learned from a VPN customer interface can be associated with a particular VRF. You can do this through the standard routing protocol process, which is known as the *routing context*. Each VRF uses a separate routing context. Chapter 8 discusses this concept fully.

Any routes learned across an interface that is associated with the particular routing protocol context are installed into the associated VRF. Any routes learned from interfaces that are *not* part of any VRF routing context are placed in the global routing table. This allows for the separation of routing information into different contexts even though the information is learned by the same routing protocol process. It effectively creates *VPN-aware* routing protocols.

Several connectivity options allow a VPN customer to attach to the MPLS/VPN backbone. The sample case study uses only RIP Version 2 and static routing, and this section reviews both of these options.

NOTE   For a full discussion on other connectivity options, such as OSPF and BGP, see Chapter 10.

PE to CE Link Configuration—Static Routing

The first option is to run static routing between the PE- and CE-routers. This static routing information is redistributed into BGP for advertisement across the MP-iBGP sessions that connect PE-routers. This is a good choice for deployment when the site is a *stub site*, that is it has only one entry point into the service provider's network because there is little to be gained by dynamically learning the customer routes via the PE-CE link.

A static route for every network (or aggregate route) beyond the CE-router must be configured into the VRF on the PE-router that connects the site (assuming other members of the VPN can reach the network). This is the same type of configuration as with normal IP routing.

NOTE   One exception to this is when the rest of the VPN uses the site for central services, such as Internet connectivity. In this case, a default route pointing to the site can be deployed and advertised to other members of the VPN using a specific route target. See the discussion on Internet connectivity in Chapter 12, "Advanced MPLS/VPN Topics," for further details.

To allow this static routing information to be advertised between PE-routers, it must be redistributed into BGP. You can achieve this by using the **redistribute** command within the BGP Address Family configuration, which is discussed in more detail in the section on MP-BGP, later in this chapter. You can use the same command to redistribute any connected VRF interface addresses into BGP.

In the case study example, the SuperCom Paris PE-router needs to be configured for static routing to both VPN customers. Each customer CE-router points by default to the PE-router, so you do not need to consider the configuration of the CE-router. The first step in this process is to configure all the relevant static routes, and to place these static routes in the correct VRF, rather than the global routing table. To acheive this objective, use the **ip route** command (with extensions for MPLS/VPN). Example 9-10 shows the relevant configuration for the SuperCom Paris router to support the EuroBank Paris and FastFoods Lyon customer sites.

Example 9-10 *ip route Command Extensions for MPLS/VPN*

```
Paris(config)# ip route vrf FastFoods 10.2.1.0 255.255.255.0 serial0
Paris(config)# ip route vrf EuroBank 196.7.25.0 255.255.255.0 serial1
```

The second step is to advertise these static routes to other PE-routers by using MP-iBGP. As previously stated, you use the **redistribute** command within the address-family configuration of the VRF to do this. Example 9-11 shows the configuration of the SuperCom Paris PE-router, which allows the previously defined static routes to be advertised to other PE-routers within the SuperCom MPLS/VPN backbone:

Example 9-11 *Redistribution of Static Routing Information into MP-iBGP*

```
hostname Paris
!
router bgp 1
!
address-family ipv4 vrf EuroBank
 redistribute static
exit address-family
!
address-family ipv4 vrf FastFoods
 redistribute static
exit address-family
```

If multiple static routes exist for a particular VPN customer and only some of these routes should be reachable by other members of the VPN, you can use a **route-map** command to control which static routes are placed into MP-iBGP during redistribution.

PE to CE Link Configuration—RIP Version 2

This connectivity option provides the facility to run RIP version 2 between the PE- and CE-routers. The information received via RIP from any VPN customer CE-router is placed into the connected VRF for the receiving interface, and then is advertised across the MPLS/VPN backbone between PE-routers.

When RIP version 2 is chosen as the routing protocol, the RIP process needs to be told which RIP routes to advertise out of which interfaces. To achieve this, use the **network** command. The **network** command tells the RIP process which interfaces are RIP-enabled and which interfaces to send RIP updates out of. In a normal RIP version 2 deployment, these RIP updates contain every RIP route within the routing table plus any directly connected interfaces that are RIP-enabled.

It obviously is not desirable, in the context of MPLS/VPN, for the RIP process to advertise all routes out of any interfaces that belong to the address range specified by the **network** command. To overcome this, use the **address-family** sub-mode within the main RIP process configuration. The router interprets any commands you enter in this sub-mode as belonging to the specified VRF. Because of this, any **network** commands you enter in the sub-mode are associated with the VRF that is configured for that address-family. Routes belonging to the VRF then are advertised by RIP but only out of the interfaces associated with the address-family. Any RIP routes that belong to the global routing table, or any other VRF, are not advertised even though the RIP process is aware of the routes.

The SuperCom San Jose PE-router in the case study runs RIP version 2 with the EuroBank San Francisco site and the FastFoods San Jose site. Example 9-12 illustrates the relevant RIP configuration.

Example 9-12 *PE to CE RIP Version 2 Configuration Example*

```
hostname San Jose
!
interface serial0
 description ** interface to Eurobank San Francisco**
 ip address 10.2.1.5 255.255.255.252
!
interface serial1
 description ** interface to FastFoods San Jose**
 ip address 195.12.2.5 255.255.255.252
!
router rip
 version 2
 !
address-family ipv4 vrf EuroBank
 version 2
 redistribute bgp 1 metric 1
 network 10.0.0.0
 no auto-summary
exit-address-family
!
address-family ipv4 vrf FastFoods
 version 2
 redistribute bgp 1 metric 1
 network 195.12.2.0
```

Example 9-12   *PE to CE RIP Version 2 Configuration Example (Continued)*

```
   no auto-summary
 exit-address-family
   !
```

Example 9-13 shows that a routing context is defined for each VRF that receives routes from the RIP process. Any routes received via RIP across interfaces associated with the VRF are placed into the VRF and are not placed into the global routing table. However, this configuration only gets the RIP-derived information into the relevant VRFs; it does not cause the routes to be advertised via MP-iBGP to other PE-routers. If this is desired, then you must configure the address-family for this specific VRF within the BGP process as in the previous static route example, and the RIP routes must be redistributed into BGP. This causes the routes to be advertised across any MP-iBGP sessions that are configured to carry VPN-IPv4 address prefixes.

NOTE   In Example 9-12, notice the statement **redistribute bgp 1 metric 1** in the RIP address-family configuration. This command is necessary so that any VPN routes learned from across MP-iBGP sessions are advertised toward the CE-router by the RIP process. Notice also that these routes are iBGP routes that normally are not redistributed when running standard BGP-4, but are successfully redistributed if the interface is associated with a VRF.

NOTE   Although RIP version 1 also works in this scenario, it is not recommended due to its lack of VLSM support and the fact that Cisco does not support its use within this environment.

NOTE   When using RIP as the PE-CE configuration, it is necessary (as in normal redistribution) to specify the BGP metric as the default metric, which is **unreachable**. In later releases of IOS, however, it is possible to carry RIP metrics transparently across the MPLS/VPN backbone through the use of the command **redistribute bgp metric transparent**. This command causes RIP to use the routing table metric for redistributed routes as the RIP metric, with the original metric being carried across the MPLS/VPN backbone in the BGP MED value.

Association of Interfaces to VRFs

After you define all relevant VRFs on the PE-router, you must tell the PE-router which interfaces belong to which VRF and, therefore, should populate the VRF with routes from connected sites. More than one interface can belong to the same VRF.

You can do this by using the **ip vrf forwarding** interface-mode command, which associates the interface with the named VRF. Both main and sub-interfaces can be defined within a VRF. Example 9-13 shows the relevant configuration for the SuperCom San Jose PE-router.

Example 9-13   *Association of Interfaces to VRFs*

```
hostname San Jose
!
interface serial0
 description ** interface to Eurobank San Francisco**
 ip vrf forwarding EuroBank
 ip address 10.2.1.5 255.255.255.252
!
interface serial1
 description ** interface to FastFoods San Jose**
 ip vrf forwarding FastFoods
 ip address 195.12.2.5 255.255.255.252
```

When the interface is associated with a particular VRF, its IP address is removed from the global routing table and from the interface. This is because an assumption is made that the address is not valid across multiple routing tables and should be reconfigured after the interface is given membership to a VRF.

NOTE   Only interfaces that run CEF switching can be associated with VRFs because the CEF switching mechanism is a necessary prerequisite for successful MPLS/VPN data forwarding as label imposition is achieved through the CEF switching path.

Multiprotocol BGP Usage and Deployment

You have seen already that you use MP-BGP, which is an extension of the existing BGP-4 protocol, to advertise customer VPN routes between PE-routers that were learned from connected CE-routers. These customer routes might be learned through standard BGP-4, RIP Version 2, static routes, or OSPF. Future versions of Cisco IOS might support additional CE-PE routing protocols.

MP-BGP is required only within the service provider backbone. Therefore, all MP-BGP sessions are *internal* BGP sessions, internal because the session is between two routers that belong to the same autonomous system.

MP-iBGP is required within the MPLS/VPN architecture because the BGP update needs to carry more information than just an IPv4 address. You have seen already that an MP-iBGP update contains a VPN-IPv4 address, MPLS label information, extended BGP communities, and possibly standard BGP communities.

NOTE   Multiprotocol BGP extensions to the existing BGP-4 protocol (RFC 1771) are defined within RFC 2283. You can find more information on the use of MP-BGP within an MPLS environment in *draft-ietf-bgp4-mpls*, which discusses using BGP-4 to carry MPLS label information.

Certain extensions to the BGP protocol that provide additional capabilities are necessary to allow BGP to carry more information than just the IPv4 address (and standard BGP attributes). When a BGP session is established between two peers, an OPEN message exchanges initial BGP parameters, such as the autonomous system number used by the BGP neighbors. This OPEN message can contain optional parameters, one of which is the **Capabilities** parameter that describes which optional capabilities the peer can understand and execute. One of these capabilities is multiprotocol extensions. These multiprotocol extensions provide BGP with the capability to carry addresses other than standard IPv4 addresses.

Two new optional, non-transitive attributes are introduced to BGP when the multiprotocol extensions capability is used. One of these attributes (Multiprotocol Reachable NLRI or MP_REACH_NLRI) announces new multiprotocol routes. The other attribute (Multiprotocol Unreachable NLRI or MP_UNREACH_NLRI) revokes the routes previously announced by MP_REACH_NLRI.

The first attribute (MP_REACH_NLRI) carries a set of reachable destinations together with the next hop information to be used for forwarding to these destinations. The second attribute (MP_UNREACH_NLRI) carries the set of unreachable destinations. Both of these attributes are optional and non-transitive. For two BGP speakers to exchange multiprotocol data, they must agree on this capability during their capabilities exchange.

When a PE-router sends an MP-iBGP update to other PE-routers, and this update contains MPLS/VPN information as previously described, the MP_REACH_NLRI attribute contains one or more triples that consist of the following:

- Address Family Information
- Next-hop Information
- NLRI (Network Layer Reachability Information)

The address-family information identifies the Network layer protocol that is being carried within the update. This is set to AFI=1 and sub-AFI=128 in the case of MPLS/VPN. You can find currently used values in RFC 1700, "Assigned Numbers."

The next-hop information is the next-hop address information of the next router on the path to the destination. In the case of MPLS/VPN, this is the advertising PE-router. The next-hop address must be of the same address family as the NLRI. To satisfy this requirement, the route distinguisher field of the next-hop is set to all zeros.

The NLRIs are encoded as one or more triples with the following format for MPLS:

Length: Total length of the label plus the prefix (RD included).

Label: (24 bits) Carries one or more labels in a stack, although a BGP update has only one label. This field carries the following parts of the MPLS shim header (described in Chapter 2, "Frame-mode MPLS Operation"):

Label Value——20 Bits

Experimental bits—3 Bits

Bottom of stack bit—1 bit

Prefix: Route distinguisher (64 bits) plus IPv4 prefix (32 bits).

Example 9-14 shows the command that identifies which labels are assigned to the particular VPN routes, and Example 9-15 shows the command to determine whether the PE-router is exchanging VPN-IPv4 address information with a neighbor.

Example 9-14 *show ip bgp vpnv4 all tags Command Usage*

```
New York# show ip bgp vpnv4 all tags
   Network           Next Hop       In tag/Out tag
Route Distinguisher: 1:27 (EuroBank)
   0.0.0.0           10.2.1.25      50/notag
   2.2.2.2/32        0.0.0.0        46/aggregate(EuroBank)
   8.8.8.8/32        10.2.1.25      51/notag
   9.9.9.9/32        10.2.1.25      52/notag
```

Example 9-15 *show ip bgp neighbor Command Usage*

```
New York# show ip bgp neighbor 194.22.15.4
BGP neighbor is 194.22.15.4,  remote AS 1, internal link
  BGP version 4, remote router ID 197.1.1.1
  BGP state = Established, up for 01:00:55
  Last read 00:00:56, hold time is 180, keepalive interval is 60
  seconds
  Neighbor capabilities:
    Route refresh: advertised and received
    Address family IPv4 Unicast: advertised and received
    Address family VPNv4 Unicast: advertised and received
  Received 13002 messages, 0 notifications, 0 in queue
  Sent 13089 messages, 0 notifications, 0 in queue
  Route refresh request: received 1, sent 2
  Minimum time between advertisement runs is 5 seconds

 For address family: IPv4 Unicast
  BGP table version 5, neighbor version 5
  Index 1, Offset 0, Mask 0x2
  4 accepted prefixes consume 144 bytes
  Prefix advertised 10, suppressed 0, withdrawn 6

 For address family: VPNv4 Unicast
```

Example 9-15 *show ip bgp neighbor Command Usage (Continued)*

```
BGP table version 20, neighbor version 20
Index 2, Offset 0, Mask 0x4
0 accepted prefixes consume 0 bytes
Prefix advertised 174, suppressed 0, withdrawn 25
```

Configuration of Multiprotocol BGP

The configuration of BGP requires several steps, and various configuration commands. It has to be configured for any PE-to-PE MP-iBGP sessions across the MPLS/VPN backbone, and for any PE-to-CE eBGP sessions for customers that want to run BGP with the service provider. Chapter 10 covers the configuration of these PE-to-CE eBGP sessions.

You saw earlier in this chapter that as part of the MP-BGP specification (RFC 2283), an *address-family* is created to allow BGP to carry protocols other than IPv4. Within the MPLS/VPN architecture, this address-family is the VPN-IPv4 address and BGP must be told that this type of address-family is carried by one of its sessions.

The default behavior when a BGP session is configured on a Cisco router is to activate the session to carry IPv4 unicast prefixes. This might represent a problem in a pure MPLS/VPN environment, where BGP is used solely to carry VPN-IPv4. Therefore, a new command is introduced to reverse this behavior so that the activation of any BGP sessions, whether IPv4 or VPN-IPv4, does not occur by default. Example 9-16 shows the syntax of this command.

Example 9-16 *BGP Default IPv4-unicast Command Usage*

```
San Jose(config)# router bgp 1
San Jose(config-router)# no bgp default ipv4-unicast
```

The next step in the configuration of MP-iBGP is to define and activate the BGP sessions between PE-routers. Some of these sessions carry VPN-IPv4 routes, some only IPv4 routes, and others carry VPN-IPv4 and IPv4 routes. The type of BGP session and the specification of which routes (VPN-IPv4 or IPv4) the session will carry are controlled through the use of *address families* within the BGP configuration for routes that are injected into and out of BGP, into and out of VRFs, and through the normal BGP configuration process for routes that belong to the global routing table. The address-family is synonymous with the *routing context*.

You must configure a BGP address-family for each VRF configured on the PE-router and a separate address-family to carry VPN-IPv4 routes between PE-routers. All non-VPN BGP neighbors (other PE-routers and other global BGP peers) have to be defined under the **router bgp** configuration mode. All VPN BGP neighbors (for example, a CE router exchanging routes with a PE-router through BGP) are defined under its associated address-family. The BGP process (with no address-family specified) is the default address-family where any sessions are configured that either are not associated with a VRF or are used to carry IPv4 routes from the global routing table.

The configuration of the BGP sessions that carry IPv4 routes from the global routing table is exactly the same as the standard BGP configuration, with the exception that the session needs to be activated. The **neighbor** command controls the activation of the session, as shown in Example 9-17. This example also shows all the relevant commands used to establish an IPv4 BGP session between the SuperCom San Jose PE-router and the New York PE-router (this example assumes that the New York router is configured already).

Example 9-17   *Activation of Standard IPv4 BGP Sessions*

```
San Jose(config)# router bgp 1
San Jose(config-router)# neighbor 194.22.15.3 remote-as 1
San Jose(config-router)# neighbor 194.22.15.3 update-source loopback0
San Jose(config-router)# neighbor 194.22.15.3 activate
```

The BGP process activates the MP-iBGP session that carries VPN-IPv4 prefixes through the use of the BGP's own address-family. This configuration creates a routing context for exchanging VPN-IPv4 prefixes. Example 9-18 shows the syntax of this command and the relevant command to configure the MP-iBGP session between the SuperCom San Jose and New York routers in the case study.

Example 9-18   *Address-Family Configuration for VPN-IPv4 Route Exchange*

```
San Jose(config)#router bgp 1
San Jose(config-router)#address-family ?
  ipv4   Address family
  vpnv4  Address family

San Jose(config-router)#address-family vpnv4
San Jose(config-router)#neighbor 194.22.15.3 activate
```

NOTE   In Example 9-18, notice that the VPNv4 **address-family** configuration needs only one command. This is because the BGP neighbor must be configured under the global BGP process, and therefore needs to be activated to carry only VPN-IPv4 prefixes.

The configuration of the **vpnv4** address-family also adds a further command to the BGP configuration. This command is **neighbor *x.x.x.x* send-community extended**. This command is added by default and is necessary because it instructs BGP to advertise the extended community attribute discussed earlier in this chapter. Example 9-19 provides the syntax of this command.

Example 9-19   *Advertisement of Extended Community Attribute*

```
San Jose(config-router)#neighbor 194.22.15.3 send-community ?
  both       Send Standard and Extended Community attributes
  extended   Send Extended Community attribute
  standard   Send Standard Community attribute
  <cr>
```

NOTE	The default behavior is to send only the extended community attribute. If the network design requires the standard community attribute to be attached to VPN routes, change the default configuration using the command **neighbor 194.22.15.3 send-community both**.

As you already know, after the VRF is populated with any customer routes, these routes need to be advertised across the MPLS/VPN backbone. MP-iBGP performs this job by carrying these routes as VPN-IPv4 prefixes across the MP-iBGP sessions between PE-routers. To allow this to happen, the routing context needs to be configured within the BGP process to tell BGP which VRF routes to advertise.

Again, you achieve this using the address-family configuration under the BGP process, using the **ipv4** option of the **address-family** command used in Example 9-18. Each VRF that injects routes into BGP needs to be configured under the BGP process using its own address-family. Also, any routes that belong to VRFs associated with these address-families must be redistributed into BGP if they are to be advertised across the PE-router's MP-iBGP sessions to other PE-routers.

Putting this all together, you can see the final configuration for the SuperCom San Jose PE-router in Example 9-20.

Example 9-20 *Final Configuration for the SuperCom San Jose PE-router*

```
hostname San Jose
!
ip vrf Eurobank
 rd 1:27
 route-target export 100:27
 route-target import 100:27
!
ip vrf FastFoods
 rd 1:26
 route-target export 100:26
 route-target import 100:26
!
interface loopback0
 ip address 194.22.15.2 255.255.255.255
!
interface serial0
 description ** interface to Eurobank San Francisco**
 ip vrf forwarding EuroBank
 ip address 10.2.1.5 255.255.255.252
!
interface serial1
 description ** interface to FastFoods San Jose**
 ip vrf forwarding FastFoods
 ip address 195.12.2.5 255.255.255.252
!
router rip
```

continues

Example 9-20 *Final Configuration for the SuperCom San Jose PE-router (Continued)*

```
 version 2
 !
address-family ipv4 vrf EuroBank
 version 2
 redistribute bgp 1 metric 1
 network 10.0.0.0
 no auto-summary
exit-address-family
!
address-family ipv4 vrf FastFoods
 version 2
 redistribute bgp 1 metric 1
 network 195.12.2.0
 no auto-summary
exit-address-family
!
router bgp 1
 no bgp default ipv4-unicast
 neighbor 194.22.15.3 remote-as 1
 neighbor 194.22.15.3 update-source loopback0
 neighbor 194.22.15.3 activate
 neighbor 194.22.15.1 remote-as 1
 neighbor 194.22.15.1 update-source loopback0
 !
address-family ipv4 vrf EuroBank
 redistribute rip metric 1
 no auto-summary
 no synchronization
exit-address-family
!
address-family ipv4 vrf FastFoods
 redistribute rip metric 1
 no auto-summary
 no synchronization
exit-address-family
!
address-family vpnv4
 neighbor 194.22.15.3 activate
 neighbor 194.22.15.3 send-community extended
 neighbor 194.22.15.1 activate
 neighbor 194.22.15.1 send-community extended
exit-address-family
 !
```

Enhanced BGP Decision Process for VPN-IPv4 Prefixes

The route target BGP extended community and the route distinguisher control the VPN-IPv4 route selection. This process occurs after routes are learned from other PE-routers across MP-iBGP sessions but before these routes are imported into any VRFs.

The first step of the BGP decision process is to group all relevant routes so they can be compared. Before the PE-router can select routes, it has to know which VPN routes exist and which of these routes should be comparable with each other by the BGP selection process. When the PE-router is provisioned for VPN service, each VRF is configured with statements that tell the PE-router which routes should be imported into the VRF. You already know that the route target BGP extended community controls this import process. Armed with this information, the PE-router does the following:

- Takes all routes with the same route target as any of the import statements within the VRF.

- Considers all routes that have the same route distinguisher as the one assigned to the VRF being processed.

- Creates new BGP paths with a Route Distinguisher that is equal to the Route Distinguisher configured for the VRF that is being processed.

All the routes are now comparable and, at this point, the BGP selection process is executed.

It is important to understand that this process can influence the amount of memory required to hold VPN routes on the PE-router. If each PE-router uses a different route distinguisher for each VRF of a particular VPN, the amount of memory needed to store all the VPN routes increases. Figure 9-8 provides an example of how the route distinguisher can influence the memory requirements of the PE-router.

Figure 9-8   *Increased PE Memory Requirement with Different Route Distinguisher*

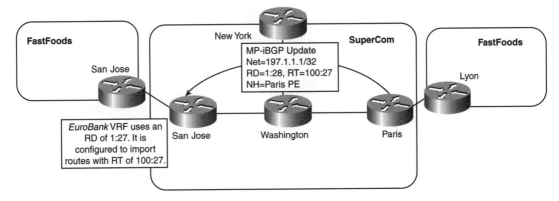

Figure 9-8 shows that the SuperCom San Jose router receives an MP-iBGP update from the Paris PE-router, and this update contains a route target of 100:27 and a route distinguisher of 1:28. The San Jose PE-router is configured to import any routes with a route target of 100:27 into the EuroBank VRF, and this it does. However, the BGP table contains two paths, one with a route distinguisher of 1:28 (the original one received) and another with a route distinguisher of 1:27, which is the route distinguisher for the EuroBank VRF on this PE-router. See Example 9-21.

Example 9-21 *Increased PE Memory with Different Route Distinguishers*

```
San Jose# show ip bgp vpnv4 all
BGP table version is 31, local router ID is 194.22.15.2
Status codes: s suppressed, d damped, h history, * valid, > best, i - internal
Origin codes: i - IGP, e - EGP, ? - incomplete

   Network          Next Hop          Metric LocPrf Weight Path
Route Distinguisher: 1:27 (default for vrf EuroBank)
*>i197.1.1.1/32     194.22.15.1                   0    100     0 ?
Route Distinguisher: 1:28
*>i197.1.1.1/32     194.22.15.1                   0    100     0 ?

San Jose# show ip bgp vpnv4 all 197.1.1.1
BGP routing table entry for 1:27:197.1.1.1/32, version 31
Paths: (1 available, best #1, table EuroBank)
  Advertised to non peer-group peers:
  10.2.1.25
  Local, imported path from 1:28:197.1.1.1/32
    194.22.15.1 (metric 10) from 194.22.15.1 (197.1.1.1)
      Origin incomplete, metric 0, localpref 100, valid, internal, best
      Extended Community: RT:100:27

BGP routing table entry for 1:28:197.1.1.1/32, version 30
Paths: (1 available, best #1, table NULL)
  Not advertised to any peer
  Local
    194.22.15.1 (metric 10) from 194.22.15.1 (197.1.1.1)
      Origin incomplete, metric 0, localpref 100, valid, internal, best
      Extended Community: RT:100:27
```

After the best routes are selected, the import process begins. This involves the process of importing routes into all VRFs and filtering any unwanted routing information from particular VRFs.

Outbound Route Filtering (ORF) and Route Refresh Features

One of the features that helps scale the MPLS/VPN architecture is its capability to keep only the relevant routes in the PE-router—each router keeps only routes for VPNs that are connected to that router. This scalability feature is achieved by importing only the VPN-IPv4 routes that are relevant to the VRFs that are configured on the PE-router.

However, the problem with this model is that all BGP routes are kept within the BGP table even though they are not used by any of the VRFs or by the global routing table. This is quite obviously a waste of resources, both in terms of memory on the PE-routers and in the advertisement of this information across the backbone to PE-routers that do not use it.

With this in mind, it obviously is desirable either to not receive or to filter any unwanted routes from the BGP table of the PE-router. You can do this a number of ways, some of which we discuss in this chapter. You can use other, more advanced options, such as the partitioning of MP-iBGP sessions between PE-routers and the deployment of route reflectors, each of which is discussed in Chapter 12.

Automatic Route Filtering on PE-routers

Because some PE-routers might receive routing information they do not require, a basic requirement is to be able to filter the MP-iBGP updates at the ingress to the PE-router so that the router does not need to keep this information in memory. Although other mechanisms exist, such as the ones discussed in Chapter 12, that prevent the PE-router from actually receiving unwanted routing information, this method might be appropriate if the size or the complexity of the network does not justify partitioning the network into segments. It also might be appropriate if the VPN information is scattered in a topology that is difficult to partition.

The *Automatic Route Filtering* feature fulfills this filtering requirement. This feature is available by default on all PE-routers, and no additional configuration is necessary to enable it. Its function is to filter automatically VPN-IPv4 routes that contain a route target extended community that does not match any of the PE's configured VRFs. This effectively discards any unwanted VPN-IPv4 routes silently, thus reducing the amount of information that the PE has to store in memory. Figure 9-9 shows how this feature is implemented.

Figure 9-9 shows that the New York PE-router receives two MP-iBGP updates. It has only one VRF configured, and it belongs to the NYBank VRF, which imports routes that contain a route target of 100:26 or 100:28.

The first update, sent by the San Jose PE-router, contains a route with a route target of 100:26. This route is accepted and imported into the NYBank VRF. The second update, sent by the Paris PE-router, contains a route with a route target of 100:27. Because the NYBank VRF is not configured to import routes that contain this route target, and because the New York PE-router has no other VRFs that use this particular route target, the update is dropped. Example 9-22 provides an example showing the update being rejected because the route target is not relevant to the New York PE-router.

Figure 9-9 *Automatic Route Filtering Feature*

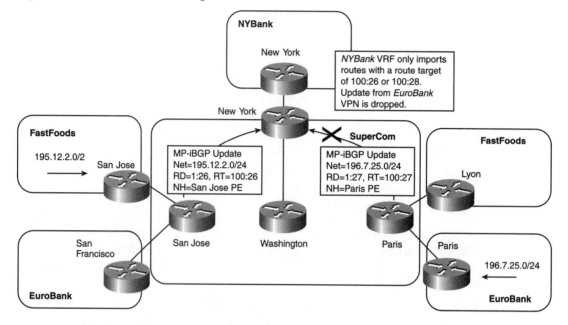

Example 9-22 *Automatic Route Filtering Feature Debug*

```
New York# debug ip bgp update

BGP(1): 10.4.1.21 rcvd UPDATE w/ attr: nexthop 10.4.1.21,
origin ?, localpref 100, metric 0, extended community RT:100:27
BGP(1): 10.4.1.21 rcvd 1:27:196.7.25.0/24 -- DENIED due to
:  extended community not supported;
```

But what if the PE-router is acting as a route reflector for other PE-routers? In this case, if it were to filter the routes automatically, the routing information would be lost. Therefore, the Automatic Route Filtering feature is acceptable only on a normal PE-router, and is disabled if the PE-router acts as a route reflector of VPN-IPv4 prefixes.

As with all service provider networks, it is safe to assume that VPN policies and VRF configurations change over time. The policy change might mean that a new customer is added (or deleted) to the VPN service, or it might mean that an existing VPN customer has a new site that needs to be commissioned into the backbone. In either case, the propagation of routing information changes, and certain PE-routers within the network need to import this information. If you refer to Figure 9-9, an example of this type of change might be that the EuroBank VPN customer needs to commission a new site in New York. Because the SuperCom New York PE-router is the best entry point into the MPLS/VPN backbone for this location, this new site is added to the New York PE-router.

The implications of this are that the New York PE-router needs all relevant routes that belong to the EuroBank VPN. However, because the New York PE-router did not have any VRFs previously configured that imported the route target used for the EuroBank VPN, it discards all routing information that was relevant to the EuroBank VPN. Therefore, further mechanisms are required in conjunction with the Automatic Route Filtering feature and these are the route refresh and ORF features.

Refreshing Routing Information Between PE-routers

When the policy of a PE-router changes, such as a new VRF is added or an existing one is modified, the PE-router needs to obtain routing information that it previously discarded. The PE-router achieves this by using a new BGP capability known as *Route Refresh*.

When this feature is used, the PE-router, shortly after its configuration is changed, requests a retransmission of routing updates from its MP-iBGP neighbors to obtain any missing VPN-IPv4 information. The delay is necessary because several changes to the inbound policy might occur at once, so it is desirable that only one Route Refresh be sent.

The routing information received in response to the Route Refresh is subject still to the filtering mechanisms already described. However, if a new route target is configured on the PE-router for import, for example, then all VPN-IPv4 addresses that contain that route target are no longer filtered at the PE.

NOTE   The Route Refresh feature is actually a new BGP capability and is documented fully in the IETF draft *draft-chen-bgp-route-refresh*. Each PE-router, during the establishment of its iBGP sessions, advertises its ability to execute this capability within its OPEN message.

Figure 9-10 provides an example of this feature, and Example 9-23 illustrates the necessary debug output.

This figure shows that a new VRF, for the EuroBank VPN, is configured on the New York PE-router (Step 1). This router sends a Route Refresh to its MP-iBGP neighbors (Step 2), in this case, the San Jose and Paris routers, which in turn re-send all their VPN-IPv4 routes (Step 3).

Example 9-23   *Route Refresh Capability Debug*

```
New York# debug ip bgp
New York# conf t
Enter configuration commands, one per line.  End with CNTL/Z.
New York(config)#ip vrf EuroBank
New York(config-vrf)# rd 1:27
New York(config-vrf)# route-target both 100:27

BGP: 194.22.15.3 sending REFRESH_REQ for afi/safi: 1/128
```

Figure 9-10 *Route Refresh Capability*

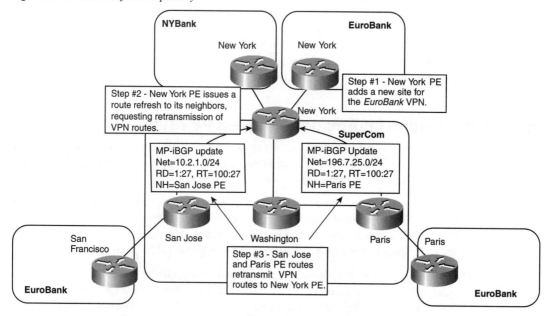

The Route Refresh feature is similar to the Cisco soft reconfiguration feature with the difference that there is no need to store unnecessary routing information on the PE-router. As with the Automatic Route Filtering feature, the Route Refresh feature is on by default and no additional configuration is necessary. Example 9-24 shows this capability using the **show ip bgp neighbor** command.

Example 9-24 *Route Refresh Capability—PE Identification*

```
New York# show ip bgp neighbor 194.22.15.1
BGP neighbor is 2.2.2.2,  remote AS 1, internal link
  BGP version 4, remote router ID 197.1.1.1
  BGP state = Established, up for 00:07:02
  Last read 00:00:02, hold time is 180, keepalive interval is 60
  seconds
  Neighbor capabilities:
    Route refresh: advertised and received
    Address family IPv4 Unicast: advertised and received
    Address family VPNv4 Unicast: advertised and received
  Received 13327 messages, 0 notifications, 0 in queue
  Sent 13434 messages, 0 notifications, 0 in queue
  Route refresh request: received 9, sent 30
  Minimum time between advertisement runs is 5 seconds
```

You also can achieve a manual refresh of VPN routing information using the **clear ip bgp** command. This command has been enhanced for the VPN environment so that it is possible to clear BGP sessions on a per-neighbor basis, or on a per–address-family basis. When this command is issued, all relevant neighbors receive a Route Refresh message and refreshed MP-iBGP or BGP information. Figure 9-11 shows a sample topology.

Figure 9-11 *clear ip bgp Command Enhancements*

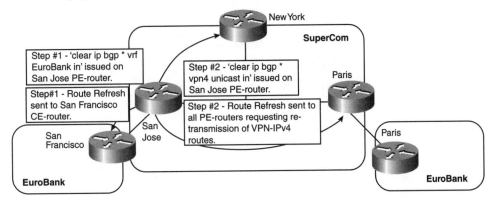

Figure 9-11 shows that the command **clear ip bgp * vrf EuroBank in** is issued on the San Jose PE-router (Step 1). This causes a Route Refresh message to be sent to the San Francisco CE-router because this is the only external neighbor that populates the EuroBank VRF through BGP.

The command **clear ip bgp * vpnv4 unicast in** also is issued on the San Jose PE-router (Step 2). This causes a Route Refresh to be sent to all PE neighbors, in this case the New York and Paris routers. Enhancing this command with a specific neighbor address causes the Route Refresh to be sent to that neighbor only, for example, the **clear ip bgp 2.2.2.2 vpnv4 unicast in** command causes the Route Refresh to be sent to the PE-router with the address 2.2.2.2. No other PE-router receives the Route Refresh message.

ORF for PE-routers

The Route Refresh and Automatic Route Filtering features provide the mechanisms to help reduce the amount of routing information that a PE-router needs to hold. However, they do not provide the capability to stop this routing information from actually arriving at the PE-router. This means that unnecessary routing information is propagated around the network only to be discarded by certain PE-routers.

The ORF feature provides this functionality and it works in conjunction with the previously described Route Refresh feature. Again, this feature is actually a new BGP capability and is exchanged during session establishment between two PE-routers through the use of the BGP OPEN message.

This feature allows a BGP speaker to advertise to downstream neighbors the outbound route filters they should use. These filters are described in **ORF** entries, which are part of the Route Refresh message. Figure 9-12 shows this message format.

Figure 9-12 *ORF Message Format*

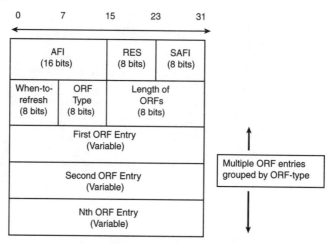

Each ORF entry carries an ORF-type that describes the format of the ORF entry within the message. Table 9-3 shows the currently defined ORF-type.

Table 9-3 *ORF—ORF-type Definitions*

ORF-type	ORF-type Value	Description
NLRI	1	The NLRI ORF-type provides address prefixes based on route filtering.
Communities	2	The Communities ORF-type provides communities-based route filtering.
Extended Communities	3	The Extended Communities ORF-type provides extended community-based route filtering.
Prefix-list	129	The Prefix-list ORF-type provides prefix-list route filtering.

After the Prefix-list ORF capability is advertised by a BGP speaker, its neighbor can push over its inbound prefix-list filter. This is useful between two PE-routers as they will apply the received prefix-list filter, in addition to their locally configured outbound filters (if any), to constrain/filter their outbound routing updates to each other. This mechanism can be used to avoid unwanted routing updates and thus help reduce resources required for routing update generation and processing.

The Extended Communities ORF-type capability is also very useful within the MPLS/VPN architecture. This is because it can filter any routes that contain a route target attribute that is not imported by the receiving PE-router. The advantage of this is that the routes are filtered before being advertised to the receiving PE-router rather than being discarded silently at the PE-router as with the Automatic Route Filtering feature.

The capability to filter routes based on their route target becomes particularly useful when BGP route reflectors are deployed within the MPLS/VPN topology. You can preconfigure each route reflector with a list of route targets that correspond to the routes that the route reflector should reflect between PE-routers. The route reflector treats all its clients, in this case the PE-routers, as a single BGP peer-group and all other route reflectors with which it has sessions as individual peers but not as members of the peer-group.

Because the set of route targets that should be reflected to a particular peer-group was preconfigured on the route reflector already, it can set the outbound route filters that contain the list of the preconfigured route targets on all its neighbor sessions. You can implement this feature using the **rr-group** command, which is discussed fully in Chapter 12.

MPLS/VPN Data Plane—Packet Forwarding

Now that the final configuration is complete, and the VPN routes are propagated across the SuperCom backbone, you can learn how to examine the MPLS label assignment and which labels are present in the label stack.

Figure 9-13 shows a portion of the example topology, which you can use to identify this label assignment. The EuroBank Paris site injects subnet 196.7.25.0/24 into the MPLS/VPN backbone, which is advertised subsequently to the EuroBank San Francisco site. The figure shows the relevant label assignments, and you can see the relevant IOS commands to see these assignments in the examples that follow.

From the perspective of the SuperCom San Jose PE-router, you can see in Example 9-25 that you can use the **show ip bgp vpnv4** *vrf-name* **tags** command to identify which VPN tag is assigned (by the originating PE-router) to the route. In the example, a tag of 38 is assigned to subnet 196.7.25.0/24. You can see this by examining the **Out tag** field in the command output.

Example 9-25 *show ip bgp vpnv4* vrf-name *Command*

```
San Jose# show ip bgp vpnv4 vrf EuroBank tags

  Network          Next Hop      In tag/Out tag
```

continues

Example 9-25 *show ip bgp vpnv4* vrf-name *Command (Continued)*

```
Route Distinguisher: 1:27 (EuroBank)
   10.2.1.0/24       0.0.0.0          38/aggregate(EuroBank)
   196.7.25.0        194.22.15.1      notag/38
```

Figure 9-13 *MPLS/VPN Label Assignment—Data Plane Forwarding*

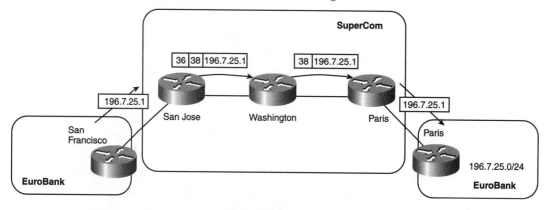

The BGP next-hop for the 196.7.25.0/24 subnet is 194.22.15.1, which is the loopback address of the SuperCom Paris PE-router. This next-hop address was learned via the SuperCom IGP and, therefore, the **show tag-switching forwarding-table** command must be used to identify the IGP label that is used to forward any packets destined for the 196.7.25.0/24 subnet. Example 9-26 shows the output for this command for the SuperCom San Jose router and for the Washington P-router that is in the path to the Paris PE-router. The example also shows the forwarding table for the Paris PE-router and highlights the 196.7.25.0/24 subnet as a VPN route by the [V].

Example 9-26 *show tag-switching forwarding-table Command*

```
San Jose# show tag-switching forwarding-table

Local  Outgoing     Prefix          Bytes tag  Outgoing   Next Hop
tag    tag or VC    or Tunnel Id    switched   interface
33     36           194.22.15.1/32      0      AT1/0/0.1  point2point
38     Aggregate    10.2.1.0/24[V]    3120

Washington# show tag-switching forwarding-table

Local  Outgoing     Prefix          Bytes tag  Outgoing   Next Hop
tag    tag or VC    or Tunnel Id    switched   interface
36     Pop tag      194.22.15.1/32    9416     AT0/1/0.1  point2point

Paris# show tag-switching forwarding-table
```

Example 9-26 *show tag-switching forwarding-table Command*

```
Local  Outgoing    Prefix            Bytes tag  Outgoing   Next Hop
tag    tag or VC   or Tunnel Id      switched   interface
38     Aggregate   196.7.25.0/24[V]  1040
```

Summary

This chapter augments the generic MPLS/VPN architecture presented in Chapter 8 with detailed protocol information and a description of the configuration tasks needed to implement a working MPLS/VPN backbone. The following are the necessary IOS configuration tasks:

- Create a VRF for every unique set of sites (each set of sites belongs to the same set of VPNs, and therefore shares exactly the same routing information and can share a VPN Routing and Forwarding table).

- Assign a unique route distinguisher to each VRF.

- Specify import and export policies for each VRF. The import policy controls the import of routes into per-VRF routing tables based on the extended communities (route targets) attached to the route. The export policy specifies the set of extended communities (route targets) that need to be attached to each route that is exported from the VRF (into the MP-BGP database).

- Establish BGP connectivity between the provider edge routers. This task is usually part of a larger design process that also establishes the desired iBGP topology to allow the network to scale as it grows (see Chapter 12 for more details on building scalable MPLS/VPN networks).

- Establish MP-iBGP between the PE-routers and allow the exchange of VPN-IPv4 routes between them.

- Configure a per-VRF routing process (or instance) for each VRF or specify the static per-VRF routes for each customer site.

- Configure the per-VRF instance of the BGP routing process and specify the redistribution of VRF routes into the BGP routing process. In some network designs, you also have to configure the redistribution from BGP into the per-VRF routing process.

In some redundant scenarios, you also have to configure the SOO setting and filter to prevent routing loops. See Chapter 10 for more details on these configurations.

Provider Edge (PE) to Customer Edge (CE) Connectivity Options

VPN Customer Access into the MPLS/VPN Backbone

We have seen in previous chapters how VPN customer routes are propagated around an MPLS/VPN backbone network, through the use of MP-BGP. These routes are taken from VPN routing and forwarding instances (VRFs), with which customer sites are associated. The population of these forwarding tables is achieved through advertisement of VPN routes across the backbone network, as discussed in Chapter 9, "MPLS/VPN Architecture Operation," and also from the receipt of routing updates from attached customers (or through static routing).

There are currently four separate ways that an MPLS/VPN backbone can receive routes from a VPN customer CE-router: BGP-4, RIP Version 2, OSPF, and static routing. In the last chapter, we examined two of these options—namely, static routing and RIP Version 2. The last two options, BGP-4 and OSPF, will be examined in this chapter. We'll also review the design choices that are available using all four possible PE-to-CE connectivity options.

NOTE   Further options may become available over time, including the support of Enhanced IGRP and Intermediate System-to-Intermediate System (IS-IS).

Regardless of which protocol is used between the PE- and CE-routers, customer VPN routes will be placed into the VRF that is associated with the interface to which the CE-router is attached. This requires that the routing protocol processes that run on the PE-router be configured so that any routing information learned from this interface can be associated with a particular VRF. We saw in the previous chapter that this is achieved through the standard routing protocol process, either as a separate process or as a routing context within the process. A separate routing context, or process, is used per VRF.

When the VRF has been populated with any routes, these routes must be advertised across the MP-iBGP sessions to other PE-routers as VPN-IPv4 (also referred to as VPNv4) prefixes. To allow this to happen, a representation of the routing context must be configured within the BGP process configuration to tell BGP which VRF routes to advertise. We saw in the previous chapter that this is achieved through the use of address families and the redistribution of routes from a particular routing context, or process, into MP-iBGP.

The redistribution of routes into MP-iBGP is necessary only when the routes are learned through any means other than BGP between the PE- and CE-routers. This includes connected subnets and static routes. In the case of routes that are learned via BGP from the CE-router, redistribution is not required because it is performed automatically, although the routing context and the BGP neighbors must be configured within the BGP process through use of an address family.

Again, a sample topology will be used throughout the first section of this chapter to assist in the explanation of the various connectivity options and their configuration. This sample topology can be seen in Figure 10-1, with all relevant address ranges for each VPN customer shown in Table 10-1.

Figure 10-1 *PE-to-CE Connectivity Options—Sample Topology*

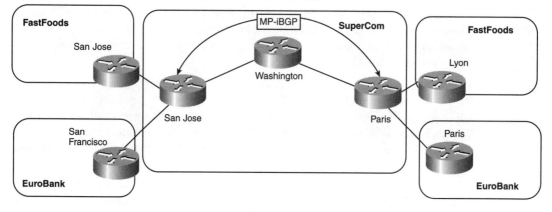

Table 10-1 *IP Address Assignment for SuperCom VPN Customers*

Company	Site	Subnet
FastFoods	San Jose	195.12.2.0/24
	Lyon	10.2.1.0/24
EuroBank	San Francisco	10.2.1.0/24
	Paris	196.7.25.0/24
SuperCom	Paris (Loopback 0)	194.22.15.1/32
	San Jose (Loopback 0)	194.22.15.2/32

BGP-4 Between Service Provider and Customer Networks

A certain number of customers that attach to the MPLS/VPN backbone will want to run BGP-4 with the service provider and exchange VPN routes across these BGP-4 sessions. Later in this chapter, we will see a sample network deployment in which this type of connectivity may be attractive, or even necessary, for the customer. With this option, all the routes that are learned from the customer CE-router will be advertised across the MPLS/VPN backbone using any existing MP-iBGP sessions between service provider PE-routers (or route reflectors). Figure 10-2 provides an illustration of this type of connectivity.

Figure 10-2   *BGP-4 Between CE- and PE-routers*

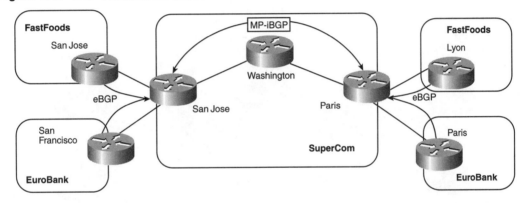

As can be seen in Figure 10-2, both the FastFoods and EuroBank VPN customers attach to the SuperCom MPLS/VPN backbone using BGP-4. With this configuration, any routes learned across the session with the EuroBank CE-routers will be placed into the VRF associated with this customer. Likewise, any routes learned across the session with the FastFoods CE-routers will be placed into these customers' respective VRF.

From the standpoint of the VPN customer, this is just a standard exterior BGP-4 session with which the exchange of IPv4 prefixes can be achieved. However, from the PE-router's perspective, although the session is a standard exterior BGP-4 session, it must understand which VPN customer the session belongs to and into which VRF the routes should be placed when received from the BGP neighbor. As with the static and RIP Version 2 examples that we saw in the previous chapter, this is achieved through the use of a routing context that is represented through an address family under the BGP process configuration.

There are two main requirements for BGP configuration in an MPLS/VPN environment. The first is the configuration of MP-iBGP sessions between PE-routers; the second is the configuration of BGP between PE- and CE-routers. To achieve this second objective, the

address family must be configured under the BGP process for each VRF that will receive
routes from a VPN customer using BGP-4.

NOTE   A separate address family entry is used per VRF, and each address family entry could have
multiple BGP neighbors (customer CE-routers) within the VRF.

Using the address assignments from Table 10-1 for the VPN customers FastFoods and
EuroBank, we can see in Figure 10-3 the necessary BGP sessions between the SuperCom
San Jose and Paris PE-routers, and each of the VPN customers.

Figure 10-3   *BGP-4 Address Assignment Between PE- and CE-routers*

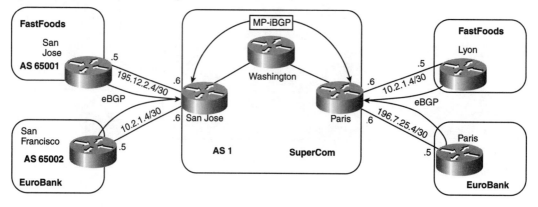

Given the address assignments within Figure 10-3, the PE-router configuration, similar to
the one in Example 10-1, can be used to configure BGP routing on the SuperCom San Jose
PE-router. Notice within this configuration the use of address families under the BGP
process for each VPN customer, and the relevant BGP session configurations for each
customer under the address-family.

Example 10-1   *PE-to-CE BGP-4 Configuration Example*

```
hostname San Jose
!
interface serial0
 description ** interface to FastFoods San Jose **
 ip vrf forwarding FastFoods
 ip address 195.12.2.6 255.255.255.252
!
interface serial 1
 description ** interface to EuroBank San Francisco **
 ip vrf forwarding EuroBank
 ip address 10.2.1.6 255.255.255.252
```

Example 10-1 *PE-to-CE BGP-4 Configuration Example (Continued)*

```
!
router bgp 1
 no bgp default ipv4-unicast
 neighbor 194.22.15.1 remote-as 1
 neighbor 194.22.15.1 update-source loopback0
 !
 address-family ipv4 vrf EuroBank
 neighbor 10.2.1.5 remote-as 65002
 neighbor 10.2.1.5 activate
 no auto-summary
 no synchronization
 exit-address-family
 !
 address-family ipv4 vrf FastFoods
 neighbor 195.12.2.5 remote-as 65001
 neighbor 195.12.2.5 activate
 no auto-summary
 no synchronization
 exit-address-family
 !
 address-family vpnv4
 neighbor 194.22.15.1 activate
 neighbor 194.22.15.1 send-community extended
 exit-address-family
```

As can be seen from Example 10-1, the SuperCom San Jose PE-router has an eBGP session with the EuroBank San Francisco CE-router. Any routes learned over this session will be placed into the EuroBank VRF. A further eBGP session exists with the FastFoods San Jose CE-router, and any routes learned across this session will be placed into the FastFoods VRF.

NOTE   The BGP-4 session between the PE- and CE-routers must be directly connected. BGP multihop is not currently supported on BGP sessions between PE- and CE-routers.

Example 10-2 provides confirmation that the BGP-4 session between the PE- and CE-router (for the EuroBank VRF) is established and that IPv4 routes will be placed into the relevant VRF.

Example 10-2 *show ip bgp neighbor Confirmation of PE-to-CE BGP-4 Session*

```
San Jose# show ip bgp neighbor
BGP neighbor is 10.2.1.5, vrf EuroBank, remote AS 65002, external link
  BGP version 4, remote router ID 10.2.1.5
  BGP state = Established, up for 00:00:38
  Last read 00:00:37,hold time is 180, keepalive interval is 60 seconds
```

continues

Example 10-2   *show ip bgp neighbor Confirmation of PE-to-CE BGP-4 Session (Continued)*

```
Neighbor capabilities:
   Route refresh: advertised and received
   Address family IPv4 Unicast: advertised and received
Received 4 messages, 0 notifications, 0 in queue
Sent 3 messages, 0 notifications, 0 in queue
Route refresh request: received 0, sent 0
Minimum time between advertisement runs is 30 seconds

For address family: VPNv4 Unicast
Translates address family IPv4 Unicast for VRF EuroBank
BGP table version 3, neighbor version 3
Index 1, Offset 0, Mask 0x2
1 accepted prefixes consume 60 bytes
Prefix advertised 0, suppressed 0, withdrawn 0
Connections established 1; dropped 0
Last reset never
```

Open Shortest Path First (OSPF) Between PE- and CE-routers

The last (currently available) PE-to-CE connectivity option to consider is the use of the Open Shortest Path First (OSPF) protocol. This option may be desirable to customers who already run OSPF within each of their sites and still want to exchange routing information between these sites using this protocol, without having to redistribute OSPF information into other protocols such as BGP-4 or RIP Version 2. If the MPLS/VPN backbone is used to connect the sites, then redistribution is not a requirement as the backbone links may be used for traffic, even if "back-door" links exist between the VPN sites, because the routes are viewed as inter-area rather than external.

The desire to restrict the amount of redistribution can be extremely important in an OSPF environment. Whenever a route is redistributed into OSPF, it is done so as an external OSPF route. The OSPF protocol dictates that external routes must be flooded across the whole OSPF domain, which increases the overhead of the protocol as well as the CPU load on all routers participating in the OSPF domain. To try to overcome this, certain area types, such as stub or totally stubby areas, can be deployed so that external routes are not sent into the area. However, this can have the drawback of sub-optimal routing because the area does not have the full topology information to make a decision on the best exit point toward the OSPF backbone for a particular external route.

Using the VPN overlay model, service providers have been capable of providing the infrastructure that can be used for the exchange of routing information between VPN customer sites. With this model, customer site routers form routing adjacencies with other site routers across Frame Relay/ATM virtual circuits and then directly exchange IP prefix information between CE-routers across these adjacencies using the OSPF protocol. With the introduction of an MPLS/VPN backbone, and hence a peer-to-peer VPN model, the exchange of site routing information becomes a challenge: Direct adjacencies between sites can no longer be formed because no direct virtual circuits exist. This means that a further mechanism is required to allow OSPF to function in this environment and to provide a seamless integration of OSPF sites into the MPLS/VPN infrastructure.

The goal of this enhancement must be to provide the same functionality within OSPF (from a customer's perspective) as seen when the overlay model is deployed, except that this functionality is provided through use of the peer-to-peer VPN model. This means that all internal VPN customer routes that belong to the same OSPF domain must be seen as either intra-area (LSA type 1 or type 2) or inter-area (LSA type 3) routes, and all external routes must be seen as either LSA type 5 or LSA type 7 routes.

NOTE	In topologies where the overlay model was previously used within the customer site, support of the OSPF protocol on the PE-to-CE link may actually reduce the complexity of a VPN customer's OSPF deployment. This will depend on how the overlay model was previously used.

In the case of point-to-point links, where multiple sub-interfaces are necessary between site routers, these links are no longer required with the introduction of MPLS/VPN because the CE-router will form a point-to-point adjacency with the PE-router. This means smaller interface configuration and fewer adjacencies for the OSPF protocol. It also implies less flooding in the event of a route change within the OSPF domain because fewer links exist within the topology.

In the case where non-broadcast multi-access (NBMA) is deployed, whether broadcast or non-broadcast, careful selection of the OSPF designated router (DR) and backup designated router (BDR) is necessary. However, with the introduction of MPLS/VPN, the PE-to-CE link will, in most cases, become a point-to-point link. Therefore, manipulation of the OSPF priority is no longer necessary because no designated router will exist. In the case where different sites are connected to the same PE-router across an NBMA network, then manipulation of the OSPF priority may still be a requirement.

The routing information learned from customer sites via OSPF is placed into the VRF that is associated with the incoming interface. This is exactly the same mechanism as is used for the other PE-to-CE connectivity options that we have already seen. These routes are then advertised across the MPLS/VPN backbone between PE-routers using MP-iBGP and are imported into relevant VRFs on other PE-routers.

To support PE-to-CE OSPF connectivity in an MPLS/VPN environment, an additional level of routing hierarchy is required for VPN sites to run independent OSPF processes and learn routes from other sites without a direct adjacency. The OSPF protocol already provides two levels of hierarchy: the backbone area 0 and any attached areas. A third level of hierarchy is provided so that we can connect sites within an MPLS/VPN backbone topology. This extra level of hierarchy is on top of area 0 (if area 0 exists).

Multiple OSPF area 0s are possible with this type of configuration, and each site may choose to run an independent area 0. However, it is mandatory that any site area 0 be attached directly with the MPLS/VPN backbone so that a partitioned area 0 topology is avoided. Based on this, two different topologies can be used—one that connects sites that utilize an area 0, and one for sites that do not. Both of these topologies are illustrated in Figure 10-4.

Figure 10-4   *PE-to-CE Connectivity—OSPF Topology Choices*

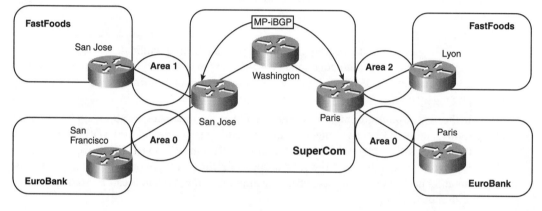

We can see from Figure 10-4 that both the FastFoods and EuroBank VPN customers are running OSPF with the SuperCom MPLS/VPN backbone, but each customer is using a different connectivity option.

- The FastFoods VPN sites are attached to the MPLS/VPN backbone through their respective areas, and no area 0 is used at either site (Option 1).

- The EuroBank VPN sites each run an OSPF area 0 that includes their PE-to-CE link with the SuperCom backbone (Option 2).

Separation of VPN Customer Routing Information

Whichever of the two connectivity options are chosen (we will look at each in detail in the sections that follow), a mechanism is needed so that the PE-router can distinguish which routes belong to which VRF. This is accomplished through association of a particular customer interface to a specific VRF (per the standard MPLS/VPN model that we have already described) and to a particular OSPF process.

A separate OSPF process is necessary for each VRF that will receive VPN routes via OSPF. This is different than the procedures used when either RIP Version 2 or BGP are deployed across the PE-to-CE link because these protocols can run different routing contexts within the same process. Due to the complexity of OSPF and the associated topology database, this option is not currently available, so a different OSPF process (with a different process-ID) is required per VRF. To support this requirement, an extension to the **router ospf** command has been provided, as shown in Example 10-3.

Example 10-3 *Extension to **router ospf** Command*

```
San Jose(config)# router ospf ospf-Process-ID VRF vrf-name
```

Using the example topology shown in Figure 10-4, we can see in Example 10-4 the use of the **router ospf** command to set up the relevant OSPF processes for the EuroBank and FastFoods VPN customers on the San Jose PE-router.

Example 10-4 *Configuration of OSPF Processes for VPN Customers*

```
hostname San Jose
!
ip vrf EuroBank
 rd 1:27
 route-target export 100:27
 route-target import 100:27
!
ip vrf FastFoods
 rd 1:26
 route-target export 100:26
 route-target export 100:26
!
interface serial 1/0
 description ** interface to EuroBank San Francisco**
 ip vrf forwarding EuroBank
 ip address 10.2.1.5 255.255.255.252
!
interface serial 1/1
 description ** interface to FastFoods San Jose**
 ip vrf forwarding FastFoods
 ip address 195.12.2.5 255.255.255.252
!
router ospf 200 vrf EuroBank
 network 10.2.1.4 0.0.0.3 area 0
!
router ospf 100 vrf FastFoods
 network 195.12.2.4 0.0.0.3 area 1
```

Given the configuration in Example 10-4, we can see in Example 10-5 both OSPF processes and the number of interfaces in each process through use of the **show ip ospf** command.

Example 10-5 *show ip ospf Confirmation of Multiple OSPF Processes*

```
San Jose# show ip ospf

Routing Process "ospf 100" with ID 195.12.2.5
 Supports only single TOS(TOS0) routes
 Supports opaque LSA
 Connected to MPLS VPN Superbackbone
 It is an area border router
 SPF schedule delay 5 secs, Hold time between two SPFs 10 secs
 Minimum LSA interval 5 secs. Minimum LSA arrival 1 secs
 Number of external LSA 0. Checksum Sum 0x0
 Number of opaque AS LSA 0. Checksum Sum 0x0
 Number of DCbitless external and opaque AS LSA 0
 Number of DoNotAge external and opaque AS LSA 0
 Number of areas in this router is 1. 1 normal 0 stub 0 nssa
 External flood list length 0
    Area 1
        Number of interfaces in this area is 1
        Area has no authentication
        SPF algorithm executed 2 times
        Area ranges are
        Number of LSA 1. Checksum Sum 0xC4E7
        Number of opaque link LSA 0. Checksum Sum 0x0
        Number of DCbitless LSA 0
        Number of indication LSA 0
        Number of DoNotAge LSA 0

Routing Process "ospf 200" with ID 10.2.1.5
 Supports only single TOS(TOS0) routes
 Supports opaque LSA
 Connected to MPLS VPN Superbackbone
 It is an area border router
 SPF schedule delay 5 secs, Hold time between two SPFs 10 secs
 Minimum LSA interval 5 secs. Minimum LSA arrival 1 secs
 Number of external LSA 1. Checksum Sum 0xCAE8
 Number of opaque AS LSA 0. Checksum Sum 0x0
 Number of DCbitless external and opaque AS LSA 0
 Number of DoNotAge external and opaque AS LSA 0
 Number of areas in this router is 1. 1 normal 0 stub 0 nssa
 External flood list length 0
    Area BACKBONE(0)
        Number of interfaces in this area is 1
        Area has no authentication
        SPF algorithm executed 6 times
        Area ranges are
        Number of LSA 7. Checksum Sum 0x4A01D
        Number of opaque link LSA 0. Checksum Sum 0x0
        Number of DCbitless LSA 0
```

Example 10-5 *show ip ospf Confirmation of Multiple OSPF Processes (Continued)*

```
Number of indication LSA 0
Number of DoNotAge LSA 0
Flood list length 0
```

When the relevant OSPF processes have been configured on the PE-router, it is now possible to learn routes from the CE-router using OSPF. These routes are placed into the relevant OSPF database, and the VPN customer VRF is populated.

NOTE   Because each OSPF process requires the use of a separate protocol descriptor block (PDB) within IOS, there is a limitation on the number of OSPF processes that can be run on each PE-router. This issue is discussed in detail in Chapter 12, "Advanced MPLS/VPN Topics," in the section "PE-router Provisioning and Scaling."

Propagation of OSPF Routes Across the MPLS/VPN Backbone

As with all other MPLS/VPN deployment options, after the VPN customer routes have been placed into the receiving VRF, they must be advertised to other PE-routers through use of MP-iBGP. Again, this behavior is not automatic, so redistribution between OSPF and BGP is required.

NOTE   It is important to note that the MPLS/VPN backbone is not a real OSPF area 0 backbone. No adjacencies are formed between PE-routers—only between PE- and CE-routers. MP-iBGP is used between PE-routers, and all OSPF routes are translated into VPN-IPv4 routes. This means that the redistribution of routes into BGP does not cause these routes to become external OSPF routes when advertised to other member sites of the same VPN.

The redistribution of VRF OSPF routes into MP-iBGP is achieved through use of the address family within the BGP configuration. Depending on which IOS revision is used, the **redistribute** command may need several options added so that all relevant routes are redistributed into BGP. The configuration for the SuperCom San Jose PE-router can be seen in Example 10-6, which shows the command with all relevant route types added.

Example 10-6 *Redistribution of VRF OSPF Routes into MP-iBGP*

```
hostname San Jose
!
router bgp 1
 no bgp default ipv4-unicast
 neighbor 194.22.15.1 remote-as 1
 neighbor 194.22.15.1 update-source loopback0
 !
 address-family ipv4 vrf EuroBank
 redistribute ospf 200 match internal external 1 external 2
 no auto-summary
 no synchronization
 exit-address-family
 !
 address-family ipv4 vrf FastFoods
 redistribute ospf 100 match internal external 1 external 2
 no auto-summary
 no synchronization
 exit-address-family
```

The final configuration step is to redistribute any routes that are contained within a particular VRF and that have been learned via MP-iBGP to other members of the VPN. This is achieved through the redistribution of routes from BGP into the relevant OSPF process, as shown in Example 10-7.

Example 10-7 *Redistribution of BGP into VRF OSPF Process*

```
hostname San Jose
!
ip vrf EuroBank
 rd 1:27
 route-target export 100:27
 route-target import 100:27
!
ip vrf FastFoods
 rd 1:26
 route-target export 100:26
 route-target export 100:26
!
router ospf 200 vrf EuroBank
 redistribute bgp 1 subnets metric 20
 network 10.2.1.4 0.0.0.3 area 0
!
router ospf 100 vrf FastFoods
 redistribute bgp 1 subnets metric 20
 network 195.12.2.4 0.0.0.3 area 1
```

When this redistribution has been configured, the PE-router becomes an area border router (ABR) and an autonomous system boundary router (ASBR) for the VPN customer site. Example 10-8 provides confirmation of this, and also shows that the EuroBank San Francisco CE-router generates a type-4 LSA (Link State Advertisement) into its attached area 1 for this ASBR.

Example 10-8 *PE-router as Autonomous System Boundary Router (ASBR)*

```
San Jose# show ip ospf

Routing Process "ospf 200" with ID 10.2.1.5
 Supports only single TOS(TOS0) routes
 Supports opaque LSA
 Connected to MPLS VPN Superbackbone
 It is an area border and autonomous system boundary router
 Redistributing External Routes from,
    bgp 1, includes subnets in redistribution

Routing Process "ospf 100" with ID 195.12.2.5
 Supports only single TOS(TOS0) routes
 Supports opaque LSA
 Connected to MPLS VPN Superbackbone
 It is an area border and autonomous system boundary router
 Redistributing External Routes from,
    bgp 1, includes subnets in redistribution

San Francisco# show ip ospf database asbr-summary

OSPF Router with ID (10.3.1.7) (Process ID 100)


                Summary ASB Link States (Area 1)

  LS age: 1339
  Options: (No TOS-capability, DC, Upward)
  LS Type: Summary Links(AS Boundary Router)
  Link State ID: 10.2.1.5 (AS Boundary Router address)
  Advertising Router: 10.3.1.7
  LS Seq Number: 80000002
  Checksum: 0x80B
  Length: 28
  Network Mask: /0
        TOS: 0  Metric: 1
```

BGP Extended Community Attribute for OSPF Routes

Whenever a PE-router receives an MP-iBGP update that contains a prefix learned via OSPF by the originating PE-router, it must be capable of identifying what type of OSPF route is contained within the update. This is necessary to allow the PE-router to generate an appropriate link state advertisement (LSA) toward the VPN customer CE-router based on the OSPF route type received across the MPLS/VPN backbone. OSPF has several route types:

- Inter-area
- Intra-area
- NSSA
- External type 1
- External type 2

To support this requirement, when the PE-router propagates OSPF routes into MP-iBGP through redistribution, the BGP extended community attribute is used to preserve and convey the OSPF attributes of the route. (This attribute was discussed in detail in Chapter 9.) The format of the attribute used for the propagation of OSPF information is as follows, and we will see the operation of this attribute in later sections:

- Extended Community 0x8000
  - 4 bytes: OSPF area number
  - 1 byte: OSPF route type (1 through 7)
  - 1 Byte: Option (used for external metric type)

As we already know, when a PE-router receives an MP-iBGP update, it must execute the BGP decision process to decide the best path to the prefix contained within the update. When this decision process is complete, the best route is passed onto the OSPF selection process for import into any relevant VRFs. Because multiple updates for the same prefix might be received, and because OSPF has its own selection process for differing route types, the BGP decision process has been enhanced to prefer intra-area OSPF routes over inter-area routes over external type 1 over external type 2 routes. This decision process is based on the OSPF route type that is conveyed within the BGP extended community attribute that accompanies the VPN-IPv4 route.

PE-to-CE Connectivity—OSPF with Site Area 0 Support

As previously stated, a couple of topologies may be used to connect VPN sites to the MPLS/VPN backbone. The first of these provides the capability for the VPN customer to run an OSPF area 0 within more than one site and to use the MPLS/VPN backbone as a Level 3 hierarchy, above area 0, to provide the connectivity between sites. With this option, the PE-to-CE link is placed into area 0, which means that the CE-router becomes an area border router (ABR) in area 0 for all other areas at the customer site. It is possible for area 0 to extend past the CE-router. In this case, the CE-router will become a backbone router, and the ABR functionality will be moved to another router somewhere else within the site. This ABR will inject summaries from other areas within the site, and these will be propagated by the CE-router to the PE for onward advertisement across the MPLS/VPN backbone.

The PE-router becomes an ASBR for the OSPF-MPLS/VPN backbone, although from the CE-router's perspective, it acts as an ABR when propagating inter-area routes between sites. This means that another site looks exactly like a non-backbone area being linked to the per-site area 0 by the PE-router acting as the ABR.

With this type of connectivity, the PE- and CE-routers form an OSPF adjacency and exchange link state advertisements (LSA) across the adjacency. The CE-router propagates summary LSAs for routes coming from the site areas toward the PE-router, and the PE-router generates summary LSAs or external LSAs for any routes coming from the OSPF-MPLS/VPN backbone. An illustration of this mechanism can be seen in Figure 10-5.

Figure 10-5   *OSPF PE-to-CE with Site Area 0 Support*

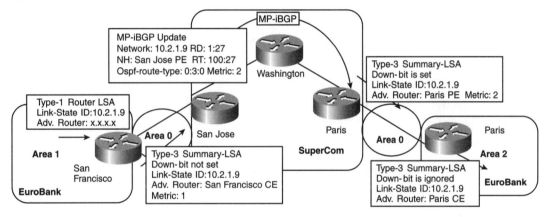

Figure 10-5 shows that the EuroBank San Francisco ABR generates a type 3 summary LSA for network 10.2.1.9 across the PE-to-CE link to the SuperCom San Jose PE-router.

This summary LSA can be seen in Example 10-9.

Example 10-9   *Summary LSA Across PE-to-CE Link*

```
San Jose# show ip ospf database summary 10.2.1.9

        OSPF Router with ID (10.2.1.5) (Process ID 200)


               Summary Net Link States (Area 0)

   Routing Bit Set on this LSA
   LS age: 214
   Options: (No TOS-capability, DC, Upward)
   LS Type: Summary Links(Network)
   Link State ID: 10.2.1.9 (summary Network Number)
```

continues

Example 10-9 *Summary LSA Across PE-to-CE Link (Continued)*

```
Advertising Router: 10.3.1.7
LS Seq Number: 80000025
Checksum: 0xA745
Length: 28
Network Mask: /32
      TOS: 0  Metric: 1
```

Example 10-10 shows that this route is placed into the EuroBank VRF and also into MP-iBGP through redistribution. The output highlights the use of the BGP 0x8000 extended community attribute for OSPF routes and shows that the 10.2.1.9/32 prefix is an inter-area route with route type 3.

Example 10-10 *Population of VRF with OSPF Routes*

```
San Jose# show ip route vrf EuroBank 10.2.1.9

Routing entry for 10.2.1.9/32
  Known via "ospf 200", distance 110, metric 2, type inter area
  Redistributing via ospf 200
  Last update from 10.2.1.6 on FastEthernet0/0, 00:02:47 ago
  Routing Descriptor Blocks:
  * 10.2.1.6, from 10.3.1.7, 00:02:47 ago, via FastEthernet0/0
      Route metric is 2, traffic share count is 1

San Jose# show ip bgp vpnv4 vrf EuroBank 10.2.1.9
BGP routing table entry for 1:27:10.2.1.9/32, version 64
Paths: (1 available, best #1, table EuroBank)
  Advertised to non peer-group peers:
  194.22.15.1
  Local
    10.2.1.6 from 0.0.0.0 (195.22.15.2)
      Origin incomplete, metric 2, localpref 100, weight 32768, valid,
      sourced, best
      Extended Community: RT:100:27 OSPF RT:0:3:0
```

Because inter-site routes may be advertised into a site from various locations, it is necessary to provide a mechanism that allows a PE-router to understand whether the route has actually originated from within the attached site, or whether it was injected by another PE-router. This mechanism is provided through use of the down-bit, which is an extension to the OSPF protocol and is part of the Options field of the generic LSA header. Any summary LSAs that are generated by the PE-routers will have the down-bit set within the LSA. As shown in Figure 10-6, this is necessary to prevent routing loops. The PE will propagate summary LSAs received from the CE into the OSPF-MPLS/VPN backbone *only* if the down-bit is *not* set.

NOTE   The down-bit is necessary only if customer CE-routers have connectivity to each other within area 0 and also have attachment to other non-backbone areas. This is because of the rule in OSPF that states: If an ABR receives a summary LSA from a non-backbone area, it should ignore the summary if it has connectivity to area 0. If the PE-to-CE link is within area 0, then this will be the case. In other situations, the down-bit may not be necessary, but the IOS implementation will set the down-bit for ALL summary LSAs that the PE-router generates, regardless of the topology of the site.

Figure 10-6   *Summary LSA Down-bit for Prevention of Loops*

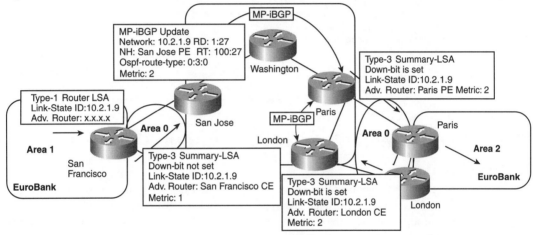

Figure 10-6 shows that the London and Paris PE-routers receive an MP-iBGP update for prefix 10.2.1.9/32 from the San Jose PE-router. In our example, the Paris PE-router generates a type 3 summary LSA into the EuroBank Paris site. This summary LSA is propagated across the site and eventually is received by the London PE-router. If this router for some reason does not have the route within the EuroBank VRF, and if the down-bit were not set, it would accept the route into the VRF and then advertise it to the San Jose and Paris PE-routers as an MP-iBGP update.

The San Jose PE-router would ignore the route because its OSPF route would be preferred. However, the Paris PE-router would now have two MP-iBGP updates for the same prefix, one from the San Jose PE-router and another from the London PE-router. Depending on which one it chose as the best route, a loop potentially would be formed where the Paris PE-router would direct the traffic to the London PE-router, which, in turn, would direct the traffic to the Paris PE-router.

If we take a look at the SuperCom Paris PE-router's summary LSA for the 10.2.1.9/32 prefix, we can see in Example 10-11 that the down-bit has indeed been set.

Example 10-11 *Use of the Down-bit for Summary LSAs*

```
Paris# show ip ospf database summary 10.2.1.9

OSPF Router with ID (10.4.1.9) (Process ID 200)


                 Summary Net Link States (Area 0)

 LS age: 1590
 Options: (No TOS-capability, DC, Downward)
 LS Type: Summary Links(Network)
 Link State ID: 10.2.1.9 (summary Network Number)
 Advertising Router: 10.4.1.9
 LS Seq Number: 80000002
 Checksum: 0x5C2F
 Length: 28
 Network Mask: /32
        TOS: 0  Metric: 2
```

PE-to-CE Connectivity—OSPF Without Site Area 0 Support

The second OSPF connectivity option is to place the PE-to-CE link into a non-backbone area. In this case, the PE-router acts as an ABR (and an ASBR) for the customer site, and forms an adjacency with the CE-router so that it can exchange LSAs. An illustration of this connectivity option can be seen in Figure 10-7.

Figure 10-7 *PE-to-CE Connectivity—Without Site Area 0 Support*

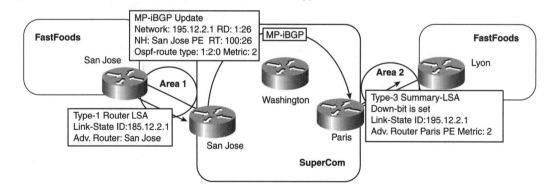

Figure 10-7 shows that the FastFoods San Jose CE-router has an adjacency with the SuperCom San Jose PE-router in OSPF area 1. The Type-1 LSA describing the 195.12.2.1/32 prefix is received by the SuperCom San Jose PE-router and is placed into the FastFoods VRF. This LSA can be seen in Example 10-12.

Example 10-12 *Router LSA for FastFoods San Jose CE-router*

```
San Jose# show ip ospf data router 195.12.2.1

        OSPF Router with ID (195.12.2.5) (Process ID 100)


                Router Link States (Area 1)

  LS age: 1707
  Options: (No TOS-capability, DC)
  LS Type: Router Links
  Link State ID: 195.12.2.1
  Advertising Router: 195.12.2.1
  LS Seq Number: 80000002
  Checksum: 0xE118
  Length: 48
   Number of Links: 2

    Link connected to: a Stub Network
     (Link ID) Network/subnet number: 195.12.2.1
     (Link Data) Network Mask: 255.255.255.255
      Number of TOS metrics: 0
        TOS 0 Metrics: 1

    Link connected to: a Transit Network
     (Link ID) Designated Router address: 195.12.2.5
     (Link Data) Router Interface address: 195.12.2.6
      Number of TOS metrics: 0
        TOS 0 Metrics: 1
```

This route is then redistributed into MP-iBGP and is advertised across the MPLS/VPN backbone as an intra-area route. This is highlighted by the OSPF route type of 1:2:0 shown in Example 10-13, where the 1 signifies that the route belongs to OSPF area 1, and the 2 signifies that the route type is intra-area.

Example 10-13 *Population of VRF with OSPF Routes for Non-area 0 Support*

```
San Jose# show ip route vrf FastFoods 195.12.2.1

Routing entry for 195.12.2.1/32
  Known via "ospf 100", distance 110, metric 2, type intra area
  Redistributing via bgp 1, ospf 100
  Advertised by bgp 1 match internal external 1 & 2
  Last update from 195.12.2.6 on FastEthernet0/0, 00:30:59 ago
  Routing Descriptor Blocks:
```

continues

Example 10-13 *Population of VRF with OSPF Routes for Non-area 0 Support (Continued)*

```
   * 195.12.2.6, from 195.12.2.1, 00:30:59 ago, via FastEthernet0/0
       Route metric is 2, traffic share count is 1

San Jose# show ip bgp vpnv4 vrf FastFoods 195.12.2.1

BGP routing table entry for 1:26:195.12.2.1/32, version 102
Paths: (1 available, best #1, table FastFoods)
  Advertised to non peer-group peers:
  194.22.15.2
  Local
    195.12.2.6 from 0.0.0.0 (194.22.15.1)
      Origin incomplete, metric 2, localpref 100, weight 32768, valid,
      sourced, best
      Extended Community: RT:100:26 OSPF RT:1:2:0
```

When the route is received by the SuperCom Paris PE-router and is imported into the FastFoods VRF, a summary LSA for the route is advertised into the FastFoods site in Lyon. This summary LSA can be seen in Example 10-14.

Example 10-14 *Summary-LSA Across PE to CE Link—Non-area 0 Support*

```
Paris# show ip ospf data summary 195.12.2.1

        OSPF Router with ID (195.12.2.9) (Process ID 100)


                Summary Net Link States (Area 1)

  LS age: 1533
  Options: (No TOS-capability, DC, Downward)
  LS Type: Summary Links(Network)
  Link State ID: 195.12.2.1 (summary Network Number)
  Advertising Router: 195.12.2.9
  LS Seq Number: 80000001
  Checksum: 0xED1F
  Length: 28
  Network Mask: /32
        TOS: 0  Metric: 2
```

VPN Customer Connectivity—MPLS/VPN Design Choices

Now that the basic mechanisms for PE-to-CE connectivity are clear, it is important to understand which method may be appropriate for which type of deployment. To assist with this investigation, a sample VPN topology for a typical VPN customer will be used, as seen in Figure 10-8.

Figure 10-8   *Typical VPN Customer Network Topology*

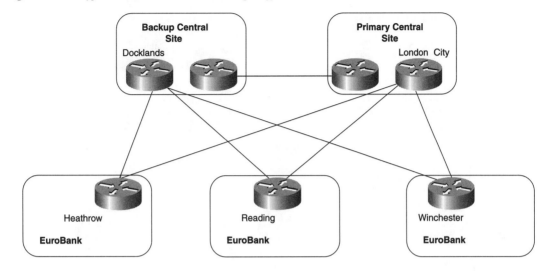

This sample topology shows that EuroBank has two central site locations, connected via Frame Relay to various remote sites. Both central site locations are connected (via fiber), and each remote site has a primary PVC to one central site location and a secondary (shadow) PVC to the backup central site. Routing between sites is provided through use of the EIGRP Interior Gateway Protocol.

The EuroBank VPN customer has decided to migrate its Frame Relay infrastructure to an MPLS/VPN solution to overcome the complexities and limitations of a private network being run across an overlay Frame Relay service. The new network infrastructure, using the SuperCom service provider's MPLS/VPN backbone, can be seen in Figure 10-9.

NOTE   For a review of the limitations of the VPN overlay model (for example, traditional Frame Relay service offered by most service providers today), refer to Chapter 7, "Virtual Private Network (VPN) Implementation Options."

Figure 10-9 *Migrated MPLS/VPN Customer Network Topology*

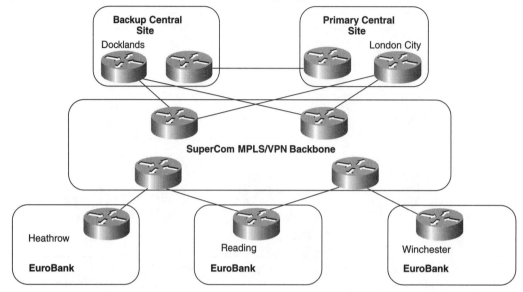

Given this network topology, we need to decide which of the four currently available PE-to-CE connectivity options should be used at each point in the network. As already discussed in the section on OSPF connectivity options, if the VPN customer is already running OSPF within each of its sites, it could decide to continue to use this protocol between PE- and CE-routers. This would be a good design choice in this case for the reasons already discussed in the OSPF section.

In our example, EIGRP is the current IGP, so the customer needs to migrate the routing protocol used across the PE-to-CE links to OSPF, BGP-4, or RIP Version 2, or use static routing so that routes can be exchanged between the EuroBank VPN sites and the SuperCom MPLS/VPN backbone. (Note that this migration is limited to the PE/CE links only.) Given the fact that some of the spoke sites have only one link into the backbone, static routing could be used on each PE-router within the SuperCom MPLS/VPN backbone—there is little point in running a dynamic routing protocol across a single link. However, some sites, such as the two central sites and the Reading spoke site, are multihomed into the backbone network. Static routing is not really an option in this case, so a more dynamic means of route advertisement is required.

The routing requirements of the spoke and central sites in our example are slightly different. In the case of the spoke sites, these sites must learn other VPN routes from the MPLS/VPN backbone so that inter-site routing is available. The central site locations, however, not only need to learn routes from other spoke sites, but they also need to apply policy in terms of traffic flow. In addition, they need to be a concentration point in terms of the number of routes that they must carry in memory (this could include Internet routes learned from the MPLS/VPN backbone). For these reasons, RIP Version 2 may be an adequate design choice for the spoke sites, but BGP-4 is an obvious choice for the central sites, because of its scaling and policy enforcement properties.

From the service provider's point of view, the use of BGP-4 between PE-routers and VPN customer CE-routers might be the protocol of choice. This is because the use of this protocol offers several advantages for the service provider:

- The service provider does not need to run multiple routing protocol processes, or routing contexts, per VRF.

- The configuration overhead is reduced, and the maintenance of the PE-router configuration is simplified.

- Redistribution between routing protocols is not necessary if the routes are learned via BGP-4.

In our example topology, BGP-4 could easily be used on each PE-to-CE link, and an autonomous system number from the private 64512–65535 range could be used in each site. This type of migration would be easy to achieve, and successful advertisement of VPN routes between sites could be provisioned.

However, if we consider another sample topology shown in Figure 10-10, you can see that the migration issues and subsequent BGP-4 deployment may become more complex as the size of the organization increases.

Figure 10-10 *VPN Customer Topology—Multiple Regions Running BGP-4*

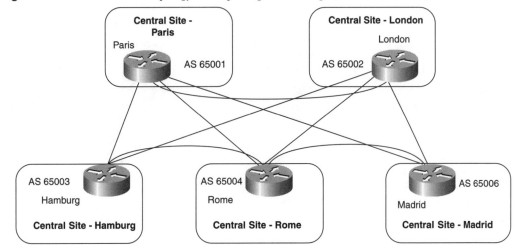

The VPN customer in Figure 10-10 has split the network into multiple regions, each connected via BGP-4. This type of topology is typical of a large (potentially multinational) customer that has chosen to split its network into separate regions, running BGP in the network core (on inter-regional links) and separate IGP process in each region. One of the reasons for using this topology would be the IGP scalability; another might be the need to apply routing policy. With this type of topology, if the customer has chosen to use a different AS number in each region and to run external BGP between regions, then replacement of the leased-line core infrastructure with an MPLS/VPN infrastructure is essentially the same as we have seen previously. However, if the same AS number is used in all regions (thus, internal BGP is used), then this type of connectivity presents some challenges for the MPLS/VPN backbone.

Migrating Customers Using iBGP in Their Network to MPLS/VPN Service

Regardless of which PE-to-CE connectivity option is chosen, after VPN routes have been advertised across the MPLS/VPN backbone and have been imported into the relevant VRFs, the next step is to advertise these routes to other sites that are associated with the VRF. If the advertisement of these routes is achieved through use of the BGP-4 protocol, we have already seen that several design choices exist between the service provider and the VPN customer sites. One such design choice is to run the same AS number within each region, as shown in Figure 10-11.

Figure 10-11 *Multiple Regions Using the Same Autonomous System Number*

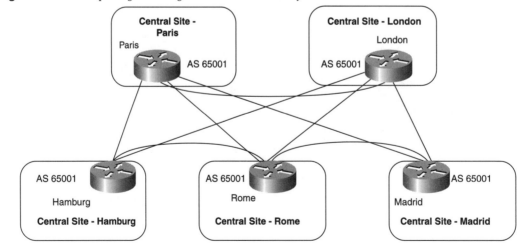

As highlighted in the previous section, this type of topology presents a problem for the BGP-4 protocol. One of the requirements of the BGP-4 protocol is that a BGP speaker should ignore any received updates that contain its own AS number within the AS_PATH. Therefore, the AS number must be removed from the AS_PATH before the route is advertised to another VPN site if different sites use the same AS number. In topologies such as the one described in Figure 10-10, in which a different AS number is used in all sites, this requirement can be met and routes can be advertised between sites without any issues. However, if internal BGP is used between sites, as in Figure 10-11, this requirement cannot be met using the standard BGP procedures.

To try to overcome this restriction, we could use a private AS number. Using this method, you might think that this private AS number could be removed by the MPLS/VPN service provider before advertisement of any routes, using the existing procedures for stripping private AS numbers when advertising routes to an external BGP neighbor. However, these procedures have the following restrictions:

- The private AS number is removed if only private AS numbers exist within the AS_PATH.

- The private AS number is removed if it is *not* equal to the neighboring AS number.

In the MPLS/VPN environment, the first restriction detailed here is met. However, because the neighboring AS number of a receiving VPN site will be the same as the originator of the route, the second restriction fails. Therefore, the PE-router will *not* remove the private AS number from the AS_PATH.

As seen in Figure 10-12, the EuroBank London site receives an update for 196.7.25.0/24, but this update contains its own AS number, 65001, within the AS_PATH. Because a BGP speaker should ignore any updates it receives that contain its own AS Number within the AS_PATH, the London CE-router ignores this update. Example 10-15 gives confirmation of this.

Figure 10-12 *Use of Private ASN with MPLS/VPN*

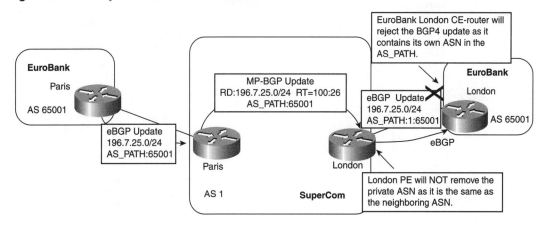

Example 10-15 *BGP-4 Rejection of Update Containing Own AS Number*

```
London# debug ip bgp update

BGP(0): 10.2.1.6 rcv UPDATE w/ attr: nexthop 10.2.1.6, origin i, ori
ginator 0.0.0.0, path 1 65001, extended community
BGP(0): 10.2.1.6 rcv UPDATE about 196.7.25.0/24 -- DENIED due to: as-
path contains our own AS;
```

Therefore, another mechanism is required so that the reuse of the AS number, whether public or private, can be supported in the MPLS/VPN environment. This mechanism is provided through use of a feature called AS Override.

Autonomous System Number Override

The AS Override feature allows the MPLS/VPN service provider to run the BGP routing protocol with a customer even if the customer is using the same AS number at different sites. This goal is achieved by rewriting the AS_PATH received from one VPN site route to contain only the MPLS/VPN backbone autonomous system number in the path. Using this mechanism, if a customer uses the same autonomous system number within each of its sites, it receives routes from other sites without failing the BGP requirement that they should not accept a route that has their own autonomous system number in the AS_PATH attribute.

This feature is necessary only if a customer's intention is to use the same autonomous system number in some or all of its sites. This feature can be used if the VPN customer uses either a private or a public autonomous system number, and it may be used in conjunction with the Site of Origin feature that we saw in the previous chapter, for the prevention of routing loops in a multi-homed scenario.

Figure 10-13 *AS Override Feature—BGP-4 Between PE- and CE-routers*

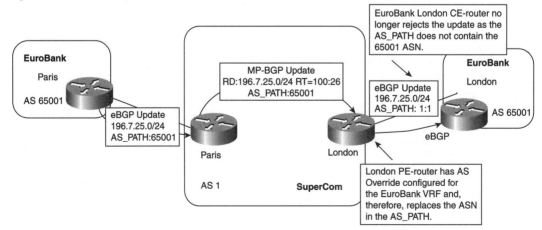

As Figure 10-13 shows, the EuroBank London site is now capable of receiving the 196.7.25.0/24 prefix from the Paris site because the AS_PATH does not contain its 65001 autonomous system number.

The AS Override feature is configured through use of the **neighbor** statement within the BGP process configuration, under the relevant address family used for the VPN customer. When configured, the PE-router checks each update before advertisement to the CE-router and performs the following operations:

- If the last autonomous system number in the AS_PATH is equal to the neighboring autonomous system number, then the PE-router will replace it with its own.

- If the last autonomous system number has multiple occurrences (which may happen with the use of AS_PATH prepend), then the PE-router will replace all the occurrences of this number with its own autonomous system number.

- The PE-router will add its own autonomous system number to the AS_PATH, per normal eBGP procedures.

Example 10-16 shows the necessary configuration for the SuperCom London PE-router to allow the EuroBank London site to receive BGP-4 updates for VPN routes that are reachable in other EuroBank sites.

Example 10-16 *AS Override Feature Configuration*

```
hostname London
!
interface serial0
 description ** interface to EuroBank London **
 ip vrf forwarding EuroBank
 ip address 10.2.1.6 255.255.255.252
!
router bgp 1
 no bgp default ipv4-unicast
 neighbor 194.22.15.2 remote-as 1
 neighbor 194.22.15.2 update-source loopback0
!
address-family ipv4 vrf EuroBank
 neighbor 10.2.1.5 remote-as 65001
 neighbor 10.2.1.5 activate
 neighbor 10.2.1.5 as-override
 no auto-summary
 no synchronization
exit-address-family
!
address-family vpnv4
 neighbor 194.22.15.2 activate
 neighbor 194.22.15.2 send-community extended
exit-address-family
```

With the configuration shown in Example 10-16, we can now see in Example 10-17 that the update for 196.7.25.0/24 is accepted by the EuroBank London CE-router and is installed into the BGP table with an AS_PATH of 1:1.

Example 10-17 *BGP-4 Update Acceptance with AS Override Enabled*

```
London# debug ip bgp update

BGP(0): 10.2.1.6 rcvd UPDATE w/ attr: nexthop 10.2.1.6, origin i, path 1 1
BGP(0): 10.4.1.22 rcvd 196.7.25.0/24
BGP(0): Revise route installing 196.7.25.0/24 -> 10.2.1.6 to main IP
table

London# show ip bgp

BGP table version is 3, local router ID is 10.2.1.5
Status codes: s suppressed, d damped, h history, * valid, > best, i - internal Origin
codes: i - IGP, e - EGP, ? - incomplete

   Network          Next Hop          Metric LocPrf Weight Path
*> 196.7.25.0       10.2.1.6                        0    1 1 i
```

Summary

We have seen in this chapter that BGP-4 and OSPF can be used to provide PE-to-CE connectivity, in addition to the static and RIP Version 2 options that we saw in the previous chapter. These protocols complete the list of currently available connectivity options, although others, such as EIGRP and IS-IS, may become available over time.

Whichever protocol is used, customer VRFs will be populated based on the routes learned from the CE-routers. To identify which VRFs should receive which routes, either routing contexts (in the case of RIP Version 2 and BGP) or a separate routing process (in the case of OSPF) is used.

MP-iBGP is used to propagate VPN customer routes between PE-routers. In most cases, except with BGP-4, redistribution is necessary to allow the routes within a VRF to be placed into the BGP table for onward advertisement.

Various design options have also been reviewed, and a sample network migration from an overlay VPN solution to an MPLS/VPN-based solution has been provided. Using this migration scenario, we've also seen that the AS Override feature may be required when BGP-4 is used across the PE-to-CE links, if the same autonomous system number is used in more than one site.

CHAPTER 11

Advanced MPLS/VPN Topologies

In Chapter 9, "MPLS/VPN Architecture Operation," we discussed the basic MPLS/VPN intranet connectivity model and learned that, in many cases, this type of solution will be adequate in providing VPN connectivity for a single organization. However, it is clear that a large majority of deployments that use the MPLS/VPN architecture will need advanced features to satisfy their topology and service requirements, and also will need to be provided with connectivity to other organizations.

Depending on the actual requirements of the network design, numerous topologies can be deployed using the MPLS/VPN architecture and its associated tools. There are too many scenarios to be able to provide examples for each and every one; instead, this chapter aims to present some of the more widely used topologies, several of which were introduced in Chapter 7, "Virtual Private Network (VPN) Implementation Options."

Intranet and Extranet Integration

Extranet support within the context of the MPLS/VPN architecture simply involves the import of routes from one VRF into a different VRF that services another VPN site. As we have seen in previous chapters, this is controlled through the use of the route target BGP extended community and import statements within the VRF that is associated with the particular VPN site. An example of this type of connectivity is illustrated in Figure 11-1.

From the figure, we can see that two separate organizations are capable of communicating directly across the MPLS/VPN backbone as they import each other's routes into their relevant VRFs.

If we examine the EuroBank London site, for example, we can see that it has its routes advertised with a route target value of 1234:17. All other PE-routers that have EuroBank sites (or FastFoods sites) attached are configured to import any routes that contain a route target with a value of 1234:17 into the EuroBank and FastFoods VRFs. These PE-routers are also configured to import any routes that contain a route target value of 1234:18, which corresponds to the FastFoods VPN, into both of these VRFs.

Figure 11-1 *Extranet VPN Connectivity Between Sites*

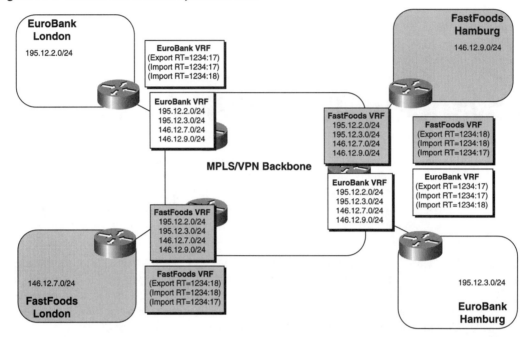

Because all the FastFoods site routes are advertised across the MPLS/VPN backbone with a route target value of 1234:18, these routes are also imported into the EuroBank and FastFoods VRFs. This means that all EuroBank and FastFoods sites have both EuroBank and FastFoods routes within their local routing table and, therefore, have connectivity across organizations.

This type of topology can be enhanced further through manipulation of the route target. In Figure 11-2, the EuroBank VPN customer has added a central site to the topology with which only EuroBank sites should be capable of communicating.

The example in Figure 11-2 shows that the EuroBank central site exports its routes with a route target value of 1234:19. Routes that contain this route target value are imported into the EuroBank VRF on all PE-routers, but *not* into the FastFoods VRF because this has not been configured to import routes with this particular route target value. This means that only the EuroBank sites are capable of accessing the central site, but they are also still capable of accessing the FastFoods sites. However, the FastFoods sites are not capable of accessing the EuroBank central site, even though they import routes from the EuroBank VPN.

Figure 11-2 *Extranet VPN Connectivity with Central Site Access*

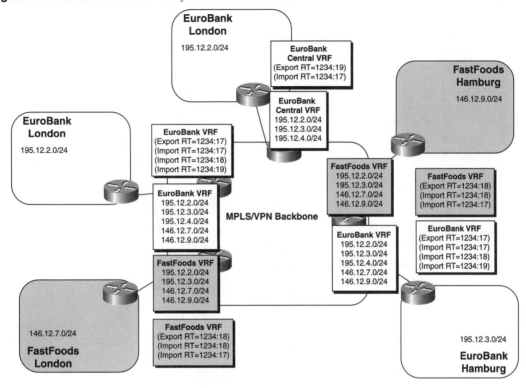

NOTE   It should be noted that with this type of connectivity, IP address space between the two different VPN customers should be unique. In our example, if the FastFoods sites were to use the same address space as the EuroBank central site (or any other EuroBank site), and vice versa, connectivity would be broken because sites would receive the same set of routes from two different locations.

NOTE   In the extranet example shown in Figure 11-2, it is possible for users from a FastFoods site to use Telnet to access the central EuroBank router (or an unprotected host at the EuroBank central site) and then access other EuroBank hosts or routers. Therefore, it is important, as with any other type of connectivity, to make sure that adequate security arrangements, such as access-list filtering, are in place to prevent this type of attack.

Central Services Topology

A second very common topology that must be implemented with MPLS/VPN technology is the central services VPN. In this topology, the client sites can access services on central servers located at one or more central sites, but they cannot communicate with each other. A number of services can be implemented with this topology, including these:

- Application hosting, in which a service provider provides access to applications residing on common servers. Application hosting can also include traditional service provider services such as hosted web sites or e-mail access.

- Access to shared equipment, including dial-in pools or voice gateways.

- Other value-added services, such as outsourced management of customer routers.

The connectivity requirements of all these services are summarized in Figure 11-3.

Figure 11-3 *Connectivity Requirements of Central Services Topology*

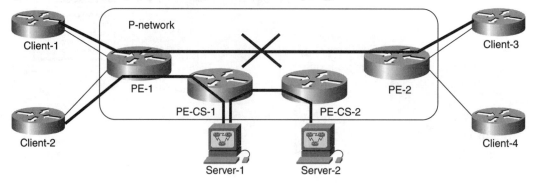

The MPLS/VPN design of the central services topology is easily inherited from the connectivity requirements. The following facts about VRFs and route distinguishers that need to be configured can be easily inferred from the requirements:

- The client sites will not communicate—every client site needs to be placed in a separate VRF.

- Every client site should use a different route distinguisher to prevent route conflict between the client sites.

NOTE	If all the client sites were on a single PE-router, they would need different route distinguishers because each VRF needs a unique route distinguisher. Because of several implementation issues, a similar rule also applies to VRFs configured on several PE-routers. In any case, the rules for the network designer are quite simple: If you want to use different VRFs (and thus different RD values) on a single PE-router, you should use different RD values even when deploying the topology across a number of PE-routers.

- The server sites will freely communicate. They can be placed in the same VRF or, if connected to different PE-routers, can use the same route distinguisher.

Based on connectivity requirements, the route import and export procedures should be as follows:

- Server sites will freely communicate. All routes from the server VRF must be exported with a route target (let's name it Server_RT) that is used as the import route target for other server VRFs.

- Client sites will reach server sites. Importing routes with Server_RT into client VRFs will achieve this goal.

- Server sites will reach client sites. All client routes will be exported with a common route target (let's call it Client_RT) and will be imported into server VRFs based on this route target.

- Client sites will not communicate. Routes exported with Client_RT will not be imported into client VRFs.

With these design rules in hand, it's easy to deploy a central services VPN solution. Let's assume that the EuroBank location in London and the FastFoods location in Hamburg need to access a common server located in Hamburg, as shown in Figure 11-4.

Figure 11-4 *Central Services in SuperCom Network*

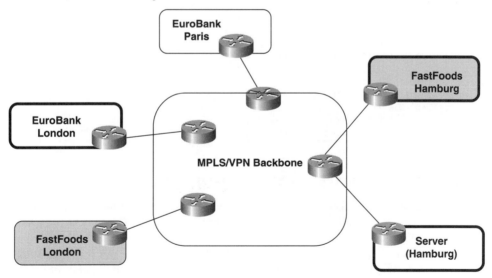

The EuroBank site and the FastFoods site are already in different VRFs with unique route distinguishers (because of their intranet VPN connectivity requirements), and we can reuse those VRFs as client VRFs to provide access to the common server. A new server VRF must be configured in Hamburg, as shown in Example 11-1.

Example 11-1 *Server VRF Configuration on Hamburg PE-router*

```
ip vrf Server_HAM
  rd 1234:713
  route-target both 1234:710    ! Server_RT
  route-target import 1234:711 ! Client_RT
```

Additionally, Server_RT must be configured as the import route target in client VRFs, and Client_RT must be configured as the export route target in the same VRFs, as shown in Example 11-2.

NOTE   These two steps complete the core MPLS/VPN configuration of central services VPN. Additional steps not covered in this section are needed, including interface configuration, routing protocol configuration, and redistribution from VRF routing protocol into MP-BGP.

Example 11-2 *Client VRF Configuration on Hamburg and London PE-routers*

```
Hamburg#
ip vrf FastFoods_HAM
  rd 1234:18
  route-target import 1234:710  ! Server_RT
  route-target export 1234:711  ! Client_RT

London#
ip vrf EuroBank_LON
  rd 1234:17
  route-target import 1234:710  ! Server_RT
  route-target export 1234:711  ! Client_RT
```

MPLS/VPN Hub-and-spoke Topology

In certain circumstances, it may be desirable to use a hub-and-spoke topology so that all spoke sites send all their traffic toward a central site location. This may be because certain central site services for a particular VPN, such as Internet access, firewalls, server farms, and so on, are housed within the hub site. Or it may be because this particular VPN customer requires that all connectivity between its sites be via the central site.

In either case, it is necessary to define a hub site that contains full routing knowledge of all spoke sites that belong to the same VPN. All traffic from the spoke sites, destined either for the central site services or for intersite connectivity, will flow via the central hub site. With this type of topology, the spoke sites export their routes to the hub site, and then the hub site re-exports the spoke site routes through a second interface (either physical or logical) using a different route target so that other spoke sites can import the routes. This causes the hub site to become a transit point for interspoke connectivity.

An example of this type of topology is shown in Figure 11-5. This figure shows two spoke sites, EuroBank London and EuroBank Hamburg, that do not have direct connectivity but that can reach each other by sending traffic via the EuroBank Paris central site.

Figure 11-5 *Hub-and-spoke Connectivity Model*

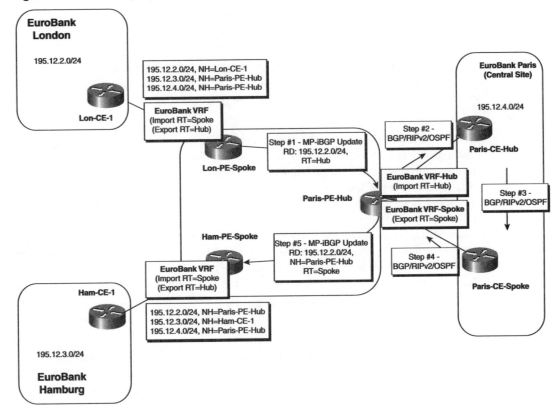

For simplicity, the relevant route targets have been given names rather than numerical values. We can see in Figure 11-5 that the EuroBank London site advertises its local prefixes, an example of which is 195.12.2.0/24, and these are placed into the EuroBank VRF on the Lon-PE-Spoke PE-router. To achieve the desired connectivity, the following steps can be taken:

1 The Lon-PE-Spoke PE-router exports all the routes from the EuroBank VRF using a route target value of Hub.

2 The hub PE-router (Paris-PE-Hub, within the figure) is configured to import the Hub route target into one of its VRFs (defined as VRF-Hub in Figure 11-5). This VRF interface attaches to the EuroBank central site and forwards all routes that are learned from the spoke sites to the CE-router (Paris-CE3-Hub), which is located within the central site.

3 The Paris-CE3-Hub CE-router advertises these routes across the central site.

4 The routes are eventually advertised back to the Paris-PE-Hub PE-router across a separate interface.

5 The Paris-PE-Hub PE-router then advertises the routes back into the MPLS/VPN backbone with a route target value of Spoke.

6 Each of the spoke PE-routers (Lon-PE-Spoke and Ham-PE-Spoke) is configured to import any routes with a route target value of Spoke into the EuroBank VRF. This means that the next-hop address for all the spoke sites, as seen by other spoke sites, is via the central site Paris-PE-Hub PE-router.

The simplest way to configure this type of connectivity would be to assign the same route distinguisher to each spoke site VRF because the spoke sites do not exchange routing information directly with each other and do not import each other's route targets. As briefly discussed in Chapter 9, this is possible when the spoke sites are not connected to the same PE-router as the hub site. This is because of the automatic VPN-IPv4 route filtering feature (also discussed in Chapter 9), which filters any routes that contain a route target that is *not* configured to be imported into any VRFs on the PE-router. In the case of a distributed hub-and-spoke model, such as the one shown in Figure 11-5, everything works fine because the spoke PE-routers are not configured to import the route target with a value of Spoke. However, if the hub-and-spoke sites are connected to the same PE-router, then it is essential to assign a different route distinguisher per spoke site VRF; otherwise, the automatic route filtering feature will *not* filter the routes with a route target value of Spoke, and essential routing information could potentially be lost.

The loss of routing information can be explained through the MPLS/VPN architecture and also through how the BGP selection process is executed within an MPLS/VPN environment. Architecturally, two or more VRFs may use the same route distinguisher if these VRFs are used by sites belonging to the same VPN *and* share exactly the same routing information. This is not the case with the hub-and-spoke topology because the hub site imports different routes from the spoke sites.

The BGP selection process applies to all routes that must be imported into the same VRF, plus all routes that have the same route distinguisher as this VRF. When the selection process is finished, only the best routes are effectively imported. In the case of the hub-and-spoke topology, if the same route distinguisher is used for each spoke site, this could result in a "best" route that is *not* imported into the VRF. This is because, if all spoke VRFs have the same route distinguisher, then each PE-router will include in the selection process not only the routes coming from the hub site, but also the routes coming from the other spoke sites (which are *not* configured to be imported). Automatic route filtering will prevent this if the topology is distributed, but it will not help if the hub-and-spoke sites are connected through the same PE-router.

NOTE   It is also worth noting that if the same route distinguisher is used on every PE-router for a particular VPN, then the topology is somewhat restricted because it requires that all spokes connected to a particular PE-router for a particular VPN use the same VRF. This is because each VRF on a PE-router must have a unique route distinguisher. This means that all spokes for a particular VPN would need to share the exact same routing information.

Deployment of the AllowAS-in Feature

Readers that are familiar with the BGP may notice a fundamental problem with the description of the hub-and-spoke topology operation given so far. This problem stems from the fact that the BGP protocol states that a BGP speaker should ignore a received update that contains within its AS_PATH attribute its own autonomous system number (ASN). If we refer back to Figure 11-5, we can see that this is in fact the case when the hub-and-spoke topology is deployed. There, the Paris-PE-Hub PE-router will advertise routes from the VRF named VRF-Hub toward the EuroBank Paris central site with the MPLS/VPN backbone ASN contained within the AS_PATH. These routes will be readvertised back toward the MPLS/VPN backbone, to be received by the Paris-PE-Hub PE-router into the VRF named VRF-spoke.

NOTE   This issue will arise only if BGP is used between the PE- and CE-routers at the hub site *and* if pervasive BGP is used within the site.

To overcome this issue so that the use of the hub-and-spoke topology becomes possible, a new feature known as AllowAS-in has been introduced so that the receiving PE-router disables the AS_PATH check for routes learned from the central site location. The use of this feature is illustrated in Figure 11-6.

Figure 11-6 *Deployment of the AllowAS-in Feature*

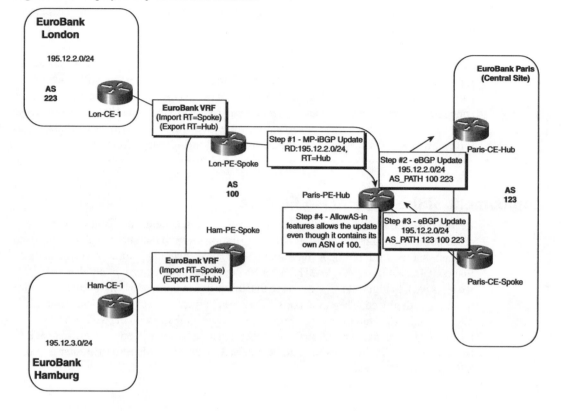

NOTE The hub-and-spoke topology may also require the deployment of the Site of Origin (SOO) attribute. This attribute was discussed in detail in Chapter 9.

The AllowAS-in feature is implemented using the command shown in Example 11-3, with the relevant configuration of the Paris-PE-Hub router shown in Example 11-4:

Example 11-3 *Configuration of the AllowAS-in Feature*

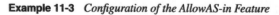

```
neighbor x.x.x.x allowas-in ASN_limit
```

NOTE   Routing loops are avoided by setting a limit of the number of occurrences of the MPLS/ VPN backbone autonomous system number in the update from the VPN hub site. This is controlled through use of the *ASN_limit* parameter within the **neighbor** command.

Example 11-4 *BGP Configuration with AllowAS-in Example*

```
router bgp 100
 !
 address-family ipv4 vrf VRF-Spoke
  neighbor 195.12.4.5 remote-as 123
  neighbor 195.12.4.5 activate
  neighbor 195.12.4.5 allowas-in 2
 exit-address-family
 !
```

NOTE   If it is possible to either advertise an aggregate from the hub site that covers the address range used by all spoke sites, or advertise a default route, then the use of the AllowAS-in feature is not necessary.

Summary

In this chapter, you've seen the versatility of MPLS/VPN technology in implementing various VPN topologies that are sometimes very hard to implement with traditional VPN technologies, ranging from Layer 2 or Layer 3 overlay VPNs to traditional peer-to-peer VPNs.

The topologies supported by MPLS/VPN can satisfy almost all customer requirements that can be formulated in terms of the IP routing model, including these:

- Simple customer virtual private networks
- Overlapping intranet/extranet networks
- Access to common servers while preventing communication between the clients
- Hub-and-spoke VPN in which all traffic must flow through the hub site for security, logging, or auditing reasons

You've also seen the extensions and modifications to traditional AS path processing needed in the BGP protocol to support some of these topologies.

CHAPTER 12

Advanced MPLS/VPN Topics

Up until this point in the book, we have been describing all the mechanisms that make up the basic MPLS-enabled VPN architecture. We have explored several different topologies and features that provide solutions to many business and services requirements.

One of the most important issues to address with any network design is how the solution will scale, both initially and in the future. This issue will be common across all deployments, so it is important to understand how to implement the architecture in a scalable and optimal way. Although many network deployments will be similar in nature, each will require a slightly different design and optimization and may have requirements that necessitate enhancements to the features that we described in previous chapters.

This chapter introduces several advanced topics that aim to address these issues. This chapter also illustrates various mechanisms that may be used during the deployment of the MPLS-enabled VPN architecture to assist with the scaling and optimization of the network infrastructure, as well as the introduction of advanced topologies to support certain types of connectivity requirements.

The SuperCom backbone topology illustrated in Figure 12-1 will be used throughout this chapter; Table 12-1 provides all the necessary IP address assignments for the service provider backbone and VPN customers.

Table 12-1   *IP Address Assignment for SP Backbone and VPN Customers*

Company	Site	Subnet
FastFoods	San Jose	195.12.2.0/24
	Lyon	10.2.1.0/24
NYBank	Denver	196.27.5.0/24
	San Francisco	196.27.6.0/24
	New York	196.27.4.0/24
EuroBank	San Francisco	10.2.1.0/24
	Paris	196.7.25.0/24
SuperCom	Paris (Loopback0)	194.22.15.1/32
	Paris (Loopback1)	194.22.16.1/32

continues

Table 12-1 *IP Address Assignment for SP Backbone and VPN Customers (Continued)*

Company	Site	Subnet
	San Jose (Loopback0)	194.22.15.2/32
	San Jose (Loopback1)	194.22.16.2/32
	New York (Loopback0)	194.22.15.3/32
	FastFoods/EuroBank RR	194.22.15.5/32
	NYBank RR	194.22.15.6/32

Figure 12-1 *SuperCom Backbone Network Topology*

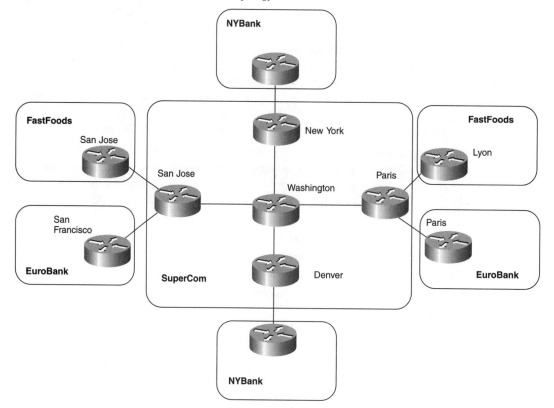

MPLS/VPN: Scaling the Solution

Many factors must be considered when planning a scalable network design. Many of these are not specific to the MPLS/VPN architecture and are therefore not covered in this book. However, certain areas within the network infrastructure are directly affected by the introduction of the MPLS/VPN architecture and must be addressed before implementation.

To understand the factors that may affect the scalability of the design, we must first consider how the MPLS/VPN service is achieved and what mechanisms are used to provision the service. This has been extensively covered in previous chapters, but in summary, we have seen that customer VPN routes are advertised across the backbone between PE-routers, and this information is then disseminated to other VPN sites. Whenever routes are advertised across a backbone network, BGP is the protocol of choice and indeed is a fundamental building block of the MPLS/VPN architecture. Therefore, we need to look at the scaling properties of this protocol, not only in terms of configuration, but also in terms of overhead for the routers that provide the BGP session endpoints and the devices that carry these sessions across the backbone.

We also need to understand how quickly routing information can be disseminated and synchronized between VPN sites in the event of a topology change in the network (for example, a link going down or coming back up)—this process is known as *convergence*. The convergence speed of the MPLS/VPN solution is of paramount importance to the customers of the VPN service who deploy their mission-critical and time-sensitive solutions across this infrastructure, so a thorough understanding of the factors that affect this convergence is imperative.

Finally, we have seen that many different sites can attach to the backbone through the same PE-device. This means that we need to investigate what issues this presents and how the PE-device can cope with deployment of additional sites.

Routing Convergence Within an MPLS-enabled VPN Network

One issue that always requires attention within any network deployment is the convergence times within the network. *Convergence* can be defined as the time taken for routers in a routing domain to learn about changes within the network and to synchronize their view of the network with other devices within the same routing domain. Interior routing protocols, by definition, converge much faster than exterior routing protocols, and this is one of their main objectives. By contrast, exterior routing protocols such as BGP-4 are designed to provide a loop-free topology between autonomous systems. Their main objective is not fast convergence, but excellent scalability and the capability to carry a large number of routes.

This has implications that must be addressed when moving to an MPLS/VPN architecture, especially if the service provider currently carries customer routes within its IGP or if the customers run their own IGP over overlay links (for example, Frame Relay DLCIs) supplied by the service provider. If the service provider already carries customer routes within BGP-4, as most do, then the implications are less obvious, although convergence times between members of a VPN will be affected by the introduction of the MPLS/VPN architecture.

Two main areas must be assessed when looking at the convergence times. The first is the speed of convergence within the service provider backbone; the second is the speed of convergence between customer sites. Both are crucial for end-to-end convergence speed as perceived by MPLS/VPN customers. Figure 12-2 provides an example that shows these two independent processes at work.

Figure 12-2   *VPN and Backbone Network Convergence*

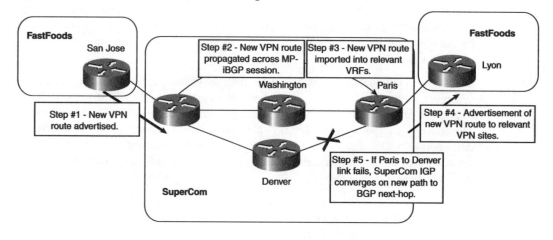

Figure 12-2 shows that the two convergence processes are completely independent. We can see in the figure that a new VPN route is advertised by the FastFoods San Jose site (Step 1). This route is propagated across the MPLS/VPN backbone (Step 2) and then is imported into the FastFoods VRF on the Paris PE-router (Step 3). The route is then advertised to the FastFoods Lyon site (Step 4). If a core link fails, such as the link between the Paris and Denver PE-routers (Step 5), then the service provider's IGP will find a new path toward the BGP next-hop (via the Washington P-router). This does not affect the convergence of the route between the two VPN sites, but it will interrupt traffic between the two VPN sites while the service provider IGP reconverges.

If a VPN site advertises a new route, or if some other change occurs within the VPN site, BGP will take care of the convergence, and the Service Provider IGP will not be affected.

Convergence Within the Service Provider Backbone

Within the service provider backbone, we are really concerned only with the convergence of the Interior Gateway Protocol and the time that it takes for any changes to be reflected in the forwarding component of MPLS. External routes are not an issue because the service provider does not hold these routes within the backbone (at least, not for the VPN service), and MPLS within the internal network is not affected by any external routing information.

Two typical designs are used by the majority of service providers for their high-speed backbones. The backbone may be built based on a pure router architecture, or it could be built on ATM technology using routers and IP-enabled ATM switches.

NOTE	The case of the backbone being built with routers connected via an ATM or Frame Relay virtual circuit is handled in the same way as the backbone built purely with routers from an MPLS convergence perspective. This is because the ATM or Frame Relay switches are not involved in IP routing, so MPLS does not see the underlying physical structure of the Layer 2 network.

We have already discussed the differences of how MPLS is deployed using these two types of technologies, and we should consider each one in turn when assessing the convergence impact that the introduction of MPLS will have.

Service Provider Backbone Convergence—Router-based Topology

The convergence times within the backbone should not be greatly affected by the introduction of MPLS if the infrastructure is based on a router-only topology. This is due to the way that allocation, retention, and distribution of MPLS labels are performed across the network. We already saw in Chapter 2, "Frame-mode MPLS Operation," how the MPLS label distribution is implemented within a router platform and non-ATM interfaces. This process can be summarized as follows:

- **Labels are distributed in unsolicited downstream mode**—The router advertises bindings as soon as it has a route in its routing table.

- **Routers use liberal retention mode**—When the router receives label bindings for the same FEC from different neighbors, all the bindings are retained. Only some of those label bindings will be used; this is based on the current next-hop for the FEC as found in the routing table of the LSR.

Note	If there is more than one neighbor for an FEC, and if one of these neighbors becomes the next-hop for the FEC after routing changes, no additional label distribution needs to take place. The LSR is ready to label switch packets immediately using the new next-hop.

- **Routers also can use independent control mode**—Each router binds and advertises its labels, regardless of whether it has received any labels. In other words, as soon as a route is in the routing table, a label is bound to it, even if the router has not received a label for that prefix from its downstream neighbor.

Whenever a change occurs within the routing table of the LSR, the MPLS process is informed immediately, and convergence occurs based on the factors mentioned previously. This is the same mechanism that is used to instruct a routing protocol that a change has occurred within the forwarding table, so the effect on convergence should be minimal. Introduction of MPLS into the core service provider backbone thus does not increase the convergence time—the overall backbone convergence time is still dictated by the convergence speed of the routing protocol used in the backbone.

Service Provider Backbone Convergence—ATM-based Topology

The convergence times within the backbone will be affected by the introduction of MPLS if the infrastructure is based on an IP-enabled ATM topology and the routers within the topology use TC-ATM interfaces that use the VPI/VCI of ATM cells to carry MPLS label information. This type of architecture was fully described in Chapter 3, "Cell-mode MPLS Operation." Again, this is because of the way that allocation, retention, and distribution of MPLS labels are performed across the backbone network. The default behavior in this type of environment can be summarized as follows:

- **Labels are distributed in downstream on demand mode**—The router will advertise label bindings only if it is specifically asked to do so by an upstream neighbor. This may have an effect on convergence because the LSR may not actually have a label binding for a requested FEC, so it will need to signal downstream to its neighbors to ask for this binding.

- **ATM-LSRs use conservative retention mode**—When the router receives label bindings for the same FEC from several neighbors, it will keep only the label binding that is received from the next-hop neighbor (as controlled by the routing table) for the particular FEC. All other label bindings will be discarded. Therefore, if a change in the topology occurs, the LSR must go through the routing protocol convergence phase, request labels from its downstream neighbor, and wait for new label-binding information to be received from its downstream neighbors before it can continue to label switch traffic.

- **ATM-LSRs will use ordered control mode**—The LSR will allocate a label for a particular FEC only if it is the egress LSR for that FEC, or if it has received a label binding for the FEC from its downstream LDP/TDP neighbors.

The overall convergence time for an ATM-based core backbone could be significantly larger than for the non-ATM core backbone because the convergence occurs in two steps:

- The interior routing protocol used in the backbone detects a link or node failure and converges around the failure spot.
- LDP/TDP must re-establish label mappings across the ATM backbone. In large ATM backbones with many ATM switches being connected in sequence (in other words, the number of hops across the ATM backbone is large), the LDP/TDP propagation time could be significant, more so if you're faced with a major trunk failure in which a large number of routers start asking for new labels all at once.

Convergence Between VPN Sites

The convergence time between VPN sites is of critical importance to the customers of the VPN service. In the traditional overlay VPN model, which we discussed in Chapter 7, "Virtual Private Network (VPN) Implementation Options," customers are capable of obtaining high-speed convergence through fine adjustment of their own Interior Gateway Protocol (IGP) timers across the virtual circuits provided by the service provider. Although high-speed convergence times are still possible through the MPLS/VPN service, it is important to understand that the responsibility of these convergence times is essentially handed over to the service provider when an MPLS-enabled VPN service is obtained.

Several factors must be considered when assessing the convergence times between VPN sites across the MPLS/VPN backbone. These factors will directly affect the convergence times between VPN customer sites and are not present within the overlay model. The end-to-end convergence delay has essentially four components:

- The advertisement of routes from a site toward the backbone (including the import of these routes into the relevant routing tables)
- The propagation of these routes across the backbone
- The import process of these routes into all relevant VRFs
- The advertisement of these routes to other sites

Each of these components can be seen in Figure 12-3.

Figure 12-3   *End-to-end Convergence Delay Components*

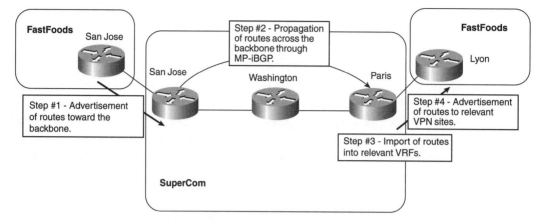

The convergence times between the CE-router and the PE-router in the ingress direction are not affected by the introduction of MPLS/VPN if the VPN service is provided through the peer model because MPLS is not run across the link. This means that whenever a CE-router advertises a route toward the PE, the time it takes for this route to be installed into the local routing table does not change. However, because most (if not all) customers will have been using the overlay model for VPN connectivity before the availability of the MPLS/VPN service, then a certain amount of impact will be felt. This is because the overlay model does not require the exchange of routing information directly between the service provider and VPN customer. With the introduction of MPLS/VPN and the resultant migration to a peer-based solution, these "ex-overlay" customers will see a change in convergence times, which will need to be addressed if they are to receive the same level of service as with their previous overlay solution.

The choice of routing protocol across the PE-to-CE link will obviously have an effect on convergence, but this is not specific to MPLS and will not be considered for discussion within this chapter. The propagation of routes across the backbone should also not be affected detrimentally by the introduction of MPLS if the customer routes were already carried within BGP. However, as already discussed, this is not the case with most customers because they will have propagated routing information across Frame Relay/ATM circuits provided by the service provider. In this case, the service provider may need to fine-tune the advertisement of VPN routing information between PE-routers so that the convergence times may be comparable with a customer's current VPN solution.

There will be a small delay incurred in getting the routes from the VRF into the BGP process, but this is no different than standard BGP, in which routes that are learned through a routing protocol other than BGP are redistributed into the BGP process.

Although there will always be a certain amount of convergence time across the backbone, this is the same whether the routes are standard IPv4 routes or VPN-IPv4 routes. This time is dictated by the interior BGP damping mechanisms—changes in the BGP tables are not propagated to BGP neighbors immediately, but they are batched and sent to the neighbors at regular intervals (the default is every five seconds). If you have deployed route reflectors in your network, a similar delay might be incurred on every route reflector. To improve the convergence of your iBGP sessions, use the **neighbor advertisement-interval** configuration command.

As each PE-router receives VPN-IPv4 routes from across the backbone, it needs to process them and place them into the relevant VRFs. This process will certainly have an effect on convergence. Whenever a BGP speaker receives an update from a BGP neighbor, it needs to correlate the update with all other updates received from other BGP neighbors. When this process is complete, the BGP router can select the best path to a given destination from all the paths available to it. This is achieved through the BGP selection process.

NOTE   A description of the BGP selection process can be found on the Cisco Systems web site, www.cisco.com, within the BGP configuration documentation.

The import process is an added phase after BGP has selected the best paths. A large number of routes, which have been learned from across the backbone, may be available for import into attached VRFs, and this can potentially be very CPU-intensive. Therefore, each BGP router uses a process known as the scanner process to deal with this task. This happens independently of the BGP router process, which is the standard mechanism used by the router to perform BGP-related tasks.

The actual import of the VPN-IPv4 routes into the relevant VRFs is performed every 15 seconds by default. This means that it can take up to a maximum of 15 seconds for a VPN-IPv4 route learned by a PE-router from a route reflector or from another PE-router to make it into local VRF routing tables. This may also be the case for any routes that are learned from any attached CE-devices. When a prefix is learned from a CE (either via eBGP or an IGP and then redistributed into BGP), the PE-router needs to

1   Attach the relevant export route target.
2   Calculate the BGP best path.
3   If there is a new best path, the BGP version number is increased by 1 and the new best path is advertised to other PE-routers.
4   If this prefix is to be imported to other local VRFs, the import is actioned at the next invocation of the import scanner process.

A further factor that can affect convergence is the invocation of the BGP scanner process to scan the BGP table and routing tables. This is a separate invocation of the process and does not occur at the same time as the importing of VPN-IPv4 routes. By default, BGP scans the BGP table and routing tables for all address families that are configured under the BGP process every 60 seconds.

This is invoked as a separate process to the BGP router process because of the potentially large amounts of information that must be scanned. Running **debug** on a PE-router will show this process being invoked every 60 seconds for each address family, and also every 15 seconds for the import of routes. An example of this, and a sample output that shows the BGP scanner process in action, can be seen in Example 12-1.

Example 12-1 *Invocation of the BGP Scanner Process*

```
San Jose# show processes cpu
CPU utilization for five seconds: 0%/0%; one minute: 0%; five minutes: 0%
 PID  Runtime(ms)  Invoked  uSecs   5Sec   1Min   5Min TTY Process
 107       67824     35013   1937   0.00%  0.00%  0.00%   0 BGP Scanner


San Jose# debug ip bgp events
BGP events debugging is on
11:08:32 GMT: BGP: Import timer expired. Walking from 8659 to 8659
11:08:47 GMT: BGP: Import timer expired. Walking from 8659 to 8659
11:09:02 GMT: BGP: Performing BGP general scanning
11:09:02 GMT: BGP(0): scanning IPv4 Unicast routing tables
11:09:02 GMT: BGP(IPv4 Unicast): Performing BGP Nexthop scanning for general scan
11:09:02 GMT: BGP(1): scanning VPNv4 Unicast routing tables
11:09:02 GMT: BGP(VPNv4 Unicast): Performing BGP Nexthop scanning for general scan
```

The scanning of the BGP table and routing tables is necessary to check for changes in the next-hop so that consistent and accurate information is reflected within the router and is passed to the BGP neighbors of the router. The same process also handles the **network** and **redistribute** commands so that any new routes that have to be originated are discovered. We will see that changes to attributes of existing routes or the addition of new routes learned from other BGP neighbors are processed using the advertisement interval.

NOTE   In theory, the scan time could cause a route to not be advertised to an external neighbor for up to 90 seconds. For example, it could take 60 seconds for the scanner process to run and thus discover a new prefix, or change to an existing prefix, and then 30 seconds for the next advertisement interval to an external neighbor.

The BGP scanner process can be tuned to help speed up the convergence times. The actual optimal settings of this process must be determined through monitoring the live implementation because each deployment and topology will be different. Tables 12-2 through 12-4 provide the commands necessary to perform this tuning. All values shown are in seconds.

Table 12-2   *Tuning of the BGP Scanner Process for IPv4 Routes*

Step	Command	Purpose
1	**router bgp** *autonomous-system*	Enable a BGP routing process, which places you in router configuration mode
2	**bgp scan-time** {5-60}	Set the next-hop validation interval for IPv4 unicast routes only

Table 12-3   *Tuning of the BGP Scanner Process for VPN-IPv4 Routes*

Step	Command	Purpose
1	**router bgp** *autonomous-system*	Enable a BGP routing process, which places you in router configuration mode
2	**address-family vpnv4 unicast**	Enter address family configuration for VPNv4 unicast routes
3	**bgp scan-time** {5-60}	Set the next-hop validation interval for the specified address family on all VPN-IPv4 prefixes learned from both PE and CE-routers

Table 12-4   *Import Process Timer for VPN-IPv4 Routes*

Step	Command	Purpose
1	**router bgp** *autonomous-system*	Enable a BGP routing process, which places you in router configuration mode
2	**address-family vpnv4 unicast**	Enter address family configuration for VPNv4 unicast routes
3	**bgp scan-time import** {5-60}	Set the import timer for VPN-IPv4 unicast routes only

In addition to the scanning and importing of routes, each PE-router needs to advertise the best routes within each VRF to all its VRF neighbors. This process will occur both on ingress into the MPLS/VPN backbone, when routes are received from CE-routers, and on egress, when routes are advertised toward CE-routers. The advertisement of these routes is different depending on whether the neighbors are eBGP neighbors (VPN clients) or iBGP neighbors (other PE-routers). By default, BGP updates are sent to eBGP neighbors every 30 seconds and to iBGP neighbors every five seconds if any update/change is available for transmission. This behavior also has an effect on convergence and can be tuned. The actual update times are controlled by the command in Example 12-2, which is the number of seconds that the router will wait between BGP update transmissions.

Example 12-2 *Tuning the Advertisement Interval of BGP Routes*

```
neighbor x.x.x.x advertisement-interval {0-600}
```

NOTE   The advertisement interval and scan time need to be tuned on CE-routers as well as PE-routers if the customer runs eBGP across the PE-to-CE link. This may not be possible in some circumstances without an IOS upgrade because the capability to manipulate these timers is a relatively new feature and may not be available within the IOS level running on the CE-router.

Similar to the tuning performed for the BGP process, you might want to fine-tune other routing protocols running between PE- and CE-routers. For example, you might change RIP Version 2 timers to allow them to propagate updates received from the BGP backbone faster.

Advertisement of Routes Across the Backbone

To provide a virtual private network service based on the MPLS architecture, we have seen that our backbone infrastructure is required to service VPN client sites in various locations. It must be capable of propagating routing information from these clients across the backbone for advertisement to other members of the VPN. Our description has shown that to achieve this fundamental requirement, one of the necessary tools is MP-iBGP between PE-routers; this is an integral part of the MPLS/VPN architecture.

The implications of this requirement are quite apparent. It is clear that a full mesh of MP-iBGP sessions will be required, and as the number of VPN clients and PE-routers increases, so will the number of MP-iBGP sessions across the backbone. This is clearly an administrative nightmare. We must also consider that the service provider backbone may be required to carry normal BGP traffic so that non-VPN clients that require Internet access can be provided for.

So as we consider the scalability of our network design, we must keep in mind that the number of BGP sessions between PE-routers could become quite large. This means that it may be necessary to employ techniques that can help cut down on the number of sessions that are required and also to manage the distribution of routing information across the network so that we propagate information only to parts of the network where it is necessary.

The actual number of BGP sessions that a BGP speaker should service depends on many factors, primarily the amount of memory within the router and the speed of the CPU. It is difficult to predict exactly how many of these sessions would constitute a maximum, and indeed you would not want to deploy a solution that used this maximum limit. Therefore, published guidelines suggest that a BGP speaker should not service more than 100 BGP sessions, and techniques should be deployed to reduce the amount of BGP sessions that are required. Two main techniques exist within BGP to reduce the number of sessions that are required between PE-routers, although these are not the only ones that may be used. These techniques are using route reflectors and using confederations, and both may be deployed within an MPLS/VPN topology.

BGP for VPN-IPv4 and IPv4 Routing Information

Before we consider the mechanisms that help us to control the scalability of the BGP session requirement, we must understand what type of routing information will be needed within the core of the network and at the edges. We have already discussed how the introduction of MPLS can be used to remove BGP information from our core routers and that label switching can be used based on the BGP next-hop address of any external routes. Although this helps the service provider scale the backbone, it does not mean that BGP information is no longer required by the customers of the service provider.

In the case of customers that belong to the MPLS/VPN service, we know that we can carry their routing information within MP-iBGP updates. But we may also want to carry IPv4 routing information across the backbone so that the global routing tables of the PE-routers are populated. Without this information on the PE-routers, we would not be able to provide full or partial Internet routing information to VPN or non-VPN customers unless we adopted advanced BGP mechanisms, such as eBGP multihop, in combination with central BGP route servers and default routes in the service provider backbone.

So in some cases, we need to provide BGP sessions that will carry VPN-IPv4 routes for the VPN customers and IPv4 routes for Internet customers. We could achieve this by configuring separate BGP sessions, one for the IPv4 routes and the other for the VPN-IPv4 routes. An example of this method can be seen in Figure 12-4. The relevant BGP session configurations for PE-routers San Jose and Paris are shown in Example 12-3, and output showing the relevant BGP sessions is shown within Example 12-4.

Figure 12-4   *Multiple BGP Sessions Between PE-routers*

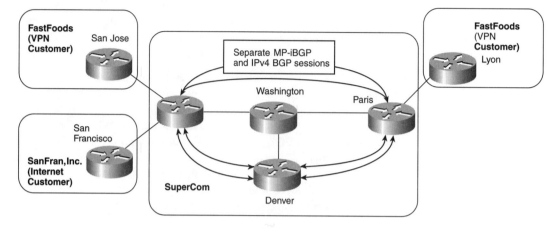

Example 12-3   *Multiple BGP Sessions Between PE-routers*

```
hostname San Jose
!
interface loopback 0
 ip address 194.22.15.2 255.255.255.255
!
interface loopback 1
 ip address 194.22.16.2 255.255.255.255
!
router bgp 1
 no bgp default ipv4-unicast
 neighbor 194.22.15.1 remote-as 1
 neighbor 194.22.15.1 update-source Loopback0
 neighbor 194.22.15.1 activate
 neighbor 194.22.16.1 remote-as 1
 neighbor 194.22.16.1 update-source Loopback1
 !
 address-family vpnv4
  neighbor 194.22.16.1 activate
  neighbor 194.22.16.1 send-community extended
 exit-address-family

hostname Paris
!
interface loopback 0
 ip address 194.22.15.1 255.255.255.255
!
interface loopback 1
 ip address 194.22.16.1 255.255.255.255
!
router bgp 1
```

Example 12-3 *Multiple BGP Sessions Between PE-routers (Continued)*

```
no bgp default ipv4-unicast
 neighbor 194.22.15.2 remote-as 1
 neighbor 194.22.15.2 update-source loopback 0
 neighbor 194.22.15.2 activate
 neighbor 194.22.16.2 remote-as 1
 neighbor 194.22.16.2 update-source loopback 1
 !
address-family vpnv4
 neighbor 194.22.16.2 activate
 neighbor 194.22.16.2 send-community extended
exit-address-family
```

Example 12-4 *Multiple BGP Sessions—**show ip bgp neighbor** Output*

```
San Jose# show ip bgp neighbor 194.22.15.1
BGP neighbor is 194.22.15.1,  remote AS 1, internal link
  BGP version 4, remote router ID 197.1.1.1
  BGP state = Established, up for 00:08:17
  Last read 00:00:17, hold time is 180, keepalive interval is 60
  seconds
  Neighbor capabilities:
    Route refresh: advertised and received
    Address family IPv4 Unicast: advertised and received
  Received 11 messages, 0 notifications, 0 in queue
  Sent 11 messages, 0 notifications, 0 in queue
  Route refresh request: received 0, sent 0
  Minimum time between advertisement runs is 5 seconds

 For address family: IPv4 Unicast
  BGP table version 1, neighbor version 1
  Index 1, Offset 0, Mask 0x2
  0 accepted prefixes consume 0 bytes
  Prefix advertised 0, suppressed 0, withdrawn 0

San Jose# show ip bgp neighbor 194.22.16.1
BGP neighbor is 194.22.16.1,  remote AS 1, internal link
  BGP version 4, remote router ID 197.1.1.1
  BGP state = Established, up for 00:08:12
  Last read 00:00:12, hold time is 180, keepalive interval is 60
  seconds
  Neighbor capabilities:
    Route refresh: advertised and received
    Address family VPNv4 Unicast: advertised and received
  Received 11 messages, 0 notifications, 0 in queue
  Sent 11 messages, 0 notifications, 0 in queue
  Route refresh request: received 0, sent 0
  Minimum time between advertisement runs is 5 seconds

 For address family: VPNv4 Unicast
  BGP table version 1, neighbor version 1
```

continues

Example 12-4   *Multiple BGP Sessions—***show ip bgp neighbor** *Output (Continued)*

```
Index 1, Offset 0, Mask 0x2
0 accepted prefixes consume 0 bytes
Prefix advertised 0, suppressed 0, withdrawn 0
```

Although the example shown in Figure 12-4 allows us to provide our desired functionality (because we are advertising VPN routes between PE-routers across MP-iBGP sessions anyway), it would be far better if we could just use these sessions for our IPv4 routes as well. Therefore, it is no surprise that MP-iBGP sessions are capable of carrying both VPN-IPv4 addresses and IPv4 addresses between PE-routers. This is controlled by the use of address families within the BGP configuration, which we discussed in Chapter 9, "MPLS/VPN Architecture Operation." A revamped configuration for PE San Jose from Figure 12-4 can be seen in Example 12-5.

Example 12-5   *MP-iBGP for VPN-IPv4 and IPv4 Route Propagation*

```
hostname San Jose
!
interface loopback 0
 ip address 194.22.15.2 255.255.255.255
!
router bgp 1

 neighbor 194.22.15.1 remote-as 1
 neighbor 194.22.15.1 update-source Loopback0

 !
 address-family vpnv4
  neighbor 194.22.15.1 activate
  neighbor 194.22.15.1 send-community extended
 exit-address-family
```

NOTE   If the same session is used for both IPv4 and VPN-IPv4 address families, then the **no bgp default ipv4-unicast** command is not required. This means that the IPv4 session need not be manually activated anymore, although this is still required to allow the VPN-IPv4 session to come active.

Example 12-6 shows that only one BGP session now exists between PE-routers San Jose and Paris, and that this session carries both IPv4 unicast and VPN-IPv4 unicast routes.

Example 12-6   *MP-iBGP Session with Two Address Families*

```
San Jose# show ip bgp neighbor 194.22.15.1
BGP neighbor is 194.22.15.1,  remote AS 1, internal link
  BGP version 4, remote router ID 197.1.1.1
  BGP state = Established, up for 00:00:05
```

Example 12-6 *MP-iBGP Session with Two Address Families (Continued)*

```
Last read 00:00:04, hold time is 180, keepalive interval is 60
seconds
Neighbor capabilities:
  Route refresh: advertised and received
  Address family IPv4 Unicast: advertised and received
  Address family VPNv4 Unicast: advertised and received
Received 20 messages, 0 notifications, 0 in queue
Sent 20 messages, 0 notifications, 0 in queue
Route refresh request: received 0, sent 0
Minimum time between advertisement runs is 5 seconds

For address family: IPv4 Unicast
BGP table version 1, neighbor version 1
Index 1, Offset 0, Mask 0x2
0 accepted prefixes consume 0 bytes
Prefix advertised 0, suppressed 0, withdrawn 0

For address family: VPNv4 Unicast
BGP table version 1, neighbor version 0
Index 1, Offset 0, Mask 0x2
0 accepted prefixes consume 0 bytes
Prefix advertised 0, suppressed 0, withdrawn 0
```

Full Mesh of MP-iBGP Between PE-routers

Now that it is clear that we can carry both VPN-IPv4 and IPv4 addresses within the same MP-iBGP sessions, we need to decide how these peering sessions between PE-routers should be deployed. The simplest way to achieve this may be to just configure a full mesh of MP-iBGP sessions between PE-routers and rely on the filtering features that we discussed in Chapter 9, such as automatic route filtering. This option can be seen in Figure 12-5.

In the topology shown in Figure 12-5, each PE-router has an MP-iBGP session with every other PE-router within the backbone. You can see that as the number of PE-routers increases, we start to encounter scaling and management problems. This is because the number of MP-iBGP sessions between the PE-routers increases at the rate of one new session per existing PE-router, for each new PE-router introduced into the network. Even more troublesome, every time you add a new router into the service provider backbone, a new BGP neighbor must be inserted into the core BGP configuration on all BGP-speaking routers in the service provider backbone to retain the full-mesh topology.

In some network deployments, this may not be an issue because the size of the infrastructure may be quite small, and this type of topology might be appropriate. However, in most cases, this type of configuration should be avoided unless the expansion of the network is known to be minimal.

Figure 12-5 *Full Mesh of MP-iBGP Between PE-routers*

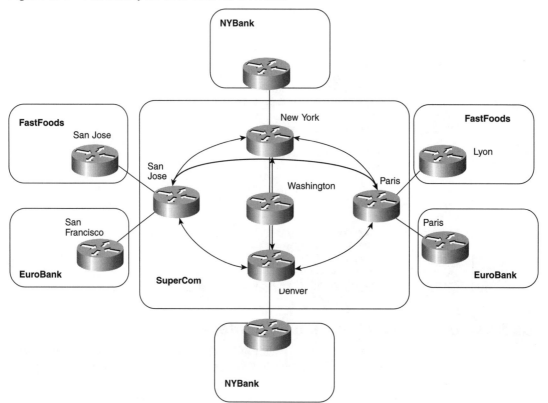

One further point of interest can be deduced from Figure 12-5: A full mesh of MP-iBGP sessions between PE-routers may not actually be required because of the nature of the distribution of VPN routing information. We have already discussed that the MPLS/VPN architecture requires that PE-routers learn routes only for VPNs that are directly connected to them. If we take a look once more at our example, we can see that the PE-routers in New York and Denver have only customers that belong to the NYBank VPN, and PE-routers San Jose and Paris have only customers that belong to the FastFoods and EuroBank VPNs. This means that PE-routers New York and Denver do not need to receive any information about the FastFoods or EuroBank VPNs, and the San Jose and Paris routers do not need to receive any information about the NYBank VPN.

Separation of MP-iBGP Sessions Between PE-routers

To help alleviate the need of a full mesh of MP-iBGP sessions between PE-routers, and to make sure that PE-routers receive only routes that are applicable to the VPNs that they service, we can partition each of the PE-routers into separate mini MP-iBGP clusters. Each of these clusters is still required to run a full MP-iBGP mesh, but the size of each mesh can be considerably reduced. The actual session requirement is based on which PE-routers need to send routing information to which other PE-routers.

Figure 12-6 provides an example of this and shows that our previous example has now been changed. MP-iBGP sessions now are provisioned only between PE-routers that hold customers that require the same VPN routing information.

Figure 12-6 *Separation of MP-iBGP Sessions Between PE-routers*

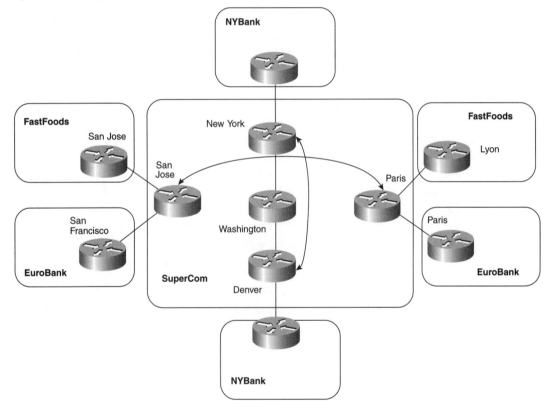

Although this solution provides the capability to separate the full-mesh MP-iBGP requirement, it does not provide a scalable solution in terms of network growth, and it eventually suffers from the same drawbacks as the previous solution. It also introduces additional complexity in the network design and deployment phases because the MP-iBGP sessions must be carefully planned before introduction of a new customer or site.

As seen in Figure 12-6, as the network grows, the number of MP-iBGP sessions grows, albeit in separate full-mesh clusters. If a further PE-router were added to this sample topology, and if this required routes for the FastFoods VPN, then a further MP-iBGP session would need to be configured to this new PE-router from both the San Jose and Paris routers.

It should be clear by now that a different mechanism is required to help scale the topology. This mechanism is provided through the use of BGP route reflectors or confederations.

Introduction of Route Reflector Hierarchy

The term *route reflection* is used to describe the operation of a BGP speaker advertising a route that was learned through an iBGP session to another iBGP peer. This practice is prohibited in normal BGP operation because the traditional BGP routing protocol had no safeguards against routing loops within an autonomous system (thus requiring a full mesh of iBGP speakers). A BGP speaker that propagates iBGP routes to other iBGP peers is called a route reflector, and such a route is called a reflected route.

With the introduction of route reflectors, the scaling of the MP-iBGP sessions becomes easier because the full-mesh requirement is eliminated. However, there will always be a finite number of sessions that can be made to the route reflector, so a hierarchical structure of route reflectors may be desirable; the design of the network should be capable of catering to its introduction. The actual number of sessions that a route reflector can service without affecting its functionality or its capability to reflect routing information is difficult to judge. It depends on many factors, such as the number of routes per session, the use of peer groups, the CPU power, and the memory resources of the route reflector.

For these reasons, formal recommendations are few, and no recommendation can really replace good design testing before full implementation. However, one scenario, using an RSP2 on a 7500 series router in one of the major core sites of the Internet, showed that it was possible to carry full Internet routing (about 40,000 routes at the time) for approximately 75 iBGP neighbors and still keep a reasonable level of CPU utilization.

NOTE   It should be noted that with the introduction of more advanced processors on various Cisco Systems platforms, this number is likely to be far greater, even though the full Internet routing table is now approximately 80,000 routes. With the introduction of peer-group support on route reflector iBGP sessions, this number will increase even further.

NOTE   In a large network, where the number of iBGP sessions on route reflectors is expected to be very high, you could deploy a design in which the route reflector does not forward any user traffic, but serves only as a route propagation device. Such a router would commonly have only one interface, deserving the name "router-on-a-stick."

As new PE-routers are introduced and the amount of neighbors or routes increases, it is good practice for processor load and memory usage to be monitored so that an optimal configuration can be maintained. If memory and CPU usage continue to increase, measures such as increased memory, higher-performance routers, or more route reflectors should be introduced into the topology.

It is always a good idea to run more than one route reflector so that a redundant configuration is provided. However, in a large-scale environment, it may be necessary to run even more than two route reflectors to help scale the topology and also provide the capability for expansion in the future. With this in mind, a suitable topology might be as shown in Figure 12-7. This topology illustrates regional ISP points of presence (POPs) connected to one or multiple core POPs. It also shows the hierarchical route reflection techniques, but it is not meant to represent an exact topology that will suit all customer needs.

Figure 12-7   *Hierarchical Route Reflection—Sample Topology*

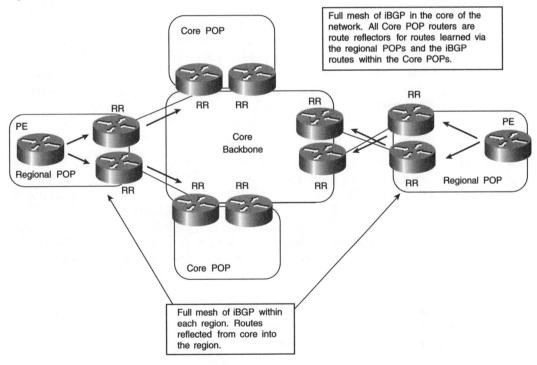

In Figure 12-7, we can see that the network can be split into separate route reflector clusters. Each router that is not a route reflector (in this case, any routers internal to the regional

POPs) is required to peer to two separate route reflectors, each of which is either in a different cluster or within the same cluster.

NOTE	For a full discussion on route reflectors and route reflector clusters, refer to the Cisco press publication *Internet Routing Architectures,* Second Edition, written by Bassam Halabi.

Previously, it was not advisable for peer clients to separate route reflector clusters because of unnecessary route propagation, sometimes referred to as routing information loops. However, this restriction was lifted, and the BGP selection process was changed so that the chances of a routing information loop were reduced considerably. However, it is still considered to be a good design practice for a BGP router to be peered only with route reflectors in the same cluster.

NOTE	The definition of a routing information loop is the unnecessary propagation of routing information, thus causing duplication of routing information. This is *not* the same as a routing loop, in which the information contained within the routing table of a particular device differs from another device, potentially causing a "ping-pong" effect of packets entering a loop between the two devices.

The route reflectors within the core of the network are peered together in a full iBGP mesh. This means that any information received from a client (the clients, in this case, are the regional POP route reflectors) by a route reflector within the core will be advertised into the other clusters via the full iBGP mesh between the route reflectors. This type of configuration provides redundancy in case one of the route reflectors fails or the path to this route reflector becomes unavailable. It also potentially provides geographic redundancy where each of the route reflectors is in a physically different location to the other.

NOTE	If more than one route reflector exists within a cluster, it is mandatory for all clients to peer with all the route reflectors within the cluster. If one client does not have all these peerings, then it is possible that the BGP information will be partitioned within the cluster.

Route Reflection of PE Routes to Aid Scaling

Although Figure 12-7 provides a good hierarchical and scalable route reflection design, in many cases, this type of topology will not be available or even required. In a standard, large-scale ISP design in which external routing information is required within the core of the network, this topology is certainly appropriate. It may also be appropriate if there is a requirement to send VPN-IPv4 routes between PE-routers within each region and across regions, or if the size of the MPLS/VPN backbone dictates that multiple route reflectors be deployed to help scale the topology.

However, with the introduction of the MPLS-enabled VPN service, our real requirement is the propagation of external routing information between PE-routers. This information should not be necessary within the core of the network unless our core routers are acting as route reflectors between regional sites, as in the example shown in Figure 12-7. This means that dedicated route reflectors may be deployed; the number of these will depend on the topology and size of the backbone network, as well as on how the reflection of routes between VPNs is performed. The level of redundancy for route reflection must also be considered, along with the geographical distribution of the BGP peering sessions, so that intraregional connectivity can be maintained in the event of a link failure from the region into the backbone.

To achieve this type of topology, we have some choices on how to reflect routes between the PE-routers. Our first choice is to deploy a number of router reflectors and then peer all PE-routers to these route reflectors. This type of topology can be seen in Figure 12-8. For the sake of simplicity, only two route reflectors are shown.

Although this type of topology achieves our objective of route reflection between PE-routers, and although all PE-routers are capable of learning VPN routes from other PE-routers, some PE-routers will receive routes for a particular VPN for which they have no members. An example of this is the San Jose PE-router. It will receive VPN routes for the NYBank VPN, but it does not have any attached customers that belong to that VPN. This means that the routes will be dropped through use of the automatic route filtering feature that we described in Chapter 9.

NOTE   It is important to understand that whenever route reflectors are deployed, there is a danger that the route reflector may select a best path that is different than the best path that would have been selected by a client if it had been fully meshed. Although this does not cause a problem in forwarding traffic, it may introduce some suboptimal routing if the chosen best path is not the closest exit point from a client's point of view. This is because the scope of route reflectors is to reduce the iBGP session requirement without having any impact on the packet forwarding scheme.

Figure 12-8   *Introduction of Route Reflection for MP-iBGP*

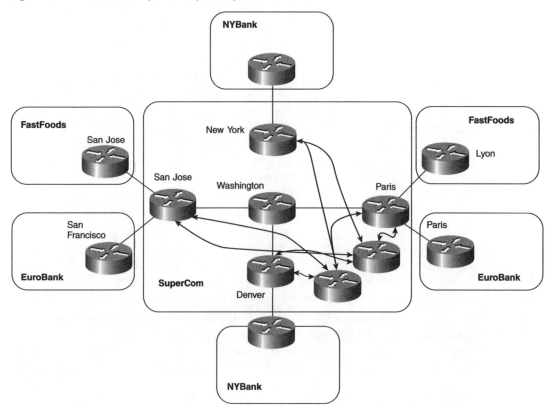

Route Reflector Partitioning

To try to overcome the unnecessary advertisement of routes to PE-routers that do not import them, we need to filter routing information at some point in the network before this information is advertised across any MP-iBGP sessions. This filtering could be achieved through mechanisms such as access lists, or it could be achieved through careful layout of the topology.

If the careful layout of the topology approach is taken, then our main objective is to split the network into multiple route reflector clusters, each servicing a certain number of VPNs. The PE-router clients of these route reflectors will then receive only routes that belong to the relevant VPNs that they service. We will see in the sections that follow that we can achieve this objective in several ways.

Our first deployment option is to split up the topology of the network so that PE-routers peer only with certain route reflectors and each PE-router services only certain VPNs. This technique is illustrated in Figure 12-9.

Figure 12-9   *Partitioning Route Reflectors Between PE-routers*

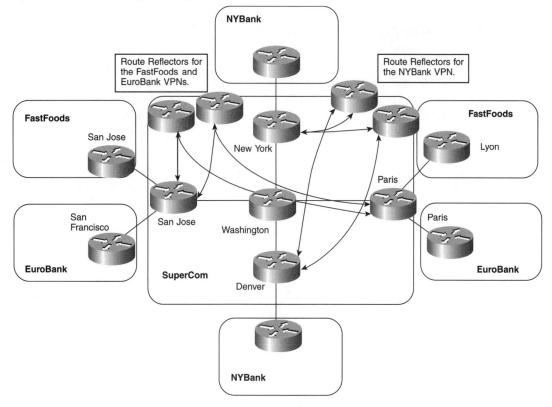

Although this approach enables us to partition the route reflection, it does not provide us with an easily adapted solution if we want to add a different VPN to an existing PE-router in the future. If we consider a situation in which an existing PE-router suddenly needs to service a VPN to which it has not provided routes previously, we would need to change the PE-router configuration. This configuration change would be necessary so that a further session to another route reflector (one that serviced the new VPN) could be obtained, to somehow filter the routes so that we sent routes only to the correct route reflectors.

If we examine the topology in Figure 12-9, we can see that if the San Jose PE-router wants to join the NYBank VPN at some point in the future, we will need to make several configuration changes. The first change would be to configure an MP-iBGP session from the San Jose PE-router to the route reflector that services the NYBank VPN. When this session configuration has been added, filters would need to be added to prevent the San Jose

PE-router from sending any routes from the FastFoods or EuroBank VPNs toward the NYBank VPN route reflector, and also from sending any NYBank VPN routes to the FastFoods or EuroBank VPN route reflector. There are obvious drawbacks to this approach, such as the configuration and management overhead.

Standard Community Filtering on PE-routers

Our requirement to filter routes before advertisement from a PE-router can be achieved through the use of standard BGP communities. This provides us with the capability to partition the route reflectors. Instead of relying on topology or extensive access lists to filter the routes, however, we can now rely on filtering based on the community value. In doing so, we are easily able to add a new VPN to an existing PE-router and just configure a session to the relevant route reflector.

With this method, we must assign a separate standard BGP community for each VRF (this could be the same as the route target, as long as its format is not extended). We also must apply outbound route filtering, based on the BGP community, when the routes from the VRF are advertised toward the route reflectors. This enables us to send only certain VPN routes to selected route reflectors so that any PE-router that has a session with the route reflector will receive the routes. This technique is demonstrated in Figure 12-10, and the relevant route target and standard BGP communities are shown in Table 12-5. This example is similar to the one in Figure 12-9; in this case, however, the San Jose PE-router needs to service all VPNs, so it has sessions to several route reflectors. For the sake of simplicity, only the San Jose PE-router MP-iBGP sessions are shown in the figure.

In our previous example, we would need to apply extensive filtering to the San Jose router to achieve our goal. However, the difference now is that each PE-router is capable of peering to multiple route reflectors and sending only the relevant routes for each VPN based on the standard BGP community value.

Table 12-5   *Route Target and Standard Communities for SuperCom Route Reflection*

VPN Name	Route Target	Standard Community Value
FastFoods	100:26	100:26
EuroBank	100:27	100:27
NYBank	100:28	100:28

Figure 12-10 *Standard Community Filtering Toward Route Reflectors*

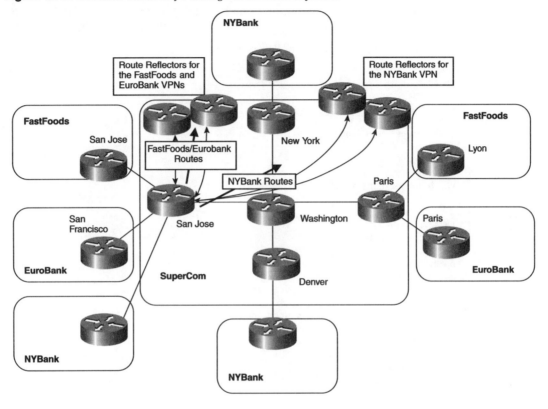

The configuration for the San Jose PE-router shown in Figure 12-10 can be seen in Example 12-7. The FastFoods/EuroBank route reflector has a BGP peering address of 194.22.15.5/32, and the NYBank route reflector has an address of 194.22.15.6/32 (per Table 12-1).

Example 12-7   *Standard Community Filtering Toward Route Reflectors*

```
interface loopback 0
 ip address 194.22.15.2 255.255.255.255
!
ip vrf FastFoods
 rd 1:26
 route-target both 100:26
!
ip vrf EuroBank
 rd 1:27
 route-target both 100:27
!
ip vrf NYBank
 rd 1:28
 route-target both 100:28
!
router bgp 1
 neighbor 194.22.15.5 remote-as 1
 neighbor 194.22.15.5 update-source loopback0
 neighbor 194.22.15.6 remote-as 1
 neighbor 194.22.15.6 update-source loopback0
!
address-family ipv4 vrf FastFoods
 neighbor 195.12.2.6 remote-as 100
 neighbor 195.12.2.6 activate
 neighbor 195.12.2.6 route-map FastFoods_routes_in in
exit address-family
!
address-family ipv4 vrf EuroBank
 neighbor 10.2.1.6 remote-as 150
 neighbor 10.2.1.6 activate
 neighbor 10.2.1.6 route-map EuroBank_routes_in in
exit address-family
!
address-family ipv4 vrf NYBank
 neighbor 196.27.6.6 remote-as 200
 neighbor 196.27.6.6 activate
 neighbor 196.27.6.6 route-map NYBank_routes_in in
exit address-family
!
address-family vpnv4
 neighbor 194.22.15.5 activate
 neighbor 194.22.15.5 send-community extended
 neighbor 194.22.15.5 route-map FastFoods_EuroBank_routes_out out
 neighbor 194.22.15.6 activate
 neighbor 194.22.15.6 send-community extended
 neighbor 194.22.15.6 route-map NYBank_routes_out out
exit address-family
!
```

Example 12-7 *Standard Community Filtering Toward Route Reflectors (Continued)*

```
ip community-list 1 permit 100:26
ip community-list 2 permit 100:27
ip community-list 3 permit 100:28
!
route-map FastFoods_routes_in permit 10
 set community 100:26
!
route-map EuroBank_routes_in permit 10
 set community 100:27
!
route-map NYBank_routes_in permit 10
 set community 100:28
!
route-map FastFoods_EuroBank_routes_out permit 10
 match community 1
!
route-map FastFoods_EuroBank_routes_out permit 20
 match community 2
!
route-map NYBank_routes_out permit 10
 match community 3
```

Route Target Attribute-based Filtering on Route Reflectors

Although the previous example of standard community-based filtering provides a workable solution, it still requires configuration on each PE-router within the backbone so that only relevant routes are sent toward the route reflectors.

A different approach to this is to apply the filtering at the route reflector. With the introduction of route target-based control of VPN-IPv4 prefixes serviced by a route reflector, it is possible to limit the number of prefixes that the route reflector has to manage. This is achieved by specifying which route targets should be accepted by the route reflector for reflection to PE-clients.

We have already described that a route reflector will not currently filter any routes by default (although, as will be seen later in this chapter, this will change with the use of the **bgp rr-group** command). This means that configuration is needed to allow for certain routes to be filtered. This can be achieved again through the use of route maps. Figure 12-11 shows an example of the FastFoods/EuroBank route reflector cluster.

With this feature, it is no longer necessary to configure each PE-router with standard communities so that outbound filtering toward the route reflector will occur. In addition, you could have multiple sessions to different route reflectors and let the route reflector take care of VPN-IPv4 prefix filtering and the correct advertisement of the routes to all relevant PE-routers within the MPLS/VPN domain. Example 12-8 shows the configuration of one of the route reflectors from Figure 12-11.

Figure 12-11 *Route Reflector Filtering Using Route Target*

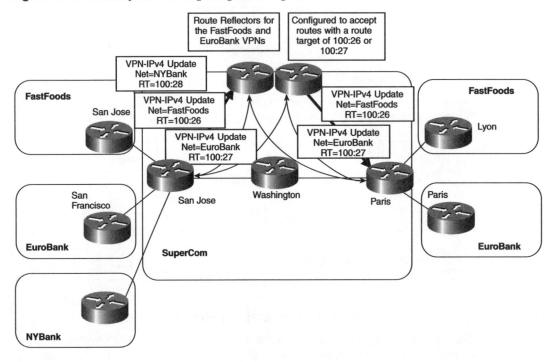

Example 12-8 *Route Reflector Extended Community Filtering Configuration*

```
router bgp 1
 no bgp default ipv4-unicast
 neighbor 194.22.15.2 remote-as 1
 neighbor 194.22.15.2 update-source Loopback0
 neighbor 194.22.15.1 remote-as 1
 neighbor 194.22.15.1 update-source Loopback0
 !
 address-family vpnv4
 neighbor 194.22.15.2 activate
 neighbor 194.22.15.2 route-reflector-client
 neighbor 194.22.15.2 send-community extended
 neighbor 194.22.15.2 route-map RTfilter in
 neighbor 194.22.15.1 activate
 neighbor 194.22.15.1 route-reflector-client
 neighbor 194.22.15.1 send-community extended
 exit-address-family
!
ip extcommunity-list 1 permit rt 100:26 rt 100:27
!
route-map RTfilter permit 10
 match extcommunity 1
```

Route Reflection and ORF Capability

Although the two previous examples have provided differing ways of filtering unwanted routing updates, both have drawbacks. In the case of standard community filtering on the PE-routers, the overhead of having to maintain multiple filters for each PE-router within the backbone is restrictive. In the case of route target filtering on the route reflectors, unwanted updates are sent toward only the route reflector to be filtered. Therefore, the ultimate solution would be to filter updates at the PE-routers so that they are not sent toward route reflectors that do not need them, but also to make this dynamic so that extensive filtering configuration is not necessary on the PE.

This solution is provided through use of the ORF capability that was described in Chapter 9. Using this capability, each route reflector is preconfigured with a list of route targets that it will accept for reflection to any PE-clients. All the PE-clients are treated as a single peer group, so the ORF capability is used to set the outbound filtering of the PE-client so that it does *not* send unwanted routes toward the route reflector. This is shown in Figure 12-12.

Figure 12-12 *Route Reflection and ORF Capability*

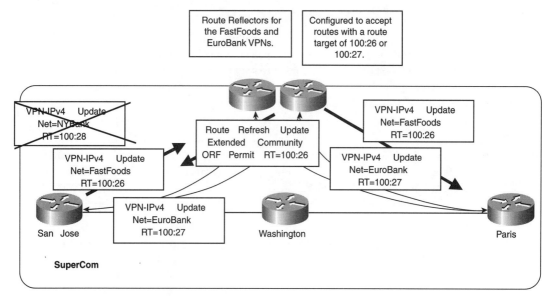

The functionality depicted in Figure 12-12 is automatic through configuration of an extended community list and route reflector group. Table 12-6 shows all the necessary commands for the route reflector configuration.

Table 12-6   *Route Reflection with ORF Capability*

Step	Command	Purpose
1	**ip extcommunity-list** *extcommunity-list number*	This command provides the facility to set up an extended community list that specifies all the permitted route target attributes that will be referenced through the **bgp rr-group** command.
2	**bgp rr-group** *extcommunity-list number ≠ name*	This command provides the facility to set up a route reflector group, which is similar in nature to a peer group. The *extcommunity-list* argument enables you to specify which extended community list should be used to indicate which routes, based on their route target, should be propagated through the ORF update to all PE-neighbors of the group.

BGP Confederations Deployment

BGP confederations are another mechanism for controlling the explosion of iBGP meshing. They can be used instead of or in combination with route reflectors. The basic functionality of BGP confederations is to split up the autonomous system into smaller, more manageable, autonomous systems, which are represented as one single autonomous system to BGP peers external to the confederation.

NOTE   For an in-depth discussion of BGP confederations, refer to the Cisco Press title *Internet Routing Architectures,* Second Edition, by Bassam Halabi, or RFC 1965, "Autonomous System Confederations for BGP."

By creating smaller autonomous system domains, or sub-ASs, it is possible to restrict the number of iBGP sessions that are required—a full mesh is required only within each sub-AS. A further advantage to this method, which may be useful in very large-scale topologies, is that separate IGPs can be deployed across the service provider backbone, which helps with the scaling of the IGP. This feature is not possible when route reflectors are used, unless the BGP next-hop addresses are leaked across sub-AS boundaries, because you cannot reset the BGP next-hop on a route reflector. (However, you can do this on a confederation boundary router.)

NOTE	Note that although confederations reduce the size of the iBGP mesh, they make it harder to partition the routing information if the separation of the IGP between sub-AS approach is taken. This is because packets must be forwarded across the confederation boundary, which in an MPLS/VPN environment means that each the edge confederation boundary routers must have access to all VPN routes (unless complex partitioning of the routes between multiple edges is deployed).

To help explain this complex subject, we will consider the topology shown in Figure 12-13. This topology depicts a service provider, Confed.Com, that has three regional POPs, located in San Jose, Paris, and London, connected in a full mesh. All relevant IP address assignments are shown in Table 12-7.

Figure 12-13 *Confed.Com Network Topology Example*

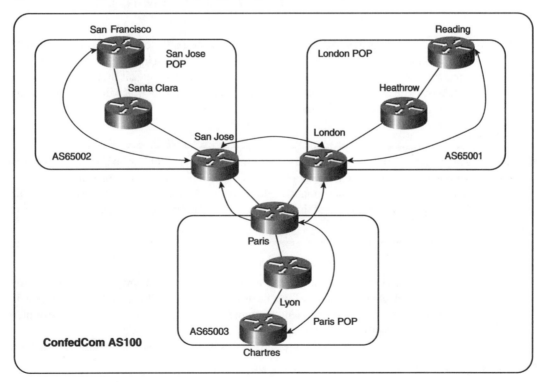

Table 12-7 *IP Address Assignments for Confed.Com Backbone*

POP	Site	Subnet
San Jose	San Jose (Loopback0)	194.17.1.1/32
	San Francisco (Loopback0)	194.17.1.2/32
	Santa Clara (Loopback0)	194.17.1.3/32
London	Reading (Loopback0)	197.58.27.3/32
	Heathrow (Loopback0)	197.58.27.2/32
	London (Loopback0)	197.58.27.3/32
Paris	Paris (Loopback0)	195.12.14.1/32
	Chartres (Loopback0)	195.12.14.3/32
	Lyon (Loopback0)	195.12.14.2/32

Figure 12-13 shows that MPLS and MP-iBGP have been deployed within each regional POP and that a full mesh of eBGP is used to connect each regional POP. Each POP is a separate sub-AS, so our requirement of an iBGP full mesh among all BGP speaking routers is relaxed. The exchange of routes and labels between the sub-ASs will differ, depending of which type of deployment option is taken.

NOTE   Although a full mesh of eBGP is used to connect each regional POP, it should be noted that within a confederation environment, the eBGP session between sub-AS's differs from normal eBGP. The attributes of any routes advertised across the session are not changed, including the BGP next-hop of the route. In addition, normal iBGP rules apply within each sub-AS.

When confederations are used, we have a couple of choices on how to design and deploy the IGP. Which choice is taken affects the use of the MPLS/VPN architecture and how it functions in this type of environment. Example 12-9 provides configuration for PE-routers San Francisco, San Jose, London, and Reading, which will be used in the examples that follow. For the sake of simplicity, the Paris POP will not be considered within the examples.

Example 12-9 *BGP Confederation—Example Configuration*

```
hostname Reading
!
ip vrf EuroBank
 rd 1:27
 route-target export 100:27
```

Example 12-9 *BGP Confederation—Example Configuration (Continued)*

```
 route-target import 100:27
!
interface loopback0
 ip address 197.58.27.3 255.255.255.255
!
router bgp 65001
 no bgp default ipv4-unicast
 bgp confederation identifier 100
 bgp confederation-peers 65002

 neighbor 197.58.27.1 remote-as 65001
 neighbor 197.58.27.1 update-source Loopback0
 neighbor 197.58.27.1 activate
 !
 address-family ipv4 vrf EuroBank
 redistribute connected
 no auto-summary
 no synchronization
 exit-address-family
 !
 address-family vpnv4
 neighbor 197.58.27.1 activate
 neighbor 197.58.27.1 send-community extended
 exit-address-family


hostname London
!
ip vrf EuroBank
 rd 1:27
 route-target export 100:27
 route-target import 100:27
!
interface loopback0
 ip address 197.58.27.1 255.255.255.255
!
router bgp 65001
 no synchronization
 no bgp default ipv4-unicast
 bgp confederation identifier 100
 bgp confederation peers 65002
 neighbor 197.58.27.3 remote-as 65001
 neighbor 197.58.27.3 update-source Loopback0
 neighbor 197.58.27.3 activate
 neighbor 10.1.1.14 remote-as 65002
 neighbor 10.1.1.14 activate
 !
 address-family ipv4 vrf EuroBank
 no auto-summary
 no synchronization
 exit-address-family
```

continues

Example 12-9 *BGP Confederation—Example Configuration (Continued)*

```
 !
 address-family vpnv4
 neighbor 197.58.27.3 activate
 neighbor 197.58.27.3 send-community extended
 neighbor 10.1.1.14 activate
 neighbor 10.1.1.14 send-community extended
 exit-address-family


hostname San Jose
 !
ip vrf EuroBank
 rd 1:27
 route-target export 100:27
 route-target import 100:27
 !
interface loopback0
 ip address 194.17.1.1 255.255.255.255
 !
router bgp 65002
 no synchronization
 no bgp default ipv4-unicast
 bgp confederation identifier 100
 bgp confederation peers 65001
 neighbor 194.17.1.2 remote-as 65002
 neighbor 194.17.1.2 update-source Loopback0
 neighbor 194.17.1.2 activate
 neighbor 10.1.1.13 remote-as 65001
 neighbor 10.1.1.13 activate
 !
 address-family ipv4 vrf EuroBank
 no auto-summary
 no synchronization
 exit-address-family
 !
 address-family vpnv4
 neighbor 194.17.1.2 activate
 neighbor 194.17.1.2 send-community extended
 neighbor 10.1.1.13 activate
 neighbor 10.1.1.13 send-community extended
 exit-address-family


hostname San Francisco
 !
ip vrf EuroBank
 rd 1:27
 route-target export 100:27
 route-target import 100:27
 !
interface loopback0
 ip address 194.17.1.2 255.255.255.255
 !
```

Example 12-9 *BGP Confederation—Example Configuration (Continued)*

```
router bgp 65002
 no bgp default ipv4-unicast
 bgp confederation identifier 100
 redistribute connected
 neighbor 194.17.1.1 remote-as 65002
 neighbor 194.17.1.1 update-source Loopback0
 neighbor 194.17.1.1 activate
 !
 address-family ipv4 vrf EuroBank
 redistribute connected
 no auto-summary
 no synchronization
 exit-address-family
 !
 address-family vpnv4
 neighbor 194.17.1.1 activate
 neighbor 194.17.1.1 send-community extended
 exit-address-family
```

BGP Confederations—Single IGP Environment

When the choice is taken to run a single IGP process across the whole BGP confederation, normal iBGP rules apply, so no BGP attributes are changed, including the next-hop for each route that is exchanged between sub-AS boundaries. We have already discussed how an MPLS LSR assigns a label for each internal route that it learns through its IGP. This does not change within a BGP confederation environment, so a label for every BGP next-hop, as assigned by each PE-router within the backbone, should exist. Label swapping can occur to all customer VPN routes.

An example of this type of connectivity can be seen in Figure 12-14. This example also shows the advertisement of a VPN route and the relevant label distribution to obtain connectivity.

Figure 12-14 shows that each sub-AS runs the same IGP process as all other sub-ASs. eBGP is used between sub-ASs, but normal iBGP rules apply across the sub-AS boundaries. This means that the next-hop of any route is not changed and must be reachable by each sub-AS. In the case of MPLS, a label must exist for the BGP next-hop so that packets can be label-switched to the egress LSR for the external destination.

In our example, the Confed.Com San Francisco PE-router receives an update for 195.12.2.0/24 from the EuroBank VPN customer. This update is populated into the EuroBank VRF and is advertised using MP-iBGP to the Confed.Com San Jose PE-router with a next-hop of 194.17.1.2/32 and a VRF label of 11. This route is then advertised across the confederation sub-AS boundary to the Confed.Com London PE-router, with the next-hop and VRF label unchanged. The London router then advertises the route to the Reading PE-router, which installs it into the EuroBank VRF.

Figure 12-14 *BGP Confederations—Single IGP Environment*

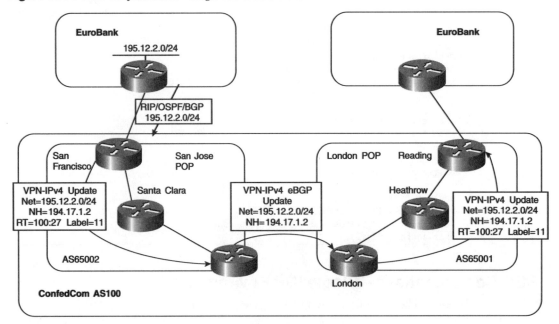

When a packet is sent from one EuroBank site to the other, because a label exists for the BGP next-hop of the route (194.17.1.2/32, in our example), the VRF label is prepended/pushed on to the packet and is label-switched across the Confed.Com backbone to the San Francisco PE-router. The packet will arrive at the San Francisco router with a one-level label stack (the top level will have been popped at the Santa Clara P-router); this label will have a value of 11, as originally set by the San Francisco router.

BGP Confederations—Multiple IGP Environment

When BGP confederations are deployed and each sub-AS uses its own IGP process, the next-hop for all BGP routes is still unchanged across sub-AS boundaries. This means that the BGP next-hop addresses must be reachable from within each sub-AS, or connectivity will be broken. You might think that by redistributing the BGP next-hop addresses between sub-AS IGP processes, connectivity could be restored. This is certainly the case in a non-MPLS environment. However, in the case of MPLS/VPN, we need to consider an example to understand whether this redistribution will allow connectivity between sub-ASs. Figure 12-15 shows a sample topology with a different IGP process in each sub-AS.

Figure 12-15 *BGP Confederations—Multiple IGP Environment*

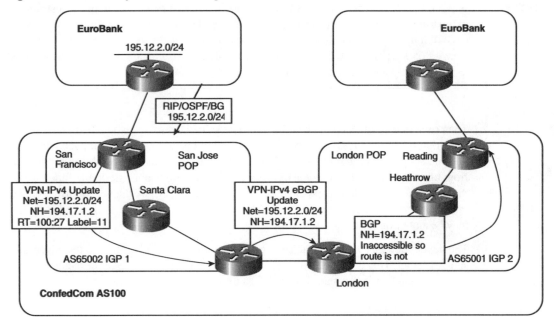

Within Figure 12-15, we can see that the San Jose PE-router learns routes from other PE-routers within its own sub-AS, AS65002, through the use of MP-iBGP. These routes are advertised across the sub-AS boundary MP-iBGP session to the London PE-router with the next-hop and label information unchanged.

The first thing to notice is that the London PE-router is incapable of advertising these routes to other PE-routers because the next-hop for the routes is inaccessible: It belongs to the IGP running within the AS65002 sub-AS. This is because of the requirement within BGP that the next-hop of the route be accessible. To rectify this situation, we could try to redistribute the BGP next-hop addresses for each route across the sub-AS boundaries, or we could configure static routes on the London PE-router. This would allow us to label-switch packets to the egress LSR.

A careful reader might notice that BGP was not mentioned as an option for the distribution of next-hop addresses between sub-AS boundaries. This is because labels are not assigned to BGP routes. Therefore, if this protocol were used to advertise the next-hop addresses from AS65002 to AS65001, label switching would not work—no label would be assigned to the next-hop addresses of VPN routes.

The problem with this approach is that multiple static host routes would be required, or redistribution between IGP processes would need to be configured. It is arguable that the reason to deploy confederations is to help scale the IGP and to hide instability in one POP from other POP sites. If this is the case, then redistribution is not a desirable function. On the other hand, the initial scope of confederations was not to hide the IGP information, but rather to reduce the number of iBGP sessions. If this is the requirement, then redistribution may be an option.

The next option that we have is to set the next-hop of all the VPN routes to the advertising sub-AS router. This would cause all routes to be advertised with a BGP next-hop that pointed to the San Jose router. Figure 12-16 illustrates this.

Figure 12-16 *Resetting of Next-hop at Subconfederation Boundary*

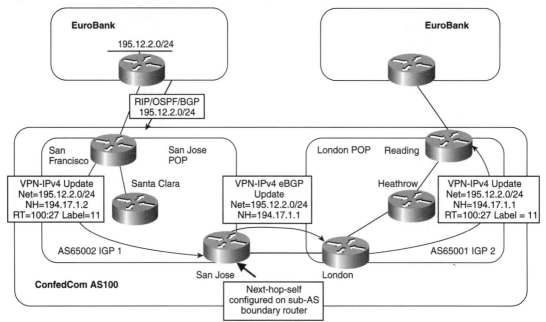

At first glance, this appears to solve the problem. However, if we consider how the Reading router will forward traffic destined for the EuroBank VPN via the San Francisco PE-router, we can see that a problem exists with this mechanism. When the Reading router received a packet, it would append a two-level label stack. The first label would be the VPN label—in our case, label 11—and the second label would be for the egress PE-router. The egress PE-router is actually the BGP next-hop of the route, so the Reading router would apply a label that corresponded to the San Jose router.

The problem with this approach is that packets would be label-switched to the San Jose router, but that router would not be capable of forwarding the packets because it would not understand the second level label (the VPN label). Therefore, a mechanism is required to allow label exchange to occur between sub-AS boundaries, but without the requirement of injecting IGP information between the sub-ASs. This is achieved by allocating a new stack of labels at the sub-AS boundary when **next-hop-self** is configured. The act of resetting the next-hop causes the PE-router to assign a new label to represent the route and advertise it outside the region across the MP-eBGP connection between confederation peers. An illustration of this technique can be seen in Figure 12-17.

NOTE   The label can also be reset by the receiving sub-AS PE-router through use of the **next-hop-self** command. This has the advantage of not having to keep a /32 route for the confederation peer within the receiving sub-AS.

In Figure 12-17, the San Jose PE-router has assigned a label of 12 to a VPN-IPv4 update that it has sent to the London PE-router. The San Jose router is capable of mapping this label to a two-level label stack to reach the San Francisco PE-router, where the VPN-IPv4 route originated. In this type of topology, if the next-hop of a VPN route is changed, one level of label is used across the sub-AS boundary; this label represents the VPN route as seen by the boundary router. The IGP label that got the packet to the boundary router will have been removed.

On the return path, the boundary router replaces this label with a two-level label stack that consists of the original VPN label, as assigned by the originating PE-router, and an IGP label to carry the packet to the originating PE-router. The subsequent forwarding sequence for the example shown in Figure 12-17 can be seen in Figure 12-18.

Figure 12-17 *Label Exchange Using MP-eBGP and **next-hop-self***

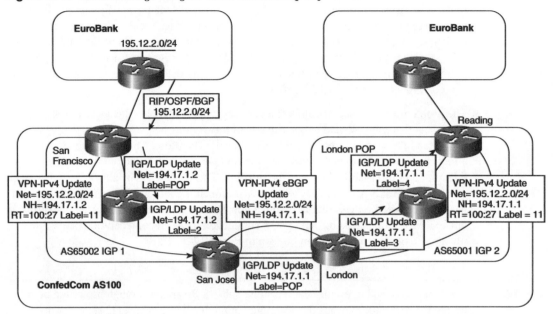

Figure 12-18 *Label Exchange Using MP-eBGP—Forwarding Example*

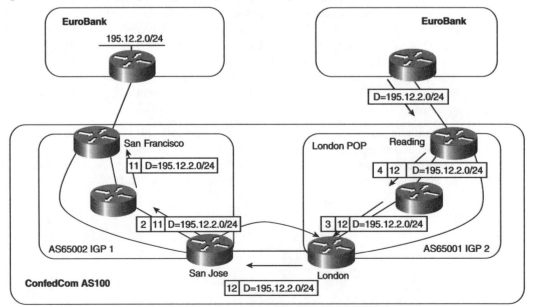

| NOTE | Only one label is used between the sub-AS peers shown in Figure 12-18 because the IGP label associated with the BGP next-hop address has a value of 2 (implicit-null) and therefore has been popped by the upstream hop, per the penultimate hop popping rules discussed in Chapter 2. |

PE-router Provisioning and Scaling

When provisioning an MPLS/VPN solution, one of the major concerns is how to scale the PE-router configuration and what limits should be drawn so that the configuration can scale. This is certainly not a trivial exercise, and numerous factors will affect this scaling, some of which we will cover during this section. There are no "magic" numbers relevant to each and every design, and the limitations that will be used very much depend on the actual deployment and design requirements.

As with all new technologies, deployment experience is generally sketchy (at best). Therefore, only limited information is available for any design decisions. An amount of theoretical data must be used. This does not mean that a successful deployment of the architecture cannot take place, although a certain amount of tuning may need to occur during the deployment phases of the design so that an optimal production environment is produced.

The first implication of the MPLS/VPN architecture to understand is that each of the PE-routers does not need to carry every route that belongs to the customers of the VPN service. This means that, potentially, the amount of memory required to hold BGP routes may be reduced. However, the information within the BGP routes is increased to include such things as extended attributes, which must be held in memory.

Multiple VRFs may be used within the PE configuration. There is no hard limit on the number of VRFs that can be configured on a PE-router—this is bounded by the number of interfaces. A certain number of data structures is required for each VRF, but this does not cause a significant amount of memory increase. Each VRF can hold as many routes as it needs. The only limit on this, as with standard BGP routing, is the amount of available memory on the PE-router. This is the real limit on PE scaling, and exactly how many routes can be held in a router will depend on such things as the number of BGP neighbors that advertise the routes and the amount of memory required to store the attributes contained within the paths of the routes.

| NOTE | To place an upper limit on the memory usage incurred by each VRF, you can use the **maximum routes** command in the VRF definition to limit the total number of routes that can reside in a VRF. You also can use **neighbor maximum-prefix** command to limit the number of routes received from a CE-router running BGP with the PE-router. |

When provisioning for PE-to-CE connectivity, it is important to bear in mind that the current IOS implementation provides a maximum of 32 protocol descriptor blocks (PDBs) per PE-router. One PDB is used per protocol instance, including static and connected. Therefore, careful design is required when provisioning the PE-router so that no more than 32 protocol instances are planned for.

If BGP is used between PE- and CE-routers, then only one BGP process is required and only 1 PDB is used. Even if you use BGP in several VRFs, they are considered as different routing contexts that run within the same BGP process. The situation is similar with RIP if multiple routing contexts within the RIP process are configured. However, if OSPF is used for PE-CE connectivity, separate OSPF processes are required (one per VRF), and one PDB is used per VRF where you run an OSPF process.

For example, consider a PE-router in which you have to run BGP with some sites, OSPF with the majority of the sites, RIP with a few sites, and static routing toward the rest of the sites. If all the sites for each routing protocol instance were contained within the same VRF, then only six PDBs would be necessary (one for BGP, one for OSPF, one for RIP, one for static routing, one for connected routing, and one for the service provider backbone IGP). However, if each site belonged to a different VRF, then the number of PDBs would increase.

Additional Connectivity Requirements—Internet Access

A common requirement within most network deployments will be that Internet access is available to some or all sites within a VPN. This Internet access may be provided through a different service provider than the one offering the MPLS/VPN service, or it may be through the same organization. If Internet access to VPN members is provided across the same infrastructure as the MPLS/VPN service offering, then this Internet access to certain member sites of a specific VPN can be achieved in several ways within the MPLS/VPN architecture.

Some deployments will require that connectivity between VPN members and the Internet be achieved through a firewall; other implementations will not. Some will require central site access only, while others will require connectivity from any site to the Internet directly across the backbone. It is important to remember that any of the methods described within this section are valid; the choice of which one to deploy will depend largely on the given topology of the customer sites and the customer connectivity and security requirements.

Again, a sample topology, shown in Figure 12-19 will serve as the reference backbone network to help explain all the Internet connectivity options.

Figure 12-19 *Internet Connectivity Reference Backbone*

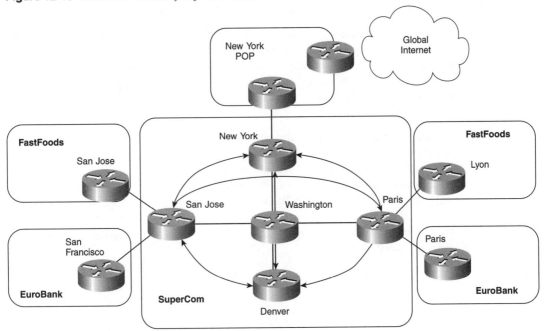

Figure 12-19 shows the SuperCom backbone that is providing an MPLS/VPN service to its VPN customers, and also provides Internet access through its New York POP. Full routing is taken from the Internet and propagated to some of the PE-routers.

NOTE   The propagation of full routing to the PE-routers is a design choice and depends on whether any of the VPN or non-VPN customers require full Internet routing. A typical example of a customer requiring full routing would be a smaller Internet service provider buying Internet connectivity from the service provider, or a multihomed customer running BGP with more than one service provider. If full routing is not a requirement, then default routing is the recommended design choice because it lowers the memory requirements and CPU load on the PE-routers.

Internet Connectivity Through Firewalls

Many customers of the service provider will not want to associate their VPN routes with Internet routes and will require that connectivity between the Internet and the VPN sites be through a security device such as a firewall. This dictates that the VPN routes are held in separate routing tables to the Internet routes, or that firewalls are present in every VPN site that wants to access the Internet directly across the backbone.

If Internet access is obtained through the MPLS/VPN backbone using any method other than central site Internet access (with one or more central sites), it is necessary for firewalls to be present at each site so that any traffic between the Internet and the VPN site will pass through the firewall. If this access is provided in a hub-and-spoke arrangement, such as central site Internet access, then not all sites require firewall services because these can be present within the central site.

This requirement is typical of Internet access from the enterprise. In this type of VPN environment, where customer sites are linked through PVCs/SVCs or IP tunnels, it is normal for Internet access to be provided through certain sites. Each site sends its Internet traffic to one or more central sites, and this traffic passes through a firewall within the central site. In the case of MPLS/VPN, in which the customer site imports a default route that is generated by one of the service provider routers, no firewall service will be available for the traffic to traverse (unless a firewall is present between the customer site and the provider backbone).

Figure 12-20 *Internet Access Through CE Running Cisco IOS Firewall Feature Set Software*

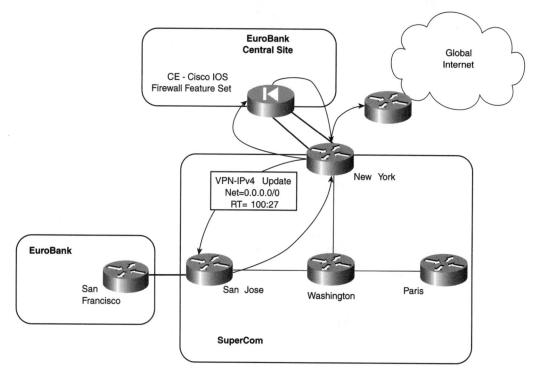

Figure 12-20 shows a topology in which Internet access for all EuroBank sites is obtained through the EuroBank's central site. This central site is capable of providing firewall services between members of the VPN and the Internet. VPN members forward their Internet traffic toward the central site because they have imported a default route with a particular route target that has been generated by the central site.

In this sample topology, the firewall service is provided through the use of the Cisco Secure Integrated software (formerly known as the Cisco IOS Firewall Feature Set) on the CE-router. This is obviously not the only possible topology; it is equally possible to house the firewall services away from the CE-router.

Two (sub)interfaces, which we will see in more detail later, have been utilized. One interface is associated with the VRF; the other is associated with the global routing table. This means that any traffic from a VPN member that follows the default route will pass through the PE-router, across the VRF interface to the CE-router, and then back up to the PE-router across the second interface. The PE-router will then route the traffic based on its global routing table.

Internet Access—Static Default Routing

In our sample topology, certain customers, such as the EuroBank VPN customer, want to obtain direct Internet access from a VPN. These customers have no requirement to receive full Internet routing, so a static default route pointing to a global next-hop address can be placed within the EuroBank VRF. This static route should point to the router that acts as the Internet gateway—in this case, the SuperCom New York router.

NOTE   Whenever a default route is placed into the VRF and this default route points to a next-hop address contained within the global routing table, any packets that use this default route will leave the VPN space and will be routed based on the global routing table at the next-hop router. This feature allows "leaking" of VPN packets into the global address space.

By placing a static default route within the EuroBank VRF, any packets that do not match any of the routes contained within the VRF will be sent to the SuperCom New York router, which provides the Internet gateway facility. This connectivity is illustrated in Figure 12-21.

Figure 12-21 *Internet Connectivity—Static Default Route*

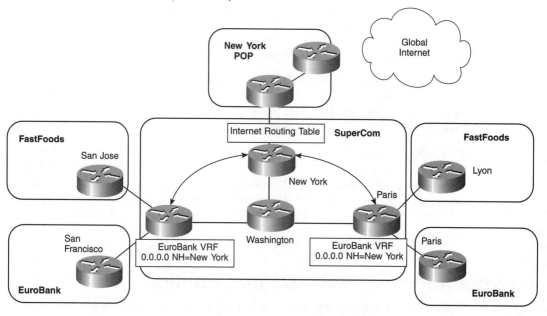

The next-hop address for the static default route should point to the interface from where the Internet routes are learned. You might be tempted to use the loopback interface address of the Internet gateway because this type of interface will never be unavailable unless the Internet gateway itself is not reachable. However, the problem with this approach is that the Internet gateway itself may be reachable, but its interface to the Internet may be down. This could cause suboptimal routing in the best case, but potentially black-hole traffic in the worst case.

In the example shown in Figure 12-21, a static default route has been configured into the EuroBank VRF on the San Jose and Paris routers, and this points to the interface of the New York router that provides the Internet gateway. This interface address must be present within the global routing table so that label switching of the packets between the PE and Internet gateway routers can occur. This means that the Internet gateway router must advertise its Internet interface address within the IGP that runs across the backbone.

NOTE	In the context of the MPLS/VPN architecture, the global routing table can be defined as the table that contains any routes other than VPN routes. These will typically include Internet routes.

When packets from a VPN customer reach the Internet gateway, they must be treated as belonging to the global routing table rather than a VRF, whether labeled or not. This means that the interface used to access the Internet must not be within the VPN—it must belong to the global routing table. If it belonged to the VPN, then when packets from a VPN customer reached the Internet gateway, a lookup within the VRF would occur rather than within the global routing table, which is where the Internet routes reside, and connectivity would not be achieved.

NOTE   It is possible to associate the Internet routing table with a VRF so that all Internet routes reside within the VRF rather than the global routing table. In this case, the interface that connects to the Internet on the Internet gateway could reside within the VRF. However, this design is strongly discouraged if you propagate full Internet routing in your network (unless you use special techniques detailed later in this chapter) because the number of routes inserted into the Internet VRF would be very large. To make matters worse, if you decide to design Internet access through an overlapping VPN structure, each customer VRF (with its unique route distinguisher) would cause the BGP process to generate another copy of all the Internet routes within the VPN-IPv4 BGP table.

In a normal routing scenario, the configuration of a static route that points to an unreachable next-hop address would not be valid. This is actually the situation that we have in the MPLS/VPN model: The next-hop of the static route is not present within the VRF.

NOTE   This situation is the case for *all* VPN routes learned through MP-iBGP in any VRF. The MP-iBGP next-hop address is always resolved in the global routing table, not within the VRF.

Because there is no redistribution between IPv4 and VPN-IPv4 routes, a method is needed to allow the PE-router to resolve the next-hop address for the Internet gateway from within the VRF. This is achieved through the use of the **global** keyword within the static default route configuration. The **global** keyword specifies that the next-hop address of the static route is resolved within the global routing table, not within the VRF. Example 12-10 provides the format of the command; the configuration for the San Jose router in Figure 12-21 can be seen in Example 12-11.

Example 12-10 *Static Default Route Configuration Command Syntax*

```
ip route vrf vrfname 0.0.0.0 0.0.0.0 Internet_GW_next-hop global
```

Example 12-11 *Static Default Route—San Jose PE Configuration*

```
hostname San Jose
!
ip route vrf EuroBank 0.0.0.0 0.0.0.0 197.22.15.6 global
```

NOTE   The label stack for the default route will contain only one label, and this will be the one assigned to the IGP route of the Internet gateway next-hop address.

The configuration of the static default route into the VRF provides an outbound route toward the Internet for members of the VPN, but what about the return path? Connectivity can be achieved only if two-way routing can occur. This means that each of the customer IP subnets (advertised by the customer as VPN routes to the PE-routers) that are used as source addresses for Internet access must be advertised through the global BGP-4 process toward the Internet. However, BGP-4 will not advertise any routes that were not learned from a BGP peer or, if sourced locally, are not contained within the global routing table of the advertising router.

We have already seen that the VPN routes are kept separate from the global routing table and are not available to be advertised through BGP-4. The easiest solution to make these routes available in the global routing table is to configure further (global) static routes so that the VPN subnets appear within the global routing table as well as the VRF. This would make them available for advertisement via BGP-4. These static routes must point to an interface, with a next-hop address specified if the outbound interface is multiaccess (such as Ethernet). Then either these routes can be redistributed into BGP, or the **network** command can be used within the BGP process. If redistribution is used, a route map can be utilized to specify which addresses to advertise.

A next-hop address for these static routes can be specified even though the next-hop is *not* present in the global routing table. In normal routing, this would not be possible because the next-hop would not be within the routing table and therefore would never be validated. However, within the MPLS/VPN environment, this type of configuration is valid. Figure 12-22 provides an example of this type of topology, with the necessary configuration for the San Jose PE-router shown in Example 12-12. Example 12-12 also shows that the static route is contained within the global routing table of the PE-router, even though the next-hop and outbound interface addresses are not present (they belong to a VRF).

Figure 12-22 *Advertisement of VPN Routes into the Global BGP-4 Process*

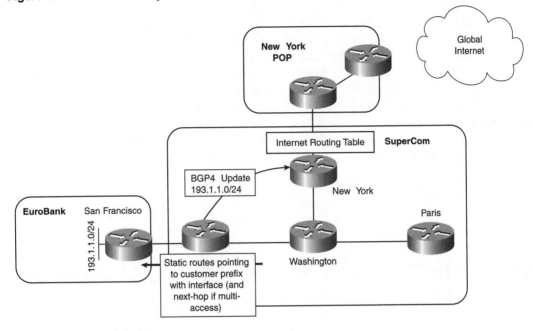

Example 12-12 *Static Route Configuration for BGP-4 Advertisement of VPN Routes*

```
hostname San Jose
!
! static route pointing to EuroBank 193.1.1.0/24 prefix
!
ip route 193.1.1.0 255.255.255.0 ethernet6/0 10.2.1.25

San Jose# show ip route
Codes: C - connected, S - static, I - IGRP, R - RIP, M - mobile, B - BGP
       D - EIGRP, EX - EIGRP external, O - OSPF, IA - OSPF inter area
       N1 - OSPF NSSA external type 1, N2 - OSPF NSSA external type 2
       E1 - OSPF external type 1, E2 - OSPF external type 2, E - EGP
       i - IS-IS, L1 - IS-IS level-1, L2 - IS-IS level-2, ia - IS-IS inter area
       * - candidate default, U - per-user static route, o - ODR
       P - periodic downloaded static route

Gateway of last resort is not set

     1.0.0.0/32 is subnetted, 1 subnets
S        193.1.1.0/24 [1/0] via 10.2.1.25, Ethernet6/0
```

If the service provider has multiple Internet exit points, then static routes for different VPN customers can be configured by pointing the next-hop address to one of the multiple Internet exit points. It may also be useful to change the autonomous system number within the AS_PATH when a VPN customer static route is redistributed into BGP so that the first autonomous system number in the AS_PATH is not the MPLS/VPN provider's, but the customer's. Example 12-13 shows a configuration that would cause the 193.1.1.0/24 prefix as shown in Example 12-12 to be advertised with an autonomous system number of 200 rather than the service provider's autonomous system number.

Example 12-13 *Setting the AS Number During Redistribution into BGP*

```
router bgp 100
 redistribute static set-as-path-EuroBank-from-tag
 !
route-map set-as-path-EuroBank-from-tag
 set aspath tag
 !
ip route 193.1.1.0 255.255.255.0 ethernet6/0 10.2.1.25 tag 200
```

Separate BGP Session Between PE- and CE-routers

Although the configuration of static routes for each VPN customer provides Internet connectivity to these customers through use of a default route, it may not be sufficient for certain network deployments, where the scalability of this solution may be restrictive.

Many implementations will require the capability to receive and advertise routes from the VPN customer sites directly with the Internet using BGP-4. The implications of this are that all Internet routes, or a subset of them, must be present on the PE-router that provides connectivity to the customer site that is receiving or sending these BGP-4 routes. This PE-router also needs to be capable of advertising the routes contained within the global routing table to the VPN customer site.

However, because these routes are not contained within the VRF of the customer VPN, a mechanism is needed to allow the PE to distribute routes from the global routing table (where the Internet routes reside) to the customer site, and to also recognize routes from the customer site that must be placed into the global table rather than the VRF. No mechanism in the MPLS/VPN implementation would give us the flexibility needed in this case, and the only way to implement the desired functionality is through a second interface to the customer, which is not part of any VRF and which belongs to the global routing table. The second interface is used to carry non-VPN specific routes between the PE- and CE-routers.

This second interface may be a separate physical interface, but it could also be a logical interface (such as a subinterface created over a Frame Relay DLCI) or a tunnel, allowing the customer and the service provider to exchange VPN and Internet data over the same physical infrastructure. A normal BGP-4 session needs to be established between the PE- and CE-routers across this second interface, and the CE-router must originate customer routes that the PE-router will propagate to the rest of the Internet from the global routing table. An example of this type of connectivity is shown in Figure 12-23.

Figure 12-23 *Internet Connectivity—Multiple (Sub)interface Model*

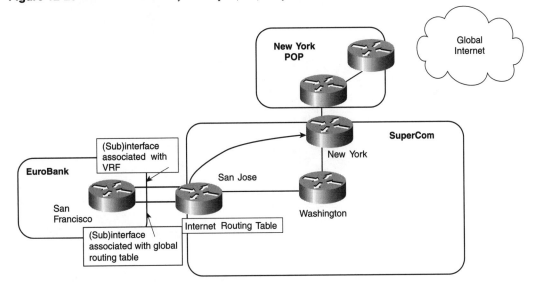

Figure 12-23 shows that two interfaces are present between the EuroBank San Francisco CE-router and the SuperCom San Jose PE-router. In this case, they are provided through use of (sub)interfaces—one of these interfaces is associated with the EuroBank VRF, and the other one is not. Using this configuration, the EuroBank CE-router can learn Internet routes via one (sub)interface and VPN routes through the other.

It is also possible to run just one interface between the PE- and CE-routers, but to configure a tunnel to carry the VPN routes. This method is illustrated in Figure 12-24.

NOTE   Running an MPLS/VPN PE-CE link across an interface that gives the customers their Internet access is potentially a large security problem. Unless you deploy very strict filtering on PE- and CE-routers, it's very easy for an intruder connected to the Internet to insert packets into your VPN. This design is thus best avoided.

Figure 12-24 *Internet Connectivity—Tunnel Interface for VPN Routes*

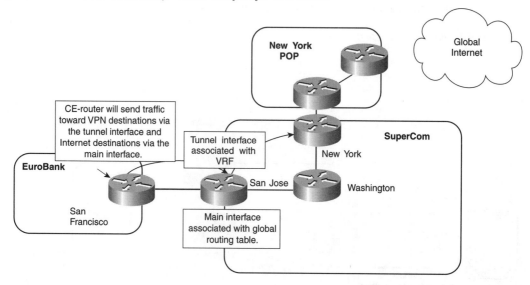

Figure 12-24 shows that the CE-router is capable of routing traffic based on the interface that the route is learned from. If a route is learned across the main interface (and these will include Internet routes), then the San Francisco CE-router will send packets via this interface. However, if the route is learned from across the tunnel interface (and all VPN specific routes will be), the San Francisco CE-router will send traffic across the tunnel. On the San Jose PE-router, packets that are received across the main interface are routed using the global routing table information, and packets received across the tunnel are routed using the EuroBank VRF forwarding table.

In certain circumstances, some MPLS/VPN solution providers may want to provide full Internet routes to different customers that have been learned from different sources. The reason for this may be administrative or policy-based, or may be simply to satisfy specific customer routing needs. The implications of this requirement are quite complex. In normal operation, Internet routes will be sent to all VPN customers with the next-hop of the advertising PE-router and the AS_PATH information of the best routes that have been learned from one or multiple Internet exit points. However, certain VPN customers may want to learn Internet routes from the same advertising PE-router but with different AS_PATH information that has been learned from another Internet exit point (this may or may not be the best path, as far as the PE-router is concerned). Figure 12-25 provides an example of this requirement.

Figure 12-25 *Internet Connectivity Through Multiple Exit Points*

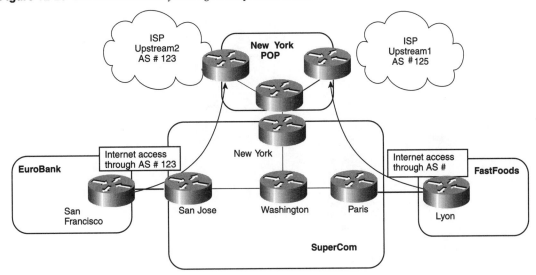

Figure 12-25 shows that two separate VPN customers, EuroBank and FastFoods, require Internet access through separate exit points within the SuperCom backbone. The actual exit point that a particular VRF will use can be resolved through the use of static default routes, as described in the previous section. However, this would not allow each VPN customer to learn or advertise routes directly through BGP-4. This means that a further mechanism is needed so that the PE-router will route traffic for different VPNs to different exit points.

In a normal routing environment, this requirement presents a problem. The PE-router will pick the best BGP route and will advertise this best route to its BGP neighbors, which would include all VPN customers that require direct Internet access. To be able to choose which exit point to use, we could try to set the BGP next-hop of any routes that are advertised from the PE- to the CE-router as the address of the desired Internet exit point. This can be seen in Figure 12-26.

Figure 12-26 shows that the EuroBank CE-router runs two separate interfaces to the PE-router. The next-hop of any Internet routes has been reset at the PE through use of a route map, and this next-hop address has been distributed to the CE by advertisement across the VRF interface. The exit point is contained within the VRF via a static route, so all traffic that matches this BGP next-hop will be sent over the VRF interface and then will use the default route within the VRF to direct the traffic to the desired Internet exit point.

Figure 12-26 *Resetting BGP Next-hop at PE-router*

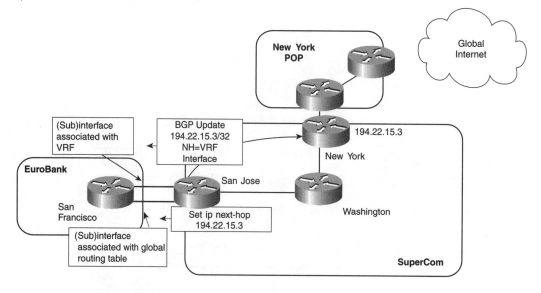

NOTE It is worth noting that with this solution, traffic flow is asymmetric. Traffic travelling from a VPN site to the Internet will take the VRF interface, while the return traffic will use the global interface.

A configuration example for this connectivity option can be seen in Example 12-14.

Example 12-14 *Resetting BGP Next-hop Configuration Example*

```
hostname San Francisco
!
interface Serial1/0
 ip address 10.2.1.6  255.255.255.252
!
interface Ethernet6/0
 ip address 10.2.1.25 255.255.255.252
!
router bgp 2
 neighbor 10.2.1.5 remote-as 1
 neighbor 10.2.1.5 update-source Loopback0
 neighbor 10.2.1.26 remote-as 1
 neighbor 10.2.1.26 update-source Loopback0
!

hostname San Jose
!
ip vrf EuroBank
```

Example 12-14 *Resetting BGP Next-hop Configuration Example (Continued)*

```
 rd 1:27
 route-target both 100:27
 !
interface Serial0/0/0
 ip address 10.2.1.5 255.255.255.252
 !
interface Ethernet0/1/0
 ip forwarding vrf EuroBank
 ip address 10.2.1.26 255.255.255.252
 !
router bgp 1
 no synchronization
 no bgp default ipv4-unicast
 neighbor 10.2.1.5 remote-as 2
 neighbor 10.2.1.5 activate
 neighbor 10.2.1.5 route-map EuroBank out
 neighbor 194.22.15.3 remote-as 1
 neighbor 194.22.15.3 update-source Loopback0
 neighbor 194.22.15.3 activate
 !
 address-family ipv4 vrf EuroBank
 redistribute connected
 redistribute static
 neighbor 10.2.1.25 remote-as 2
 neighbor 10.2.1.25 activate
 no auto-summary
 no synchronization
 exit-address-family
 !
route-map EuroBank permit 10
 set ip next-hop 194.22.15.3
 !
ip route vrf EuroBank 0.0.0.0 0.0.0.0 194.22.15.3 global
ip route vrf EuroBank 194.22.15.3 255.255.255.255 10.1.1.13 global
```

The problem with this configuration is that no BGP routes will be accepted across the
interface because the next-hop address will not be a directly connected interface. Of course,
this could be remedied by changing the next-hop of the route on the CE-router when it
receives the route. Example 12-15 shows **debug** output that confirms this.

Example 12-15 *Reset BGP Next-hop debug*

```
San Francisco# debug ip bgp updates

BGP(0): 10.2.1.5 rcv UPDATE about 197.1.1.1/32 -- DENIED due to: non-connected next-
hop;
BGP: 10.2.1.5 Non-local next-hop 194.22.15.3
```

Even though this approach is possible, it has two main drawbacks. First, two separate
interfaces (or logical/[sub]interfaces) are required. Second, it does not address the

AS_PATH information issue—we will potentially lose the desired information if the route via our selected exit point is not chosen as the best path via the BGP process on the PE-router.

To address this type of connectivity requirement so that only one interface is used and the AS_PATH information is maintained, the use of the eBGP multihop feature is required. With this feature, we can exchange VPN customer Internet routes directly with the exit point and make use of a default route within the VRF to direct all Internet traffic to this exit point without having to reset the BGP next-hop of the routes. Figure 12-27 provides an illustration of this technique.

Figure 12-27 *Use of eBGP Multihop for Internet Connectivity*

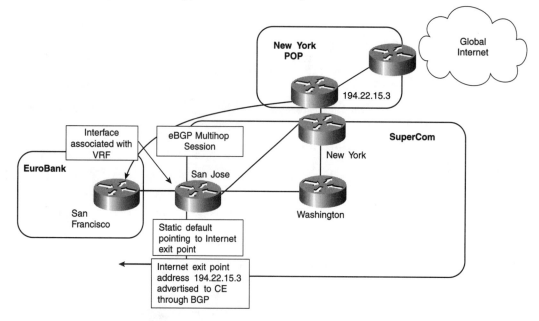

Figure 12-27 shows that the EuroBank San Francisco router runs a direct eBGP multihop session with the desired Internet exit point. The address used for this session, and the BGP next-hop of all routes, is placed into the EuroBank VRF (through a static route) and is advertised across the PE-to-CE BGP session. Reachability of the CE-router must also be given to the Internet gateway router. The relevant configuration of the San Francisco and San Jose routers is illustrated in Example 12-16.

Example 12-16 *Use of eBGP Multihop Configuration Example*

```
hostname San Francisco
!
interface Loopback0
 ip address 1.1.1.1 255.255.255.255
!
```

Example 12-16 *Use of eBGP Multihop Configuration Example (Continued)*

```
router bgp 2
 neighbor 194.22.15.3 remote-as 1
 neighbor 194.22.15.3 ebgp-multihop 255
 neighbor 194.22.15.3 update-source Loopback0
 neighbor 10.2.1.26 remote-as 1
 neighbor 10.2.1.26 update-source Loopback0
 neighbor 10.2.1.26 activate
!


hostname San Jose
!
ip vrf EuroBank
 rd 1:27
 route-target both 100:27
!
router bgp 1
 no synchronization
 no bgp default ipv4-unicast
 neighbor 194.22.15.3 remote-as 1
 neighbor 194.22.15.3 update-source Loopback0
 neighbor 194.22.15.3 activate
 !
 address-family ipv4 vrf EuroBank
 redistribute connected
 redistribute static
 neighbor 10.2.1.25 remote-as 2
 neighbor 10.2.1.25 activate
 no auto-summary
 no synchronization
 exit-address-family
 !
 address-family vpnv4
 neighbor 194.22.15.3 activate
 neighbor 194.22.15.3 send-community extended
 exit-address-family
!
! static route pointing to San Francisco CE Loopback so that it can be
! redistributed into the IGP so that the Internet exit point can reach
! the eBGP multihop peering address
!
ip route 1.1.1.1 255.255.255.255 Serial0/0/0
!
! static default route for EuroBank VRF pointing to Internet exit point
! loopback address
!
ip route vrf EuroBank 0.0.0.0 0.0.0.0 194.22.15.3 global
!
! static route pointing to the eBGP multihop peering address of the
! Internet exit point so that the CE-router is able to reach it. This
! static route will be advertised toward the CE-router
!
ip route vrf EuroBank 194.22.15.3 255.255.255.255 10.1.1.13 global
```

The eBGP multihop operation can be summarized as follows:

1 The CE-router is configured with a BGP session to the Internet exit point using eBGP multihop. The peer address for this session should be placed into the VRF through use of a static route. The BGP next-hop address for all routes that will be learned from this peer should also be within the VRF.

2 The CE-router has a further BGP session with the PE-router via the VRF interface. This is used to learn the BGP next-hop for all the routes and also the peer address of the eBGP multihop session. This need not necessarily be BGP—it could be any other protocol that is supported on a PE-to-CE link.

3 The CE-router receives routes from the Internet exit point (full or partial) with a next-hop that corresponds to the Internet exit point.

4 The CE-router forwards all Internet traffic toward the VRF interface of the PE-router because this is where the BGP next-hop address has been learned.

5 The PE-router has a default route within the VRF routing table that points to the Internet exit point.

Internet Connectivity Through Dynamic Default Routing

In many cases, VPN customers will require Internet access through a specific exit point, but they may consider that the use of static default routes is not dynamic enough. This Internet access may be provided through the service provider's exit points, or it may be provided through a customer central site. In either case, a default route pointing to the Internet exit point is sufficient. However, it is certainly desirable for this default route to be available to the VRF through a dynamic mechanism rather than through static configuration.

Dynamic Default Routing—Route Target Assignment

Central site Internet access is common with many VPN deployments. We have already seen how multiple exit points can be used through configuration of static routes into the customer VRFs. However, a dynamic method is required so that Internet access is provided only through use of a default route if the exit point is actually available.

One method of achieving this aim is to use BGP extended community route target attributes that correspond to a default route. This default route will point to the relevant central site that provides the Internet access and will be contained within the VPN customers' VRF. An example of this type of connectivity can be seen in Figure 12-28.

Figure 12-28 *Central Site Internet Connectivity Using Default Routing*

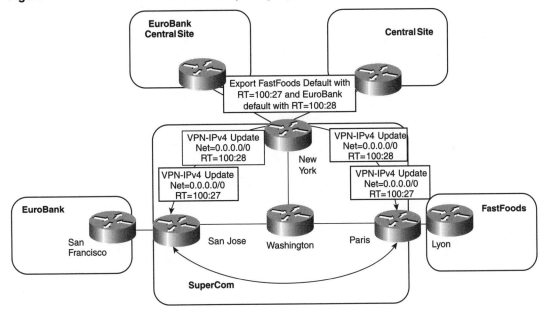

Figure 12-28 shows that the New York PE-router exports the default route from the EuroBank VRF with a route target of 100:28, and the default route from the FastFoods VRF with a route target of 100:27. When these routes are imported into the EuroBank and FastFoods VRFs at other PE-routers, all Internet traffic will be sent toward the correct central site exit point for each of the VPNs.

If this default route is learned from across the PE-to-CE link, then no further configuration is necessary. However, if the default route must be generated from within the VRF, then use of the **network 0.0.0.0** command within the BGP VRF configuration should be utilized. This can be seen in Example 12-17.

Example 12-17 *Generation of Default Route from Within the VRF*

```
Hostname San Jose
!
ip vrf EuroBank
 rd 1:27
 route-target both 100:27
!
router bgp 1
 neighbor 194.22.15.3 remote-as 1
 neighbor 194.22.15.3 update-source Loopback0
!
 address-family ipv4 vrf EuroBank
```

continues

Example 12-17 *Generation of Default Route from Within the VRF (Continued)*

```
 neighbor 10.2.1.25 remote-as 2
 neighbor 10.2.1.25 activate
 network 0.0.0.0 mask 0.0.0.0
!


San Jose # show ip bgp vpnv4 vrf EuroBank tags

Network            next-hop      In tag/Out tag
Route Distinguisher: 100:27 (EuroBank)
0.0.0.0            10.2.1.25        29/notag


San Jose # show ip bgp vpnv4 vrf EuroBank 0.0.0.0

BGP routing table entry for 1:27:0.0.0.0/0, version 17
Paths: (1 available, best #1, table EuroBank)
  Advertised to non peer-group peers:
  194.22.15.3 10.2.1.25
  Local
    10.2.1.25 from 0.0.0.0 (194.22.15.2)
      Origin IGP, metric 0, localpref 100, weight 32768, valid,
      sourced, local, best
      Extended Community: RT:100:27
```

Association of the Global Routing Table with a VRF

Although the previous example is fine for a single customer that wants to gain access to the Internet through its own central site, it is not sufficient if multiple customers require access to the Internet through use of a dynamic default route. In this case, a route target can be associated with each Internet exit point within the service provider backbone. Each VPN customer will gain Internet access through the exit point that is associated with the route target imported into the VRF. This is similar to the example shown in Figure 12-28, except that either the default route will point to one of the service provider's Internet exit point interfaces (instead of a customer central site), or it will be treated as an aggregate route by the advertising PE-router and a lookup of the Layer 3 header will be performed.

If the advertising PE-router has only one interface toward the Internet, then the default route that it generates may point toward this interface. This interface need not be associated with a VRF. Because this default route is associated with an outgoing interface, all incoming traffic that holds the relevant VPN label that will have been assigned to the default route will be label-switched out of the interface. The implications of this are that the next router in the path must be capable of routing the packet based on the global routing table. Example 12-18 provides a configuration to allow the generation of a default route with a specific Internet exit point route target.

Example 12-18 *Generation of Default Route Outside a VRF*

```
hostname San Jose
!
ip vrf Internet_access
 rd 1:29
 route-target export 100:29
 !
router bgp 1
 !
 address-family ipv4 vrf Internet_access
 redistribute static
 network 0.0.0.0 mask 0.0.0.0
 !
ip route vrf Internet_access 0.0.0.0 0.0.0.0 atm2/0/0.1

San Jose # show ip bgp vpnv4 vrf Internet_access 0.0.0.0

BGP routing table entry for 1:29:0.0.0.0/0, version 24
Paths: (1 available, best #1, table Internet_access)
  Advertised to non peer-group peers:
  194.22.15.3
  Local
    0.0.0.0 from 0.0.0.0 (194.22.15.2)
      Origin IGP, metric 0, localpref 100, weight 32768, valid,
      sourced, local, best
      Extended Community: RT:100:29

San Jose # show tag forwarding vrf Internet_access

Local   Outgoing    Prefix          Bytes tag  Outgoing    next-hop
tag     tag or VC   or Tunnel Id    switched   interface
38      Untagged    0.0.0.0/0[V]    0          AT2/0/0.1   point2point
```

If multiple exit points exist from the same PE-router, as in Figure 12-29, then a default route pointing to an interface would not allow load balancing across multiple exit point interfaces. Traffic would be switched out of one interface only, based on the configured default route. It is certainly possible to configure multiple default routes so that load balancing on the same PE-router can be achieved; however, this can lead to sub-optimal routing if the chosen exit point is not the shortest path.

Figure 12-29 *Multiple Internet Exit Points on PE-routers*

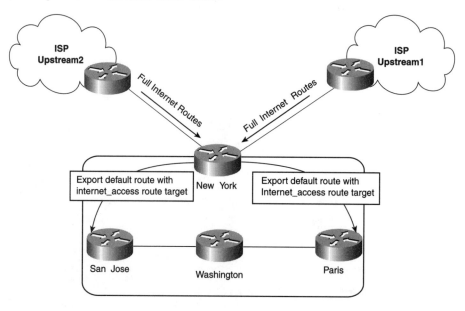

Figure 12-29 shows that the New York PE-router has two interfaces that connect to the Internet. Full Internet routing is received through both interfaces, and the best routes are selected through the standard BGP decision process. To take advantage of this decision process and thus send all Internet traffic along the best path, each Internet exit point interface must be associated with the same VRF.

If the association of the global routing table with a VRF approach is taken, it is necessary to make sure that the full Internet routes exist within the VRF so that the destination of the packet can be resolved at the end of the label-switched path (LSP). When the routes reside within the VRF, and only a default route is required by VPN customers, then the default route within the VRF should be generated as an aggregate label so that a lookup within the VRF will be performed on all packets that use the default route. If the default is not generated as an aggregate, and if multiple exit points exist, then routing will still be successful. However, it could be suboptimal or, in extreme cases, a routing loop. This problem is illustrated in Figure 12-30.

Figure 12-30 *Sub-optimal Routing with Multiple Internet Exit Points*

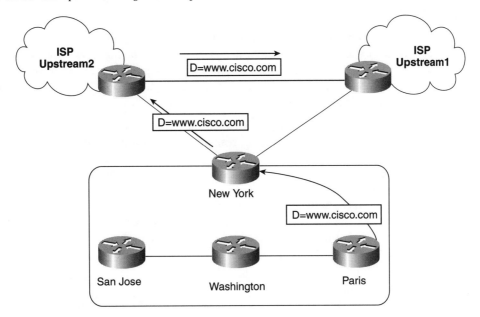

Imagine that you configure an Internet VRF in the New York router and then insert all routes received from both upstream ISPs into that VRF. You also configure static default routes pointing toward these upstream ISPs. A default route is then propagated (with a specific route target) to all other PE-routers and is imported into all relevant VRFs on the Paris PE-router. When traffic is sent to the Paris PE-router from a VPN customer that uses one of these VRFs, this traffic is sent to the New York PE-router. The New York PE-router has two default routes: One of these points to the Upstream1 ISP, and the other points to the Upstream2 ISP. Both of these defaults are contained within the Internet access VRF, and the same label is assigned to both default routes within this VRF.

In this case, the Paris PE-router will send any packets (if a no more specific route exists within the VRF) toward the New York PE-router with two labels. One label is used for the default route, and the other label is used to get the packet to the New York router.

The first label will be popped one hop before the New York PE-router so that it will receive a packet with just the label for the default route attached. Because the same label is assigned to both of the default routes within the VRF, the New York router is capable of performing load balancing across the two upstream links. This means that it will send the packet to either the Upstream1 or Upstream2 routers as an unlabeled IP packet after removing the default route label.

If we assume that the packet is sent to the Upstream2 router, then this router will route the packet as normal, based on the information in its global routing table. However, the best path toward a particular destination might be via the Upstream1 ISP, so the packet will be sent toward the Upstream1 router, as displayed in Figure 12-30. Therefore, there is the potential for suboptimal routing.

To remedy this situation, it is possible to generate a default route that contains an aggregate label. As we have already described, an aggregate label causes a PE-router to perform a lookup within the relevant VRF. If full Internet routes are available within this VRF, then optimal routing can be achieved. In our example, the generation of an aggregate label can be achieved by assigning only one static default route on the New York PE-router. This static route can be configured to point to a next-hop address that is a loopback address on the PE-router. The loopback interface need *not* be part of the VRF. The static route is placed into the VRF and is treated as an aggregate label, which means that a lookup in the VRF is performed for any packet using this label.

Additional Lookup in the Global Routing Table

If full Internet routes are available on the PE-router, then it's also possible to perform an additional lookup in the global routing table if a destination prefix is not available within the local VRF. The consequence of this is that a default route cannot be present within the VRF. However, with this feature, there is not necessarily the need for a default route within the PE configuration or for the association of the global routing table with a VRF. An example of this type of connectivity is shown in Figure 12-31.

Figure 12-31 shows that any traffic sent toward the SuperCom San Jose PE-router will be initially routed based on the content of the VRF that is associated with the attached customer. If this lookup fails, then an additional lookup will be performed within the global routing table of the PE-router.

WARNING   Additional lookup can present a security risk in an MPLS/VPN network. For example, the packet sent from the San Jose FastFoods site toward the Lyon FastFoods site might escape into the global Internet if the Lyon FastFoods site is not reachable in the FastFoods VRF (for example, because of link failure between Paris and Lyon). In the worst case, the packets will be propagated beyond the boundaries of the SuperCom network and can be intercepted by an intruder beyond the domain of the SuperCom network. The same issue also exists when using a static global default. This is a general issue that should be fully understood if default routing or additional lookup is to be deployed.

Figure 12-31 *Additional Lookup in the Global Routing Table*

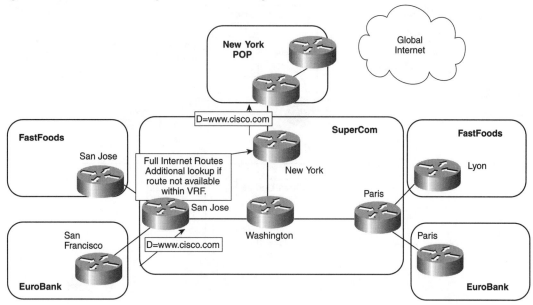

This feature can be enabled through use of the **ip vrf forwarding** *name* **[fallback global]**
configuration command.

Internet Connectivity Through a Different Service Provider

Some customers of the MPLS/VPN provider may want to obtain their Internet access
through a different provider, or they may want to obtain access through both the MPLS/
VPN provider and another Internet service provider. In either case, a combination of the
previously described techniques should allow for this type of connectivity requirement.

Many different topologies are possible in this environment, too many to describe each one
in detail. However, Figure 12-32 shows one such topology in which the EuroBank VPN
customer is capable of accessing the Internet either through the MPLS/VPN backbone or
through a separate provider.

Figure 12-32 *Internet Connectivity Through a Different Service Provider*

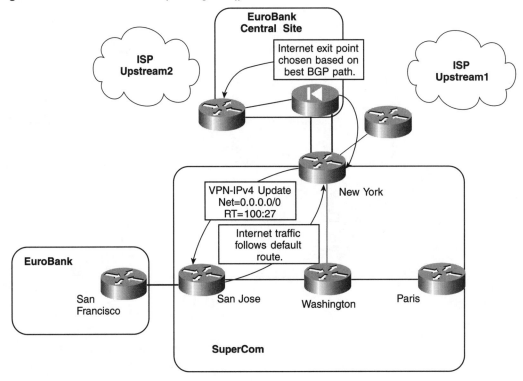

Figure 12-32 shows that the EuroBank VPN sites gain access to the Internet through a central site, which includes firewall protection. When the traffic arrives at the central site, it will be sent to the Internet through one of two exit points, either Upstream1 or Upstream2, and this will be based on the best BGP path.

Summary

We have seen in this chapter that scaling any large-scale service provider backbone is a challenge. This does not change with the introduction of the MPLS/VPN architecture, and attention should certainly be directed toward this task.

Convergence is quite obviously a very major issue, both for the service provider and for the customers of the VPN service. We have seen that whenever a VPN service is provided through use of the MPLS/VPN architecture, the convergence of the backbone network and the customer networks are affected in different ways. We have also seen that careful tuning of routing protocol timers, and other parameters, may be necessary so that customers may realize comparable convergence times as with their traditional VPN services.

The advertisement of VPN routing information between customer sites is achieved through the use of MP-iBGP. With the potential for substantial growth in PE-routers supporting the VPN service, and the number of BGP sessions between PE-routers that will be required to support this growth, some scaling issues inevitably may need to be addressed. Several options to reduce the number of BGP sessions were presented during this chapter, including the use of BGP confederations and route reflectors,

Internet connectivity will almost certainly be a requirement for every VPN customer that attaches to the service provider backbone network. This connectivity may be provided in many ways, each of which must be accommodated by the MPLS/VPN backbone. This chapter has presented several common scenarios, including central site access, any-to-any access, and connectivity through firewalls. Although these scenarios do not cover every possible topology, the techniques presented are the necessary tools to successfully provision this type of connectivity in most network deployments.

CHAPTER 13

Guidelines for the Deployment of MPLS/VPN

Introduction to MPLS/VPN Deployment

Whenever a new technology is introduced, there are always issues to address and design choices to make so that the deployment can reach a successful conclusion. This is no different in the case of the MPLS/VPN architecture and its introduction into the network.

This chapter builds on the previous chapter, which provided information on the scaling properties of the MPLS/VPN architecture. This chapter aims to highlight some of the issues that you will face and to provide some suggestions on techniques and methodologies to overcome these problems. It also presents some of the issues with a traditional backbone environment and shows how the introduction of the MPLS/VPN architecture affects the service provider. To assist in the illustration of these techniques, we will use the SuperCom backbone network that we have seen in previous chapters.

These suggestions should not be viewed as a replacement to thorough design and migration planning, or as a substitute to extensive design testing. The purpose of these guidelines is to highlight some of the issues that you might face and to provide solutions that may be appropriate to certain network deployments.

IGP to BGP Migration of Customer Routes

Whenever a service provider allows access into its network infrastructure, whether for VPN service or for some other type of service such as Internet connectivity, a fundamental requirement exists to pass traffic across the network between customer access points. This requirement presents a problem for the service provider because each of the external destinations that is advertised toward, and therefore reachable by, the service provider and its customers must be known by all transit routers that will carry customer traffic across the backbone. The reason for this is that as a packet traverses the service provider network, each router in the packet's path must analyze the Layer 3 header of the packet and route it based on its destination IP address. Because the destination of the packet is for an external network, if external routing information were not held by the service provider's transit routers, then the packet would be dropped—the destination would not exist within the forwarding table of internal routers.

Figure 13-1 provides an example of why P-routers within the SuperCom core backbone require access to external routing information:

Figure 13-1 *Full Routing Requirement for P-routers*

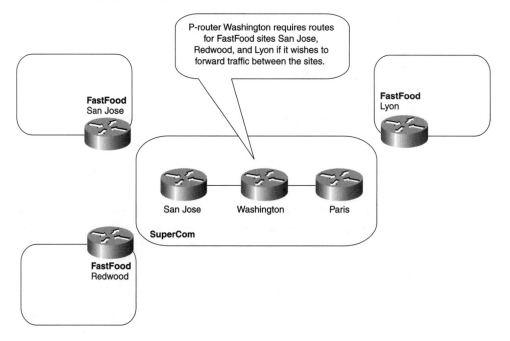

Figure 13-1 shows that if FastFood sites San Jose, Redwood, and Lyon want to communicate across the SuperCom backbone network, then P-router Washington needs to know each of their address ranges so that it can forward traffic.

In a typical service provider environment, a couple of choices exist to allow customer routes to be carried across the core network. These two choices are either to carry the customer routes within the service provider's own Interior Gateway Protocol (IGP), or to carry the customer routes using an exterior routing protocol, most commonly BGP. In either case, internal transit routers within the core of the network (the P-routers, in MPLS/VPN terminology) must hold this routing information.

Figure 13-2 shows a typical environment. In this case, the service provider has elected to carry its customer's routes within BGP. As you can see, each of the internal routers that provide transit across the backbone (San Jose, Washington, and Paris within the SuperCom backbone) needs to hold external routing information so that it can analyze the Layer 3 header of any incoming packets and route the traffic based on its destination IP address. This information is provided through use of a full mesh of iBGP sessions between the SuperCom backbone routers.

Figure 13-2   *External Routing Requirement Within the Core*

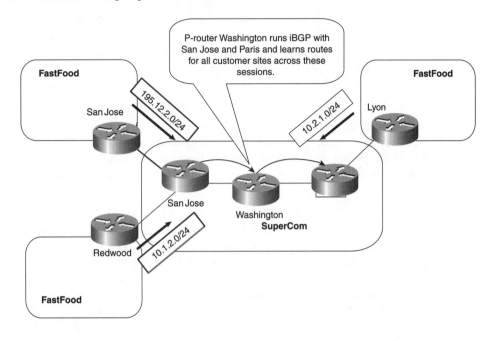

NOTE   Traditional BGP setup would require a full mesh of iBGP sessions among all routers (edge or core) that *originate* routes into BGP. If any of the core routers do not originate routes into BGP (which will be a high percentage, in most backbone networks), then they do not need to be fully meshed. However, they still need an iBGP session with all edge routers—this is clearly a nonscalable environment in large network topologies.

Scalability mechanisms, such as route reflectors or BGP confederations, which we discussed in Chapter 12, "Advanced MPLS/VPN Topics," relax the full-mesh requirement and make iBGP networks scalable. These BGP concepts are covered in more details in the Cisco Press publication *Internet Routing Architectures*, Second Edition, by Bassam Halabi.

In most cases, the service provider elects to carry customer routes within BGP so that any instability within its customer networks does not affect the service provider's core IGP and so that the size of the internal routing protocol structure can be kept to a minimum. However, if the number of customer routes is small, some service provider's will elect to carry the routes within the IGP.

NOTE In most large service provider backbones, the number of customer routes quickly grows beyond the scaling capabilities of any IGP, whether EIGRP, OSPF, or IS-IS. The service providers who initially decide to carry customer routes within their IGP sooner or later will face a challenging migration process: They will be forced to migrate their customer routes to BGP because of scalability and stability issues.

In most backbone environments, reachability to these external customer destinations is necessary only so that end-to-end customer connectivity can be achieved. The backbone devices themselves, described previously as P-devices, do not actually source traffic toward these destinations, so they need to know about them only for the reasons that we have already described.

One of the goals that the MPLS architecture hopes to achieve is to increase the scalability of IP-based networks. This scalability enhancement is provided in several ways, some of which we discussed in the previous chapter. One such way is for internal routers (P-routers) to forward packets to external destinations without having to carry external routing information. We have already seen within this chapter that this is certainly a desirable mechanism and that this eliminates some of the existing scalability issues that a service provider faces. It also fits in nicely with our desire to carry customer routes within BGP, but with the added advantage that this BGP information is *not* required within the core of the network.

MPLS is capable of achieving this functionality because, within the backbone network, labels are not generated for BGP routes, but are generated for the next-hop addresses of these routes. This means that packets destined for external BGP destinations are sent across the service provider backbone with labels that correspond to the egress router that advertised the external route. Because these packets are labeled inside the backbone, each core router does not need to analyze the IP header and can label-switch the packet toward the egress PE-router. Because the router does not need to look at the IP header, it therefore does not need to learn BGP routing information to forward the packet. The consequence of this is that BGP information is required only at the edge of the network so that customer routes can be distributed across the backbone and between PE-routers. An example of this can be seen in Figure 13-3.

Figure 13-3 *BGP Routing Across an MPLS Core Network*

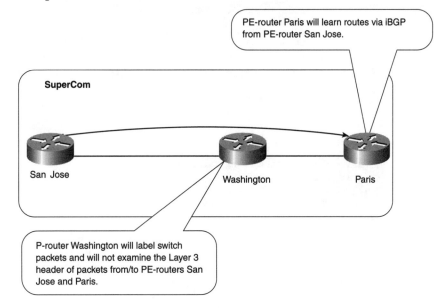

Figure 13-3 shows an example in which BGP information is not required within the core of the network. When MPLS is enabled within the SuperCom backbone, P-router Washington can switch packets based on their labels, so it does not need to hold BGP information. Examples 13-1 and 13-2 show the routing table and LFIB for PE-router Paris in Figure 13-3.

Example 13-1 *Routing Table Output for BGP and IGP Routes*

```
Paris# show ip route
      194.22.15.0/32 is subnetted, 1 subnets
C        194.22.15.1 is directly connected, Loopback0
      194.22.15.0/32 is subnetted, 1 subnets
i L1     194.22.15.2 [115/51765] via 10.2.1.26, Ethernet6/0
      10.0.0.0/8 is variably subnetted, 3 subnets, 2 masks
i L1     10.1.1.12/30 [115/51765] via 10.2.1.26, Ethernet6/0
B        10.1.2.0/24 [200/0] via 194.22.15.2, 00:19:01
C        10.2.1.24/30 is directly connected, Ethernet6/0
B     195.12.2.0/24 [200/0] via 194.22.15.2, 00:19:01
```

Example 13-1 shows that all BGP derived routes are learned with a next-hop address of 194.22.15.2, which is the BGP next-hop address used by the SuperCom San Jose router to advertise BGP routes toward the Paris router across its iBGP session.

NOTE   This behavior is due to the use of **next-hop-self** within the BGP configuration. In a standard BGP implementation, this command is not enabled by default, and it must be explicitly configured. The advantage of this type of configuration is that the service provider does not need to inject any external interface addresses into its IGP. Refer to the section "VPN Routes and Next-hop Forwarding," later in this chapter, for further information on this topic.

Example 13-2 *LFIB Output for BGP Routes*

```
Paris# show tag forwarding 10.1.2.0
Local   Outgoing    Prefix         Bytes tag   Outgoing    Next Hop
tag     tag or VC   or Tunnel Id   switched    interface
28      28          10.1.2.0/24    0           Et6/0       10.2.1.26

Paris# show tag forwarding 195.12.2.0
Local   Outgoing    Prefix         Bytes tag   Outgoing    Next Hop
tag     tag or VC   or Tunnel Id   switched    interface
28      28          195.12.2.0/24  0           Et6/0       10.2.1.26

Paris# show tag forwarding tag 28
Local   Outgoing    Prefix         Bytes tag   Outgoing    Next Hop
tag     tag or VC   or Tunnel Id   switched    interface
28      28          194.22.15.2/32 0           Et6/0       10.2.1.26
```

Example 13-2 shows that the label applied to all BGP routes is actually the label used to reach the next-hop for that BGP route. You can see from the sample output that both BGP routes (10.1.2.0/24 and 195.12.2.0/24) have the same label; this label is actually the one assigned to the next-hop address, 94.22.15.2/32, which is the Loopback1 interface address of the San Jose PE-router

Multiprotocol BGP Deployment in an MPLS/VPN Backbone

As already discussed in Chapter 8, "MPLS/VPN Architecture Overview," and Chapter 9, "MPLS/VPN Architecture Operation," the introduction of a VPN service based on the MPLS architecture requires MP-iBGP sessions between all PE-routers that hold routing information for the same VPN or set of VPNs. Because these sessions are iBGP sessions, and the number of PE-routers could potentially be high, this presents a scaling issue due to the sheer number of MP-iBGP peering sessions required between PE-routers. This is not an uncommon situation when BGP is deployed because of the nature of iBGP, which requires that each iBGP speaker run a direct BGP session with every other iBGP speaker that originates routes into BGP.

We have already discussed certain methods that are available to the designer to aid in the scaling of these peering sessions. We recommend in this environment that BGP route reflectors be deployed so that the number of required internal BGP peering sessions is considerably reduced. A further possibility is the introduction of BGP confederations. Both of these methods were discussed in detail in Chapter 12.

Even when these methods are deployed, BGP may still have issues with scaling. When routing information changes occur, a router must scan the whole BGP table for each of its neighbors. This process causes a BGP update to be built on each iteration of the scanning process. If multiple neighbors exist, then multiple BGP updates are built. This has a detrimental effect on the router's resources (CPU load and memory). Therefore, the use of BGP peer groups is further recommended if the router uses the same outbound policies toward each BGP neighbor. The introduction of peer groups will allow the BGP router to create in memory just one single update for all members of the peer group.

When changes occur within the topology, the BGP table is scanned only once. A single outbound BGP update is built for one of the neighbors that is a member of the peer group (also called the peer group leader) and is sent to every member of the peer group.

NOTE	The router automatically chooses the peer group leader. You cannot influence the selection of the peer group leader, but you can monitor which neighbor becomes the peer group leader by using the **show ip bgp neighbor** command.

Because the same update is sent to all members of a peer group, you must configure the same outbound policy for every neighbor that is a member of that peer group.

NOTE	Cisco IOS also enforces this requirement by preventing you from configuring any per-neighbor BGP parameter that might affect outbound updates on individual BGP neighbors that are also members of a peer group.

VPN Routes and Next-hop Forwarding

As has already been highlighted, a PE-router may learn customer VPN routes through various different sources. These routes may be learned through a VPN instance of an internal routing protocol such as RIP Version 2 or OSPF, through static routing, or through an external routing protocol such as BGP. Regardless of how these customer VPN routes are learned, all of them must be advertised to other PE-routers; this is achieved through utilizing MP-iBGP in the way that we described in the "Multiprotocol BGP Usage and Deployment" section of Chapter 9. Therefore, when the MPLS/VPN architecture is introduced into the network, all customer VPN routes will be carried by BGP across the backbone and will not be injected into the service provider's IGP.

When the routes are learned through any other method other than BGP, these routes must be injected into MP-iBGP through redistribution. In all cases, routes learned through VPN routing instances must be readvertised in BGP with the PE as the next-hop. This is because the label advertised with the route is assigned by the originating PE-router. This is not the case, by default, when learning routes through non-VPN eBGP.

In a standard BGP implementation, the default behavior of an eBGP speaker that has sessions to external neighbors is to advertise, unchanged, any routes that it learns from these neighbors to all internal neighbors. Therefore, the next-hop attribute of the route contains the IP address of the external neighbor that announced the route. Additional processing takes place when the same route is propagated through several BGP sessions between routers connected to the same multiaccess media. In that case, the next-hop is set to the interface IP address of the first router that announced the route across a BGP session over that multiaccess media.

The effect of this is that all the links that are used to carry the non-VPN eBGP sessions need to be known within the IGP of the service provider. This behavior should not really be necessary in many cases, and these links need to be known only within the service provider IGP if they must be reachable for some reason (for instance, for network management of the links). Therefore, a mechanism is needed that will allow a non-VPN BGP-speaking router to advertise external routes without having to inject the external link IP addresses into the internal IGP. This can be achieved through use of the **next-hop-self** command within the BGP configuration; an example of this can be seen in Example 13-3.

NOTE   As will be seen later, this command is not necessary for VPN because, by default the PE-router will announce the route with itself as the next-hop.

Example 13-3 *Use of **next-hop-self** for BGP Route Advertisement*

```
router BGP <AS #>
!
 neighbor x.x.x.x remote-as <remote-as-#>
 neighbor x.x.x.x next-hop-self
```

NOTE   In a non-VPN environment, the IP subnets of links connecting the customers to the service provider backbone are usually not inserted into BGP by the service provider. Therefore, if the service provider wants to perform any network management of the customer-to-provider links, such as do SNMP requests on the customer router or ping IP addresses on the customer-to-provider links, they still must carry those subnets within the IGP. On the other hand, if the service provider only monitors link availability by reading SNMP tables on the PE-router, the IP subnet connecting the customer to the provider does not have to be reachable by other parts of the provider backbone.

Note also that just monitoring the SNMP tables on the PE-router does not guarantee that you'll be able to discover connectivity problems—the physical link might appear operational but does not pass any customer traffic. Also, if the link belongs to a VPN customer and is associated with a VRF, the link address will not be reachable within the service provider's IGP address space because it will have been removed from the global routing table.

We have already seen that when MPLS/VPN is introduced into the network, PE-routers will propagate VPN routes through the use of MP-iBGP. We have also seen that the PE-routers need to propagate labels that point toward the egress PE-router that announces these VPN routes.

Because each PE-router that announces VPN routes is the endpoint of any label-switched path (LSP) toward the VPN destination, the architecture requires that the PE-router announce itself as the BGP next-hop for the route so that label forwarding can occur and so that the PE-router can switch the packet based on the content of the second level label that corresponds to the relevant VRF and outbound interface for the route.

As previously stated, to guarantee successful forwarding of labeled VPN packets across the provider backbone, each PE-router will announce itself as the next-hop for any routes that it sends across MP-iBGP sessions by default; there is no need to specify this within the configuration of the PE-router. This next-hop address should be one of the loopback addresses of the advertising PE-router because this type of interface is always available.

NOTE   The PE-router will use the address specified within the **update-source** parameter of the **neighbor** command. This should be one of the loopback addresses.

The proper handling of the BGP next-hop is a necessary condition only for proper forwarding of VPN data. The ingress PE-routers also need a label toward the BGP next-hop (the loopback address of the egress router) in their forwarding table so that they can set the top MPLS label of the VPN packets to the label that has been assigned for the egress PE-router's loopback address. This means that all PE loopback addresses must be carried within the service provider's IGP, but they need not be host routes (although the use of host routes facilitates better usage of service provider address space—see the "PE-router Loopback Address Configuration" section, later in this chapter).

NOTE	Also refer to Chapter 8 and Chapter 9 for a further detailed discussion of VPN packet forwarding across the service provider backbone.

All internal links within the backbone must be enabled for MPLS switching so that a TDP/LDP relationship can be formed and so that the distribution of labels between adjacent LSRs can be achieved. If a router-only backbone is used, a label will be assigned to every internal route by the LSR, and this is determined by what is contained with the routing table. In normal Frame-mode MPLS operation, these labels will be advertised to upstream neighbors using downstream label distribution procedures. However, a label is required only for these internal links if packets will be sent directly to them. To prevent the advertisement of all these labels, the filtering techniques already discussed in Chapter 5, "Advanced MPLS Topics," should be deployed.

NOTE	Note that such filters will prevent only the advertisement of these labels, not their origination and subsequent insertion into the router's LFIB.

PE-router Loopback Address Configuration

Whenever a loopback address is configured and assigned an IP address, it is desirable for this IP address to be seen as a /32 host route within the IGP. This saves on address space and requires the use of only one address from a block of addresses for this particular interface. This is not strictly necessary or specified within the MPLS/VPN architecture, but it is certainly recommended.

In the case where the IGP is Open Shortest Path First (OSPF), then the loopback address should always be configured with a /32 mask. This is because OSPF will always set the address of a loopback interface to a host route, regardless of the configured mask for that interface. This OSPF behavior can be overridden by forcing the OSPF process to see the loopback address as a point-to-point link by using the **ip ospf network point-to-point** command within the loopback configuration. However, it is more advisable to use a /32 host route for the loopback address to conserve address space.

The implications of this behavior are pretty severe within an MPLS environment and will cause a loss of connectivity if not strictly adhered to. This is because if the loopback address is configured with a mask that is not /32—for instance, /24—there will be a difference between the OSPF route within its database and the LDP/TDP label. The LDP/TDP binding will refer to a route with a mask of /24 because the routing table of the LSR knows the loopback address as a *connected* /24 route.

In Figure 13-4, when LSR San Jose exchanges label bindings for all its routes with other LSRs, which will include a binding for its loopback interface, it will include a label binding for the loopback /24 route, not the /32 route that is contained within the OSPF database. All other LSRs will not use any label bindings that they receive if there is no corresponding route within their local routing table.

Figure 13-4   *PE Loopback Address Assignment*

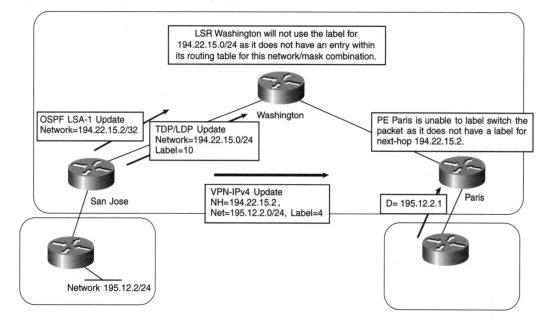

This means that when LSR Washington in Figure 13-4 receives the /24 label binding for 194.22.15.0/24 from LSR San Jose (it will not have received an IGP update for this route— it will have received a /32 route via OSPF because this is what is contained within the OSPF database of LSR San Jose), this /24 label binding will never be considered for use. Thus, connectivity to any destinations that use an address within the /24 subnet as a next-hop will be lost.

Summarization of PE Loopback Addresses

We have already seen that whenever a PE-router advertises a customer VPN route or any other external route to another PE-router, it does so with itself as the BGP next-hop. This next-hop address will be the address used for the MP-iBGP peering to other PE-routers, which will typically be one of its loopback interfaces. This can be seen in Figure 13-5, with sample configuration and router output shown in Examples 13-4 and 13-5.

Figure 13-5 *MP-iBGP Update Next-hop Assignment*

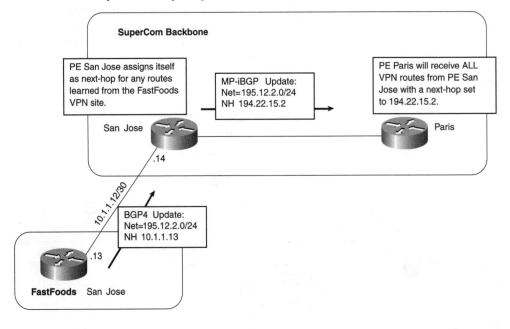

Figure 13-5 shows that PE-router San Jose receives an update from a VPN neighbor that is running BGP-4 across the PE-to-CE link for prefix 195.12.2/24. PE-router San Jose then advertises this route to PE-router Paris, but with the next-hop set to 194.22.15.2, which is the loopback address used by the San Jose PE-router for the MP-iBGP session to PE-router Paris.

Example 13-4 *MP-iBGP Update Configuration*

```
hostname San Jose
!
ip vrf FastFoods
 rd 1:26
 route-target both 100:26
!
interface Loopback0
 ip address 194.23.16.1 255.255.255.255
!
interface Loopback1
 ip address 194.22.15.2 255.255.255.255
!
interface serial0
 ip vrf forwarding FastFoods
 ip address 10.1.1.14 255.255.255.252
!
router bgp 1
 no bgp default ipv4-unicast
```

Example 13-4 *MP-iBGP Update Configuration (Continued)*

```
 neighbor 194.22.15.1 remote-as 1
 neighbor 194.22.15.1 update-source loopback1
!
 address-family ipv4 vrf FastFoods
 redistribute connected
 neighbor 10.1.1.13 remote-as 2
 neighbor 10.1.1.13 activate
 no auto-summary
 no synchronization
 exit-address-family
 !
address-family vpnv4
 neighbor 194.22.15.1 activate
 neighbor 194.22.15.1 send-community extended
 exit-address-family
!

hostname Paris
!
interface Loopback0
 ip address 194.22.15.1 255.255.255.255
!
router bgp 1
 no bgp default ipv4-unicast
 neighbor 194.22.15.2 remote-as 1
 neighbor 194.22.15.2 update-source Loopback0
!
 address-family vpnv4
 neighbor 194.22.15.2 activate
 neighbor 194.22.15.2 send-community extended
 exit-address-family
!
```

Example 13-5 *MP-iBGP Update show ip route vrf Output*

```
San Jose# show ip route vrf FastFoods 195.12.2.0
Routing entry for 195.12.2.0/24
  Known via "bgp 1", distance 20, metric 0
  Tag 2, type external
  Last update from 10.1.1.13 on serial0, 01:01:58 ago
  Routing Descriptor Blocks:
  * 10.1.1.13, from 10.1.1.13, 01:01:58 ago, via serial0
      Route metric is 0, traffic share count is 1
      AS Hops 1

Paris# show ip bgp vpnv4 vrf FastFoods 195.12.2.0
BGP routing table entry for 1:26:195.12.2.0/24, version 15
Paths: (1 available, best #1, table FastFoods)
Flag: 0x208
```

continues

Example 13-5 *MP-iBGP Update **show ip route vrf** Output (Continued)*

```
  Not advertised to any peer
  2
    194.22.15.2 (metric 40000) from 194.22.15.2 (194.22.15.2)
      Origin IGP, metric 0, localpref 100, valid, internal, best
      Extended Community: RT:100:26
```

NOTE   Notice that PE-router San Jose has a loopback0 interface that has an IP address of
194.23.16.1; this address is not used as the BGP next-hop. However, if the peering session
between PE-router San Jose and PE-router Paris is changed so that the configuration of PE-
router Paris reflects 194.23.16.1 as the MP-iBGP session endpoint, all routes will be
advertised with a next-hop of 194.23.16.1 from PE-router San Jose.

You might think that with multiple PE-routers spread across the network, it may be
desirable to summarize the loopback address ranges to help reduce the size of the routing
table. However, when MPLS is used within the core of the network, the addresses that are
used for the loopback interfaces of PE-routers must *not* be summarized anywhere within
the network because this will cause a loss of connectivity across the backbone. This is
regardless of whether the advertised routes are for VPN customers or non-VPN customers.

To understand the need to avoid summarization, we must consider how internal routers will
forward packets based on their MPLS information. We have already seen that regardless of
whether the route is for a non-VPN or a VPN customer, a next-hop is used that corresponds
to the advertising PE-router. This means that whenever a packet is forwarded to an external
destination, a label is appended to the packet that corresponds to the BGP next-hop of the
route, this being the egress PE-router. This label will be the first label in the MPLS label
stack; as mentioned previously, it will be the label that corresponds to the egress PE-router's
loopback interface address. An illustration of this is shown in Figure 13-6.

If the BGP next-hop were summarized by any P-routers within the core, they would become
the endpoint of the label-switched path (LSP) for the route. In other words, the top label,
pointing toward the egress PE-router, would be removed, and the P-router would be faced
with a packet that it might not be capable of recognizing. The implications of this are
slightly different for non-VPN and VPN routes.

In the case of non-VPN routes, the user data is sent across the provider backbone with only
one MPLS label, pointing toward the egress PE-router. Whenever the P-router becomes a
summarization point, it advertises the **implicit-null** label to upstream neighbors for each
summarized route, requesting them to remove the top label. When the top label is removed,
the P-router is faced with a pure IP packet. This means that the P-router would need to use
information from its own routing table to forward the packet. Because no BGP information
is advertised to P-routers, connectivity is lost and all packets for destinations covered by the
summary would be dropped.

Figure 13-6   *MPLS Two-Level Label Stack*

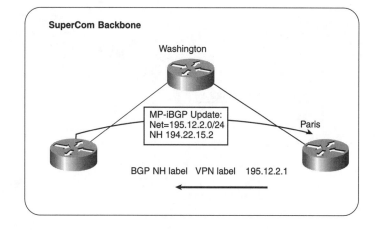

NOTE   Theoretically, it is still possible to summarize loopback addresses in non-VPN networks *if*
the router doing the summarization also carries full BGP routing. However, we definitely
advise against such practice.

In the case of VPN routes, if the BGP next-hop address is summarized somewhere within
the backbone at a point that is between two PE-routers exchanging MP-iBGP routes, then
any VPN connectivity between these two routers is lost.

After the top MPLS label is removed, the P-router is faced with a labeled packet with the
second label in the original MPLS label stack as its top label. This second label, imposed
on the VPN packet by the ingress PE-router, was assigned to the VPN destination by the
originating egress PE-router. Because we know that the labels have only local significance,
the meaning of this label is completely unknown to the P-router.

In this case, the upstream P-router looks for a label corresponding to the /32 of the BGP
next-hop. Because it does not have a downstream label for this route, it treats it as *untagged*.
When the P-router removes the top label and finds another label underneath, it discards the
packet, resulting in no connectivity to the VPN destination. This behavior prevents packets
from being forwarded along an incorrect LSP.

Figure 13-7 provides an example of a customer VPN route being advertised between two
PE-routers, and illustrates the problem of summarizing the PE loopback addresses.

Figure 13-7 *Summarization of PE Loopback Addresses*

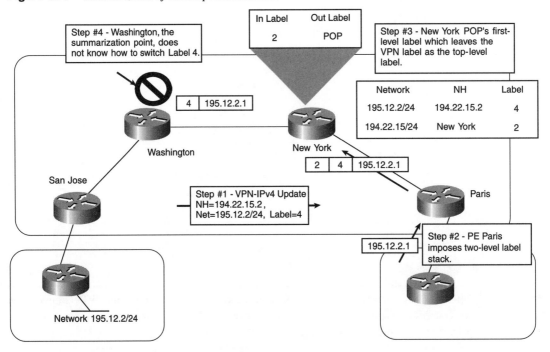

Figure 13-7 shows that PE-router San Jose advertises a VPN route for network 195.12.2/24 to PE-router Paris using its MP-iBGP session. When a packet for a host on network 195.12.2/24 arrives on PE-router Paris, it imposes a two-level stack of labels to the packet (with the top label being the label advertised by the SuperCom New York router for the next-hop, and the next label being the label advertised by the San Jose PE-router for the final VPN destination) and forwards it toward the SuperCom New York P-router.

When the New York router receives the packet, it POPs the first-level label (because it received the implicit-null label from the Washington P-router) and forwards the packet to the Washington P-router with a one-level label stack. When the Washington router receives the packet, it has a top label that corresponds to the external route as advertised by PE-router San Jose to PE-router Paris via MP-iBGP. However, the Washington router has no information available to be capable of switching the packet based on a label assigned by some other router (in this case, the San Jose PE-router); connectivity to network 195.12.2/24 is lost as the packet is dropped.

NOTE	It should be noted that the number of internal routes may actually increase within the core of the network because of the requirement that summarization of PE loopback addresses is prohibited. Therefore, the size of the IGP will be close to the number of PE-routers within the backbone.

MPLS/VPN Deployment on LAN Interfaces

Most media types provide the capability to partition the physical interface into one or multiple (sub)interfaces. Because each logical interface can belong to any VRF, this capability provides the functionality to apply multiple VRFs to the same physical interface so that multiple VPNs can share the same interface. Our discussion in Chapter 12 on Internet access for MPLS/VPN clients provides an illustration of one such topology in which this type of functionality might be required.

This capability to partition the physical interface is not available when using LAN interfaces that do not support virtual LANs (for example, standard Ethernet interfaces or Token Ring)—it is not possible to configure (sub)interfaces on these types of media. It is also not possible to associate a VRF to a secondary IP address because each VRF must be assigned to an interface, whether physical or logical, and not an IP address.

NOTE	Each interface can belong to only one VRF to allow the router to uniquely identify the forwarding table used for packets received through the interface in question. Two or more VRFs on the same interface would lead to ambiguities in many scenarios.

The implications of this are that standard 10-Mbps Ethernet does not provide the capability to have some hosts on one VPN and others on a totally separate VPN. In certain topologies, such as multiple customers on the same LAN segment, and for particular services, such as shared servers, this might be a very desirable function. One possible solution to this problem is to run multiple tunnels from the PE-router to each customer CE-router across the Ethernet. This option can be seen in Figure 13-8, which shows that each tunnel interface can be associated with a particular VRF to thus provide the required functionality.

Figure 13-8   *Tunnel Interfaces Between PE and CE Across LAN Media*

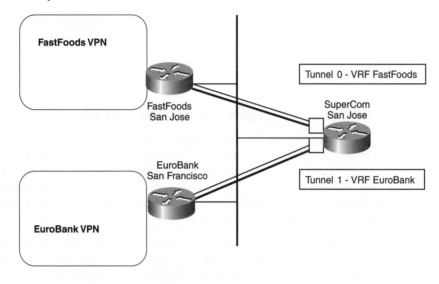

NOTE	The tunnel setup shown in Figure 13-8 reduces the security and isolation between the VPNs usually provided by the MPLS/VPN architecture. Every CE-router can capture packets exchanged between the PE-router and any other CE-router, resulting in loss of confidentiality. The intruder using one CE-router can also inject tunneled IP-over-IP packets with the source address of another CE-router, effectively inserting data into another VPN.

A further option is available when the interface to the shared media supports virtual local-area networks (VLANs)—for example, Fast Ethernet interfaces that are capable of supporting ISL. These VLANs can be mapped to different VPNs by associating the VLAN (sub)interface to a particular VRF.

NOTE	There are two conditions for successful deployment of this scenario: The interface must support VLANs, and the router must use the CEF switching path for a particular VLAN technology.

For example, Cisco IOS 12.0(7)T supports CEF switching only for ISL-based VLANs, not for 802.1q-based VLANs, so you cannot run MPLS/VPN across 802.1q-based VLANs in that particular level of IOS.

In this type of environment, Catalyst VLAN switches are connected to routers forwarding traffic from a number of ISL VLANs. The performance of this solution can be further improved with the VIP distributed ISL capability in the Cisco 7500 series router, where each VIP card can route ISL-encapsulated VLAN IP traffic. This functionality can be seen in Figure 13-9, which shows two scenarios. The first scenario shows a PE-router that is connected to a shared server that services multiple VPN clients. Each (sub)interface is used for a specific VPN access into the shared server.

NOTE   This type of configuration would require that the shared server be capable of servicing multiple application instances simultaneously, as well as handling VPNs that use the same address space. Although this is technically possible, research into specific server functionality is outside the scope of this publication.

The second scenario shows CE-routers connected to a PE-router through a VLAN-capable switch; each CE-router belongs to a separate VPN and is referenced through a unique (sub)interface by the PE-router.

Figure 13-9   *ISL Support for PE-routers*

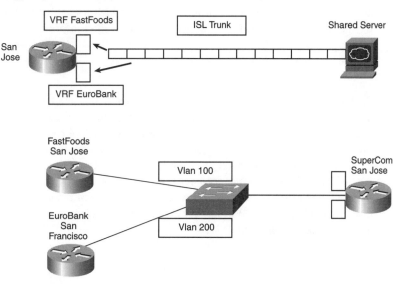

A partial configuration for PE-router San Jose in the second scenario of Figure 13-9 can be seen in Example 13-6. This example shows that the PE-router configuration of the Fast Ethernet interface is split into two (sub)interfaces, and these are configured to belong to particular VLANs and VRFs.

Example 13-6 *Fast Ethernet (Sub)interfaces and ISL Support*

```
interface FastEthernet2/1.1
 encapsulation isl 100
 ip vrf forwarding FastFoods
!
interface FastEthernet2/1.2
 encapsulation isl 200
 ip vrf forwarding EuroBank
```

Network Management of Customer Links

As with any network solution, the management and provisioning of customer links and of the internal service provider infrastructure are an important part of the deployment. In addition, the configuration and subsequent changes to this configuration are also high on the agenda. We have already discussed the role of the network management NMC in previous chapters, and we have also seen a typical topology that provides this type of activity.

NOTE   The applications that can provide this type of functionality within an MPLS-enabled VPN environment have not been included in this publication and have not been the focus of the research into this book. However, the Cisco VPN Solutions Center product offering will be available for management and provisioning of an MPLS-enabled VPN network. Refer to the Cisco Systems web site, www.cisco.com, for further information on this product offering.

Without the use of specific applications that have been designed to assist in the management and provisioning of the VPN service, it is still possible to manage the network by manipulating the route target attribute of certain VPN-IPv4 routes so that they may be imported by a network management station somewhere within the service provider network. Indeed, even if this type of application is deployed, it really addresses only the PE side of the problem. If a managed network service of CE-routers is a requirement, then manipulation of the route target is necessary. This type of managed network service was discussed in Chapter 7, "Virtual Private Network (VPN) Implementation Options"; an example is shown in Figure 13-10.

Figure 13-10 *Network Management VPN Topology*

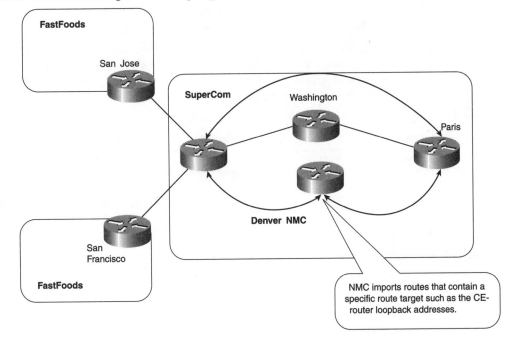

Although this type of solution may not be appropriate for all deployments—and certainly many customers will utilize SNMP for management of their customer links—it may be of interest in some cases. The techniques described may be useful for other applications of the MPLS/VPN architecture as well.

To be able to provide this type of service through use of the mechanisms that make up the MPLS/VPN architecture, we need to define what problem we are actually trying to overcome. In this case, the ultimate goal is to be able to pick out certain routes as belonging to specific areas of interest, such as identification of customer links for network management purposes. There are many ways to approach this problem—these will be visited in the following sections—and several solutions are available to the network designer.

Advertisement of Routes with Different Extended Communities

Our objective can be summarized as follows: to provide a service in which all customer routes become eligible for import into the Network Management VPN, and to make sure that we can import only the routes that are significant for the network management application. To achieve this objective, a number of options can be used. The first option, and probably the easier to implement, is to advertise all routes from a particular VPN with two separate BGP route target extended communities. You might think that it should be possible to import some routes into one set of VRFs and then to import the others into another set by using this method.

In our example, this would involve the first route target attribute being imported by members of the relevant VPN, and the second route target attribute being imported by the network management stations. If we refer to the example shown in Figure 13-10, we can define the relevant route target attributes as specified within Table 13-1.

Table 13-1   *Route Target Attributes for Dual Advertisement Example*

Customer Name	VPN Routes RT	NMC Routes RT
FastFoods	100:26	100:94

The following example shows a sample configuration that will cause the originating PE-router to send an update for each prefix within the VRF with two separate route target attributes.

Example 13-7   *Advertisement of Same Routes with Two Route Targets*

```
ip vrf FastFoods
 rd 1:26
 route-target import  100:26
 route-target export 100:26
 route-target export 100:94
 !
```

Running **debug** on the advertising/receiving PE-routers shows that each prefix is advertised only once, but this advertisement contains two separate route target attributes.

Example 13-8   *Debug Output for Advertisement of Routes with Two Route Targets*

```
San Jose # debug ip bgp update
BGP(1): 194.22.15.1 send UPDATE (format) 1:26:195.12.2.0/24 nexthop 194.22.15.2,
metric 0, path, extended community RT:100:26 RT:100:94

Paris # show ip bgp vpnv4 vrf FastFoods 195.12.2.0
BGP routing table entry for 1:26:195.12.2.0/24, version 13
Paths: (1 available, best #1, table FastFoods)
  Not advertised to any peer
  Local
    194.22.15.2 from 194.22.15.2 (194.22.15.2)
      Origin incomplete, metric 0, localpref 100, valid, internal,
      best
      Extended Community: RT:100:26 RT:100:94
```

The route targets attached to the BGP routes make every route from the customer VPN eligible for import into customer VRFs and the Network Management VRF. The end result of this setup would be that all customer routes would also end up in the Network

Management VRF, which would, in the worst case, hold all the routes of all the VPN customers. Because some customers might have overlapping IP addresses, the resulting routing tables would be even more interesting.

We don't control the export process in this case, so it is necessary to apply import filters (implemented as import maps, which were discussed in detail in Chapter 11, "MPLS/VPN Advanced Topologies") so that only the relevant routes are imported into specific VRFs. In our example, the goal is to import the subnets that connect the CE-routers with the PE-router into VRFs that are referenced by Network Management VPNs, and to import all other VPN routes into the relevant customer VPN. Both of these VPNs should not hold routes that belong to the other.

Figure 13-11 *Advertisement of Routes with Two Route Targets*

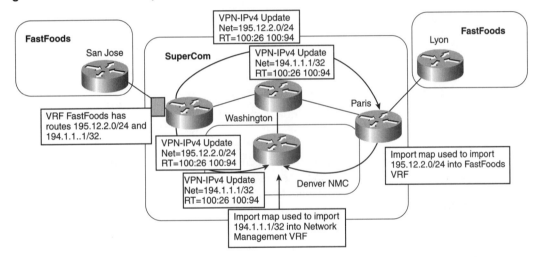

Figure 13-11 shows an example of the advertisement of the routes from a VRF using two separate route target attributes. When these routes are received by SuperCom routers Paris and Denver, they must be filtered and imported into the relevant VRFs. This can be achieved through use of import maps.

The import maps can filter based on IP prefix, standard BGP community, or extended community. Extended community support was introduced in Cisco IOS 12.0(7)T. Before IOS 12.0(7)T, no facility was available to filter imported routes based on route target, which meant that you usually had to rely on IP prefix lists (or standard IP access lists) to specify the import filter, and these could become quite large. The solution was obviously very restrictive and not at all scalable.

An example follows to illustrate where this type of filtering may become restrictive. Although this example is exaggerated, it illustrates the problem and shows that the resultant access list could end up with 201 entries. This is not only a headache in terms of configuration, but it is also very restrictive when trying to manage the configuration of the service.

Example 13-9   *Route Filtering Using Import Maps Without Extended Community Support*

```
A site is receiving 300 routes; 100 of these routes have a route target of 1:100, a
further 100 have a route target of 1:200, and the other 100 have a route target of
1:300.
The site requirement is such that only routes with a route target of 1:100 or 1:200
and only one route with a route target of 1:300 can be imported into the site VRF.
If the site routes cannot be summarized, then the worst-case scenario is that the
access list will require 201 entries. The resultant configuration would be as
follows:
ip vrf sample
 route-target import 1:100
 route-target import 1:200
 route-target import 1:300
 import map RouteFilter
!
route-map RouteFilter
 match ip address 1
!
access-list 1 permit 192.1.1.1 255.255.255.0
access-list 1 permit 193.1.1.1 255.255.255.0
...
```

In the example shown in Figure 13-11, in which we want to import some routes into the Network Management VPN and others into the customer VPN, the necessary configuration to allow each of the VRFs to be populated with the correct routes would be as shown in Example 13-10. Import maps are used to filter each route so that only the correct routes are placed into the VRFs of the PE-router.

Example 13-10 *Configuration Example for Import Filtering into VRFs*

```
hostname Paris
!
ip vrf FastFoods
 rd 1:26
 route-target import 100:26
 import map FastFoodRoutesOnly
!
route-map FastFoodRoutesOnly
 match ip address 1
!
access-list 1 permit 195.12.2.0 255.255.255.0
```

Example 13-10 *Configuration Example for Import Filtering into VRFs (Continued)*

```
!
hostname Denver
!
ip vrf NetworkManagement
 rd 1:94
 route-target import 100:94
 import map NetworkManagement
!
route-map NetworkManagement
 match ip address 2
!
access-list 2 permit 194.1.1.1
```

This configuration highlights a problem with using two separate route targets with import maps. Because each route carries both route target attributes, it is not possible to pick out the relevant routes through the route import process designed in the MPLS/VPN architecture (extended community attribute route target), so we need to base the route import decision on IP access lists. This means that there is little point in advertising the routes with different route targets within our scenario, and the same route target can be used for all routes.

NOTE   The advertisement of the same set of routes with different route targets may be useful in certain topologies. For example, if a site wants to import routes from only one other site within its VPN, then it could import a different route target advertised from that site rather than importing the default VPN route target. If it did not do this, then it would need to deploy an extensive import map so that it filtered out all unwanted routes.

Use of Standard BGP Communities for Route Filtering

As an alternative to the previous approach of advertising a set of routes with two separate route target attributes, it is possible to use the same method but with standard BGP communities within the import map filters instead of filtering based on the IP prefix.

This approach has some obvious advantages, primarily the reduction in the amount of entries that are required within the access lists used to implement the filters on the receiving PE-routers. However, we need to understand whether it will allow us to achieve our ultimate goal of picking out specific routes for import into our Network Management VPN in a scalable manner.

Figure 13-12 *Route Filtering Using Standard BGP Communities*

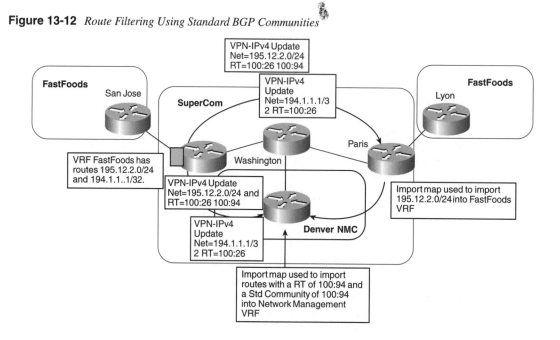

Figure 13-12 provides an illustration of this method. Using this approach, every customer route is marked with two route targets, as in our previous example: the FastFoods and the Network Management route targets. However, only the routes that are destined for the Network Management VRF are marked with a standard BGP community. This standard BGP community can then be used in the import map for the Network Management VRF. This means that the SuperCom PE-router Denver will import only routes into the Network Management VRF that contain a specific route target (in this case, 100:94) and the configured standard community (defined also as 100:94).

NOTE   Both route target attributes are necessary because all VPNs will use the same route target to import routes that are pertinent to the Network Management VPN.

NOTE   Note that the standard and extended communities differ in their format, so care must be taken on the value that is used. Standard communities use a 32-bit format, while extended community use a 64-bit format.

An IP prefix list may also be used to match on a certain prefix or prefix length. In the following example, this facility has been used by the SuperCom Paris router. Also notice that the **both** keyword is required within the BGP VPNv4 configuration so that the PE-router knows that it must send both standard and extended BGP community attributes. The configurations for all relevant routers in Figure 13-12 are as shown in Example 13-11.

Example 13-11 *Use of Standard Communities to Control Route Import into VRF*

```
hostname San Jose
!
ip vrf FastFoods
 rd 1:26
 route-target import 100:26
 route-target export 100:26
 route-target export 100:94
!
router bgp 1
 neighbor 194.22.15.3 remote-as 1
 neighbor 194.22.15.1 remote-as 1
!
address-family vpnv4
 neighbor 194.22.15.3 activate
 neighbor 194.22.15.3 send-community both
 neighbor 194.22.15.3 route-map FilterRoutes out
 neighbor 194.22.15.1 activate
 neighbor 194.22.15.1 send-community extended
!
access-list 1 permit 194.1.1.1
!
route-map FilterRoutes permit 10
 match ip address 1
 set community 100:94
!
route-map FilterRoutes permit 20
!

hostname Denver
!
ip vrf NetManagement
 rd 1:94
 route-target import 100:94
 route-target export 100:94
 import map NetManagement
!
ip community-list 1 permit 100:94
!
route-map NetManagement
 match community 1
!

hostname Paris
!
ip vrf FastFoods
```

continues

Example 13-11 *Use of Standard Communities to Control Route Import into VRF (Continued)*

```
 rd 1:26
 route-target import 100:26
 route-target export 100:26
 import map FastFoodRoutesOnly
 !
ip extcommunity-list 1 permit rt 100:26
 !
ip prefix-list FastFoods seq 10 permit 195.12.2.0/23 ge 24
 !
route-map FastFoodRoutesOnly
 match extcommunity 1
 match ip address prefix-list FastFoods
 !
```

This sample configuration shows several things of interest. SuperCom routers Denver and Paris will learn routes from PE-router San Jose with two separate route targets. The Denver router will import only routes that have a route target of 100:94 *and* a standard BGP community of 100:94. The Paris router will import only routes that have a route target of 100:26 *that* fall within the range of the prefix-list.

Because prefix 195.12.2.0/24 falls within the **permit** statement of the prefix list on router Paris, it will be imported into the FastFoods VRF. Notice that this is the only route that will be imported into this VRF, although both routes will be considered for import because they contain the route target of 100:26. (The output from **show ip bgp vpnv4 all** in Example 13-12 confirms this. Notice how the FastFoods VRF has both routes, but the NetManagement VRF has only one—the route that contains both the standard and extended community attributes.)

To verify the correct import of various customer routes into VRFs on the SuperCom routers, the following example illustrates all the relevant commands showing that the standard BGP community 100:94 is not attached to the route 195.12.2.0/24. The route is therefore not imported into the NetManagement VRF.

Example 13-12 *Imported Routes Using Standard BGP Communities*

```
Paris# show ip bgp vpnv4 all

   Network          Next Hop          Metric LocPrf Weight Path
Route Distinguisher: 1:26 (default for vrf FastFoods)
 *>i195.12.2.0/24    194.22.15.2                0    100     0 ?
 *>i194.1.1.1/32     194.22.15.2                0    100     0 ?

Denver# show ip bgp vpnv4 all
Network          Next Hop          Metric LocPrf Weight Path
Route Distinguisher: 100:94 (default for vrf NetManagement)
 *>i194.1.1.1/32     194.22.15.2                0    100     0 ?

Paris# show ip bgp vpnv4 all 195.12.2.0
BGP routing table entry for 1:26:195.12.2.0/24, version 7
```

Example 13-12 *Imported Routes Using Standard BGP Communities (Continued)*

```
Paths: (1 available, best #1, table FastFoods )
  Not advertised to any peer
  Local
     194.22.15.2 from 194.22.15.2 (194.22.15.2)
       Origin incomplete, metric 0, localpref 100, valid, internal,
       best
       Extended Community: RT:100:26 RT:100:94

Paris# show ip bgp vpnv4 all 194.1.1.1
BGP routing table entry for 1:26:194.1.1.1/32, version 265
Paths: (1 available, best #1, table NULL)
  Not advertised to any peer
  Local
     194.22.15.2 from 194.22.15.2 (194.22.15.2)
       Origin incomplete, metric 0, localpref 100, valid, internal,
       best
       Community: 100:94
       Extended Community: RT:100:26 RT:100:94

Denver# show ip bgp vpnv4 all 194.1.1.1
BGP routing table entry for 1:94:194.1.1.1/32, version 27
Paths: (1 available, best #1, table NetManagement)
  Not advertised to any peer
  Local, imported path from 1:94:194.1.1.1/32
     194.22.15.2 from 194.22.15.2 (194.22.15.2)
       Origin incomplete, metric 0, localpref 100, valid, internal,
       best
       Community: 100:94
       Extended Community: RT:100:26 RT:100:94

Denver# show ip bgp vpnv4 vrf NetManagement

  Network          Next Hop         Metric LocPrf Weight Path
Route Distinguisher: 100:94 (default for vrf NetManagement)
*>i194.1.1.1/32     194.22.15.2           0    100      0 ?
```

The method described in the previous paragraphs enables us to achieve our objective and provides a method of selectively picking certain routes for import into specific VRFs. However, the major drawback to this method is that each PE-router that wants to import selective routes needs to have filters configured to match on the standard community attribute. So, what is really needed is a method that allows us to selectively *export* routes with specific route targets that can be imported using one statement on any receiving PE-routers.

You might think that to achieve this, we could change the route target extended community attribute in the same way as the standard community attribute in the previous example. However, setting extended community attributes through route maps applied to route redistribution, or to BGP neighbors, is not supported; this type of change must be implemented using export maps, as will be seen in the next section. The following example shows the error that is produced if you try to change the route target through a route map.

Example 13-13 *Changing Route Target Using a Route Map*

```
Paris(config-route-)# set extcommunity rt 100:100
% "ExtendedCommOut" used as BGP outbound route-map, set extcommunity rt not
supported
```

Advertisement of Routes with Different Route Targets Using Export Maps

The previous example provided us with a working solution to the CE-router management problem, but the solution was complex and suboptimal (it would be fair to call it a workaround, not a solution). We have not been able to provide the capability to advertise routes with different route target attributes from the originating PE-router.

As previously stated, what is needed is a mechanism by which the originating PE-router can selectively advertise certain routes with a route target that is different than other routes that it is also advertising from the same VRF. This mechanism is provided through the use of export maps within the VRF configuration.

In our SuperCom backbone example, if this feature is used, then we now can advertise our network management routes with one route target and then advertise the rest of our routes with a totally separate route target. This is illustrated in Figure 13-13.

Figure 13-13 *Export of Routes with Different Route Targets*

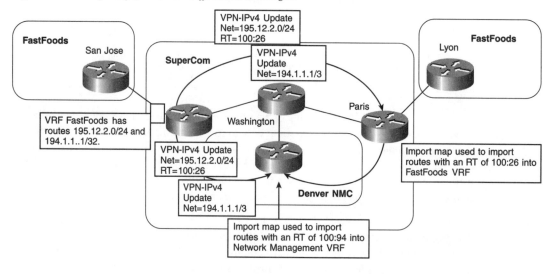

Figure 13-13 shows that two routes are advertised from the SuperCom PE-router San Jose, and each of these has a different route target. The SuperCom PE-router Paris is configured to import routes with one of the route targets into the FastFoods VPN, and router Denver is configured to import routes with the other route target into the Network Management VPN. The resultant configurations for all the relevant routers can be seen in Example 13-14.

Example 13-14 *Export of Routes with Different Route Targets*

```
hostname San Jose
!
ip vrf FastFoods
 rd 1:26
 export map FastFoodsExport
 route-target import 100:26
!
access-list 1 permit 194.1.1.1
access-list 2 permit any
!
route-map FastFoodsExport permit 10
 match ip address 1
 set extcommunity rt 100:94
!
route-map FastFoodsExport permit 20
 match ip address 2
 set extcommunity rt 100:26
!

hostname Paris
!
ip vrf FastFoods
 rd 1:26
 route-target export 100:26
 route-target import 100:26
!

hostname Denver
!
ip vrf NetManagement
 rd 1:94
 route-target export 100:94
 route-target import 100:94
!
```

In some networks, the service providers base the connectivity toward their customers on static routes configured on PE-routers. If the customer is a VPN customer, the route would obviously be configured within the context of the customer VRF. To advertise these static routes to other members of the VPN or to other VPNs, they must be redistributed into MP-iBGP. In this environment, the PE-router configuration can be simplified significantly by using a tag that can be associated with the static route to signify the set of VPNs into which the route should be exported.

Ideally, the tags assigned to static routes would be used during their redistribution into MP-iBGP to set the route target of the route. The real solution, however, is slightly more complex because you cannot set route target during route redistribution. In addition, the original route tag is lost at the moment that the route target is set with the export map. The only parameters that can be used in both route maps are standard BGP communities that serve as a link between the tags assigned to static routes and MPLS/VPN route targets.

When the static routes toward the VPN customer are redistributed into MP-iBGP, a route map is used to match the static route tag and to set a corresponding standard BGP community. When the standard BGP community is set, it can then be used to specify which route target should be used for the route when it is exported through MP-iBGP to other PE-routers. Example 13-15 provides a sample configuration that shows a static route for prefix 193.1.1.1/32 being placed into the FastFoods VPN with a standard BGP community of 100:1. When this route is advertised via MP-iBGP, its route target is set to 100:5.

Example 13-15 *Tagging Static Routes for Redistribution into MP-iBGP*

```
hostname San Jose
!
ip vrf FastFoods
 rd 1:26
 export map FastFoodsExport
 route-target import 100:26
!
access-list 1 permit 194.1.1.1
access-list 2 permit any
!
ip community-list 101 permit 100:1
!
router bgp 1
!
 address-family ipv4 vrf FastFoods
 redistribute static route-map static FastFoodStatics
 exit address-family
 !
ip route vrf FastFoods 193.1.1.1 255.255.255.255 serial 0/1 tag 100
!
route-map FastFoodsExport permit 10
 match ip address 1
 set extcommunity rt 100:94
!
route-map FastFoodsExport permit 20
 match community 101
 set extcommunity rt 100:5
!
route-map FastFoodsExport permit 30
 match ip address 2
 set extcommunity rt 100:26
!
route-map static_FastFoodStatics permit 10
 match tag 100
 set community 100:1
```

NOTE   Notice that within the configuration of the San Jose router, there is no **route-target export** command within the FastFoods VRF configuration. This is because the default route target for this VRF has been set to 100:26 within the export map. (The third **permit** statement allows everything that does not match the first two statements.)

If two route target attributes for the same prefix are required, then the default may be configured within the export map by using the **set extcommunity rt** command and specifying the default plus any other required route targets.

If it is desirable to remove the standard BGP community attributes that were specified in Example 13-15, then the following configuration could be added. This will strip the standard BGP community before it is advertised across the MP-iBGP sessions.

Example 13-16 *Removal of Standard BGP Community Attributes Before Advertisement*

```
ip community-list 102 permit 100:1
!
address-family vpnv4
 neighbor 194.22.15.1 activate
 neighbor 194.22.15.1 send-community both
 neighbor 194.22.15.1 route-map drop community out
!
route-map drop_community permit 10
 set comm-list 102 delete
```

Use of Traceroute Across an MPLS/VPN Backbone

Although the use of traceroute between VPN sites should not be a huge issue for the service provider, it may be a major issue for the customers of the VPN service who may want to see the internal structure of the backbone network. There may also be confusion on the part of the customer when a hub-and-spoke topology is deployed because the hub router will appear twice in the traceroute. The service provider can decide, based on customer demand, whether this internal structure is shown.

Regardless of which choice is taken, it is interesting to understand the mechanisms involved and the packet flow from one site to another. To achieve this, we should consider a traceroute that is initiated from one CE-router to another CE-router in a different site, or from a host in one site to a host in a different site. An example of the CE-to-CE case can be seen in Figure 13-14.

In the scenario shown in Figure 13-14, when the traceroute is started on the FastFoods San Jose CE-router, it will create an IP/UDP packet with a source IP address set to the outgoing interface address of the CE-to-PE link and the destination address set to the address of the FastFoods Lyon CE-router (Step 1). The Time-to-Live (TTL) of the packet will be set to 1, and an ICMP time exceeded message will be received back from the first router within the packet's path—in this case, the SuperCom San Jose PE-router (Step 2). No MPLS is involved at this stage.

Figure 13-14 *The Traceroute from CE to CE Across MPLS Backbone*

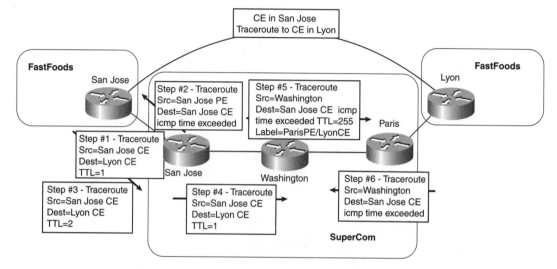

The FastFoods San Jose CE-router will now send a new packet, but this time the TTL will be set to 2 (Step 3). The receiving SuperCom San Jose PE-router will accept the packet and treat the TTL as valid. The packet will be switched based on the content of the local VRF; at this point, the packet will enter into the SuperCom MPLS/VPN backbone (Step 4).

The MPLS architecture as described in *draft-ietf-mpls-arch* provides two choices on how the PE-router can treat the TTL field of the packet when it first enters the MPLS backbone. These choices dictate whether to propagate the TTL value into the TTL field of the label header. In the Cisco Systems implementation of the architecture, this choice is determined through configuration, as shown in Table 13-2. The default configuration is to propagate the TTL.

Table 13-2   *Propagation of TTL into TTL Field of Label Header*

Step	Command	Purpose
1	**tag-switching ip propagate-ttl**	Propagate the TTL into the TTL field of the label header.
2	**no tag-switching ip propagate-ttl**	Do *not* propagate the TTL into the TTL field of the label header.

NOTE	The **propagate-ttl** command has two effects: It propagates the IP TTL into the label header, *and* it propagates the label TTL into the IP header (where the packet exits the MPLS/VPN backbone).

Assuming that TTL propagation is enabled within the SuperCom backbone, the SuperCom San Jose PE-router will now forward the packet with a label stack imposed to reach the FastFoods Lyon CE-router. This label stack will have the TTL of the original IP packet contained within the header.

NOTE	If this packet were to flow through ATM switches, then the TTL would not be examined again. This is because there is no concept of TTL within an ATM environment, which is treated as one hop within the MPLS environment. Refer to the MPLS architecture draft, *draft-ietf-mpls-arch* for further information on TTL and loop prevention in an ATM environment. Also refer to the discussion on this subject in Chapter 5.

If the packet flows through a router-based MPLS backbone—for example, across the SuperCom backbone—then when the packet reaches the next LSR in the path (the Washington *P-router*, in the SuperCom network), the TTL is examined, and its value is decreased by 1. The value of the TTL is now found to have reached 0. In a normal IP environment, the router will now generate an ICMP time exceeded message with itself as the source address and the source address contained within the IP packet as the destination address. The original packet would then be dropped.

If the router generating the ICMP response is a P-router (Washington, in our case), it will not have any information about the originator of the packet (that information is stored only in the PE-routers). Thus, it cannot route the **ICMP time exceeded** packet back because it has no route toward the offending packet originator in its routing table. However, it does still have the original label stack that was imposed by the first PE-router in the path—San Jose, in our example—and it will use this to forward the **ICMP time exceeded packet** toward the destination (Step 5 in Figure 13-14). This process can be seen in Example 13-17.

Example 13-17 *ICMP Time Exceeded and MPLS Packet Debug*

```
Packet is received with TTL set to 1 by the P-router:
Washington# debug tag-switching packet
TAG: PO2/0: recvd: CoS=0, TTL=1, Tag(s)=27/81
TTL expires, and an ICMP time exceeded message is generated with the P-router as
source and the destination as the source address of the originating CE-router.
Washington# debug ip icmp
ICMP: time exceeded (Time To Live) sent to 194.22.15.1 (destination was 195.12.2.2)
```

continues

Example 13-17 *ICMP Time Exceeded and MPLS Packet Debug (Continued)*

```
The new ICMP message is forwarded using the original label stack, although the
internal label of 27 has been change to allow the packet to be label-switched across
the MPLS backbone:
Washington# debug tag-switching packet
TAG: PO4/0: xmit: CoS=6, TTL=255, Tag(s)=28/81
```

The packet is now label-switched to the SuperCom Paris router, which connects to the
FastFoods Lyon CE-router. However, this is not the real destination of the packet—the
FastFoods San Jose CE-router is.

When the packet arrives at the SuperCom Paris router, if the label is not an aggregate label,
then the packet is forwarded to the destination CE-router, FastFoods Lyon. Then FastFoods
Lyon will route the packet back toward the MPLS core, to be label-switched to the
FastFoods San Jose CE-router. However, if the label is an aggregate label, then the Paris
PE-router will perform a lookup in the VRF for the FastFoods VPN and will find that the
packet should be forwarded back through the MPLS core toward the FastFoods San Jose
CE-router (Step 6 in Figure 13-14).

If the internal topology of the MPLS network is to be hidden from customers, then turning
off TTL propagation will achieve this objective because the IP TTL will not be copied into
the label TTL (the value of 255 is instead), and the MPLS/VPN backbone will be seen as
one IP hop.

Summary

In this chapter, we have highlighted several issues that will be common to most
implementations of the MPLS/VPN architecture.

MPLS/VPN requires BGP throughout the service provider network to support the exchange
of VPN routes between the PE-routers. The infrastructure that must be put in place for the
MPLS/VPN technology can also be utilized to migrate customer routes from the existing
IGP routing protocol run within the service provider backbone to BGP. This results in a
cleaner network design, a more stable core network, and a more scalable solution in the
long run. Most of the MPLS/VPN implementations will also have to implement BGP
scalability mechanisms, from route reflectors to confederations (assuming that **next-hop-
self** is used between sub-AS boundaries) to reduce the full-mesh requirement imposed on
iBGP sessions by the BGP protocol and to performance optimizations made possible by
BGP peer groups in the Cisco Systems IOS.

Another important consideration in MPLS/VPN deployment is the usage of loopback
interfaces as the endpoints of MP-iBGP sessions and related BGP next-hop issues.
Although the MPLS/VPN architecture does not mandate it, the common guideline of
configuring /32 subnets on loopback interfaces should be followed if at all possible. The
subnets assigned to loopback interfaces should not be summarized in the IGP run in the

service provider network—summarization of these loopback addresses will result in loss of VPN connectivity.

MPLS/VPN is usually deployed across WAN links connecting PE-routers with CE-routers. However, in some cases the PE-router and the customer router are linked with shared LAN media. In these scenarios, MPLS/VPN is best configured in combination with virtual LAN technologies (ISL, for example), and care should be taken to avoid any MTU issues such as the ones discussed in Chapter 5. Alternatively, IP-over-IP tunnels can be used, resulting in degraded security of the overall solution.

We have also seen several examples of how customer routers can be managed by the service provider (the same scenario applies to any common service offered by the service provider to its customers), and we have explored what issues are likely to occur based on the method chosen to implement the service.

CHAPTER 14

Carrier's Carrier and Inter-provider VPN Solutions

Our description of the MPLS/VPN architecture so far has assumed that all VPN customer sites are connected to a single service provider backbone across PE-to-CE links, and that the exchange of routing information across these links occurs without the need of MPLS, and without any direct exchange of routing information between customer sites. We have also highlighted the fact that a customer may choose to use the MPLS/VPN service to connect sites because this provides a more scalable way of providing VPN connectivity when compared to traditional methods such as the overlay or peer-to-peer models (described in Chapter 7, "Virtual Private Network (VPN) Implementation Options").

However, it is possible that these customer sites may actually belong to an Internet service provider (ISP) (where the ISP is a VPN customer of the service provider offering connectivity or bandwidth services). In addition, the customer sites could be dispersed across a wide geographical area, so they might need to attach to multiple service providers to obtain their VPN service throughout their organization.

All these possibilities require that extensions be provided to the basic MPLS/VPN architecture that we have so far described, to help scale the deployment and maintain connectivity between VPN sites when inter-site traffic crosses service provider boundaries. These extensions are provided through the carrier's carrier and inter-provider VPN architectures, and they are described also within RFC 2547bis.

As with all complex subjects, example topologies will be used throughout this chapter to help describe these architectural extensions. An example topology in which the carrier's carrier architecture may be appropriate can be seen in Figure 14-1.

Figure 14-1 provides the topology of the SuperCom MPLS/VPN backbone and shows that two VPN customers, EuroISP1 and EuroISP2, attach to the backbone in various points of presence (POP) locations. Each of these customers is an Internet service provider (ISP); the customers exchange full Internet routing information between their POP sites. Both of these VPN customers use the SuperCom network as transport between their sites.

Figure 14-1 *SuperCom Base Network Topology*

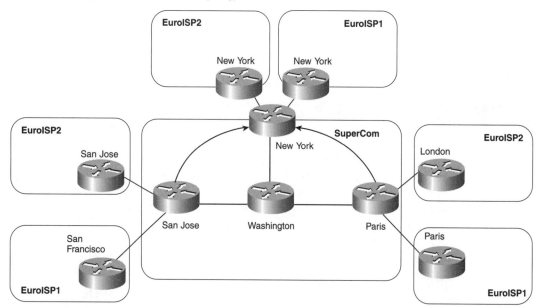

Carrier's Carrier Solution Overview

The carrier's carrier MPLS/VPN solution is targeted at ISPs (or MPLS/VPN service providers) that are VPN customers of another service provider that provides connectivity or pure bandwidth services across an MPLS/VPN backbone. These VPN customers usually require inter-POP connectivity (including the capability to carry full Internet routing information) across the MPLS/VPN backbone and also adopt their own peering and routing policies

No restrictions within the MPLS/VPN architecture prevent this type of connectivity from being possible, using the functionality that we have already described in previous chapters. However, it is important to understand the implications of providing this service and to determine whether the mechanisms already described within the MPLS/VPN architecture are adequate to supply inter-POP connectivity.

Before reviewing how this type of connectivity can be provided, it is essential to make some distinctions between route types so that the following explanations become clear. We know that the carrier's carrier solutions are targeted at VPN customers that are ISPs, so we can assume that these customers will also be providing connectivity for their own external customers. This means that the ISP will have routes that belong to its own internal network and routes that will belong to external customers, or peering points. Figure 14-2 illustrates these types of routes.

Figure 14-2 *ISP Route Types—Internal and External Routing Information*

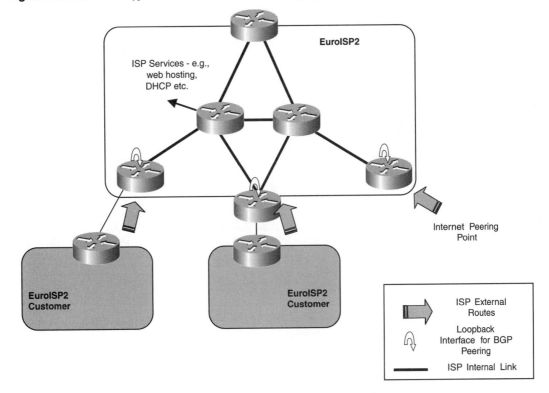

Within the figure, we can see that all the ISP internal links, internal services, and loopback interfaces can be classed as internal routes. We will see later in this chapter that not all of these routes need to be advertised between ISP sites. All routes learned via Internet peering points or from customers of the ISP can be classed as external routes. For the rest of this chapter, we will refer to each of these route types as either ISP-customer internal or ISP-customer external routes to help provide the distinction of whether the route will be advertised across the MPLS/VPN backbone (ISP-customer internal) or directly between ISP VPN customer sites (ISP-customer external).

To fully appreciate the implications of this type of connectivity, we should review what will happen if the exchange of routing information between ISP sites is achieved by advertising all possible routes (both internal and external) across the PE-to-CE links. Figure 14-3 provides an example of this type of deployment.

Figure 14-3 *PE-to-CE Exchange of Internet Routes*

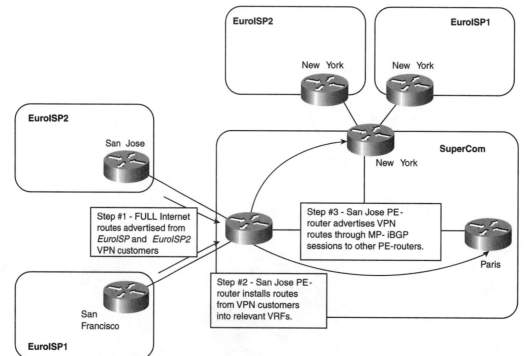

As seen in Figure 14-3, the amount of routing information that the ISP may hold—and, therefore, exchange between POP sites—may be substantial. The most likely scenario is that the ISP will hold full Internet routes, as is the case in our sample topology, although partial routing may be an option. This will almost certainly still present a substantial number of routes that must be exchanged between POP sites.

NOTE   Partial routing in the majority of cases is not an option because the customers of the ISP will usually require full Internet routing information.

In Figure 14-3, the EuroISP1 and EuroISP2 VPN customers each want to advertise full Internet routes to other POP sites across the MPLS/VPN backbone. To achieve this, these routes are advertised toward the San Jose PE-router, which must install them into the relevant VRFs—in this case, full routes into the EuroISP1 VRF and full routes into the EuroISP2 VRF.

NOTE	The routes must be installed into a VRF because the MPLS/VPN backbone is providing only bandwidth services between VPN sites, not Internet peering services in which the routes would reside within the global routing table.

If only one ISP customer attaches to the MPLS/VPN backbone, then the worst-case scenario is that full Internet routes will be advertised toward the PE-router from every ISP site. However, as illustrated in Figure 14-3, it is apparent that as more ISP customers require connectivity across the MPLS/VPN backbone, the exchange of routing information presents some major scaling issues that must be addressed.

This exchange of ISP-customer external routing information between sites via the MPLS/VPN backbone is not very optimal. If you consider the amount of routing information that each PE-router will need to hold, potentially multiple copies of full Internet routes, and also the amount of label space that will be required per VRF (one label per route), you can see that the basic architecture is not going to provide a scalable method for this type of connectivity. You can also see that if each ISP advertises all routes toward the backbone, this presents a major increase in the amount of routing protocol traffic traversing the MPLS/VPN backbone, even though much of this information is not actually required by the service provider that provides the VPN service. Therefore, an alternative method of route exchange is needed in this type of environment to overcome these limitations—this is provided through use of the carrier's carrier architecture.

Carrier's Carrier Architecture—Topologies

Several possible topologies require different services from the MPLS/VPN backbone. Some ISPs will not run MPLS within their own sites, while others will run MPLS but will not provide VPN services to their customers. Some ISPs will run MPLS within their own network and will also provide a VPN service to their customers. In all cases, it is necessary to differentiate between routes that will be presented to the MPLS/VPN backbone and those that will be advertised directly between sites but not advertised to the backbone network (on a CE-router/PE-router session).

External routing information for a particular VPN customer is not necessary within the MPLS/VPN backbone because label switching is performed based on BGP next-hop addresses. This is no different than the standard MPLS/VPN model that we have seen previously. However, in the case of ISP connectivity, our goal is to exchange external routing information between ISP sites, but without having to advertise this information toward the MPLS/VPN backbone and then between PE-routers within the backbone using MP-iBGP. This means that, within an ISP's VRF, the PE-routers in an MPLS/VPN backbone should not carry routes that have been learned by that ISP from its own external BGP peerings or customers.

Only the ISP's internal routes need to be advertised by the ISP sites toward the backbone for subsequent import into relevant VRFs on the PE-router. These routes will include any internal routes that must be reachable by other members of the ISP VPN, such as BGP next-hop addresses and iBGP peering addresses, and any internal networks that provide inter-POP services, such as web hosting, server farms, and central DHCP services.

Using the route types that we defined in the previous section, we can make the distinction that ISP-customer internal routes will be advertised toward the MPLS/VPN backbone, and ISP customer external routes will not.

ISP with No MPLS Deployment Within POP Sites

Having reviewed the VPN connectivity requirements of an ISP, it is clear that we should avoid the exchange of ISP-customer external routing information between POP sites through advertisement of this routing information toward the MPLS/VPN backbone. Because of this requirement, the carrier's carrier architecture can be introduced so that the MPLS/VPN backbone is not overloaded with unnecessary external routing information.

In our first example of this architecture, the ISP may not run MPLS within its own POP sites. ISP-customer external routing information is exchanged between POP sites through the use of iBGP. This type of connectivity can be seen in Figure 14-4.

Figure 14-4 *Carrier's Carrier—No MPLS Within ISP Sites*

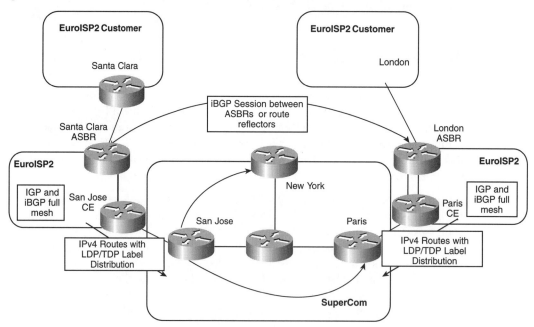

In Figure 14-4, we can see that ISP EuroISP2 wants to exchange external routing information from its Santa Clara site with other POP sites and then use the MPLS/VPN backbone to send traffic toward external destinations that are reachable through these other POP sites.

Each autonomous system boundary router (ASBR) within the ISP's sites runs an iBGP session with all other ASBRs in other POP sites so that ISP-customer external routing information can be exchanged between the sites. The BGP next-hop address for these routes must be advertised to the MPLS/VPN backbone because these addresses will subsequently be used for label switching from one site to another. This is achieved through normal routing protocol exchange across the CE-to-PE links and is no different than the mechanisms that we have already seen within the MPLS/VPN architecture.

NOTE   Standard iBGP rules apply where a full mesh between sites, and within sites, is required or where the use of route reflectors can be deployed to help with the scaling of the solution. If route reflectors are deployed—and this is certainly recommended—then iBGP sessions between sites can be restricted to route reflector peerings. A full mesh of iBGP sessions between route reflectors, and within each site, is still required.

All internal routes (that should be reachable by other members of the VPN) will be distributed between sites via the MPLS/VPN backbone, so each of the BGP next-hop addresses for ISP-customer external routes will be present in the VRF for the specific ISP and will be used to validate the ISP-customer external routes that are learned across the direct iBGP sessions between sites.

In our example, the San Jose PE-router will have a route within the EuroISP2 VRF that corresponds to the EuroISP2 Santa Clara ASBR router. This is because this address is used as the BGP next-hop for all routes that are advertised from the Santa Clara router to other POP sites within the EuroISP2 VPN.

The BGP next-hop addresses, and any other routes that reside within the VRF, are advertised across the MPLS/VPN backbone using MP-iBGP. They are then imported into the relevant VRFs on receiving PE-routers. In our example, the Paris PE-router will receive an MP-iBGP update that corresponds to the BGP next-hop address used by the EuroISP2 Santa Clara ASBR router for all of its ISP-customer external routes that it advertises across its iBGP session with the London ASBR. When the routes are within the VRF, they are advertised across the PE-to-CE links to all relevant VPN sites.

You might think that this is all that needs to be done to provide connectivity between ISP sites. However, as Figure 14-5 shows, packets sent from the ISP site using the information provided across their iBGP sessions are dropped at the first PE-router in the path to the destination.

Figure 14-5 *ISP External Traffic—Routing Requirement at PE-router*

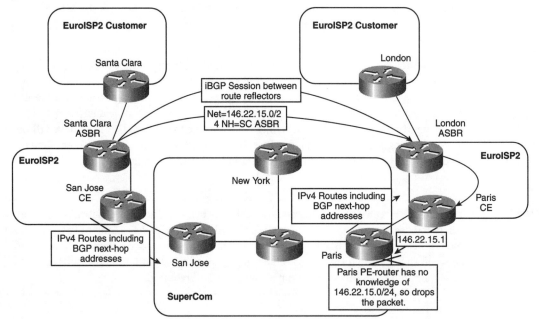

As seen in Figure 14-5, packets sent from the EuroISP2 Paris CE-router to the SuperCom Paris PE-router are dropped. This is because the PE-router has no knowledge of ISP-customer external VPN routing information (in our example, the 146.22.15.0/24 subnet) within its VRF and cannot route the packet. For this reason, each PE-to-CE link must be configured to run LDP/TDP label distribution procedures so that MPLS labels can be exchanged between the PE- and CE-routers. This is achieved through use of the **mpls ip** command, as shown in Example 14-1:

Example 14-1 *Configuration of LDP/TDP on PE-to-CE Link*

```
interface serial0/1
 description ** PE to CE link running LDP/TDP label distribution
 ip vrf forwarding EuroBank
 mpls ip
```

Once labels have been exchanged, the CE-router is capable of imposing a label for the BGP next-hop address that it has learned from the PE-router. The PE-router then can label-switch the incoming packet rather than try to route it based on information within the VRF.

Therefore, the EuroISP2 CE-routers in San Jose and Paris run LDP/TDP label distribution with the SuperCom backbone PE-routers so that they can learn labels for the BGP next-hop addresses of ISP-customer external routes from other POP sites, and also ISP-customer internal networks, across these sessions. However, because these routes were learned via

BGP, the LDP/TDP label distribution is modified in this environment so that it can carry labels for BGP routes (the default behavior is to carry labels only for internal routes).

NOTE   When the **mpls ip** (or **tag-switching ip**) command is configured on a VRF interface, the PE-router will automatically assign a label to any routes that are learned from across the MPLS/VPN backbone. The default behavior of a VRF interface is to assign labels only to routes that are learned from any attached CE-devices rather than routes learned via the MPLS/VPN backbone. This means that when the **mpls ip** (or **tag-switching ip**) command is added to the VRF configuration, there are two label assignments: one for incoming routes from the CE-routers (standard MPLS/VPN VRF mechanism), and one for outgoing routes learned from across the MPLS/VPN backbone. This second label assignment essentially maps a new label to the label that will be received within the MP-iBGP update for the route.

These labels are assigned by the PE-router and correspond to any routes that are learned across MP-iBGP sessions and imported into the VRF. Because the ISP sites are not running MPLS, no specific label values are advertised by the CE-router toward the PE. However, every internal route within the site will have the implicit-null label assigned by the CE-router, and this will be advertised across the link to the PE-router. ISP-customer external routes that are advertised across the direct iBGP sessions between ISP sites will also have no associated labels because no LDP/TDP label distribution between the ASBRs (or route reflectors) will exist across these iBGP sessions.

Any labels used by the CE-routers must be controlled by the PE-router. This is achieved through the association of the label with a specific route contained within the VRF. In addition, the PE-router keeps track of the label values that have been assigned to each of the VRFs so that it can track which label mappings have been advertised to which CE-routers and through which interfaces, to eliminate the possibility of label spoofing.

Figure 14-6 provides an illustration of the relevant label assignment for the topology already discussed in Figure 14-4. For simplicity, no IP address assignment is shown, and the router names are used to represent relevant IP addresses.

This figure shows that the EuroISP2 Santa Clara ASBR router learns prefix 146.22.15.0/24 from one of its customers. This route is advertised to internal BGP neighbors within the EuroISP2 Santa Clara site, and to other EuroISP2 sites, with a BGP next-hop address of SC-ASBR (this will be the loopback interface address used for the iBGP session). The EuroISP2 San Jose CE-router advertises the BGP next-hop address for the route—in this case, the address of the Santa Clara ASBR router (SC-ASBR)—across the link to the SuperCom San Jose PE-router using the routing protocol configured for the link.

Figure 14-6   *Carrier's Carrier—No MPLS Within ISP Sites (Label Assignment)*

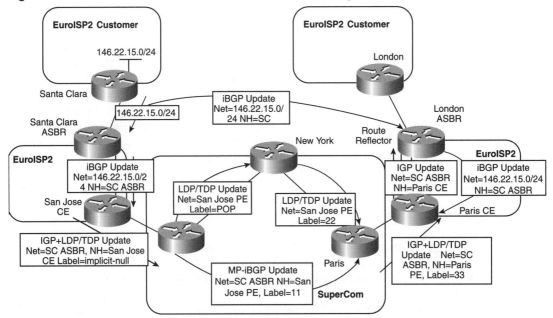

NOTE   The routing protocol used across the PE-to-CE link may be any of the currently supported protocols, such as RIP Version 2, OSPF, or BGP. We will see later that when MPLS is also deployed within the VPN site, then BGP may not (currently) be used as the PE-to-CE link protocol because the CE-router cannot allocate labels to routes that are learned via BGP.

The SuperCom San Jose PE-router installs the SC-ASBR prefix into the EuroISP2 VRF and advertises it, along with an assigned label, to all other PE-routers using MP-iBGP. In Figure 14-6, the Paris PE-router receives the MP-iBGP update for the SC-ASBR prefix and imports it into the EuroISP2 VRF. Because the Paris PE-router is configured for LDP/TDP label assignment, it assigns a new label to this route. The PE-router then advertises the route across the PE-to-CE link using the standard routing protocol mechanisms, either IGP or BGP. The PE-router also advertises a label mapping using LDP/TDP with the relevant label assignment for the route.

NOTE	Note that if any protocol other than BGP is used across the PE-to-CE link, then redistribution from the VRF into the routing protocol running across the link is necessary, just as in the standard MPLS/VPN procedures that we have described in previous chapters.

When the Paris CE-router receives the update for the SC-ASBR prefix, it advertises it using its IGP (or iBGP, if received via a PE-to-CE eBGP session) to the London ASBR.

NOTE	The BGP next-hop address—SC-ASBR, in our example—can be learned across the VPN site via iBGP. However, this means that BGP synchronization must be disabled. When a BGP route is validated through other BGP routes—which is the case, in our example—you must make sure that the BGP next-hop route is not subject to synchronization.

Figure 14-7 shows the subsequent packet flow when the London ASBR receives a packet destined for a host on network 146.22.15.0/24.

Figure 14-7 *Carrier's Carrier—No MPLS Within ISP Sites (Traffic Flow)*

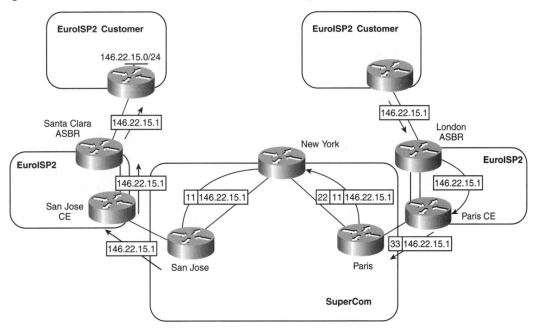

If we follow the packet flow shown in Figure 14-7, we can see that the London ASBR receives a packet destined for a host on network 146.22.15.0/24. The London ASBR looks up the 146.22.15.0/24 prefix within its forwarding table and finds a BGP route with a next-hop pointing to the Santa Clara ASBR router. This next-hop address has been learned via the EuroISP2 IGP (or possibly iBGP, if synchronization has been disabled), as advertised by the Paris CE-router. The London ASBR thus routes the packet toward the Paris CE-router.

When the Paris CE-router receives the packet, it also looks up the destination of 146.22.15.0/24 within its forwarding table and finds that the next-hop for this route is reachable via the SuperCom Paris PE-router. It also finds that a label of 33 has been assigned to this next-hop address. This is the same principle as with the basic MPLS architecture, where a label is not assigned to the BGP route; instead, we use the label that has been assigned to the next-hop of that route. The packet thus is sent to the Paris PE-router with a label of 33, which corresponds to the BGP next-hop address of the EuroISP2 Santa Clara ASBR.

When the SuperCom Paris PE-router receives the labeled packet (with label value 33), it knows that the label corresponds to the VPN route SC-ASBR as learned from its MP-iBGP session with the San Jose PE-router. This means that it swaps the label value of 33 to a label stack that will be used to reach the originating PE-router (the San Jose router, in this example). The Paris PE-router then label-switches the packet to the San Jose PE-router using the standard MPLS/VPN mechanisms that we have already seen.

The San Jose PE-router uses the VPN label to switch the packet to the EuroISP2 San Jose CE-router. Because MPLS has not been deployed within the site, no outgoing labels exist within the PE-router for the VPN prefix, so the packet is sent as an unlabeled packet. The EuroISP2 San Jose CE-router is then capable of routing the packet using its forwarding table.

ISP with MPLS Deployed Within POP Sites

Although our previous example provides a scalable solution to allow the ISP to connect its POP sites across an MPLS/VPN backbone, it still requires that traditional Layer 3 routing occur within each site and that ISP-customer external routing information be carried by all transit routers within each site. For these reasons (although, of course, these are not the only ones), an ISP customer of the MPLS/VPN backbone may choose to deploy MPLS locally within its own site and label-switch traffic end to end, from ingress ASBR to egress ASBR in another POP site.

In this environment, iBGP sessions are still required between site ASBR routers, just as in our previous example, so that ISP-customer external routing information can be learned from other sites. A full mesh of iBGP between ASBRs (or route reflectors) is also still necessary, although a full mesh of iBGP sessions is no longer required within each site. This is because label switching will be performed across the site, so internal transit routers that do not have direct customer connectivity do not need to carry external routing information. This is the same situation as described in Chapter 1, "Multiprotocol Label Switching (MPLS) Architecture Overview," where internal routers within an MPLS domain do not need to hold BGP routing information because they will forward packets based on their label values, not their Layer 3 address.

As in the previous connectivity example, only the BGP next-hop addresses and ISP-customer internal routes are required to be propagated through use of MP-iBGP across the MPLS/VPN backbone and via the site IGP so that label forwarding will be successful across the backbone and within the VPN site. This means that iBGP sessions are required only between site ASBRs and any edge routers that will receive incoming customer traffic and that, therefore, need to perform label imposition on the incoming packets.

Each CE-router within a POP site is required to inject all routes that it learns from across the PE-to-CE link, just as in the basic MPLS/VPN model, into its local IGP process. This is necessary so that labels can be assigned end to end and so that next-hop reachability of all ISP-customer external routes can be assured.

As can be seen, this type of connectivity is exactly the same mechanism as used in our previous example, with the exception that MPLS is used locally within the ISP POP sites. MPLS label switching is performed within the site, but with only one label in the label stack, pointing to the egress LSR (the BGP next-hop address of the route), which will be the ingress ASBR in the originating POP site for the FEC. An example of this type of connectivity can be seen in Figure 14-8.

Figure 14-8 *Local MPLS Deployment—No Label Distribution Between Sites*

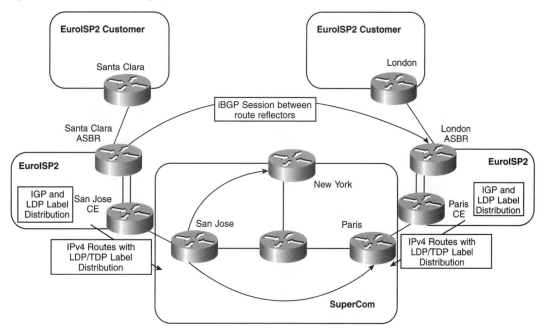

Figure 14-8 shows that each EuroISP2 site runs MPLS with LDP/TDP label distribution. When a packet enters one of the VPN sites, the ingress router performs a Layer 3 lookup within the global IP routing table to determine how to route the packet (standard packet classification). When this classification is done, a label is applied to the packet and is used to forward the packet toward the BGP next-hop of the route.

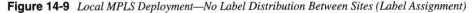

NOTE   In the initial release of the carrier's carrier architecture, it is a requirement that BGP not be run between CE- and PE-routers if MPLS is deployed within the ISP site. This is because the CE-router cannot allocate labels to any BGP routes that it learns from the PE-router. Static RIP Version 2 or OSPF (and in the future, possibly IS-IS and EIGRP) must be used so that the routes learned from the PE are seen as internal routes by the CE, which then allocates labels accordingly.

The label assignment used for this type of connectivity is shown in Figure 14-9. This figure provides an example of a route advertised from the Santa Clara ASBR router to the London ASBR router and shows the relevant label assignments.

Figure 14-9 *Local MPLS Deployment—No Label Distribution Between Sites (Label Assignment)*

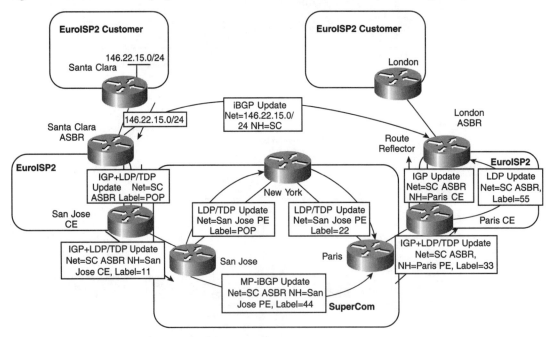

In Figure 14-9, labels are advertised both within the MPLS/VPN backbone, as with our previous example, and within each ISP site. After all the labels have been distributed through LDP/TDP, label switching can occur, both in the MPLS/VPN backbone and within each ISP site. However, no label distribution occurs across the intersite iBGP sessions, so the egress LSR—in our example, the Santa Clara ASBR—must perform an IP lookup for each packet to determine how it should be forwarded.

Using this example, Figure 14-10 shows the traffic flow and subsequent label assignment for a packet sent toward the 146.22.15.0/24 subnet from a customer attached to the EuroISP2 London site.

Figure 14-10 *Local MPLS Deployment—No Label Distribution Between Sites (Traffic Flow)*

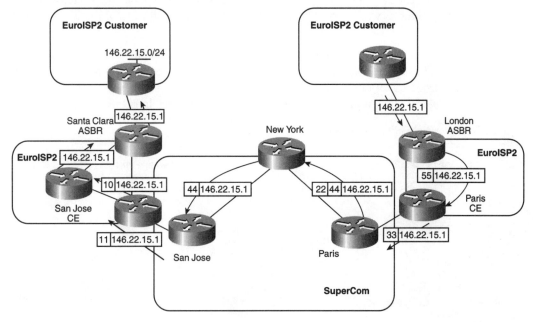

Before forwarding, the EuroISP2 London ASBR router assigns a label to any packets that are received from locally attached customers. In our example, a label value of 55 is prepended to the packet and is label-switched to the Paris CE-router across the EuroISP2 site. The Paris CE-router label switches the packet toward the Paris router, swapping the label value of 55 with a value of 33. When the SuperCom Paris PE-router receives the labeled packet, it swaps the label value of 33 for a label stack that corresponds to the VPN route and egress PE-router (the San Jose PE, in our example), and then label-switches the packet across the MPLS/VPN backbone. When the San Jose PE-router receives the packet, it uses the VPN label to forward the packet, with a label value of 11, to the EuroISP2 San Jose CE-router.

When the EuroISP2 San Jose CE-router receives the labeled packet, it label-switches it across the POP site to the Santa Clara ASBR router, which uses its global routing table to forward the packet toward the 146.22.15.0/24 subnet.

Hierarchical Virtual Private Networks

Some ISP customers of the MPLS/VPN backbone may want to provide MPLS/VPN services for their own customers. The implications of this are that VPN-IPv4 routes and their corresponding labels must be exchanged between ISP sites and must be imported into relevant VPN customer VRFs within the ISP site. This is essentially the same model as the carrier's carrier architecture that we have already seen, except that the ISP-customer external routes will be contained within a VRF rather than the global routing table of the ISP.

This type of connectivity is known as hierarchical VPN, sometimes referred to as recursive VPN. Its deployment is similar to our previous examples, except that Multiprotocol iBGP is introduced for the distribution of prefix and label information between ISP sites. A sample topology using this connectivity option can be seen in Figure 14-11.

Figure 14-11 *Hierarchical VPN Connectivity*

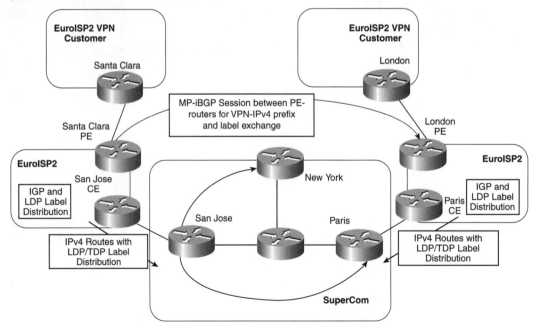

Within each ISP site in Figure 14-11, the PE-routers hold VRF routing information for any VPN customers that are attached to the POP MPLS/VPN backbone. This is no different than the standard MPLS/VPN architecture, so VPN-IPv4 prefixes are assigned to customer VPN routes and are distributed between ISP sites using MP-iBGP with BGP extended community attributes (Route Target and Site of Origin).

Because each POP site may hold several PE-routers, a full mesh of MP-iBGP is necessary among all PE-routers within the ISP MPLS/VPN topology. However, again, route reflectors can be deployed to cut down on the number of required peering sessions. In the example shown in Figure 14-11, it would be possible, for example, for the EuroISP2 London and Santa Clara PE-routers to be route reflectors for their own EuroISP2 site. You could even deploy totally separate devices and make each PE-router a route reflector client so that MP-iBGP updates can be successfully reflected to all PE-routers that need the VPN information contained within the updates.

Figure 14-12 provides an example of the relevant label assignment for the 146.22.15.0/24 prefix, which is learned from a VPN customer of the EuroISP2 Santa Clara site.

Figure 14-12 *Hierarchical VPN Connectivity (Label Assignment)*

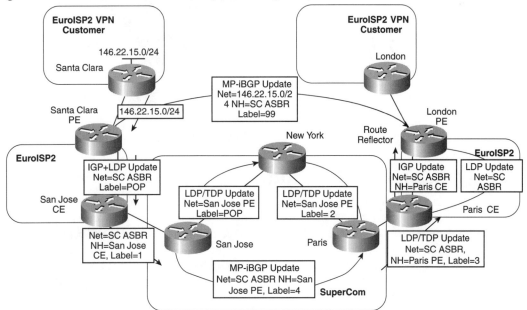

The figure shows again that labels are advertised both within the MPLS/VPN backbone and within each ISP site, for each of the ISP-customer internal routes. ISP-customer external routes are distributed between sites as VPN-IPv4 routes (instead of IPv4 routes as with the carrier's carrier solution). This means that the iBGP session between sites becomes an MP-iBGP session so that VPN-IPv4 routes, and their associated labels, can be successfully advertised.

The actual traffic flow for a packet destined for a host on the 146.22.15.0/24 subnet and arriving at the EuroISP2 London PE-router is illustrated in Figure 14-13.

Figure 14-13 *Hierarchical VPN Connectivity (Traffic Flow)*

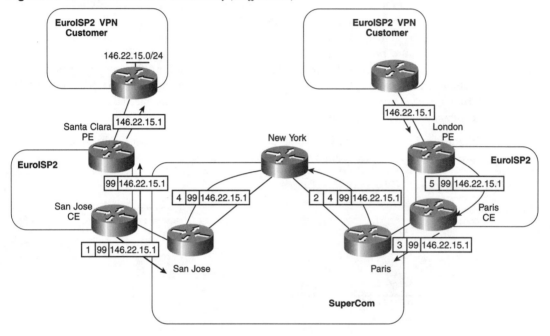

Inter-provider VPN Solutions

The last connectivity option to consider is the case in which a VPN customer, or ISP customer, wants to obtain VPN service through multiple service providers. This situation will most likely arise because of geography—certain sites will need to attach to one service provider, and others will need to attach to another service provider. This means that transit between one site and another site may pass through multiple MPLS/VPN backbones. Within the MPLS/VPN architecture, this connectivity requirement is known as Multi-provider or inter-provider VPN.

The problem with this connectivity requirement is that VPN information needs to be passed between MPLS/VPN service providers so that they can route traffic for a particular VPN successfully. This type of service is not available with the description of the MPLS/VPN architecture that we have seen so far. A new mechanism is needed so that prefix and label exchange can occur in a scalable manner between MPLS/VPN domains. Figure 14-14 provides an illustration of a topology in which this type of connectivity may be required.

Figure 14-14 *Inter-provider VPN Connectivity—Topology Example*

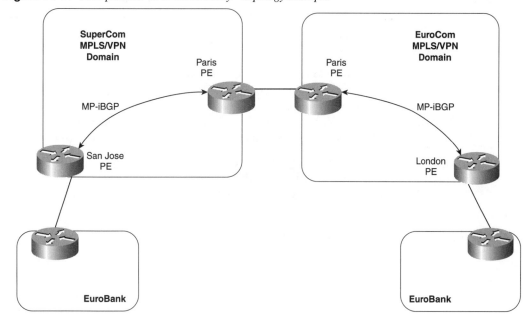

This sample topology shows that the EuroBank VPN customer has sites in San Jose and London. Because of the geography, the San Jose site attaches to the SuperCom MPLS/VPN backbone via the San Jose PE-router, and the London site attaches to the EuroCom MPLS/VPN backbone via the London PE-router. This type of connectivity requires inter-provider route exchange of VPN customer prefixes.

There are actually two ways to provide this type of inter-provider connectivity, although others may become available over time. The first is to exchange VPN-IPv4 prefixes/labels across the service provider MPLS/VPN domain boundaries. In our example, this would mean between the SuperCom Paris PE-router and the EuroCom Paris PE-router. The second option is to deploy multi-hop eBGP sessions between customer sites, or between service provider VPN-IPv4 route reflectors, and then exchange VPN-IPv4 prefixes/labels directly across these sessions.

NOTE   Future enhancement will allow for direct eBGP route exchange with labels and also the capability to turn off **next-hop-self** for eBGP sessions from route reflectors. Both of these features are necessary so that the next-hop PE addresses of any routes that are advertised across multi-hop MP-eBGP sessions can be passed between service providers without conversion to VPNv4 routes.

Inter-provider VPN—Exchange of VPN-IPv4 Across Boundaries

This first option allows the same functionality as the standard MPLS/VPN architecture that we have already seen, except that the customer is attached to multiple service providers instead of just one.

Each customer site attaches to its local MPLS/VPN backbone and exchanges routes, including all external routes, with the provider across its PE-to-CE link. Because the exchange of routing information between the customer and the MPLS/VPN backbone includes external routes, this solution is not really suitable in the situation where the customer is an ISP, for the same reasons that were discussed in the previous section.

These routes belong to VPN customers, so they are allocated labels by the service provider PE-router and are advertised across the MPLS/VPN backbone as VPN-IPv4 routes using MP-iBGP between PE-routers. Figure 14-15 shows the basic structure of this type of connectivity.

Figure 14-15 *Inter-provider VPN—Exchange of VPN-IPv4 Between Service Providers*

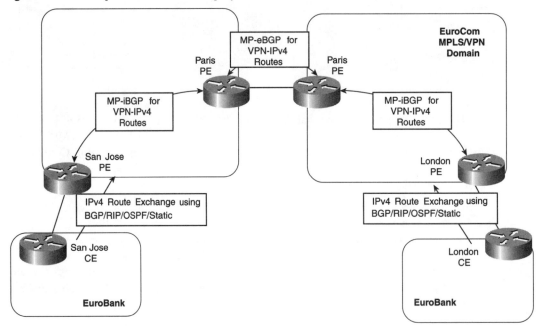

Figure 14-15 shows that each service provider establishes a direct MP-eBGP session with the other provider and exchanges VPN-IPv4 addresses with labels across this link. In the figure, this session is established between the two Paris PE-routers. Because these routers provide connectivity between two separate MPLS/VPN domains, we can refer to them as PE-ASBR routers. No IGP or LDP/TDP label distribution occurs across this link, so both service provider networks are completely separate. This means that they do not need to exchange any of their internal prefix or MPLS label information. The configurations for the PE-routers shown in Figure 14-15 can be seen in Example 14-2.

Example 14-2 *Inter-provider VPN—Exchange of VPNv4 Across Service Provider Boundaries (Configuration Example)*

```
SuperCom PE Routers

hostname San Jose
!
ip vrf EuroBank
 rd 1:27
 route-target export 100:27
 route-target import 100:27
!
interface Loopback0
 ip address 194.22.15.2 255.255.255.255
!
router bgp 1
 no bgp default ipv4-unicast
 neighbor 194.22.15.1 remote-as 1
 !
 address-family ipv4 vrf EuroBank
 redistribute connected
 redistribute static
 no auto-summary
 no synchronization
 exit-address-family
 !
 address-family vpnv4
 neighbor 194.22.15.1 activate
 neighbor 194.22.15.1 send-community extended
 exit-address-family

hostname Paris
!


interface Loopback0
 ip address 194.22.15.1 255.255.255.255
!
router bgp 1
 no bgp default ipv4-unicast
 no bgp default route-target filter
 neighbor 194.22.15.2 remote-as 1
 neighbor 195.26.19.1 remote-as 2
 !
 address-family ipv4 vrf EuroBank
 no auto-summary
 no synchronization
 exit-address-family
 !
```

Example 14-2   *Inter-provider VPN—Exchange of VPNv4 Across Service Provider Boundaries (Configuration Example) (Continued)*

```
address-family vpnv4
neighbor 195.26.19.1 activate
neighbor 195.26.19.1 send-community extended
neighbor 194.22.15.2 activate
neighbor 194.22.15.2 next-hop-self
neighbor 194.22.15.2 send-community extended
exit-address-family


EuroCom PE Routers

hostname Paris
!


interface Loopback0
 ip address 195.26.19.1 255.255.255.255
!
router bgp 2
 no bgp default ipv4-unicast
 no bgp default route-target filter
 neighbor 195.26.19.2 remote-as 2
 neighbor 194.22.15.1 remote-as 1
 !
 address-family ipv4 vrf EuroBank
 no auto-summary
 no synchronization
 exit-address-family
 !
 address-family vpnv4
 neighbor 195.26.19.2 activate
 neighbor 195.26.19.2 next-hop-self
 neighbor 195.26.19.2 send-community extended
 neighbor 194.22.15.1 activate
 neighbor 194.22.15.1 send-community extended
 exit-address-family

hostname London
 !
ip vrf EuroBank
 rd 1:27
 route-target export 100:27
 route-target import 100:27
 !
interface Loopback0
 ip address 195.26.19.2 255.255.255.255
!
router bgp 2
 no bgp default ipv4-unicast
 neighbor 195.26.19.1 remote-as 2
 !
```

continues

Example 14-2 *Inter-provider VPN—Exchange of VPNv4 Across Service Provider Boundaries (Configuration Example) (Continued)*

```
address-family ipv4 vrf EuroBank
redistribute connected
no auto-summary
no synchronization
exit-address-family
!
address-family vpnv4
neighbor 195.26.19.1 activate
neighbor 195.26.19.1 send-community extended
exit-address-family
```

NOTE   Notice within the configuration shown in Example 14-2 that you do not need to configure any VRFs on the border PE-routers. This is because the automatic route filtering feature, which we discussed in Chapter 9, "MPLS/VPN Architecture Operation," has been disabled through use of the **no bgp default route-target filter** command.

In the example shown in Figure 14-15, if the SuperCom San Jose PE-router advertised a route via MP-iBGP to the SuperCom Paris PE-router, then if this router advertised the route to the EuroCom Paris PE-router with the same VPN label, connectivity would be lost. This is because no LDP/TDP label distribution occurs across this link. Therefore, when a packet is forwarded by the EuroCom Paris PE-router toward the SuperCom network, the label stack will contain one entry. This entry will be the VPN label as received through MP-eBGP, but the SuperCom Paris PE-router will not know how to forward the packet because it did not allocate the label. This is the same situation that we saw in Chapter 12, "Advanced MPLS/VPN Topics," in our discussion of BGP confederations.

For this reason, when MP-eBGP is used between two PE-ASBR routers, the advertising PE-router allocates a new label for the route before it advertises it across the MP-eBGP session to the other PE-router. This behavior is enabled by default on an MP-eBGP session, but it can also be controlled by the **next-hop-self** command if the receiving PE-ASBR router wants to allocate a different label for use by its interior neighbors.

The interface that is used to establish the MP-eBGP session between the two service providers does *not* need to be associated with any VRF. This is because labels already will be assigned to the routes when learned via MP-eBGP. The label allocation for this type of connectivity can be seen in Figure 14-16.

Figure 14-16 shows that each of the inter-provider PE-routers—in this case, the SuperCom Paris and EuroCom Paris routers—allocates a new label to represent each VPN route that it receives across its internal MPLS/VPN domain.

Figure 14-16 *Exchange of VPN-IPv4 Routes Between Service Providers (Label Allocation)*

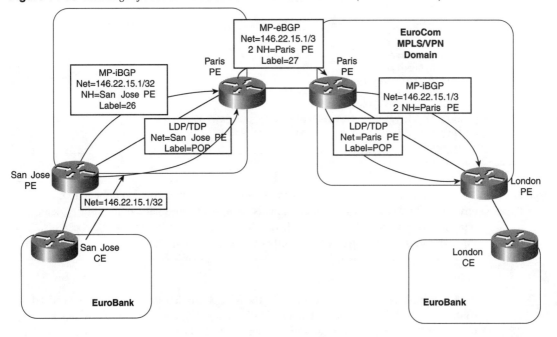

NOTE   Figure 14-16 shows only one link between PE-ASBR routers within each MPLS/VPN domain. Of course, this is a simplified topology to illustrate the techniques and label allocation, but in a real deployment of this architecture, the label stack within each MPLS/VPN domain will carry two labels: an internal label to reach the advertising PE-ASBR router, and a VPN label.

The relevant label assignments for all PE-routers are shown in Example 14-3.

Example 14-3 *Inter-provider VPN—Label Assignment Example*

```
EuroCom PE Routers

London# show ip bgp vpnv4 all tags

Network          Next Hop       In tag/Out tag
Route Distinguisher: 1:27 (EuroBank)
    146.22.15.1/32     195.26.19.1        notag/39

Paris# show ip bgp vpnv4 all tags

Network          Next Hop       In tag/Out tag
```

Example 14-3   *Inter-provider VPN—Label Assignment Example (Continued)*

```
Route Distinguisher: 1:27 (EuroBank)
    146.22.15.1/32      10.2.1.10        39/27


SuperCom PE Routers


Paris# show ip bgp vpnv4 all tags


Network           Next Hop      In tag/Out tag
Route Distinguisher: 1:27 (EuroBank)
    146.22.15.1/32    194.22.15.2        27/26


San Jose# show ip bgp vpnv4 all tags


Network           Next Hop      In tag/Out tag
Route Distinguisher: 1:27 (EuroBank)
    146.22.15.1/32    0.0.0.0          26/aggregate(EuroBank)
```

NOTE   The allocation of a new label by the EuroCom Paris PE-ASBR router is not strictly
necessary. This is because label switching will be successful even if this router does not
allocate a new label, as long as a host route for the adjacent PE-ASBR router is contained
within the IGP of the receiving MPLS/VPN backbone. Therefore, configuration of **next-
hop-self** on this PE-router, in respect of routes that it advertises to internal MP-iBGP
neighbors, can be disabled, if desired. However, this is not recommended because it implies
that redistribution of peer addresses into the IGP must occur.

In our example, this means that a /32 route for the SuperCom Paris PE-ASBR interface
address (which attaches to the EuroCom Paris PE-ASBR router) would need to be
redistributed into the EuroCom MPLS/VPN domain. This /32 host route is created by
default and does not need to be configured. However, it must be redistributed into the
receiving service provider's IGP. Without this host route, label switching will fail because
the interface between service providers is directly connected and **next-hop-self** is not
performed on the receiving PE-ASBR router. As with any directly connected interface, the
IGP label is popped one hop before the receiving PE-router. In our example, this would
cause the EuroCom Paris PE-ASBR router to receive a packet with only the VPN label;
because it did not allocate the label, label switching would fail.

This label is used across the inter-provider link and is swapped for the original label stack
by the receiving PE-ASBR router. An example of this is shown in Figure 14-17. Again, for
the sake of simplicity, only one hop across each MPLS/VPN domain is used; only the VPN
labels are shown because the internal label will have been removed due to penultimate
hopping. However, in a typical deployment, a two-level label stack will be required across
each service provider network, one for the VPN label and the other to reach the egress PE
for the destination of the packet.

Figure 14-17 *Exchange of VPN-IPv4 Routes Between Service Providers (Traffic Flow)*

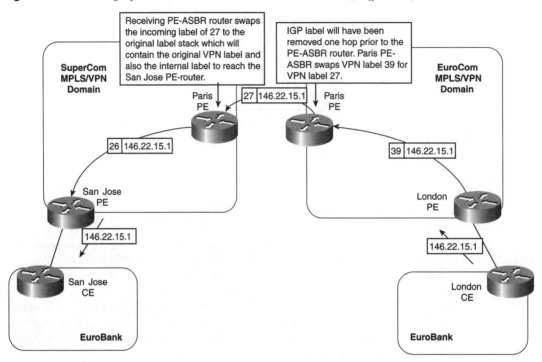

This figure shows that each inter-provider PE-ASBR router assigns its own label, which it associates with the relevant label stack to reach a particular VPN destination. Therefore, when a packet is sent from the EuroBank London site to prefix 146.22.15.1/32 in the EuroBank San Jose site, the labels that are used across the SuperCom and EuroCom MPLS/VPN domains are as shown in Figure 14-17.

Inter-provider VPN—Multi-hop eBGP Between Customer Sites

The second option with this type of connectivity is the direct exchange of VPN information between sites using MP-eBGP or MP-iBGP. This is the same scenario as with the hierarchical VPN solution that we saw previously, except that the session between customer sites may be eBGP rather than iBGP (unless, of course, each site uses the same ASN, in which case it will be iBGP). MP-eBGP will be used across the inter-provider session. If the session between VPN sites is eBGP, then BGP multi-hop must be used.

This connectivity option may be useful if the customer of the MPLS/VPN backbone is an ISP that wants to exchange large amounts of routes with other sites, and if some of those sites are attached to a separate MPLS/VPN service provider. An example topology for this type of connectivity can be seen in Figure 14-18.

Figure 14-18 *Inter-provider VPN—Multi-hop eBGP Between Customer Sites*

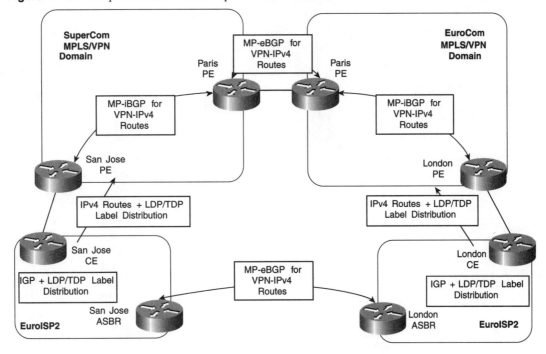

Figure 14-18 shows that ISP-customer external routes are exchanged between ISP sites through the use of MP-eBGP or MP-iBGP. The BGP next-hop addresses for these routes are exchanged with the MPLS/VPN backbone and then are advertised between service providers.

The label allocation for this type of connectivity is shown in Figure 14-19. Again, for simplicity, a one-hop MPLS/VPN backbone is shown for each of the service providers.

The label allocation is the same as shown in our example of the hierarchical VPN scenario. The only difference is that the customer routes, in this case, are advertised using MP-eBGP as opposed to MP-iBGP between sites. In addition, the BGP next-hop addresses are advertised between MPLS/VPN domains as VPN-IPv4 prefixes. Figure 14-20 shows the subsequent traffic flow for a packet sent from the EuroISP2 London site to a host on the 146.22.15.0/24 subnet.

Figure 14-19 *Inter-provider VPN—Multihop eBGP Between Customer Sites (Label Allocation)*

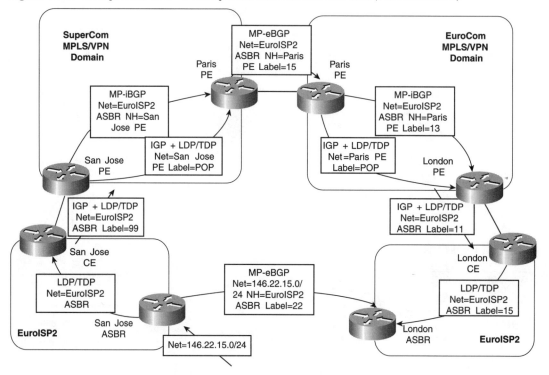

Summary

In this chapter, we have seen that when a customer of a service provider's MPLS/VPN backbone is an Internet service provider (ISP), it is imperative that any external routes that need to be advertised between the ISP sites be achieved through multi-hop iBGP sessions. This is necessary so that large volumes of external routes—potentially full Internet routes—do not get advertised toward the MPLS/VPN backbone and between PE-routers within that backbone.

This requirement is achieved through use of the carrier's carrier architecture, which allows LDP/TDP sessions between the CE-router and the PE-router. The carrier's carrier architecture provides several connectivity options, depending on whether MPLS is deployed within the ISP's own sites or whether the ISP is providing a VPN service for its customers.

Although the standard MPLS/VPN architecture will be adequate in many cases, some customer deployments will require a topology that is geographically split, and the need will arise to use different service providers to obtain VPN service. This type of deployment (also called inter-provider VPN) requires that VPN information be exchanged between service providers over MP-eBGP sessions. Again, several deployment options are available, each

of which provides full connectivity between customer sites, regardless of whether the
customer is an enterprise customer, an ISP, or even another MPLS/VPN service provider.

Figure 14-20 *Inter-provider VPN—Multi-hop eBGP Between Customer Sites (Traffic Flow)*

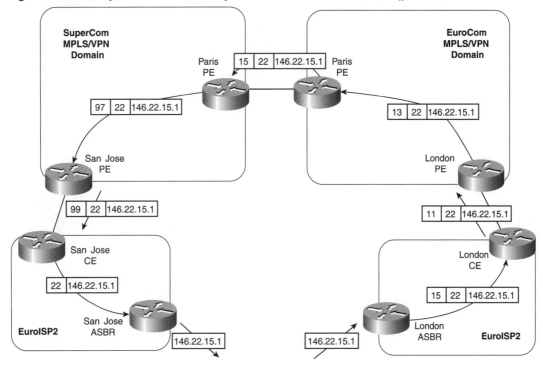

CHAPTER 15

IP Tunneling to MPLS/VPN Migration Case Study

In Chapter 6, "MPLS Migration and Configuration Example," we examined a sample migration of the TransitNet service provider network to a backbone based on the MPLS architecture. The primary reason for this migration was to remove the necessity to hold external routing information within the core. However, a further reason for the migration was to allow the service provider to offer advanced and more scalable services, such as virtual private networks, to its customers, using the MPLS technology.

During this chapter, we will see the evolution of the migrated TransitNet MPLS network to support Virtual Private Networks (VPNs) using the MPLS architecture. The case study that follows provides a sample VPN migration from an IP tunneling deployment to an MPLS-based solution. The topology used within the case study is not meant to illustrate a fully redundant network and, therefore, does not consider all aspects of resiliency and redundancy in the design.

The goal of this case study is to provide an insight into the steps necessary for a successful migration and the preliminary pre-deployment network design that must occur before migration to an MPLS-based VPN solution. The sections that follow do not provide a full migration path or all the details that are necessary to move from one technology to another. However, they do provide pointers on some of the necessary actions and can be used as a template when planning for this type of migration.

For simplicity, the example shows a VPN service that is provided to only one large customer, called SampleNet, although multiple customers could be supported using the same model. Many of the techniques described within this example can be used across multiple topologies and network deployment requirements.

Figure 15-1 provides a reminder of the migrated TransitNet MPLS backbone network, which we reviewed during Chapter 6. For simplicity, only one Internet exit point is shown within the topology, and the physical connectivity of the BGP route reflectors is not provided.

Figure 15-1 *TransitNet MPLS Backbone Network*

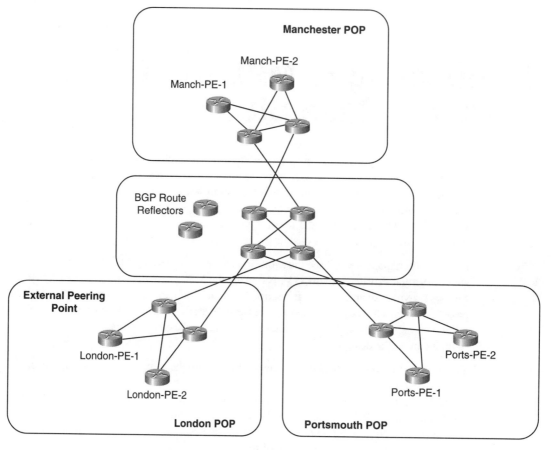

Existing VPN Solution Deployment—IP Tunneling

The existing IP tunneling-based solution for the SampleNet VPN customer is provided through the use of generic route encapsulation (GRE) tunnels to a central hub location in a hub-and-spoke arrangement (see Figure 15-2). Connectivity between sites is strictly via the central site because the customer is able to accept sub-optimal routing as a trade-off for the complexity and cost associated with a full-mesh topology. Internet access is provided within the central site location. This type of topology is a fairly common one, although this is rapidly changing as the need for any-to-any connectivity increases.

Figure 15-2 *SampleNet VPN Connectivity Using GRE Tunnels*

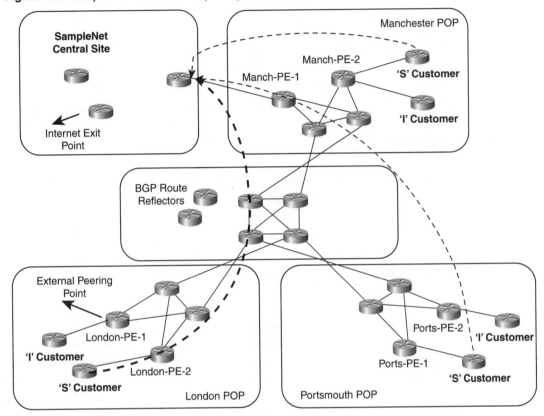

Figure 15-2 illustrates that all remote SampleNet sites, referred to as S customer sites within the figure, run a direct GRE tunnel with the SampleNet central site. Connectivity between SampleNet sites and also Internet access for these sites is provided through the central site location.

The topology shown in Figure 15-2 also shows other customers, referred to as I customers, that attach to the TransitNet backbone for connectivity to the Internet. Given this topology, the goal of the TransitNet service provider is to simplify the VPN configuration and also provide optimal routing across its backbone so that VPN customers can communicate directly with other sites that belong to the VPN, and other local Internet customers, without having to route via the central SampleNet site.

Definition of VPNs and Routing Policies for PE-routers

The first phase in the migration planning is to define the requirements for deployment of the MPLS/VPN solution and to assign the necessary naming conventions and routing policies for each of the customers that will use the VPN service. These requirements are based on the required connectivity of VPN customers and are no different from the existing VPN infrastructure except that the technology used to provide the services has changed.

Within the topology of the TransitNet backbone, four groups of interfaces must be available within the final MPLS/VPN structure. These interfaces are based on the type of customer that is connected via the interface, or the service that is available across the interface. These interfaces are defined as follows:

- **S customer**—This type of interface is used to connect to a SampleNet VPN site.

- **S Internet**—This type of interface is defined as belonging to the main SampleNet site from where Internet connectivity is provided for members of the SampleNet VPN.

- **I customer**—This type of interface is used to connect to a customer who wants to use the standard Internet connectivity provided by the TransitNet backbone network.

- **Global Internet**—This type of interface is used to connect to another Internet service provider and is not associated with any VPN.

With these interface definitions in mind, it is now necessary to define the relevant VPNs that will make up the new MPLS/VPN service. Before this can be done, the specific connectivity requirements of each customer must be defined. Within the TransitNet backbone, we have already seen that there are two types of customer sites: those that belong to the SampleNet VPN, and those that belong to a customer who wants to obtain Internet access from the TransitNet backbone.

Each SampleNet site, defined previously as an S customer, must be capable of communicating with every other S customer and also the SampleNet central site, defined as S Internet. These sites must also be capable of communicating with all other Internet customers directly across the backbone, but they must *not* be capable of accessing the Internet via the global Internet interface located within the TransitNet London POP. All SampleNet site addresses will be advertised toward the Internet from within the central SampleNet site.

All non-SampleNet customers, defined as I customers, must be capable of communicating with all S customers directly across the TransitNet backbone and also the Internet via the global Internet interface located within the TransitNet London POP. They must *not* be capable of accessing the Internet via the S Internet interfaces. They must also have their addresses advertised using BGP-4 so that they are reachable from the Internet.

Given these connectivity requirements, the following VPNs can be defined and will be sufficient to provide the required connectivity among all types of customers. The use of these VPN definitions will be examined and explained in the sections that follow.

Table 15-1   *VPN Definitions for the TransitNet MPLS/VPN Backbone*

VPN Name	VPN Definition
Snet_Customer	Sites that belong to the SampleNet VPN
Snet_Internet	Sites that provide Internet access for the SampleNet VPN
Internet_Customer	Sites that belong to standard Internet customers

Definition of VRFs Within the Backbone Network

The next step in the migration planning process is to define the actual VRFs that will be used to provide the MPLS/VPN service. As discussed in previous chapters, within the MPLS/VPN architecture, a VPN can be thought of as a "community of interest" in which members of a VPN share the same routing information. This routing information is populated into a site-specific VRF that may or may not be shared between sites connected to the same PE-router. Therefore, for ease of configuration, the same definitions shown in Table 15-1 as used for the VPNs in the previous section may be used to define the VRFs on each PE-router within the TransitNet MPLS network. Each customer interface will then be associated with a specific VRF.

To make each customer route unique within the backbone, a route distinguisher must be assigned to each VRF. This route distinguisher can be allocated based on which VPN customer connects via the interface. This means that the value of the route distinguisher will be the same for each VRF that belongs to (or, more accurately defined, contains routes for) a particular VPN, and that particular VPN is directly attached to the VRF.

NOTE   This definition is adequate within the TransitNet backbone because, except in the case of any VPN customer Internet access, after full deployment of the MPLS/VPN architecture, no hub-and-spoke topology (or any other topology that requires the definition of different VRFs) that could cause the connectivity issues discussed in Chapter 11, "Advanced MPLS/VPN Topologies," will be necessary.

When the VRFs and route distinguishers have been defined, it is necessary to allocate the relevant route target attributes based on the service definitions for each customer. These route targets will be used within the import and export policies for each VRF to provide the necessary connectivity requirements between customers.

The same values for both the route distinguisher and the route target can be used per VPN because they are completely orthogonal and therefore are not comparable. This may help to reduce the complexity of the configuration, but it may lead to confusion and misunderstanding of the usage of each entity. Therefore, different values will be used for each within the configuration of the TransitNet backbone (see Table 15-2). Notice that the ASN of the service provider is used for the first part of both the route distinguisher and the route target.

Table 15-2 *TransitNet Route Target Attribute Definitions*

VPN Name	Route Target Attribute	Route Distinguisher
Snet_Customer	1234:16	1234:100
Snet_Internet	1234:17	1234:101
Internet_Customer	1234:18	1234:102

The VPN service offering will be provided by the import and export of the route target attributes as defined in Table 15-2. Extranet support will be available by the import of more than one route target attribute into the VRF of a particular site. The next phase of the deployment planning is to define these import/export policies for each of the customers connected to the TransitNet MPLS/VPN backbone.

VRF and Routing Polices for SampleNet VPN Sites

All SampleNet VPN sites will belong to the VPN defined as Snet_Customer. These sites must have access to all other SampleNet sites directly across the TransitNet MPLS backbone (rather than through the central site, as with the currently deployed GRE tunneling solution), and they must also have direct access to Internet customers who attach to the TransitNet backbone. A further requirement is that these sites must be provided with Internet access, but via the central SampleNet network rather than through the external BGP peering point within the TransitNet London POP (although they should be reachable from the Internet via this external BGP peering point). This access will require that the address range used for the SampleNet VPN sites be advertised using BGP-4 from the SampleNet central site toward the Internet.

BGP-4 will not be used across the PE-to-CE link to SampleNet sites. This means that a static route within the VRF will be configured to point to the SampleNet sites' IP address range. This static route must be redistributed from the Snet_Customer VRF into MP-BGP so that the IPv4 addresses can be advertised across the TransitNet MP-iBGP sessions as VPN-IPv4 addresses for import by other PE-routers.

The import and export polices that will be used for this VPN can be seen in Table 15-3.

Table 15-3   *SampleNet VRF Import/Export Policies*

VRF Snet_Customer	
Import and export	1234:16 (Snet_Customer)
Import only	1234:17 (Snet_Internet)
Import only	1234:18 (Internet_Customer)

This table shows that the Snet_Customer VRF will export its local routes using the route target value 1234:16, and these routes will be imported by all other Snet_Customer VPN sites, the Snet_Internet VRF, and Internet_Customer sites. Routes that contain a route target value of 1234:17 (Snet_Internet) or 1234:18 (Internet_Customer) will be imported to allow communication with all other directly attached Internet customers and Internet access via the central SampleNet network.

VRF and Routing Policies for SampleNet Internet Access

The SampleNet central site, which provides Internet access for members of the Snet_Customer VPN, will belong to the VPN defined as Snet_Internet. This central site is the same site that is currently used as the hub in the GRE tunneling solution.

The route target attribute assigned to Snet_Internet has a value of 1234:17. This route target must be exported from the Snet_Internet VRF so that all members of the Snet_Customer VPN can import it into their VRF so that Internet connectivity is provided throughout the SampleNet network (for Internet locations that are not directly attached to the TransitNet backbone network). The only route, which is advertised from the Snet_Internet VRF, is the default route, which is learned from the SampleNet central site EIGRP process. This default route will be used by any SampleNet site that does not have a more specific route within its routing table. Internet access will *not* be provided for SampleNet customers via the external BGP peering point in the TransitNet London POP.

The link between the Snet_Internet PE-router (Manch-PE-1 within the TransitNet backbone) and the SampleNet central site will run RIP Version 2 to exchange internal routing information. This is necessary so that SampleNet customer routes that have been imported into the Snet_Internet VRF can be advertised to the SampleNet main site, and so that the default route can be learned dynamically. The RIP Version 2 routes, which include any routes learned from across the TransitNet MPLS/VPN backbone, will be redistributed into the main SampleNet site EIGRP process at the CE-router within the SampleNet central site. This connectivity is discussed in more detail in the migration strategy section later in this chapter.

The import and export policies used for this VPN can be seen in Table 15-4.

Table 15-4 *SampleNet Internet Access VRF Import/Export Policies*

VRF Snet_Internet	
Import and export	1234:17 (Snet_Default)
Import only	1234:16 (Snet_Customer)

VRF and Routing Policies for Internet Access Customers

All Internet customers that attach to the TransitNet MPLS/VPN backbone network will belong to the same Internet_Customer VPN. This VPN is necessary so that direct connectivity between these types of customers and the SampleNet VPN sites is possible. All routes will be exported and imported into the VRF using the route target value of 1234:18. For optimal routing, these customers will be able to gain direct connectivity with SampleNet VPN sites across the MPLS/VPN backbone by importing the Snet_Customer VPN routes that contain the 1234:16 route target.

Internet connectivity for these customers will be provided via the external BGP peering point within the TransitNet London POP. Because only one exit point exists, and because there is no requirement to provide full or partial routes to any Internet customers, all PE-routers will carry only the default route, which is provided through configuration of a static default route that points to the Internet exit point. This means that all customers that belong to the Internet_Customer VPN will follow a default route to the TransitNet London POP, where the external BGP peering point is located.

The import and export policies used for this VPN can be seen in Table 15-5.

Table 15-5 *Internet Customer VRF Import/Export Policies*

VRF Internet_Customer	
Import and export	1234:18 (Internet_Customer)
Import only	1234:16 (Snet_Customer)

MPLS/VPN Migration—Staging and Execution

When all the policies and design specifics have been decided, then the migration to an MPLS/VPN solution can take place. Much of the preliminary migration work, such as the migration of customer routes into BGP, and the deployment of MPLS within the internal network infrastructure, will have already been completed at this stage. However, as with all deployments, it is good practice to review the currently deployed solution to make sure that all prerequisite items have been completed. In the case of a migration to MPLS/VPN, these prerequisites will include all the things discussed in Chapter 6.

Within our case study example, the SampleNet central site will require some attention because it will be necessary to migrate the VPN sites in a staged manner rather than as a complete switchover to the new solution.

Migration of the SampleNet Central Site

The migration of the SampleNet central site location is tricky because it requires that connectivity between VPN sites be maintained throughout the migration. To achieve this goal, it will be necessary to make some changes to the current central site configuration to allow the GRE tunnel endpoints to be reachable and to ensure that the central site is capable of learning other VPN site prefixes that will be advertised across the TransitNet backbone using MP-iBGP. Figure 15-3 shows the current central site connectivity into the TransitNet backbone.

Figure 15-3 *SampleNet Central Site Connectivity*

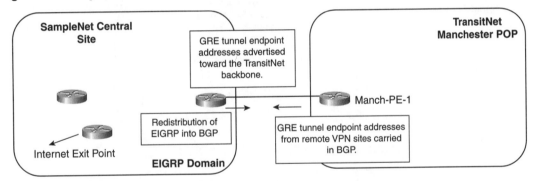

This figure shows that the TransitNet Manch-PE-1 PE-router connects via an ATM PVC to the SampleNet central site, and uses BGP to advertise the GRE tunnel endpoints from other VPN sites toward the central site and to receive updates that contain the prefix information contained within the central site. At the central site, redistribution occurs among the routing protocol running at the central site, EIGRP, and BGP so that any prefixes that must be available to other members of the VPN are reachable.

As previously mentioned, during the migration, it will be necessary for the TransitNet service provider to maintain VPN connectivity for SampleNet sites via the existing GRE tunneling method as sites are moved onto the new MPLS/VPN infrastructure. This means that a certain amount of suboptimal routing will occur. (This is discussed in more detail in the following sections, although this suboptimal routing is already apparent in the existing

GRE tunneled solution.) This also requires the addition of a further ATM PVC between the Manch-PE-1 PE-router and the central SampleNet site.

This new PVC will be used to carry traffic from SampleNet VPN sites that have been migrated over to the new MPLS/VPN solution. The use of this link is necessary to allow for connectivity between GRE tunneled sites and MPLS/VPN sites during the migration, and this link will ultimately be used as a replacement to the existing PVC when a full migration has been completed. This solution can be seen in Figure 15-4, which provides the topology and traffic flow during the migration stage.

Figure 15-4 *SampleNet Central Site Migration Scenario*

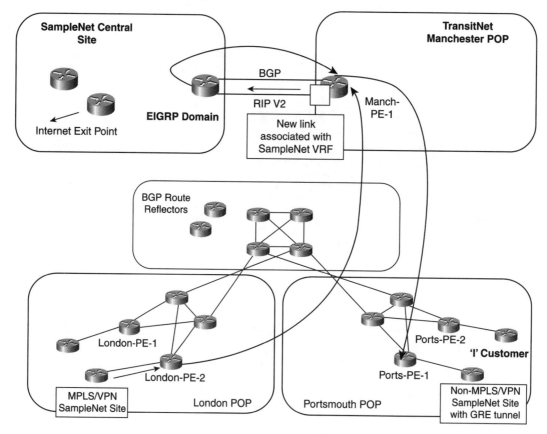

Figure 15-4 shows that one of the links (ATM PVC) to the central SampleNet site will carry BGP routes, and the other will run RIP Version 2. At this stage of the deployment, all routes learned across the BGP sessions will be standard BGP-4 routes, *not* VPN-IPv4 routes, so everything will flow across this link and will be advertised toward the central site. During the migration, the only routes that will be advertised across the link will be from non-

MPLS/VPN SampleNet customers that are still using the GRE tunneling configuration. It is necessary for these routes to be advertised to the main site so that two-way connectivity is established. The only routes that will be learned from the main site across this link are the GRE tunnel endpoint addresses.

The second link will be configured to run RIP Version 2, and this will carry any routes that have been placed into the VRF associated with the link. This VRF will belong to the Snet_Internet VPN and will learn only the default route from the central site that will have been redistributed from EIGRP (central site routing protocol) into RIP Version 2. Until customer routes are moved into the Snet_Customer VPN, the default route will be the *only* route contained within the Snet_Internet VRF. No routes will be advertised toward the central SampleNet site across this link until the Snet_Internet VRF is populated with routes that match the Snet_Customer route target value of 1234:16.

The traffic flow from a non-MPLS SampleNet site to an MPLS/VPN SampleNet site will traverse the main site and be sub-optimal. This is because the non-MPLS customer traffic will be resolved by using the global routing table where the MPLS/VPN SampleNet site routes will not reside. This means that the traffic will enter the GRE tunnel and exit at the main SampleNet site. This site will have learned the MPLS/VPN site routes via the redistribution of RIP Version 2 into EIGRP and therefore will send the traffic back to the TransitNet backbone for delivery to the MPLS/VPN site. On the return path, because the MPLS/VPN sites will have learned the default route from the central site, any routes that are not part of the VRF (such as non-MPLS sites) will be reachable through use of the default route.

When all SampleNet sites have been moved over to the MPLS/VPN solution, then the original ATM PVC to the central SampleNet site may be removed. The routing will become optimal across the TransitNet backbone and will be based upon the information contained within the Snet_Customer VRF.

The steps necessary to migrate the main SampleNet site are as follows:

- **Initialization of the second ATM PVC to the SampleNet central site**—The second link will be provided by way of an ATM PVC that will be in a shutdown state. This PVC should be activated at this stage.

- **Configuration of RIP Version 2**—RIP Version 2 should be configured across the new link to carry the MPLS/VPN routes to the SampleNet central site.

- **Redistribution between routing protocols configuration**—The necessary redistribution configuration should be applied, which includes the redistribution of the EIGRP default route into RIP Version 2, and RIP Version 2 routes into EIGRP, at the SampleNet central site router.

- **Configuration of MPLS/VPN**—When all of the link and routing protocol configuration has been completed, the PE-router that attaches to the SampleNet central site can be configured for MPLS/VPN. At this stage, no traffic will traverse the second ATM PVC because no SampleNet VPN sites will have been moved into the VPN. Several configuration steps are necessary:

    — Configure the Snet_Internet VRF, including the route distinguisher and route target import/export policies, as per Example 15-1.

    — Associate the new link with the Snet_Internet VRF using the command **ip vrf forwarding Snet_Internet** within the interface configuration of the link to the central SampleNet site.

    — Configure the RIP Version 2 address family to advertise the VRF routes toward the SampleNet central site. The VPN routes learned from other PE-routers via MP-iBGP are redistributed into RIP Version 2 and are advertised to the CE-router using the configuration in Figure 15-2.

Example 15-1 *Snet_Internet VRF Configuration Example*

```
ip vrf Snet_Internet
 rd 1234:101
 route-target export 1234:17
 route-target import 1234:17
 route-target import 1234:16
```

Example 15-2 *RIP Version 2 Configuration for the Snet_Internet VRF*

```
router rip
 version 2
 !
 address-family ipv4 vrf Snet_Internet
 version 2
 redistribute bgp 1234 metric 1
 no auto-summary
 exit-address-family
```

Configuration of MP-iBGP on BGP Route Reflectors

During the initial MPLS migration of the TransitNet backbone that we reviewed in Chapter 6, all relevant route reflectors were put into place. The MP-iBGP session configuration should follow the standard BGP session configuration, in which each of the PE-routers is peered with two route reflectors for redundancy. Separate route reflectors specific to MP-iBGP may be deployed, depending on the measured overhead of having both IPv4 and VPN-IPv4 addresses reflected on the same set of route reflectors. Either configuration is possible, and if the same set of route reflectors is used, only one BGP session is required to carry both IPv4 and VPN-IPv4 routes. Because the TransitNet BGP sessions will carry only VPN-IPv4 routes and the default route after the migration, the use of one set of route reflectors that can process both IPv4 and VPN-IPv4 routes will be adopted.

Because peer groups have been used within the TransitNet BGP configuration, all MP-iBGP neighbors should be associated with a VPN-IPv4 peer group to ease the configuration and also to lower the burden of the route reflector in terms of the number of updates that it must build. The following steps are necessary on the route reflectors:

- **Configuration of the VPN-IPv4 BGP peer group**—Within the BGP configuration, a peer-group must be defined to include all neighbors that will receive MP-iBGP updates from the route reflector. Because the TransitNet service provider has deployed route reflectors, this configuration is necessary only on the route reflector, not on all PE-routers. An example configuration can be seen in Example 15-3.

- Configuration of **no bgp default ipv4-unicast**—This configuration command is necessary under the BGP configuration so that any new BGP sessions that are configured do not immediately become active as standard BGP-4 sessions. If this command is not configured, then the default behavior is to attempt to establish a BGP-4 session (which will carry IPv4 prefixes) with the specified neighbor. This is not really an issue because a VPN-IPv4 session can also be established, but it means that an IPv4 session will exist even though it is not necessary.

- **Configuration of the VPNv4 address family**—Within the BGP configuration of the route reflector, it is necessary to define an address family that will carry MP-iBGP updates. As part of this configuration, each neighbor must be activated using the **neighbor** *neighbor-address* **activate** command before the association with the peer group. This configuration (with fictitious neighbor addresses) can be viewed in Example 15-4.

Example 15-3 *TransitNet Route Reflector Peer Group Configuration*

```
router bgp 1234
 neighbor VPNv4 peer-group
 neighbor VPNv4 remote-as 1234
 neighbor VPNv4 update-source Loopback0
```

Example 15-4 *TransitNet Route Reflector Address Family Configuration*

```
router bgp 1234
 !
 address-family vpnv4
  neighbor VPNv4 activate
  neighbor VPNv4 route-reflector-client
  neighbor VPNv4 send-community extended
  neighbor 194.27.1.1 peer-group VPNv4
  neighbor 194.27.1.2 peer-group VPNv4
  neighbor 194.27.1.3 peer-group VPNv4
 exit-address-family
```

None of the newly created MP-iBGP sessions will become active at this point because the other end of the MP-iBGP sessions will not have been configured.

Configuration of MP-iBGP on TransitNet PE-routers

Each PE-router within the network will need to be configured to run an MP-iBGP and standard BGP-4 session to the pair of route reflectors within the core of the TransitNet backbone. The configuration for the MP-iBGP sessions is the same address-family configuration under the BGP process as was performed on the route reflectors, except that the neighbor addresses used are the loopback addresses of the route reflectors.

When this configuration has been entered, the MP-iBGP sessions should become active. However, no updates will be received except for the default route from the Snet_Internet VRF because no VRFs will have been created and no customer interfaces have been associated with any VRFs. The default route update from the Snet_Internet VRF will not be used at this point as it has not been imported into any VRFs within any of the PE-routers.

When the MP-iBGP sessions become active, the following configuration steps will be necessary on each of the PE-routers to provide the relevant VRFs and BGP configuration for successful migration of VPN sites to the MPLS/VPN solution:

1 **Creation of the relevant VRFs**—Each PE-router within the TransitNet network should now be configured with all of the relevant VRFs that will be used on that PE-router. This can be achieved using a similar configuration to the one shown in Example 15-5.

2 **Configuration of the static default route within the Internet_Customer VPN**— Each customer that belongs to the Internet_Customer VPN will need to be capable of reaching the Internet gateway router for Internet connectivity.

3 **Creation of address families within the BGP configuration**—An address family must be created for each of the VRFs under the BGP configuration. This is necessary so that the routes contained within the VRF are advertised across the MP-iBGP sessions between PE-routers. Example 15-6 provides the necessary configuration to allow the MP-iBGP sessions to carry routes from the Snet_Customer and Internet_Customer VPNs.

Example 15-5 *TransitNet PE-router VRF Configuration*

```
ip vrf Snet_Customer
 rd 1234:100
 route-target export 1234:16
 route-target import 1234:16
 route-target import 1234:17
 route-target import 1234:18
 !
ip vrf Internet_Customer
 rd 1234:102
 route-target export 1234:18
 route-target import 1234:18
 route-target import 1234:16
```

Example 15-6 *TransitNet PE-router BGP VRF Address Family Configuration*

```
router bgp 1234
!
address-family ipv4 vrf Snet_Customer
 no auto-summary
 no synchronization
 redistribute static
exit-address-family
!
address-family ipv4 vrf Internet_Customer
 no auto-summary
 no synchronization
 redistribute static
exit-address-family
```

Migration of VPN Sites onto the MPLS/VPN Solution

The last stage of the MPLS/VPN migration involves the movement of existing VPN customers onto the new infrastructure. All the relevant PE configurations for all the VRFs and the MP-iBGP sessions have been completed by this stage. The last few steps that are necessary are as follows:

1 **Move existing VPN customers into their respective VRFs**—Each VPN site may be moved into the relevant VRFs by associating the connecting interface with the VRF. This is achieved through use of the **ip vrf forwarding** *vrf-name* command within the interface configuration. This action removes the IP address of the interface from within the configuration, so this address must be reconfigured.

2 **Create static routes**—Static routes for each of the VPN site's prefixes must be configured so that they are placed into the relevant VRF.

3 **Removal of GRE tunneling configuration for the SampleNet VPN**—When all SampleNet sites on the TransitNet PE-router have been migrated onto the MPLS/VPN solution, the GRE tunnels to the SampleNet central site can be removed.

Summary

In this chapter, you've seen a potential migration strategy from a classical IP-over-IP VPN implementation toward an MPLS/VPN-based implementation of VPN services. This strategy does not cover every customer need and should serve only as a starting point for your own migration strategy, of course, because every network has its own specific requirements. Still, a number of common steps must be followed in every network migration toward an MPLS/VPN-based backbone.

Start with these preparatory steps:

Step 1   Document the connectivity needs of your customers, and design your service solutions based on these needs.

Step 2   Design VRFs, route targets, and route distinguishers to satisfy the connectivity needs of various customer types.

Step 3   Define the numbering and naming policies for VRFs, route targets, and route distinguishers.

Step 4   Migrate your backbone to an MPLS-enabled backbone—see Chapter 6 for an example.

Step 5   If needed, establish a new route-reflector hierarchy to satisfy the needs of MP-BGP route propagation.

Migrate your IP-over-IP VPN customers by following these steps:

Step 1   Establish central site(s) for every network that will serve as transition points during the upgrade process.

Step 2   Define VRFs for the VPN central site(s).

Step 3   Use virtual circuits or separate physical links to connect the central site(s) to a VPN, as well as keep it connected to the global IP backbone to preserve existing IP-over-IP VPN tunnels.

Step 4   Establish VPN routing information exchange between the central site(s) and PE-routers. Verify that the routing information sent by the central site router(s) is correctly received and propagated by the PE-routers.

Step 5   Migrate a pilot site to the new VPN. Verify that the routing information is properly exchanged between the sites still connected via IP-over-IP tunnels and the new VPN sites. Verify application-level connectivity between the old and new sites.

Step 6   Migrate remaining customer sites to the new VPN.

Step 7   Remove global connectivity from the central site(s).

Similar steps can be followed when migrating Frame Relay or ATM-based VPN customers to an MPLS/VPN-based solution.

INDEX

Numerics

802.1q VLANs, 337

A

address families, 191
  routing context, configuring, 193–194
  VPN-IPv4, configuring, 192
address space, overlapping, 148
advertisements
  AS-override, 180
  Extended Community attribute, 192–193
  PE routers, requirements for, 167
aggregates, 29
  penultimate hop popping, 41
allocating labels
  across ATM-LSR domains, 56–61
  distribution methods, 34–36
  independent control, 57
  VC merge, 58–61
AllowAS-in feature, deploying, 245–247
any-to-any connectivity
  intranet model, 168–169
  extranet model, 138
application hosting, 240
applications, control protocols, 19–20
architecture
  Cell-mode MPLS, control plane, 51–53
  Edge-LSRs, 18
  MPLS/VPN, 13, 145–146
    Extended Communities ORF-type
      capability, 203
    FECs, 16
    inter-PE router routing, 156–157
    intranet topology, 168–169
    overlapping addresses, 174
    route distinguishers, 157
    route targets, 155–156
    scalability, 157
    sites, 153
    SOO, 177, 180
area 0 (OSPF), PE-to-CE connectivity, 213, 220–224

arguments, tag-switching advertise-tags command, 75
AS Override, 232–234
ASN (Autonomous System Number), assigning to route distinguishers, 175
assigning
  interfaces to VRFs, 188
  labels. See bindings
  loopback addresses to PE-routers, 328
  route distinguishers to VRFs, 391–392
  unique numbers to route distinguishers, 175–176
associating VRF with global routing table, 310–311, 314
ATM (Asynchronous Transfer Mode)
  backbone networks
    migration to Cell-mode MPLS, 108–110
    migration to Frame-mode MPLS, 106–108
  Cell-mode MPLS, 49, 69
    control-plane connectivity, 52–53
    limitation, 50
  Frame-mode MPLS, 67–69
  heterogeneous MPLS-mode operation, 69
  Layer 3 lookup, 50
  LSRs, 13–15
    convergence, 61–62
    domains, 50
    Edge-LSRs, 13–15, 50
    IP connectivity, 51
    labeled packet forwarding, 55–56
    loopback interfaces, 53
  service provider backbone, convergence, 254
  switches
    control-plane implementation, 54
    ordered control, 57
  VCs, 49
attributes (BGP), 171
  community, removing, 351
  Extended Community, 177
    advertising, 192–193
    format, 182
    OSPF route propagation, 220
    route target, 178–179
  MP_REACH_NLRI, 189
  MP_UNREACH_NLRI, 189

D

L

M

R

W

CCIE Professional Development

Cisco LAN Switching

Kennedy Clark, CCIE; Kevin Hamilton, CCIE

1-57870-094-9 • AVAILABLE NOW

This volume provides an in-depth analysis of Cisco LAN switching technologies, architectures, and deployments, including unique coverage of Catalyst network design essentials. Network designs and configuration examples are incorporated throughout to demonstrate the principles and enable easy translation of the material into practice in production networks.

Advanced IP Network Design

Alvaro Retana, CCIE; Don Slice, CCIE; and Russ White, CCIE

1-57870-097-3 • AVAILABLE NOW

Network engineers and managers can use these case studies, which highlight various network design goals, to explore issues including protocol choice, network stability, and growth. This book also includes theoretical discussion on advanced design topics.

Large-Scale IP Network Solutions

Khalid Raza, CCIE; and Mark Turner

1-57870-084-1 • AVAILABLE NOW

Network engineers can find solutions as their IP networks grow in size and complexity. Examine all the major IP protocols in-depth and learn about scalability, migration planning, network management, and security for large-scale networks.

Routing TCP/IP, Volume I

Jeff Doyle, CCIE

1-57870-041-8 • AVAILABLE NOW

This book takes the reader from a basic understanding of routers and routing protocols through a detailed examination of each of the IP interior routing protocols. Learn techniques for designing networks that maximize the efficiency of the protocol being used. Exercises and review questions provide core study for the CCIE Routing and Switching exam.

Cisco Systems

Cisco Press

www.ciscopress.com

Cisco Career Certifications

Cisco CCNA Exam #640-507 Certification Guide
Wendell Odom, CCIE

0-7357-0971-8 • AVAILABLE NOW

Although it's only the first step in Cisco Career Certification, the Cisco Certified Network Associate (CCNA) exam is a difficult test. Your first attempt at becoming Cisco certified requires a lot of study and confidence in your networking knowledge. When you're ready to test your skills, complete your knowledge of the exam topics, and prepare for exam day, you need the preparation tools found in *Cisco CCNA Exam #640-507 Certification Guide* from Cisco Press.

CCDA Exam Certification Guide
Anthony Bruno, CCIE & Jacqueline Kim

0-7357-0074-5 • AVAILABLE NOW

CCDA Exam Certification Guide is a comprehensive study tool for DCN Exam #640-441. Written by a CCIE and a CCDA, and reviewed by Cisco technical experts, *CCDA Exam Certification Guide* will help you understand and master the exam objectives. In this solid review on the design areas of the DCN exam, you'll learn to design a network that meets a customer's requirements for perfomance, security, capacity, and scalability.

Interconnecting Cisco Network Devices
Edited by Steve McQuerry

1-57870-111-2 • AVAILABLE NOW

Based on the Cisco course taught worldwide, *Interconnecting Cisco Network Devices* teaches you how to configure Cisco switches and routers in multi-protocol internetworks. ICND is the primary course recommended by Cisco Systems for CCNA #640-507 preparation. If you are pursuing CCNA certification, this book is an excellent starting point for your study.

Designing Cisco Networks
Edited by Diane Teare

1-57870-105-8 • AVAILABLE NOW

Based on the Cisco Systems instructor-led and self-study course available worldwide, *Designing Cisco Networks* will help you understand how to analyze and solve existing network problems while building a framework that supports the functionality, performance, and scalability required from any given environment. Self-assessment through exercises and chapter-ending tests starts you down the path for attaining your CCDA certification.

CISCO SYSTEMS
CISCO PRESS

www.ciscopress.com

Cisco Press Solutions

Enhanced IP Services for Cisco Networks
Donald C. Lee, CCIE

1-57870-106-6 • AVAILABLE NOW

This is a guide to improving your network's capabilities by understanding the new enabling and advanced Cisco IOS services that build more scalable, intelligent, and secure networks. Learn the technical details necessary to deploy Quality of Service, VPN technologies, IPsec, the IOS firewall and IOS Intrusion Detection. These services will allow you to extend the network to new frontiers securely, protect your network from attacks, and increase the sophistication of network services.

Developing IP Multicast Networks, Volume I
Beau Williamson, CCIE

1-57870-077-9 • AVAILABLE NOW

This book provides a solid foundation of IP multicast concepts and explains how to design and deploy the networks that will support appplications such as audio and video conferencing, distance-learning, and data replication. Includes an in-depth discussion of the PIM protocol used in Cisco routers and detailed coverage of the rules that control the creation and maintenance of Cisco mroute state entries.

Designing Network Security
Merike Kaeo

1-57870-043-4 • AVAILABLE NOW

Designing Network Security is a practical guide designed to help you understand the fundamentals of securing your corporate infrastructure. This book takes a comprehensive look at underlying security technologies, the process of creating a security policy, and the practical requirements necessary to implement a corporate security policy.

CISCO SYSTEMS
CISCO PRESS

www.ciscopress.com

Cisco Press Solutions

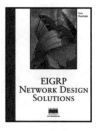

EIGRP Network Design Solutions
Ivan Pepelnjak, CCIE

1-57870-165-1 • AVAILABLE NOW

EIGRP Network Design Solutions uses case studies and real-world configuration examples to help you gain an in-depth understanding of the issues involved in designing, deploying, and managing EIGRP-based networks. This book details proper designs that can be used to build large and scalable EIGRP-based networks and documents possible ways each EIGRP feature can be used in network design, implmentation, troubleshooting, and monitoring.

Top-Down Network Design
Priscilla Oppenheimer

1-57870-069-8 • AVAILABLE NOW

Building reliable, secure, and manageable networks is every network professional's goal. This practical guide teaches you a systematic method for network design that can be applied to campus LANs, remote-access networks, WAN links, and large-scale internetworks. Learn how to analyze business and technical requirements, examine traffic flow and Quality of Service requirements, and select protocols and technologies based on performance goals.

Cisco IOS Releases: The Complete Reference
Mack M. Coulibaly

1-57870-179-1 • AVAILABLE NOW

Cisco IOS Releases: The Complete Reference is the first comprehensive guide to the more than three dozen types of Cisco IOS releases being used today on enterprise and service provider networks. It details the release process and its numbering and naming conventions, as well as when, where, and how to use the various releases. A complete map of Cisco IOS software releases and their relationships to one another, in addition to insights into decoding information contained within the software, make this book an indispensable resource for any network professional.

CISCO SYSTEMS

CISCO PRESS

www.ciscopress.com

Cisco Press Solutions

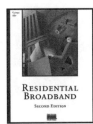

Residential Broadband, Second Edition

George Abe

1-57870-177-5 • AVAILABLE NOW

This book will answer basic questions of residential broadband networks such as: Why do we need high speed networks at home? How will high speed residential services be delivered to the home? How do regulatory or commercial factors affect this technology? Explore such networking topics as xDSL, cable, and wireless.

Internetworking Technologies Handbook, Second Edition

Kevin Downes, CCIE, Merilee Ford, H. Kim Lew, Steve Spanier, Tim Stevenson

1-57870-102-3 • AVAILABLE NOW

This comprehensive reference provides a foundation for understanding and implementing contemporary internetworking technologies, providing you with the necessary information needed to make rational networking decisions. Master terms, concepts, technologies, and devices that are used in the internetworking industry today. You also learn how to incorporate networking technologies into a LAN/WAN environment, as well as how to apply the OSI reference model to categorize protocols, technologies, and devices.

OpenCable Architecture

Michael Adams

1-57870-135-X • AVAILABLE NOW

Whether you're a television, data communications, or telecommunications professional, or simply an interested business person, this book will help you understand the technical and business issues surrounding interactive television services. It will also provide you with an inside look at the combined efforts of the cable, data, and consumer electronics industries' efforts to develop those new services.

Performance and Fault Management

Paul Della Maggiora, Christopher Elliott, Robert Pavone, Kent Phelps, James Thompson

1-57870-180-5 • AVAILABLE NOW

This book is a comprehensive guide to designing and implementing effective strategies for monitoring performance levels and correctng problems in Cisco networks. It provides an overview of router and LAN switch operations to help you understand how to manage such devices, as well as guidance on the essential MIBs, traps, syslog messages, and show commands for managing Cisco routers and switches.

CISCO SYSTEMS

CISCO PRESS

www.ciscopress.com

Cisco Press Fundamentals

IP Routing Primer

Robert Wright, CCIE

1-57870-108-2 • AVAILABLE NOW

Learn how IP routing behaves in a Cisco router environment. In addition to teaching the core fundamentals, this book enhances your ability to troubleshoot IP routing problems yourself, often eliminating the need to call for additional technical support. The information is presented in an approachable, workbook-type format with dozens of detailed illustrations and real-life scenarios integrated throughout.

Cisco Router Configuration

Allan Leinwand, Bruce Pinsky, Mark Culpepper

1-57870-022-1 • AVAILABLE NOW

An example-oriented and chronological approach helps you implement and administer your internetworking devices. Starting with the configuration devices "out of the box;" this book moves to configuring Cisco IOS for the three most popular networking protocols today: TCP/IP, AppleTalk, and Novell Interwork Packet Exchange (IPX). You also learn basic administrative and management configuration, including access control with TACACS+ and RADIUS, network management with SNMP, logging of messages, and time control with NTP.

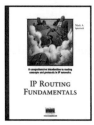

IP Routing Fundamentals

Mark A. Sportack

1-57870-071-x • AVAILABLE NOW

This comprehensive guide provides essential background information on routing in IP networks for network professionals who are deploying and maintaining LANs and WANs daily. Explore the mechanics of routers, routing protocols, network interfaces, and operating systems.

Cisco Press Fundamentals

Internet Routing Architectures, Second Edition

Sam Halabi with Danny McPherson

1-57870-233-x • AVAILABLE NOW

This book explores the ins and outs of interdomain routing network design with emphasis on BGP-4 (Border Gateway Protocol Version 4)--the de facto interdomain routing protocol. You will have all the information you need to make knowledgeable routing decisions for Internet connectivity in your environment.

Voice over IP Fundamentals

Jonathan Davidson and James Peters

1-57870-168-6 • AVAILABLE NOW

Voice over IP (VoIP), which integrates voice and data transmission, is quickly becoming an important factor in network communications. It promises lower operational costs, greater flexibility, and a variety of enhanced applications. This book provides a thorough introduction to this new technology to help experts in both the data and telephone industries plan for the new networks.

For the latest on Cisco Press resources and Certification and

Training guides, or for information on publishing opportunities, visit

www.ciscopress.com

Cisco Press

Committed to being your long-term resource as you grow as a Cisco Networking professional

CISCO SYSTEMS

CISCO PRESS

Help Cisco Press **stay connected** to the issues and challenges you face on a daily basis by registering your product and filling out our brief survey. Complete and mail this form, or better yet ...

Register online and enter to win a FREE book!

Jump to **www.ciscopress.com/register** and register your product online. Each complete entry will be eligible for our monthly drawing to win a FREE book of the winner's choice from the Cisco Press library.

May we contact you via e-mail with information about **new releases, special promotions** and customer benefits?

❐ Yes   ❐ No

E-mail address _____

Name _____

Address _____

City _____ State/Province _____

Country _____ Zip/Post code _____

Where did you buy this product?

❐ Bookstore   ❐ Computer store/electronics store

❐ Online retailer   ❐ Direct from Cisco Press

❐ Mail order   ❐ Class/Seminar

❐ Other_____

When did you buy this product? _____ **Month** _____ **Year**

What price did you pay for this product?

❐ Full retail price   ❐ Discounted price   ❐ Gift

How did you learn about this product?

❐ Friend   ❐ Store personnel   ❐ In-store ad

❐ Cisco Press Catalog   ❐ Postcard in the mail   ❐ Saw it on the shelf

❐ Other Catalog   ❐ Magazine ad   ❐ Article or review

❐ School   ❐ Professional Organization   ❐ Used other products

❐ Other_____

What will this product be used for?

❐ Business use   ❐ School/Education

❐ Other_____

Cisco Press

How many years have you been employed in a computer-related industry?

❏ 2 years or less   ❏ 3-5 years   ❏ 5+ years

Which best describes your job function?

❏ Corporate Management   ❏ Systems Engineering   ❏ IS Management
❏ Network Design   ❏ Network Support   ❏ Webmaster
❏ Marketing/Sales   ❏ Consultant   ❏ Student
❏ Professor/Teacher   ❏ Other _____

What is your formal education background?

❏ High school   ❏ Vocational/Technical degree   ❏ Some college
❏ College degree   ❏ Masters degree   ❏ Professional or Doctoral degree

Have you purchased a Cisco Press product before?

❏ Yes   ❏ No

On what topics would you like to see more coverage?

_____
_____

Do you have any additional comments or suggestions?

_____
_____

Thank you for completing this survey and registration. Please fold here, seal, and mail to Cisco Press.

MPLS and VPN Architectures (1-58705-002-1)

Cisco Press
Customer Registration—CP0500227
P.O. Box #781046
Indianapolis, IN 46278-8046

Place
Stamp
Here

ciscopress.com

Cisco Press
201 West 103rd Street
Indianapolis, IN 46290